Contributions to Management Science

The series *Contributions to Management Science* contains research publications in all fields of business and management science. These publications are primarily monographs and multiple author works containing new research results, and also feature selected conference-based publications are also considered. The focus of the series lies in presenting the development of latest theoretical and empirical research across different viewpoints.

This book series is indexed in Scopus.

More information about this series at http://www.springer.com/series/1505

Hasan Dincer • Serhat Yüksel
Editors

Strategic Priorities in Competitive Environments

Multidimensional Approaches for Business Success

Springer

Editors
Hasan Dincer
Istanbul Medipol University
Kadiköy, Istanbul, Turkey

Serhat Yüksel
Istanbul Medipol University
Besiktas, Istanbul, Turkey

ISSN 1431-1941 ISSN 2197-716X (electronic)
Contributions to Management Science
ISBN 978-3-030-45022-9 ISBN 978-3-030-45023-6 (eBook)
https://doi.org/10.1007/978-3-030-45023-6

This Springer imprint is published by the registered company Springer Nature Switzerland AG.
The registered company address is: Gewerbestrasse 11, 6330 Cham, Switzerland

Contents

BSC-Based Evaluation for the Factors Affecting the Performance of Wind Energy Companies

Hasan Dinçer, Serhat Yüksel, Gözde Gülseven Ubay, and Hüsne Karakuş

Abstract This study aims to identify the significant factors which improve the performance of wind energy companies. For this purpose, a detailed literature review is conducted, and eight different performance evaluation criteria are identified based on four dimensions of balanced scorecard (BSC) approach. In the evaluation process of these factors, fuzzy DEMATEL approach is taken into consideration. The results indicate that internal process and learning and growth are the most important dimensions of BSC regarding the wind energy investment projects. Moreover, it is also concluded that the most important criteria are technological background and research and development. Hence, it is recommended that wind energy companies should mainly pay attention to technological development in order to be successful in such a complex investment which requires high engineering knowledge. In this context, the equipment and information technology software should be effective in these countries. Owing to this issue, the risk of having deficiencies can be minimized. Additionally, high technology can be obtained with a lower cost by making extensive research and development activities.

1 Introduction

Energy is a very important element for all countries in the world. Countries and international organizations compete with each other to dominate energy from past to present (Khare et al. 2016). With its increasing importance especially with the industrial revolution, energy has become an irreplaceable phenomenon in the daily life of both people and companies. With the technology advancing all over the world, people's needs for electrical energy are progressing in direct proportion. Today, producing sufficient amount of cheap and clean energy in parallel with

H. Dinçer (✉) · S. Yüksel · G. G. Ubay · H. Karakuş
The School of Business, İstanbul Medipol University, Istanbul, Turkey
e-mail: hdincer@medipol.edu.tr; serhatyuksel@medipol.edu.tr; gozde.ubay@std.medipol.edu.tr; husnekarakus@st.medipol.edu.tr

H. Dincer, S. Yüksel (eds.), *Strategic Priorities in Competitive Environments*, Contributions to Management Science, https://doi.org/10.1007/978-3-030-45023-6_1

rapidly growing population for countries is one of the basic problems of both economic and social life (Eti et al. 2020). The main reasons for this problem can be the exhaustible energy resources, fluctuations in prices, foreign dependency of the countries while providing energy and environmental effects (Dinçer et al. 2019).

With the environmental awareness, which has become popular especially since the 1970s, measures to prevent pollution of the atmosphere have been taken by many countries, but countries have been reduced to a certain level of carbon emission with legal obligations such as the Kyoto Protocol and the Paris Agreement (Pischke et al. 2019). For this reason, it is of great importance to use the generated energy with high efficiency, to evaluate the potential of alternative and renewable energy sources as well as the existing energy sources day by day (Kumar et al. 2017; Zhou et al. 2019). Although most of the global energy is derived from fossil fuels today, renewable energy sources also play a critical role in reducing dependence on fossil fuels such as coal, oil and natural gas, and thus reducing carbon emissions (Zhang et al. 2020).

With the environmental consciousness, which has become popular especially since 1970s, measures to prevent pollution of the atmosphere have been taken by many countries, and countries have also been reduced to a certain level of carbon emission by legal obligations (Wang et al. 2019). For this reason, it is quite significant to use the generated energy with high efficiency, to evaluate the potential of alternative and renewable energy sources as well as the existing energy sources. Although most of the global energy is derived from fossil fuels today, renewable energy sources also play a critical role in reducing dependence on fossil fuels such as coal, oil and natural gas, and thus reducing carbon emissions.

Many types of renewable energy sources have been recently discovered by countries in recent years. Wind energy, which is one of the most preferred methods of countries that are sensitive to the environment and want to localize their energy resources. This energy depends on many other factors such as local and geographical differences as well as pressure differences, temporal and local change due to the inhomogeneous warming of the earth, rotation of the earth, surface friction (Dinçer and Yüksel 2019). Although wind energy has taken place in the lives of people in the form of mills throughout the history, electricity production from wind energy has remained behind other renewable energy sources since it was unpredictable for many years (Hossain 2020). However, wind energy has been accepted as one of the most efficient renewable energy sources, with the decline in investment costs over the years and the fact that the wind has become much more predictable and measurable with technological developments.

One of the main dynamics of economic growth and development is the realization of energy investment projects, which affect the financial and financial situation of countries, both directly and indirectly, with successful planning. At this point, investments in renewable energy sources, especially wind energy, are of great importance. Wind energy, which is defined as an alternative energy source, has gained importance as the primary energy source for many countries. For this reason, many investments are made in this field both on state and private sectors and many project-based studies have been successfully implemented. The fact that the governments have made incentives to produce and use wind energy has also accelerated this transition period (Zhu and Liao 2019). Wind energy investments to countries make an important contribution to the nationalization of the energy of that country, while introducing the countries with a cleaner energy type. Foreign dependency in any sector is an issue that is a burden on countries and needs to be solved. The equipment and parts used when producing wind energy are easily available from every country. For this reason, although wind energy is costly during the installation phase, since the countries will be able to produce their own energy after the installation, there is a significant decrease in the foreign dependencies of these countries in the energy sector (Cole and Banks 2017).

Although one of the key players playing a role in this process is the government of the country, the share of companies operating in the energy sector is also quite large. The private sector and its actors are in every area of our lives by developing and producing equipment, project and investment, assembling the equipment it produces, building the facility, operating the plant and producing energy, supplying and selling this energy. With the exponentially increasing technological developments, the energy sector has become a constantly growing dynamic sector due to the demand of more and more energy every day. This situation has a vital importance for the private sector, which is the main producer and consumer of energy. Because energy in production, distribution, trade, consumption and financing stages all over the world, it is in a decisive position at every point in the value chain. The positive development experienced in the renewable energy costs we have mentioned before has been mainly led by the private sector.

However, all areas where the private sector is active must be covered in order for the energy transformation to be implemented with all its elements. The significance of this is that as the traditional one-way energy system from the manufacturer to the consumer experiences revolutionary transformations, the private sector's roles increase and grow with differentiation and growth (Maulidia et al. 2019). In order to keep up with this transformation, the private sector needs to be prepared today to take on these new roles and responsibilities. Although the role of state and state support in renewable energy production is great, this support is sometimes not sufficient and leads companies to turn to other sources that generate more profit (Zhang et al. 2016). Therefore, the main action is the performance of companies investing in renewable energy. It is possible to create an energy transformation success story in the world with the correct definition of this performance, a correct orientation and a patient study. In addition to the direct economic contribution of this energy transformation, which will be carried out under the leadership of the private sector, to the actors involved in the process, employment growth, technology development and knowledge that will support the economy of the countries applying renewable energy is also an important plus.

Therefore, the role and importance of companies in this field is very important in wind energy investments, which have accelerated by the efforts of countries to produce their own energy in recent years. Sustainability, which is one of the main pillars of the energy transformation, is a concept that has taken place in the business world for many years (Al-Hamamre et al. 2017). When we look at it from a global perspective, private sector companies that do or want to do business worldwide publish sustainability reports in addition to financial reports. These reports bring the goals and progress of the companies regarding sustainability to the attention of their stakeholders. For this reason, examining the sustainability performances of these companies at certain intervals and giving guidance according to these reviews makes a great contribution to the rapid development of the wind energy sector in the field of energy and enables investments in this area to become more efficient (Heiskanen et al. 2018). At this point, determining the factors affecting the performance of companies investing in wind energy in many ways is of great importance.

For this reason, in this study, it is aimed to determine the factors affecting the performance of wind energy companies in many ways to fill this shortcoming in the literature. In this context, a large literature review was carried out first. As a result, an analysis with BSC was made under the finance, customer, internal process and learning and growth categories to examine the multiple factors affecting the performance of wind energy companies. In this analysis, the financial part emphasizes the point that companies want to be reached by their stakeholders, while the customer part emphasizes the point that companies want to be reached by their customers. Additionally, the internal process section states the business process that companies develop to satisfy their customers and stakeholders. On the other side, the learning and growing section covers the changes and improvements that companies must make to achieve their goals (Nørreklit et al. 2018). In order to make this analysis, fuzzy DEMATEL approach is taken into the account.

While determining the performances of the companies in the past, all relevant data were tried to be made financial. While fields are represented correctly, fields without financial data are left out (Akkermans and Van Oorschot 2018). The biggest advantage of using BSC in this study is that companies look at determining the performance not only financially but also from a multi-dimensional perspective. In other words, owing to considering this approach, it can be possible to use both financial and nonfinancial issues. It is believed that this situation is the most significant contribution of this study while comparing with the others. Another important point is that fuzzy multi-criteria decision-making approaches are rarely considered in the studies. Hence, by making analysis with fuzzy DEMATEL, it is thought that this study can have methodological advantage.

2 Literature Review

There are many factors that companies take into consideration in their efforts to increase their performance. One of these factors is related to finance. This factor has been addressed by many researchers in the literature. Aras et al. (2018) analyzed a model regarding the performance management of Turkish banks. On the other hand, Turkish deposit banks operating in the 2012–2014 period were included in the scope of the review. The said study was examined with the TOPSIS method. As a result, it was emphasized that while increasing the performance of banks, it should give importance to financial reports, management practices, economy and social changes.

Sunderaraman et al. (2019) also examined the issue of changes in consumer behavior that affect financial capacity. For this purpose, Australia and the United States are included in the review. This study was tested by multiple regression method. As a result, it has been determined that individuals who have behavioral disorders in financial terms have a negative effect on company performance. On the other hand, it was also identified that these individuals reduced financial capacity and this situation reflected negatively on the performance of the company.

There are different studies on the financial factor in the literature. Hili et al. (2016) examined the issue that the risks that arise financially affect the company performance in their study. USA, Europe and developing countries are included in the scope of the study. Especially the problems arising in capital investment funds are examined. As a result, it has been determined that the problems arising in capital investment funds will have a negative impact on company performance. Wang et al. (2016) investigated a study in which suggestions for problems arising in information management systems were determined. This study has been tested with fuzzy logic method. As a result, it has been determined that companies should carry out policies to reduce the problems that arise in the information management process in order to increase their performance and profitability. It has been studied on other issues that companies must consider in order to increase their financial performance. Song et al. (2017) examined the impact of environmental management on financial performance. The Chinese companies for the years between 2007 and 2011 have been included in the evaluation. As a result, it was determined that companies should give importance to environmental management in order to increase their performance. On the other hand, it was emphasized that environmental management has a positive effect on the profitability of the company.

Customers are another factor that companies consider in order to improve their performance. Companies need to pay attention to customer satisfaction in order to increase their performance. In this context, the needs and expectations of the customer should be taken into consideration first. This issue has been handled by many researchers in the literature. Sarvari et al. (2016) examined the ways to reach customer segmentation by taking demographic and monetary issues into consideration. Pizza companies operating in Turkey in the work in question was taken into the examination scope. As a result, it has been determined that in order to increase the performance of the company, it is necessary to consider the needs and expectations of the producer and consumer. There are other studies that emphasize customer needs to increase company performance. Kim and Park (2019) examined how the services offered by companies affect customer behavior. In this study, firms' performances were evaluated on the basis of the Markov chain model. Consequently, it was determined that products should be created according to customer expectations in order to increase the performance of companies.

The services offered by companies affect the customer behavior towards the company. Therefore, companies need to pay attention to the services they offer to their customers in order to increase their performance. This issue has been handled by many researchers in the literature. Bharadwaja et al. (2018) examined the relationship between customer behavior and service-oriented organizational behavior. A detailed literature review was carried out regarding the study in question. As a result, it has been determined that the behaviors of service-oriented organizations change according to the gender of the customer. On the other hand, it was emphasized that the customers want to receive service according to the gender of the employees. Therefore, it is stated that companies should give importance to customer relations in order to increase their performance. Hosseini et al. (2017) examined the relationship between the health company's power to distribute products to a particular region and customer demands. Health companies are included in the scope of the examination. The study was tested using the Analytical Hierarchy method (AHP). It was emphasized that health companies should attach importance to the distribution network in order to increase their performance. On the other hand, the stronger the distribution network, the more customer demands are determined. It is involved in studies where it is determined how to achieve customer expectations. Sisodia et al. (2020) examined the importance of comments made on the website for businesses. Travel information and 800 customer reviews of the travel advisor site are included in the review. The study was examined with unigram, bigram and trigram methods. Hence, it has been determined that the way to increase the performance of the companies is to meet the expectations of the customer. On the other hand, it was emphasized that companies should give importance to websites in order to understand customer expectations.

Another factor that should be considered in order to increase the performance of the company is intra-company communication. In the literature, this issue has been addressed by many researchers. Hassell and Cotton (2017) investigated the effect of video-mediated communication on team performance. This study was examined by one-way analysis of variance (anova). As a result, it has been determined that internal communication affects the performance of the company. On the other hand, video-mediated communication has been found to have a negative impact on the employee's performance. Therefore, it has been determined that the way to increase internal performance is not through video communication. Yap et al. (2017) also examined the effect of modifying the designs of projects on project performance and effective communication. In the study, Malaysia Construction Projects were included in the scope of the study. The study was examined with qualitative research methods. Consequently, it was determined that when the changes were made in the project, both time and cost were lost. On the other hand, it has been determined that the way of learning new design processes depends on the communication between the employees in the project. Therefore, it was emphasized that companies should reduce the problems arising from the changes in the project with internal communication.

Other studies have been conducted to examine the impact of internal communication on performance. Villa et al. (2017) studied the effect of effective communication systems on the performance of humanitarian organizations. Somalia was included in the scope of the study. The study was examined by survey and structural equation model (SEM). As a result, it has been determined that humanitarian organizations can continue their existence and efforts to increase their performance through strong communication. On the other hand, it was emphasized that humanitarian aid provided would be more when internal communication was good. De

Waal and Goedegebuure (2017) examined the effect of management practices on company performance. The study was examined by linear regression analysis method. As a result, it has been identified that there is a positive relationship between strong management practices and increasing their corporate performance. Additionally, it was emphasized that internal communication is important in strengthening management practices.

Another factor that the company should consider in order to increase its performance is the technological infrastructure. In the literature, this issue has been addressed by many researchers. In this context, Khoshnevis and Teirlinck (2018) examined how R&D resources are based on firms and how they affect company performance. In the study, Belgium was included in the scope of the examination. This study was tested with data envelopment analysis. As a result, it was emphasized that the effect of R&D activities on increasing the performance of the company is important. On the other hand, it is determined that firms use different research budgets differently according to their size. In this framework, it was emphasized that the performances of companies vary depending on their R&D activities. Other studies have been conducted to determine the impact of research and technology on company performance. Varmazyar et al. (2016) examined the effect of research and technology on company performance and proposed a model. The research and technology organization (RTO) in Iran was included in the study. The study was tested with BSC, multi-criteria decision-making method (MCDM), DEMATEL, TOPSIS and MOORA methods. Thus, it has been determined that there are many financial and non-financial variables that affect the performance of the companies. It was defined that one of these variables is the work done by research and technology organization companies. On the other hand, it was emphasized that the performance of the company, which forms the research and technological infrastructure, is also increasing and therefore companies should improve themselves in the field of research and technology. It is very difficult for companies with weak technological infrastructure to improve their performance. Zhang et al. (2019) examined the economic and environmental impacts of geothermal energy. In the study, China was included in the scope of the study. As a result, it has been concluded that the environmental performance of geothermal energy is quite high and it cannot be made because it is economically and technologically insufficient. In this context, it was emphasized that the government should provide incentives and train personnel who can produce technology.

In addition, companies need to consider personnel selection in order to improve their performance. This issue has been handled in the literature for different purposes. Lee and Tseng (2018) investigated the criteria to be used when selecting staff. This study was tested by multi-criteria decision making (MCDM), VIKOR Analysis and Entropy method. As a result, it has been determined that companies need to make personnel selection very well in order to show their performance in the best way. On the other hand, it was emphasized that the experts should evaluate the criteria they care about when choosing personnel. Makhamara et al. (2016) examined the effect of criteria used in recruitment evaluations in the health sector on employee performance. In the study, the health sector in Kenya was included in the scope of the analysis. This study has been tested with the survey method. As a result, it has been determined that the criteria sought in recruitment evaluations in each sector are different and that the employees perform according to the criteria considered when hiring. In this context, it was stated that the company should evaluate the criteria of the personnel it has chosen to perform at its best.

As a result of the literature review, it has been frequently encountered that many researchers deal with finance, customer, internal communication, technological infrastructure and personnel quality. In some of the related studies, countries were examined, but in others, companies were evaluated. Issues such as internal communication, management practices and company performance, and the status of R&D activities within the company are emphasized. In these studies, methods such as survey method, TOPSIS, multiple regression, one-way variance analysis, data envelopment analysis, multi-criteria decision-making methods (MCDM), DEMATEL method, MOORA, VIKOR were used. Therefore, there is a need for a study in which different methodology is considered. In this study, BSC-based factors are taken into account to reach the conclusion. Therefore, it is believed that this study has a positive influence on the improvement of the literature.

3 An Analysis on Wind Energy Companies

This part of the study is related to the performance evaluation on wind energy companies. Within this context, BSC-based criteria are identified in the first manner. Secondly, necessary information will be provided regarding fuzzy DEMATEL approach. Thirdly, the significance levels of these criteria are identified by using this methodology.

3.1 Determining the BSC-Based Criteria of Performance Measurement

As a result of literature review, eight performance measurement criteria are identified. In this framework, the dimensions of BSC approach are taken into the account. This approach is used to measure the performance of companies. The BSC method has four different dimensions. The most important advantage of this method compared to others is that both financial and non-financial factors are taken into account. In other words, in addition to the financial figures of companies, other factors such as customer, internal processes and training and development are also taken into account (Dinçer et al. 2017). In this way, it will be possible to measure the performance of companies more accurately. Table 1 gives information about these criteria.

Table 1 indicates that there are eight different criteria for the performance assessment of wind energy companies regarding four dimensions of BSC approach. With respect to the dimension of finance, cost and return on investment are taken

Table 1 Performance measurement criteria

Dimensions	Criteria	Literature background
Finance	Cost (C1)	Aras et al. (2018); Hili et al. (2016)
	Return on investment (C2)	Song et al. (2017); Sunderaraman et al. (2019)
Customer	Customer expectation (C3)	Wang et al. (2016); Sarvari et al. (2016); Dinçer et al. (2020)
	Problem solving (C4)	Kim and Park (2019); Bharadwaja et al. (2018)
Internal process	Effective communication (C5)	Hosseini et al. (2017); Sisodia et al. (2020)
	Technological background (C6)	Hassell and Cotton (2017); Villa et al. (2017); Kalkavan and Ersin (2019)
Learning and growth	Research and Development (C7)	Yap et al. (2017); de Waal and Goedegebuure (2017)
	Qualified personnel (C8)	Zhang et al. (2019); Khoshnevis and Teirlinck (2018)

into consideration. The main reason is that these two factors have an important impact on the profitability of wind energy companies. In addition to them, regarding customer dimension, understanding the expectations is very significant. Similarly, immediately solving the problems of the customers also plays a key role for this situation. On the other side, communications should be effective and wind energy companies should have necessary technological background to improve their performance. In the final dimension, these companies should make investment on research and development and qualified personnel should be employed.

3.2 *Defining the Importance Levels of these Criteria*

These selected criteria are weighted in the final part of the analysis. In this context, fuzzy DEMATEL is considered. This approach is a popular type of multi-criteria decision-making models. It is mainly used to find more significant factors. Because of this issue, it can be said that this approach is very helpful to reach decision under the complex environment. The main reason of selecting DEMATEL is that impact relationship analysis can be conducted by using this model. For this purpose, evaluations from three decision makers are provided. These people have at least 15-year experience in wind energy companies. The decision makers make evaluations by considering five different scales that are none (N), low (L), medium (M), high (H) and very high (VH). After that, these scales are converted into fuzzy numbers (Lin 2013). Hence, triangular fuzzy numbers of each three decision makers for direct relation matrix are obtained. In the next stage, initial direct relation matrix is created by considering the averages of three direct relation matrix. The details of initial direct relation matrix are illustrated on Table 2.

Next, the values in the initial direct relation matrix are normalized. In this process, all values are divided to the maximum value of the rows. The details of the normalized direct relation matrix are summarized in Table 3.

Table 2 Initial direct relation matrix

Criteria	C1			C2			C3			C4			C5			C6			C7			C8		
C1	0.00	0.00	0.00	0.33	0.58	0.83	0.08	0.17	0.42	0.17	0.42	0.67	0.00	0.08	0.33	0.00	0.00	0.25	0.00	0.17	0.42	0.00	0.25	0.50
C2	0.33	0.58	0.83	0.00	0.00	0.00	0.25	0.50	0.75	0.00	0.00	0.25	0.17	0.42	0.67	0.00	0.08	0.33	0.00	0.00	0.25	0.00	0.25	0.50
C3	0.17	0.42	0.67	0.25	0.50	0.75	0.00	0.00	0.00	0.00	0.00	0.25	0.25	0.50	0.75	0.00	0.00	0.25	0.00	0.00	0.25	0.00	0.25	0.50
C4	0.25	0.50	0.75	0.00	0.25	0.50	0.25	0.50	0.75	0.00	0.00	0.00	0.25	0.50	0.75	0.17	0.25	0.50	0.17	0.33	0.58	0.00	0.25	0.50
C5	0.00	0.00	0.25	0.00	0.00	0.25	0.00	0.25	0.50	0.00	0.00	0.25	0.00	0.00	0.00	0.25	0.50	0.67	0.17	0.25	0.50	0.00	0.25	0.50
C6	0.67	0.92	1.00	0.67	0.92	1.00	0.67	0.92	1.00	0.67	0.92	1.00	0.67	0.92	1.00	0.00	0.00	0.00	0.25	0.50	0.75	0.58	0.83	1.00
C7	0.67	0.92	1.00	0.58	0.83	1.00	0.67	0.92	1.00	0.33	0.50	0.75	0.75	1.00	1.00	0.42	0.67	0.83	0.00	0.00	0.00	0.33	0.58	0.83
C8	0.17	0.33	0.58	0.08	0.17	0.42	0.00	0.17	0.42	0.00	0.00	0.25	0.25	0.50	0.67	0.17	0.33	0.58	0.17	0.25	0.50	0.00	0.00	0.00

Table 3 Normalized direct relation matrix

Criteria	C1			C2			C3			C4			C5			C6			C7			C8		
C1	0.00	0.00	0.00	0.05	0.09	0.12	0.01	0.02	0.06	0.02	0.06	0.10	0.00	0.01	0.05	0.00	0.00	0.04	0.00	0.02	0.06	0.00	0.04	0.07
C2	0.05	0.09	0.12	0.00	0.00	0.00	0.04	0.07	0.11	0.00	0.00	0.04	0.02	0.06	0.10	0.00	0.01	0.05	0.00	0.00	0.04	0.00	0.04	0.07
C3	0.02	0.06	0.10	0.04	0.07	0.11	0.00	0.00	0.00	0.00	0.00	0.04	0.04	0.07	0.11	0.00	0.00	0.04	0.00	0.00	0.04	0.00	0.04	0.07
C4	0.04	0.07	0.11	0.00	0.04	0.07	0.04	0.07	0.11	0.00	0.00	0.00	0.04	0.07	0.11	0.02	0.04	0.07	0.02	0.05	0.09	0.00	0.04	0.07
C5	0.00	0.00	0.04	0.00	0.00	0.04	0.00	0.04	0.07	0.00	0.00	0.04	0.00	0.00	0.00	0.04	0.07	0.10	0.02	0.04	0.07	0.00	0.04	0.07
C6	0.10	0.14	0.15	0.10	0.14	0.15	0.10	0.14	0.15	0.10	0.14	0.15	0.10	0.14	0.15	0.00	0.00	0.00	0.04	0.07	0.11	0.09	0.12	0.15
C7	0.10	0.14	0.15	0.09	0.12	0.15	0.10	0.14	0.15	0.05	0.07	0.11	0.11	0.15	0.15	0.06	0.10	0.12	0.00	0.00	0.00	0.05	0.09	0.12
C8	0.02	0.05	0.09	0.01	0.02	0.06	0.00	0.02	0.06	0.00	0.00	0.04	0.04	0.07	0.10	0.02	0.05	0.09	0.02	0.04	0.07	0.00	0.00	0.00

Table 4 Weights of Dimensions and Criteria

Dimensions	Weights of dimensions	Criteria	Weights of criteria
Finance	0.2201	Cost (C1)	0.1124
		Return on investment (C2)	0.1077
Customer	0.2092	Customer expectation (C3)	0.1042
		Problem solving (C4)	0.1050
Internal process	0.2977	Effective communication (C5)	0.1086
		Technological background (C6)	0.1892
Learning and growth	0.2730	Research and Development (C7)	0.1730
		Qualified personnel (C8)	0.1000

After creating normalized direct relation matrix, the values are divided into three which are x_l, x_m and x_u. In the next aspect, defuzzification process is occurred. As a result, the weights of the dimensions and criteria are identified. The details are given on Table 4.

Table 4 indicates that internal process and learning and growth are the most important dimensions of BSC with respect to the wind energy investment projects. Additionally, it is also identified that technological background is the most important criterion. Moreover, research and development has also second highest weight. On the other side, customer expectations and qualified personnel have lower significance in comparison with others.

4 Conclusion

Wind energy investments are very important for a country. The most important advantage of these investments is that they do not pollute the environment during the energy production process. In this way, it is possible to prevent many health problems. In addition, wind energy investments will reduce the countries' external dependence on energy. As a result of this situation, decreases may occur in the current account deficit problem of the countries. Besides these issues, these investments will contribute to the economic development of the country. In addition, it will be possible to contribute to reducing the unemployment rate with the new job opportunities to be created. As can be understood from these issues, it is important to develop strategies to increase wind energy investments effectively.

It is very obvious that the performance of the wind energy companies in a country should be high because of both social and economic issues. In this study, it is also aimed to evaluate the items to improve the performance of these companies. For this purpose, BSC-based eight different performance measurement criteria are defined by conducting a detailed literature review regarding wind energy companies. On the other side, fuzzy DEMATEL methodology is taken into account to find which criteria are more significant. The results show that technological background and research and development are the most important items in this framework. However, customer expectations and qualified personnel have lower importance by comparing with other factors.

It is understood that wind energy companies should mainly pay attention to technological development. Wind energy project is a complex investment which requires high engineering knowledge. Hence, these companies should have necessary technological background to be successful in this process. In this framework, attention should be paid to having modern technology in the equipment used. Otherwise, the equipment will constantly produce problems, which will increase the company's costs. In addition to the aforementioned issue, the fact that these companies have effective information technology software will also contribute to minimizing the disruptions to be experienced. On the other hand, as a result of the extensive research and development activities, it will be possible to have high technology with low cost.

The main limitation of this study is the fact that the analysis is only performed for wind energy companies. In the future studies, a comparative analysis can be conducted with making analysis on both wind and solar energy. In addition to this issue, different country groups can also be evaluated regarding the success of energy investment projects. Owing to this kind of analysis, it can be possible to see which countries have problems in this framework. Hence, necessary recommendations can be provided for the improvement of these projects. Another important point is that different methodologies can be taken into account to increase the originality of the studies.

References

Akkermans, H. A., & Van Oorschot, K. E. (2018). Relevance assumed: A case study of balanced scorecard development using system dynamics. In *System dynamics* (pp. 107–132). London: Palgrave Macmillan.

Al-Hamamre, Z., Saidan, M., Hararah, M., Rawajfeh, K., Alkhasawneh, H. E., & Al-Shannag, M. (2017). Wastes and biomass materials as sustainable-renewable energy resources for Jordan. *Renewable and Sustainable Energy Reviews, 67*, 295–314.

Aras, G., Tezcan, N., & Furtuna, O. K. (2018). Multidimensional comprehensive corporate sustainability performance evaluation model: Evidence from an emerging market banking sector. *Journal of Cleaner Production, 185*, 600–609.

Bharadwaja, S., Lee, L., & Madera, J. M. (2018). Customer evaluations of service-oriented organizational citizenship behaviors: Agentic and communal differences. *International Journal of Hospitality Management, 70*, 120–129.

Cole, P., & Banks, G. (2017). Renewable energy programmes in the South Pacific–are these a solution to dependency? *Energy Policy, 110*, 500–508.

de Waal, A., & Goedegebuure, R. (2017). Investigating the causal link between a management improvement technique and organizational performance. *Management Research Review, 40*(4), 429–450.

Dinçer, H., & Yüksel, S. (2019). Multidimensional evaluation of global investments on the renewable energy with the integrated fuzzy decision-making model under the hesitancy. *International Journal of Energy Research, 43*(5), 1775–1784.

Dinçer, H., Hacıoğlu, Ü., & Yüksel, S. (2017). Balanced scorecard based performance measurement of European airlines using a hybrid multicriteria decision making approach under the fuzzy environment. *Journal of Air Transport Management, 63*, 17–33.

Dinçer, H., Yüksel, S., & Martinez, L. (2019). Balanced scorecard-based analysis about European energy investment policies: A hybrid hesitant fuzzy decision-making approach with quality function deployment. *Expert Systems with Applications, 115*, 152–171.

Dinçer, H., Yüksel, S., & Pınarbaşı, F. (2020). Kano-based measurement of customer expectations in retail service industry using IT2 DEMATEL-QUALIFLEX. In *Handbook of research on positive organizational behavior for improved workplace performance* (pp. 349–370). Hershey, PA: IGI Global.

Eti, S., Kalkavan, H., Dinçer, H., & Yüksel, S. (2020). Predicting the role of Islamic banking on sustainable economic development: An analysis for Turkey with ARIMA model. In *Handbook of research on creating sustainable value in the global economy* (pp. 146–164). Hershey, PA: IGI Global.

Hassell, M. D., & Cotton, J. L. (2017). Some things are better left unseen: Toward more effective communication and team performance in video-mediated interactions. *Computers in Human Behavior, 73*, 200–208.

Heiskanen, E., Apajalahti, E. L., Matschoss, K., & Lovio, R. (2018). Incumbent energy companies navigating energy transitions: Strategic action or bricolage? *Environmental Innovation and Societal Transitions, 28*, 57–69.

Hili, J., Pace, D., & Grima, S. (2016). Equity mutual fund performance evaluation: An emerging market perspective. In *Contemporary issues in Bank financial management (Contemporary studies in economic and financial analysis)* (Vol. 97). Bingley, UK: Emerald Group Publishing Limited.

Hossain, M. R. (2020). Python based location analysis of wind mills in urban environment. *GeoJournal*, 1–19.

Hosseini, A., Johansson, S., & Westberg, M. (2017). Design and performance evaluation of a healthcare distribution network towards maintaining a direct-to-customer policy. *International Journal of Advanced Logistics, 6*(2), 68–79.

Kalkavan, H., & Ersin, I. (2019). Determination of factors affecting the south east Asian crisis of 1997 probit-logit panel regression: The south east Asian crisis. In *Handbook of research on global issues in financial communication and investment decision making* (pp. 148–167). Hershey, PA: IGI Global.

Khare, V., Nema, S., & Baredar, P. (2016). Solar–wind hybrid renewable energy system: A review. *Renewable and Sustainable Energy Reviews, 58*, 23–33.

Khoshnevis, P., & Teirlinck, P. (2018). Performance evaluation of R&D active firms. *Socio-Economic Planning Sciences, 61*, 16–28.

Kim, W. S., & Park, K. (2019). Performance evaluation of deterministic flow lines considering multiclass customer and random setups. *Journal of Manufacturing Systems, 53*, 109–123.

Kumar, A., Sah, B., Singh, A. R., Deng, Y., He, X., Kumar, P., & Bansal, R. C. (2017). A review of multi criteria decision making (MCDM) towards sustainable renewable energy development. *Renewable and Sustainable Energy Reviews, 69*, 596–609.

Lee, C. C., & Tseng, H. C. (2018, January). Integrating fuzzy membership function, entropy method and VIKOR to select qualified and stable employee. In *2018 international conference on information management and processing (ICIMP)* (pp. 26–31). Piscataway, NJ: IEEE.

Lin, R. J. (2013). Using fuzzy DEMATEL to evaluate the green supply chain management practices. *Journal of Cleaner Production, 40*, 32–39.

Makhamara, F. H., Waiganjo, E. W., & Kwasira, J. (2016). Influence of strategic recruitment and selection on employee performance in the health sector in Kenya. *Strategic Journal of Business & Change Management, 3*(21), 347.

Maulidia, M., Dargusch, P., Ashworth, P., & Ardiansyah, F. (2019). Rethinking renewable energy targets and electricity sector reform in Indonesia: A private sector perspective. *Renewable and Sustainable Energy Reviews, 101*, 231–247.

Nørreklit, H., Kure, N., & Trenca, M. (2018). Balanced scorecard. In *The international encyclopedia of strategic communication* (pp. 1–6). Hoboken, NJ: Wiley.

Pischke, E. C., Solomon, B., Wellstead, A., Acevedo, A., Eastmond, A., De Oliveira, F., et al. (2019). From Kyoto to Paris: Measuring renewable energy policy regimes in Argentina, Brazil, Canada, Mexico and the United States. *Energy Research & Social Science, 50*, 82–91.

Sarvari, P. A., Ustundag, A., & Takci, H. (2016). Performance evaluation of different customer segmentation approaches based on RFM and demographics analysis. *Kybernetes, 45*(7), 1129–1157.

Sisodia, D. S., Nikhil, S., Kiran, G. S., & Shrawgi, H. (2020). Performance evaluation of learners for analyzing the hotel customer sentiments based on text reviews. In *Performance Management of Integrated Systems and its applications in software engineering* (pp. 199–209). Singapore: Springer.

Song, H., Zhao, C., & Zeng, J. (2017). Can environmental management improve financial performance: An empirical study of A-shares listed companies in China. *Journal of Cleaner Production, 141*, 1051–1056.

Sunderaraman, P., Cosentino, S., Lindgren, K., James, A., & Schultheis, M. T. (2019). An examination of financial capacity and neuropsychological performance in chronic acquired brain injury (CABI). *Brain Injury, 33*(8), 991–1002.

Varmazyar, M., Dehghanbaghi, M., & Afkhami, M. (2016). A novel hybrid MCDM model for performance evaluation of research and technology organizations based on BSC approach. *Evaluation and Program Planning, 58*, 125–140.

Villa, S., Gonçalves, P., & Odong, T. V. (2017). Understanding the contribution of effective communication strategies to program performance in humanitarian organizations. *Journal of Humanitarian Logistics and Supply Chain Management, 7*(2), 126–151.

Wang, J., Ding, D., Liu, O., & Li, M. (2016). A synthetic method for knowledge management performance evaluation based on triangular fuzzy number and group support systems. *Applied Soft Computing, 39*, 11–20.

Wang, S., Li, W., Dincer, H., & Yuksel, S. (2019). Recognitive approach to the energy policies and Investments in Renewable Energy Resources via the fuzzy hybrid models. *Energies, 12*(23), 4536.

Yap, J. B. H., Abdul-Rahman, H., & Chen, W. (2017). Collaborative model: Managing design changes with reusable project experiences through project learning and effective communication. *International Journal of Project Management, 35*(7), 1253–1271.

Zhang, H., Zheng, Y., Ozturk, U. A., & Li, S. (2016). The impact of subsidies on overcapacity: A comparison of wind and solar energy companies in China. *Energy, 94*, 821–827.

Zhang, L. X., Pang, M. Y., Han, J., Li, Y. Y., & Wang, C. B. (2019). Geothermal power in China: Development and performance evaluation. *Renewable and Sustainable Energy Reviews, 116*, 109431.

Zhang, G., Zhou, S., Xia, X., Yüksel, S., Baş, H., & Dincer, H. (2020). Strategic mapping of youth unemployment with interval-valued intuitionistic hesitant fuzzy DEMATEL based on 2-tuple linguistic values. *IEEE Access, 8*, 25706–25721.

Zhou, P., Zhou, P., Yüksel, S., Dinçer, H., & Uluer, G. S. (2019). Balanced scorecard-based evaluation of sustainable energy investment projects with IT2 fuzzy hybrid decision making approach. *Energies, 13*(1), 1–20.

Zhu, Z., & Liao, H. (2019). Do subsidies improve the financial performance of renewable energy companies? Evidence from China. *Natural Hazards, 95*(1–2), 241–256.

Do FED's and CBRT's Policies Affect Turkish Banks' External Borrowings, Financial Impacts and Investment Performances?

Bulent Yaman, Nildag Basak Ceylan, and Ayhan Kapusuzoglu

Abstract The aim of this study is to demonstrate whether FED's and CBRT's monetary polies affected Turkish banks' external borrowings, financial impacts and investment performances. At the end of 2008, FED had to reduce its monetary policy interest rates to near zero as a response to house market collapse. To support its policy, FED started to purchase papers, which resulted in record level of balance sheet and had some spillover effects on emerging markets who enjoyed cheap and abundant liquidity during that period. During the same period, CBRT introduced ROM facility by which banks were able to use foreign exchange to meet their Turkish lira reserve requirements. The Event Study results indicate that FED's policy had significant effects on Turkish banks' external borrowings. Moreover, both regression model and VAR system also indicate that FED's and CBRT's monetary policies may affect banks' external borrowing levels.

1 Introduction

As a response to house market collapse, FED had to reduce its monetary policy interest rates to near zero levels at the end of 2008. FED started to purchase direct obligations and MBSs because the impact of the collapse could not be mitigated solely by conventional policies. However, as the initial stimulus plan was not

---

The views expressed in the study are those of the authors and do not represent the official views of the Central Bank of the Republic Turkey. Moreover, this study is based on Bulent Yaman's Ph. D. Dissertation in Ankara Yildirim Beyazit University, Graduate School of Social Sciences, Ankara, Turkey.

B. Yaman
Central Bank of the Republic of Turkey, Ankara, Turkey
e-mail: bulent.yaman@tcmb.gov.tr

N. B. Ceylan (✉) · A. Kapusuzoglu
Ankara Yildirim Beyazit University, Ankara, Turkey
e-mail: nbceylan@ybu.edu.tr; akapusuzoglu@ybu.edu.tr

H. Dincer, S. Yüksel (eds.), *Strategic Priorities in Competitive Environments*, Contributions to Management Science, https://doi.org/10.1007/978-3-030-45023-6_2

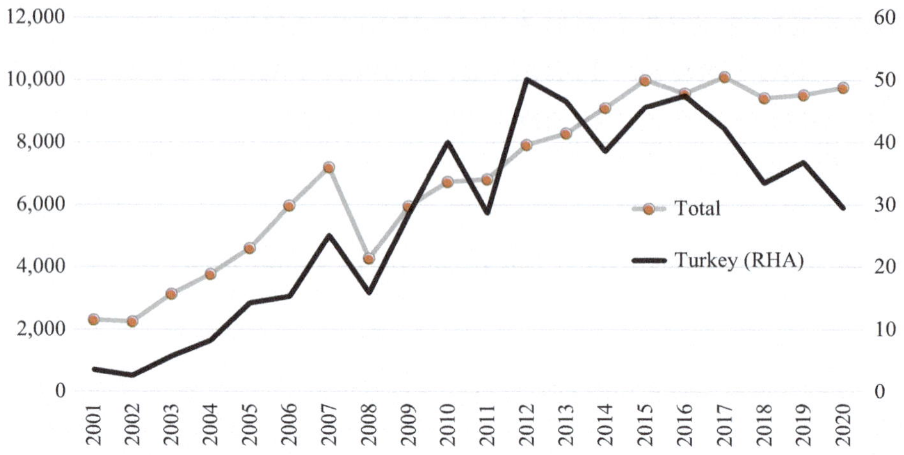

Fig. 1 US portfolio investments (billion US dollar). Source: CPIS

enough to heal the economy, FED included the long-term Treasury securities in its purchase program. As a result of these large-scale asset purchases, the balance sheet of the FED reached to 4.5 trillion US dollar from 0.9 trillion US dollar. Expansion of FED's balance sheet by purchasing securities in large scales at the secondary market during the low-level interest rates is called unconventional monetary policies. Although FED bought several types of securities at the secondary market, the large scale asset program's main drivers were the purchases of US Treasury Securities and Mortgage-Backed Security.

The FED's unconventional monetary policy had some spillover effects on global asset markets, (Belke and Dubova 2018a, b and Belke and Fahrholz 2018). According to IMF (International Monetary Fund 2013a, b), unconventional monetary policies positively affected emerging countries at their early stages through higher global growth. Higher equity prices, lower costs of capital and borrowing rates were observed in emerging market countries during this period. According to the Institute of International Finance, emerging market economies attracted about 1.7 trillion US dollar portfolio inflows between May 2009-November 2015. It can be said that some portion of the liquidity resulted from FED's large scale asset purchases (roughly 3.5 trillion US dollar) went to emerging countries. Especially countries with current account deficits accessed this liquidity to finance their external deficits. As a result, external borrowings of the private sectors of these fund receiving countries increased to record high levels. Moreover, according to IMF's Coordinated Portfolio Investment Survey (CPIS), US outflows exceeded 10 trillion US dollar and Turkey received about 50 billion US dollar (Fig. 1).

Moreover, at the same time, banks increased their external borrowings thanks to the favorable global liquidity conditions (Fig. 2).

All in all, whether the FED's unconventional monetary policy and CBRT's ROM facility affect Turkish banks' external borrowing levels or not is measured in this study. The monetary policy actions (mainly announcements) of developed countries affect other countries mainly through portfolio, liquidity and mainly signaling

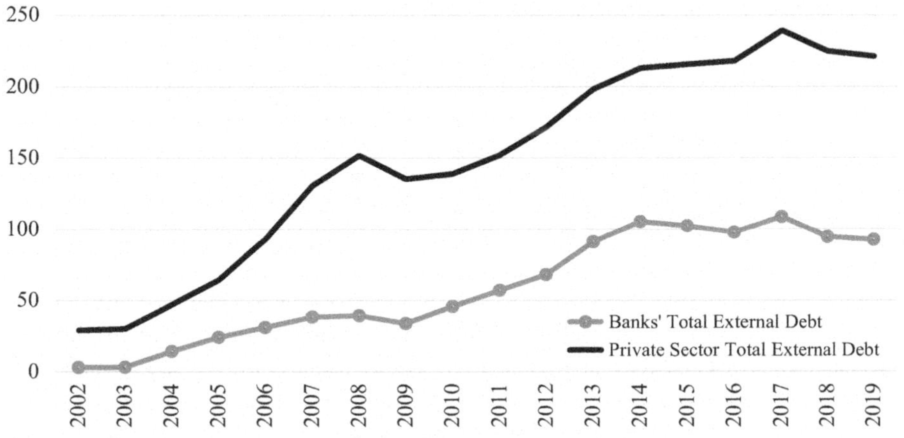

Fig. 2 Turkish Banks' external borrowings (billion US dollar). Source: CBRT

channels by using. In this respect, one of the contributions of this study is to measure the effects of FED's balance sheet changes on the Turkish banks' external borrowing level instead of the portfolio inflows in the form of equity and bonds. Moreover, the related literature measures the effects of the policies by looking only equity return or the yield of the bonds.

1.1 FED's Unconventional Monetary Policy

Near zero level policy rates with constraints on moving them significantly below zero, as using conventional monetary tools were not accommodative, FED started to employ unconventional monetary policies by injecting US dollar liquidity to the market through asset purchases of;

- 175 billion US dollar in direct obligations of Fannie Mae, Freddie Mac, and the Federal Home Loan Banks and 1.25 trillion US dollar in MBS guaranteed by Fannie Mae, Freddie Mac, and Ginnie Mac between December 2008 and August 2010.
- 300 billion US dollar of long-term Treasury papers and an additional $600 billion of longer-term Treasury securities. Moreover, FED started to buy long-term Treasury securities at a pace of $45 billion per month, following the completion of the maturity extension program in December 2012.
- 40 billion US dollar of additional MBS per month to further increase policy accommodation starting in September 2012.

In addition to the large-scale asset purchase program, FED launched Maturity Extension Program to extend the average maturity of its Treasury security holdings to reduce the longer-term interest rates and to support its unconventional monetary policy.

1.2 CBRT's Reserve Option Mechanism

Banks in Turkey started to be able to use foreign exchange for their Turkish lira reserve requirements with certain ratios at the end of 2011. The facility was later called Reserve Option Mechanism (ROM). The reserve option ratio (ROR) and the reserve option coefficient (ROC) are two main parameters that are used to calculate how much foreign exchange can be settled against Turkish lira reserve requirements. Let's suppose that Bank A has to hold 1.000 Turkish lira reserve requirements for its Turkish lira liabilities upon the upcoming reserve requirement period; ROR is 80%, ROC is 10,000 (which means banks can hold 10,000 Turkish lira equivalent of foreign exchange) per unit of Turkish lira reserve requirement) and finally foreign exchange rate of USDTRY is 40,000. In this case, Bank A may hold up to 200 US dollar (Turkish lira requirements $*$ROR$*$ROC/USDTRY Rates = 1.000$*$0.80$*$1,00/40000) for its 1.000 Turkish lira reserve requirements in foreign exchange. In this case, Bank A is able to fulfil its reserve requirement by using 200 US dollar plus 200 Turkish lira (as 80% of 1.000 Turkish lira partially matched FX in accordance with ROM) instead of using 1.000 Turkish lira. If the interest rates and the liquidity conditions are similar for foreign exchange (mainly US dollar) and Turkish lira, the ROM facility is not expected to change banks' balance sheet items. As historically, the cost of Turkish lira funding is higher than that US dollar especially during the FED's unconventional monetary policy period. As the difference between the costs of funding encourage banks to utilize ROM facility near the maximum levels, banks' balance sheets substantially affected. As ROM is used as a kind of swap transaction by which banks are able to receive Turkish lira liquidity from CBRT by placing foreign exchange in CBRT, banks reduced their cross-currency swap position.

One of the other balance sheet items which may had been affected by the ROM facility was the external borrowing levels of Turkish banks. As presented in Fig. 3, there is a sharp increase in external borrowing level at the end of 2011.

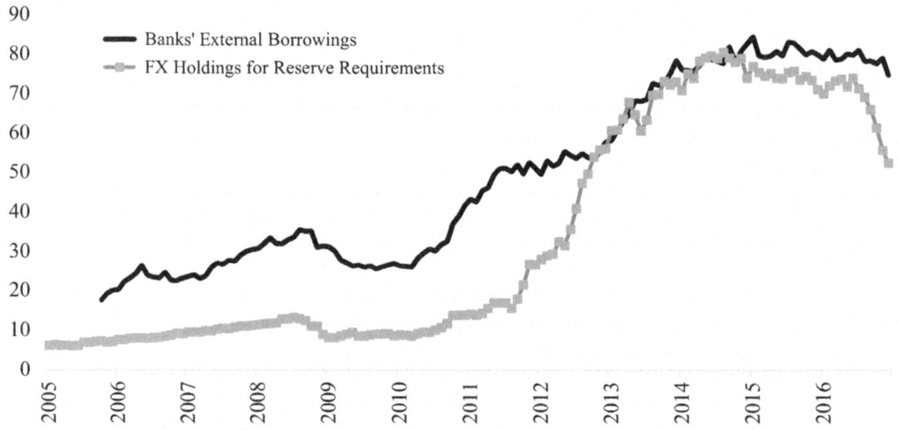

Fig. 3 Turkish Bank's external borrowings and ROM usage (billion US dollar). Source: BRSA

2 Literature Review

Shortly after FED started to employ unconventional monetary policy in 2008 by large scale asset purchases along with near zero policy interest rates, related literature started to emerge. Using large scale asset purchase programs along with near zero policy rates was not a common strategy and later called as "unconventional monetary policy". Namely one of the first comprehensive studies is done by Neely (2010). According to Neely (2010), FED's large-scale asset purchases have significant impacts on foreign exchange and bond markets of selected countries. The currencies depreciate against US dollar and bond yields decrease significantly. According to Chen et al. (2011), FED's monetary policy shocks affect capital inflows and asset prices in emerging countries and the effects are stronger during unconventional monetary policy phase. Hausman and Wongswan (2011) indicates that although global equity indexes are significantly affected by the target surprises; FX rates and long-term interest rates are more exposed to the path surprises. On the other hand, Morgan (2011) indicates that although Emerging Asian Countries received portfolio inflows and some of their currencies appreciated during the first and second phases of FED's unconventional monetary era, FED's asset purchases have no significant effect on financial markets of Emerging Asia.

According to Hayo et al. (2012), FED's monetary policy actions and communications significantly affect equity returns in emerging countries. Glick and Leduc (2012) indicate that due to FED's large-scale asset purchase announcements, US dollar depreciates, the long term interest rates and commodity prices decrease according to the phases of FED's asset purchase programs. The results of the event study of Aït-Sahalia et al. (2012) indicate that FED's unconventional monetary policy announcements are accompanied by reductions in interbank credit and liquidity risk premia domestically and had positive international impacts on Japan and the Euro Area. Glick and Leduc (2013) indicate that US dollar generally depreciates against other currencies due to FED policy surprises. IMF (2013a, b) also indicates that asset prices, corporate leverage and foreign exchange rate exposure increased rapidly in many emerging countries as a result of unconventional monetary policies. However, the effects differ among phases of these programs. According to Bruno and Shin (2013), international capital flows into the banking sector is decreased by a contractionary shock coming from FED.

According to Moore et al. (2013), FED's asset purchases have significant effects on the portfolio inflows into emerging countries mainly via bond markets. By using several empirical studies, Lim et al. (2014) result that FED's quantitative easing policy positively affect loan, portfolio and direct investment inflows into emerging countries. According to Chen et al. (2014), FED's unconventional monetary policy shocks significantly affect capital inflows and asset prices in emerging countries compared to conventional policies. Bauer and Neely (2014) indicate that as a result of FED monetary policy surprises, a significant decline in bond yields in most of the other countries is measured. Ahmed and Zlate (2014) indicate that main drivers of the capital inflows to emerging countries are the growth rate differentials, interest rate differences and global risk aversion during FED's unconventional monetary policy.

According to Rogers et al. (2014), FED's asset purchases result US dollar to depreciate and long-term Treasury yields of other countries to decrease. Gilchrist et al. (2014)'s event study results indicate FED's unconventional monetary policy announcements lower sovereign yields of other advanced countries. According to Korniyenko and Loukoianova (2015), although FED's unconventional monetary policy is mixed effects on emerging countries, it has significant and positive effects on the growth rate of broad money and liquidity in advanced economies. Bhattarai et al. (2015) and Tillmann (2016), FED's unconventional monetary policy actions and announcements significantly affect FX rates, Treasury bond yields and equity prices in emerging countries. The VECM results of Chen et al. (2015) indicate that FED's unconventional policies resulted in reduction in corporate and term spreads. Bowman et al. (2015)'s event study results indicate that there are significant effects of FED's monetary policy announcements on emerging countries assets. Fratzscher et al. (2016a, b) indicate that first and second phases of FED's unconventional monetary policy announcements cause a portfolio rebalancing in the US and emerging countries, respectively. Lim and Mohapatra (2016) indicates that a lower bound quantitative easing of FED affects gross inflows about 5% above trend for the average developing economy. Lo Duca et al. (2016) indicates that FED's unconventional monetary policy asset purchases play an important role in increasing bond issuance in the non-financial corporate bond segment in both emerging and advanced countries. According to Barroso et al. (2016), FED's unconventional monetary policy has significant and positive effects on Brazilian economy particularly through FX rates, equity prices and economic activity in Brazil.

3 Data Sources, Definitions and Model Free Results

The empirical methods used in this study are based on monthly data set for the period of December 2005 to December 2016. The data set covers both FED's unconventional monetary policy and CBRT's ROM facility periods. For the ROM data, be-weekly data is available at the CBRT's web site. In addition, the FED's balance sheet data can be reached by weekly from FED's web site. The foreign exchange rates of USDTRY are collected from CBRT's web site on a daily. VIX, EMBI and Credit Default Swaps (CDS) can be reached as tick data via Bloomberg LP. For the credit ratings of Turkey, the big three credit agencies' information can be reached their web sites on a daily basis. As the dependent variable, we prefer to use Turkish banks' external borrowings derived from balance sheets obtained from Banking Regulation and Supervision Agency of Turkey (BRSA)'s and CBRT's web sites. Although most of the data can be obtained daily, the dependent variable is available

Table 1 Summary statistics of all variables

Name	Source	Average	STD	Median	Min	Max
External borrowing	CBRT	50	23	50	18	85
FED's balance sheet	FED	2.668	1.352	2.779	823	4.500
ROM	CBRT	15	17	0	0	44
USDTRY	CBRT	18,512	0,5639	16,650	11,639	35,249
VIX	CBOE	20.0	8.8	17.2	10.4	59.9
Spread	CBRT and FED	9.5%	2.8%	9.7%	4.6%	16.2%
CDS	Bloomberg LP	218	67	203	118	487
EMBI	JP Morgan	275	82	253	169	639
Credit rating	S&P, Fitch, Moody'S	–	–	–	0,00	1,00

only in monthly bases. Model free summary statistics of all variables are presented at Table 1.

4 Empirical Analysis

In this part, it is tried to demonstrate whether FED's unconventional monetary policy and CBRT's ROM facility affect external borrowing of Turkish banks. There are several types of analyses to measure the impact of FED's unconventional monetary policy on selected assets of emerging countries. Among them, event study can be considered as the most widely used one. However, as ROM facility has only one event (the day when ROM facility was launched by CBRT), it is not suitable for the event study. Therefore, FED's monetary policy can be studied only by event study. The second approach is a linear regression model OLS. As OLS requires some specific rules for the residuals and the selected variables, some of the variables that are used in the event study are excluded in the OLS. Finally, VAR systems have been started to be preferred for this topic recently. Therefore, a VAR system is set to measure FED's and CBRT's policy effects on external borrowings of Turkish banks.

4.1 Event Study

Compared with other econometric studies, "Event Study" has the advantages of being clear and simple. Moreover, event studies are intensely used to evaluate the effects of FED's QE2 on various markets (Hamilton (2011). Hausman and Wongswan (2011), Morgan (2011), Aït-Sahalia et al. (2012) Glick and Leduc (2012 and 2013), Moore et al. (2013), Gilchrist et al. (2014), Rogers et al. (2014), Bauer and Neely (2014), Chen et al. (2014) and Barroso et al. (2016) use event study method when investigating the effects of asset purchases of FED on capital flows, long-term interest rates, exchange rates, equity indexes, commodity and financial conditions abroad. In event study method, it is assumed that the causality runs in one direction, therefore, in this study, FED's asset purchases is assumed to affect the external borrowing of Turkish banks.

4.1.1 Events

The announcement and speech days of FED as mentioned by Chodorow-Reich (2014), Bauer and Neely (2014) and Chen et al. (2014) are defined as events presented at Table 2.

4.1.2 Structure

Although there is not a single methodology to employ event study, the general structures of McKinlay (1997) and Brown and Warner (1980, 1985) are used in this study. After defining the events, the "estimation window" and "event window" should be identified. Estimation window is the period that is considered normal days during which no surprise in it. The estimation window is determined as the period between 60 months before the event date and 6 months before the event date, where the event date (time zero) refers to the dates of FED's unconventional monetary policy announcements. Therefore, (−60,−6) denotes the estimation window and (−5, +5) is the event window. In this framework, the arithmetic, expected and abnormal returns of asset i are demonstrated at Eqs. (1)–(3) respectively.

Table 2 FED's unconventional monetary policy related events

Date	Phase	Explanation
25.11.2008	I	FED indicates purchases of up to 100 bio USD in agency debt and up to 500 bio USD in agency MBS at **intermeeting policy announcement**
01.12.2008	I	FED's chairman states that "FED could purchase longer term Treasury securities in substantial quantities" **intermeeting policy announcement**
16.12.2008	I	FED indicates "exceptionally low level of the federal funds rate for some time"
18.03.2009	I	FED indicates purchases of up to additional 100 bio USD in agency debt, up to 750 bio USD in agency MBS and 300 bio USD in Treasury securities.
10.08.2010	II	FED indicates reinvestment principal payments from first phase of QE purchases in Treasury
03.11.2010	II	FED indicates purchases of 600 bio USD in Treasury securities
21.09.2011	II	FED indicates maturity extension program
13.09.2012	III	FED indicates purchases of 40 bio USD per month of agency MBS, maintaining the federal funds rates at zero to mid-2015.
12.12.2012	III	FED indicates increase of 40 bio USD per month agency MBS purchases to 85 bio USD

$$R_{i,t} = \frac{P_{i,t} + P_{i,t-1}}{P_{i,t-1}} \quad (1)$$

$$\overline{R}_i = \frac{1}{55} \sum_{t=-60}^{-6} R_{i,t} \quad (2)$$

$$AR_{i,t} = R_{i,t} - \overline{R}_i \quad (3)$$

Where $\overline{R_i}$ is the average return of the asset class of $_i$ for the estimation window which starts 60 months before the event date and ends 6 months before the event date. Therefore, abnormal return (AR_i) of time t is the difference between return of time t and normal return. After defining abnormal returns, it is important to test the results to compare indicators' significance levels. For the selected event studies, crude dependence adjustment (CDA) developed and defined by Brown and Warner is used for the test statistic computed by dividing the mean abnormal returns of event date with the standard deviation of abnormal returns. According to Brown and Warner, as long as the abnormal returns are normally, independently and identically distributed, the test statistic will be distributed with Student-T. For a specific indicator over an event window (−5, +5), the cumulative abnormal return (CARi) and CDA's test statistic are defined at Eq. (4) and (5), respectively.

$$CAR_i(-5, +5) = \sum_{t=-5}^{+5} AR_{i,t} \quad (4)$$

$$t_{CAD} = \frac{CAR}{s(CAR)} \quad (5)$$

After setting up the structure of the event study analysis, the variables reactions to FED's unconventional monetary policy is interpreted.

4.1.3 Main Findings

Graphs in the Fig. 4. show the reactions of selected variables to FED's related actions for following 5 months. As stated before, Event 1–3 are considered as QE1, and Event 4–6 are considered as QE2. If the ratio of CAR/sCAD of a variable is higher or lower than ±2, the FED's unconventional monetary policy action (Event) has significant effects on the selected variable. Moreover, negative sign of the ratio of CAR/sCAD indicates that the variable decreases as a result of the Event. The selected variables are External Borrowing Level, External Borrowing Leverage Ratio, USDTRY Rates, Policy Rate Differences, VIX, Turkey CDS Spreads and EMBIs. The results are revealed according to variable basis to separate the effects of different phases of the FED's unconventional monetary actions.

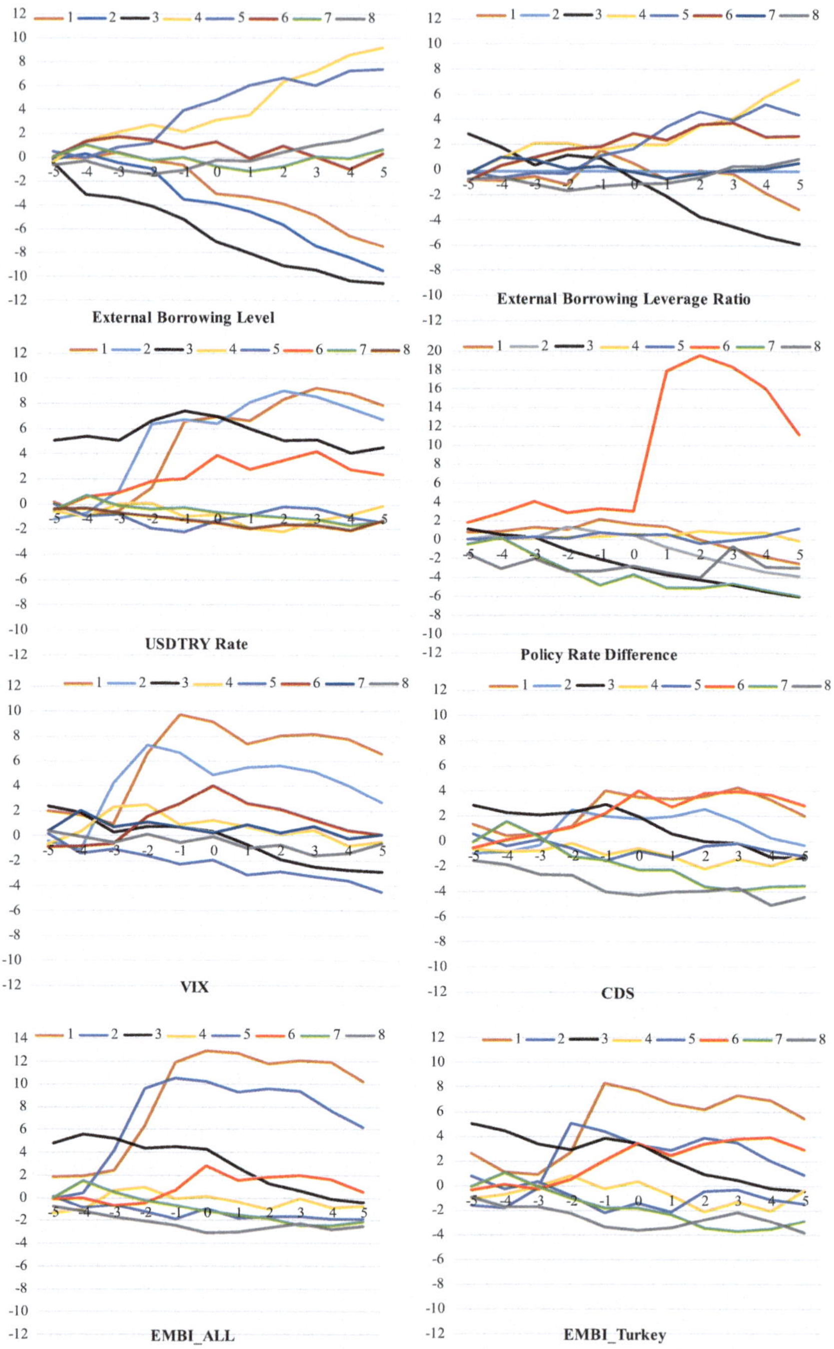

Fig. 4 All event comparisons per indicator (CAR/s(CAR) Results)

- **External Borrowing Level:** During the first phase of QE, Turkish banks' external borrowing levels are decreased. However, Turkish banks start to significantly increase their external borrowing levels during second phase of QE. This results are in line with the results of Chen et al. (2011) indicating FED's spillover effects on foreign exchange flows to emerging countries; of Lim et al. (2014) indicating the quantitative easing of FED positively affect loan inflows to emerging countries; of Chen et al. (2014) indicating US policy shocks significantly affect capital flows and asset prices in emerging countries; of Lim and Mohapatra (2016) indicating quantitative easing affects inflows to developing countries. Moreover, the findings are in line with Fratzscher et al. (2016a, b) who measure that announcements made during the second phase of QE caused a portfolio rebalancing into emerging countries.
- **VIX:** When FED announced to start purchasing of mortgage market papers (Event 1) and longer-term securities (Event 2) at the first time, VIX responded very significantly. On the other hand, VIX decreased significantly when FED announced to start purchasing of additional securities (Event 5) at the end of 2010. Therefore, it can be stated that FED's unconventional monetary policy announcements result in decrease in the market volatility during the second phase of QE. The results similar to Fratzscher et al. (2016a, b) who indicate that policy announcements mainly cause a portfolio rebalancing into more risky segments in the US during the first phase.
- **External Borrowing Leverage Ratio:** Announcements of the first phase of QE related have negative and significant effects on the leverage (debt ratio) of Turkish banks, which implies that banks external borrowings in terms of total assets decrease during the first phase of QE. On the other hand, the debt ratio was positively and significantly affected during the second phase of QE. Therefore, the structure and thus leverage of the banks' balance sheet is affected by the announcements of QE1 and QE2 differently. As there are no papers regarding the impact of the QE on the capital structure of banks, one of the contributions of the study is demonstrating the impacts of FED's unconventional monetary policy on banks' leverages. According to the results, Turkish banks leverage is decreased as a result of the QE1. On the other hand, announcements related to QE2 encourage banks to increase their leverage ratio. This result is in line with our expectations.
- **USDTRY Exchange Rate:** The QE1 announcements significantly and negatively affect the exchange rates. During the first phase of QE, Turkish lira depreciates against US dollar. Although QE2 announcements had positive impacts on the USDTRY exchange rates, its significance level not so high compared to that of QE1. Therefore, the results are not in line with Morgan (2011) indicating some of the Emerging Asian Countries' currencies appreciated during the first and second phases of FED's quantitative easing purchases. Glick and Leduc (2013) also indicate that US dollar depreciate against other currencies due to the monetary policy surprises of FED. On the other hand, results are supported by Barroso et al. (2016) indicating that FED's unconventional monetary policy has significant and positive effects on Brazilian exchange rates.

- **Policy Rate Difference:** The results indicate that policy rate difference decreases generally due to the unconventional monetary policy announcements. However, policy interest rate difference is affected mostly by the final announcement described as Event 8. Although first phase of QE has not significant impacts on the policy rate difference in general, policy rate difference became narrower after QE2. The findings are parallel with the results of Ahmed and Zlate (2014) stating that interest rate differences between central banks explain the capital private inflows to emerging countries.
- **CDS of Turkey**: When FED announced to start unconventional monetary policy at first time (Event 1), the CDS increased significantly. It is not in line with Chen et al. (2011) who indicate that announcements of first phase of QE significantly reduce emerging Asian CDSs. On the other hand, CDS level decreases as a result the third phase announcements of QE, which in line with Chen et al. (2011).
- **EMBI_All**: Reactions of EMBI to announcements are very similar to that of VIX. As presented at Fig. 25, the first phase QE announcements resulted in increase in the EMBI significantly. On the other hand, EMBI was negatively affected from the announcements of the third phase of QE. The results imply that the EMBI decreases as a result of FED's unconventional monetary announcements. However, results are not similar to Hayo et al. (2012) who indicate an ascending EMBIG spread implies moving capital into equity markets in times of higher bond returns.

EMBI_Turkey: Similar to the EMBI_All, first two (Event 1 and 2) announcements of FED result in increased EMBI_Turkey. The announcements of third phase QE negatively and significantly affect EMBI_Turkey. Therefore, it can be stated that EMBI_Turkey increases as a result of first phase QE announcements and decreases third phase QE announcements. As emerging market financial indicators are expected to be adversely affected by QE1 and positively affected by QE2, the results are not as expected.

The results of the event study support the argument that the FED's unconventional monetary policy announcements have significant effects on the selected indicators of Turkey. On the other hand, the significance levels and the signs of financial indicators vary according to the QE phases. In general, as a result of the announcements during the first phase of FED's unconventional monetary policy, the level of external borrowings and the leverage of Turkish banks decrease. According to the literature, FED's first phase announcements have positive effects on financials of US, however negative on emerging countries. On the other hand, Turkish banks' external borrowing level and external borrowing leverage ratio increase during the second phase of QE. The results are also in line with the literature indicating that FED's second phase of QE has positive effects on the financials of emerging countries. On the other hand, the effects on other selected variables are mixed.

4.2 *Regression Analysis*

Although event study method is one of the most widely used empirical method for analyzing the effects of FED's unconventional monetary policy surprises on various asset classes of emerging countries, regression analysis is employed by several scholars as well. In this respect, we also used regression analysis to measure the effects of the FED's unconventional monetary policy and CBRT's ROM facility on Turkish banks' external borrowings.

4.2.1 Model

To conduct empirical analysis, a linear regression model is set up similar to Ahmed and Zlate (2014), Cerutti et al. (2014), Chung et al. (2014), Korniyenko and Loukoianova (2015) The baseline model is;

$$\mathrm{DEBT_t} = \alpha + \beta\mathrm{FED} + \gamma\mathrm{ROM} + \delta\mathrm{X} + \varepsilon \tag{6}$$

where *Debt* stands for external borrowing level of Turkish banks in billions of the US dollar, *ROM* denotes ROM utilization level of Turkish banks in billions of the US dollar. α, β, γ, and δ are the parameters to be estimated and ε represents the residual component of the model. Moreover, *X* denotes a vector of control variables. The X vector is composed according to the literature review stated above. The variables are;

$$\mathrm{X} = \begin{pmatrix} X_1 \\ X_2 \\ X_3 \\ X_4 \end{pmatrix} = \begin{pmatrix} DIF \\ VIX \\ FX \\ GR \end{pmatrix} \tag{7}$$

where interest rate differences respect to US is DIF; volatility index is VIX; USDTRY exchange rates is FX; and the dummy variable that represent investment grade criterion of Turkey is GR. While investors invest in a country, they prefer that the country receives investment grade from at least one credit rating agency. Generally, if a country has investment grades from two of the three credit rating agencies, that country will be placed on investment radars of the most of the investors and funds managements globally. Therefore, investment grade criterion is included to the model as a dummy variable. The dummy variable's value is "1" if Turkey receives at least two investment grades from the three rating agencies at a given month, otherwise zero. Using investment grade or credit rating of country such a way as one of the explanatory variables in the model when analysing policy effects is one of the contributions of this work.

According to the literature, we expect positive and significant relationships between FED's unconventional monetary policy asset purchases and ROM utilization, and the external borrowings of Turkish banks. However, we expect negative relationship between VIX and the level of the external borrowing of Turkish banks. If global risk appetite decreases (higher VIX), investors become less willing to lend abroad. Therefore, the external borrowing level of Turkish banks is expected to be adversely affected by the increase of the VIX.

On the other hand, the results regarding to exchange rates and interest rate difference are contradictory. The cost of borrowing may increase due to USDTRY exchange rate, which forces Turkish banks to decrease their external borrowing limits. However, depreciation in a domestic currency may encourage foreign lenders as well. The increase in the differentiation in interest rates may increase the cost of the external borrowing, which makes the external borrowing more costly and discourages banks to borrow externally. On the other hand, higher interest rate difference offers higher returns to the foreign investors.

4.2.2 Regression Results

At the first stage of the regression analysis, the base model presented in Eq. (8) is run and its empirical statistics interpreted. Later, the residuals and the variables of the base model is checked. As it is presented at Table 3, almost all of the variables have unit root according to Augmented Dicey-Fuller test statistics at the first differences.

To have a model that is not has any issues regarding its residuals and variables is the prerequisite to show the relationship between FED's and CBRT's policy actions and Turkish banks external borrowings. The modified model is presented at Eq. (9). Before demonstrating modified model's statistic results, it is critical to test the residuals against normality, correlation and heteroscedasticity.

$$\begin{aligned}\Delta(DEBT_t) = \alpha + \beta\Delta(FED_{t-2}) + \gamma\Delta(ROM_{t-2}) + \delta_1\Delta(DIF_{t-2}) + \delta_2\Delta \mathrm{VIX} \\ + \delta_3\Delta \mathrm{FX} + \delta_4\Delta(\mathrm{GR}_{t-2}) + \varepsilon\end{aligned} \quad (8)$$

Jarque-Bera Test is preferred to test the normality of the residuals of the modified model presented at Eq. (8) and indicates the residuals of the modified model are

Table 3 Augmented Dickey-Fuller test statistics of variables

Variables	Probability*	First diff
FED's balance sheet	0.8645	0.0000
Reserve option mechanism	0.9426	0.0000
Interest rate difference	0.2234	0.0000
VIX	0.0141	0.0000
USDTRY rates	0.9999	0.0000
Investment grade criterion	0.5066	0.0000
Residuals	0.0657	0.0000

*One sided p-values

Table 4 Regression test results of the modified model

Variable	Coefficient	Std. error	t-statistic	Prob.
Constant	0.267813	0.152057	1.761260	0.0806
FED's balance sheet**	0.000902	0.001699	0.530758	0.5965
Reserve option mechanism**	0.150546	0.076595	1.965488	0.0516
Interest rate difference**	5.334921	13.93513	0.382840	0.7025
VIX	0.033710	0.032262	1.044866	0.2981
USDTRY rates	4.643948	2.186920	2.123511	0.0357
Investment grade criterion**	3.751673	1.152285	3.255856	0.0015
	Values			
R-squared	0.184269			
Adjusted R-squared	0.145114			
S.E. of regression	1.603637			
Sum squared resid	321.4563			
Log likelihood	−246.0438			
F-statistic	4.706145			
Prob (F-statistic)	0.000237			
Mean dependent var.	0.415009			
S.D. dependent var.	1.734411			
Akaike info criterion	3.833997			
Schwarz criterion	3.986873			
Hannan-Quinn criterion	3.896119			
Durbin-Watson stat	1.935286			

Table reports coefficient estimates of OLS regressions of 1 month change of external borrowing of banks. Sig.level: %5

*All variables are used with their first difference

**Second lags of the variables are used

***Accumulated Response to Cholesky One S.D. Innovations ± 2 S.E

normally distributed. Moreover, the residuals of the modified model is tested for correlation. The Breusch-Godfrey Serial Correlation LM Test indicates that there is no correlation among the residuals of the modified model. Furthermore, the residuals of the modified model are tested for the heteroscedasticity by using Breusch-Pagan-Godfrey test and the test results indicate that modified model's residuals are homoscedastic. Finally, the residuals of the modified model are tested against stationary by using Augmented Dickey-Fuller Test statistics and residuals are stationary.

After modifying the base model by using the first difference of the all variables and passing the tests of the residuals for normality, correlation and heteroscedasticity, the regression results of the modified model are presented at Table 4. As a result of the modifications on the variables to have a robust model, we had to give up the explanatory power of the model. Therefore, the adjusted R^2 decreased to 14% from 95%. Moreover, the results of t-statistics of the variables have changes.

4.2.3 Main Findings

The regression model presented Eq. (8) provides us satisfactory expected results in terms of the expectations and literatures, respectively. FED's unconventional monetary policy actions and thus balance sheet expansion and CBRT's ROM facility have positive affect on the banks' external borrowing levels. On the other hand, surprisingly the ROM facility had statistically the more significant independent variable in the model compared to the FED's balance sheet expansion. Therefore, it may be interpreted that CBRT's ROM facility may have impacts on external borrowings of Turkish banks than that of FED's asset purchases unintentionally. Moreover, to having investment grade from two of the major three credit rating agencies is one of the most important independent variables which drives banks to borrow externally thanks to FED maintaining low level of borrowing costs. Therefore, it can be said that when Turkey has investment grades from two of the three credit rating agencies, the level of the external borrowing of the banks increases.

When the policy interest rate difference becomes wider, the level of external borrowing increases due to the increasing return of the lenders abroad. Moreover, the relationship between exchange rates and capital flows is as expected. The test results indicate that the depreciated exchange rates have positive effect on the external borrowing of the banks. On the other hand, VIX do have neither expected sign nor the significant t-statistics according to the test results.

4.3 VAR

According to the literature review, some of the scholar prefer to use VECM rather than the VAR models as a result of their variables' preferences. As "Intercept (no trend) in CE and test VAR" and perform Trace and Maximum Eigenvalue Tests indicate no co-integration at the 5% level, there is no need to use Vector Error Correction (VEC) or nonstationary regression methods to estimate the co-integrating equation.

4.3.1 VAR System

In the VAR system, it is critical to demonstrate how FED's unconventional monetary policy and CBRT's ROM facility decisions transform to the external borrowing of Turkish banks. In a period, due to abundant global liquidity and low level of borrowing costs due to FED's asset purchases and ROM facility, it is assumed that banks increased their external borrowing level. In the VAR model, the ordering of the variables may directly affects the ordering of the system is; (1) FED for FED's Balance Sheet, (2) VIX for VIX, (3) FX for USDTRY exchange rates, (4) ROM for ROM facility and (5) DEBT for External Borrowings of Turkish Banks. Similar to

Bruno and Shin (2013), to identify the impacts of the shocks, VAR system is set as follows;

$$T(L)y_t = \varepsilon_t \tag{9}$$

where T(L) is a matrix of polynomial with a lag operator (L), yt is an "n x 1" data vector. Moreover, ε_t is a vector of disturbances and serially not correlated. It is a five variable VAR system with the Cholesky restrictions. Lagrange Multiplier Test result indicates that there are no autocorrelation among the residuals according to the test statistics. Moreover, according to the stability condition test results, the eigenvalues are less than one and the formal test confirms no root lies outside the unit circle. Therefore, the system satisfies the stability condition and is stationary. Furthermore, the majority of the lag criteria including Akaike and Hannan-Quinn Information Criterion suggest using one lag for the system.

4.3.2 Impulse Response Analysis

After uncovering the latent variables and estimating VAR parameters, impulse response functions can be derived. For this purposes, the impulse response functions of all endogenous variables are separated into ROM (Fig. 5) and FED's unconventional monetary (Fig. 6) actions.

As FED's asset purchases have indirect impacts on the global risk appetite, VIX immediately and sharply increases as a response to a shock of FED's asset

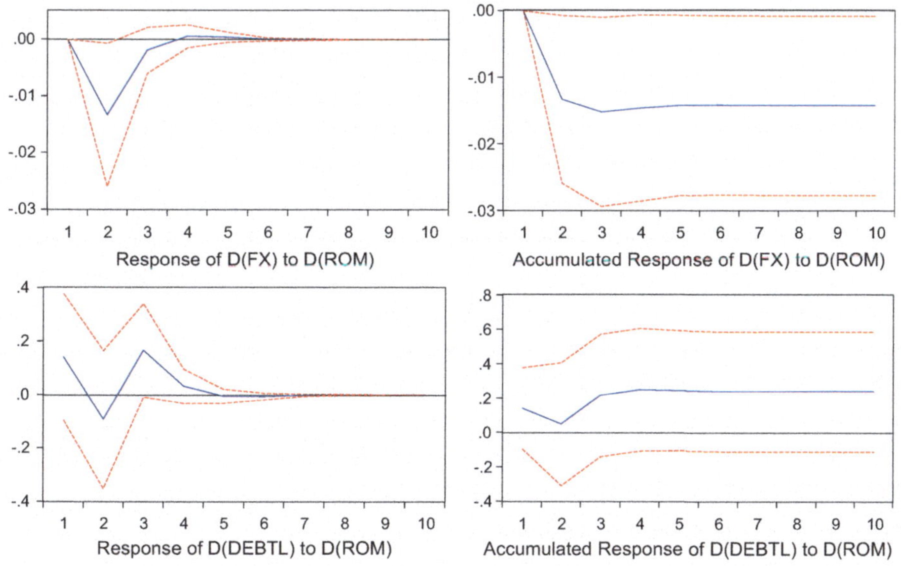

Fig. 5 Responses to CBRT's ROM

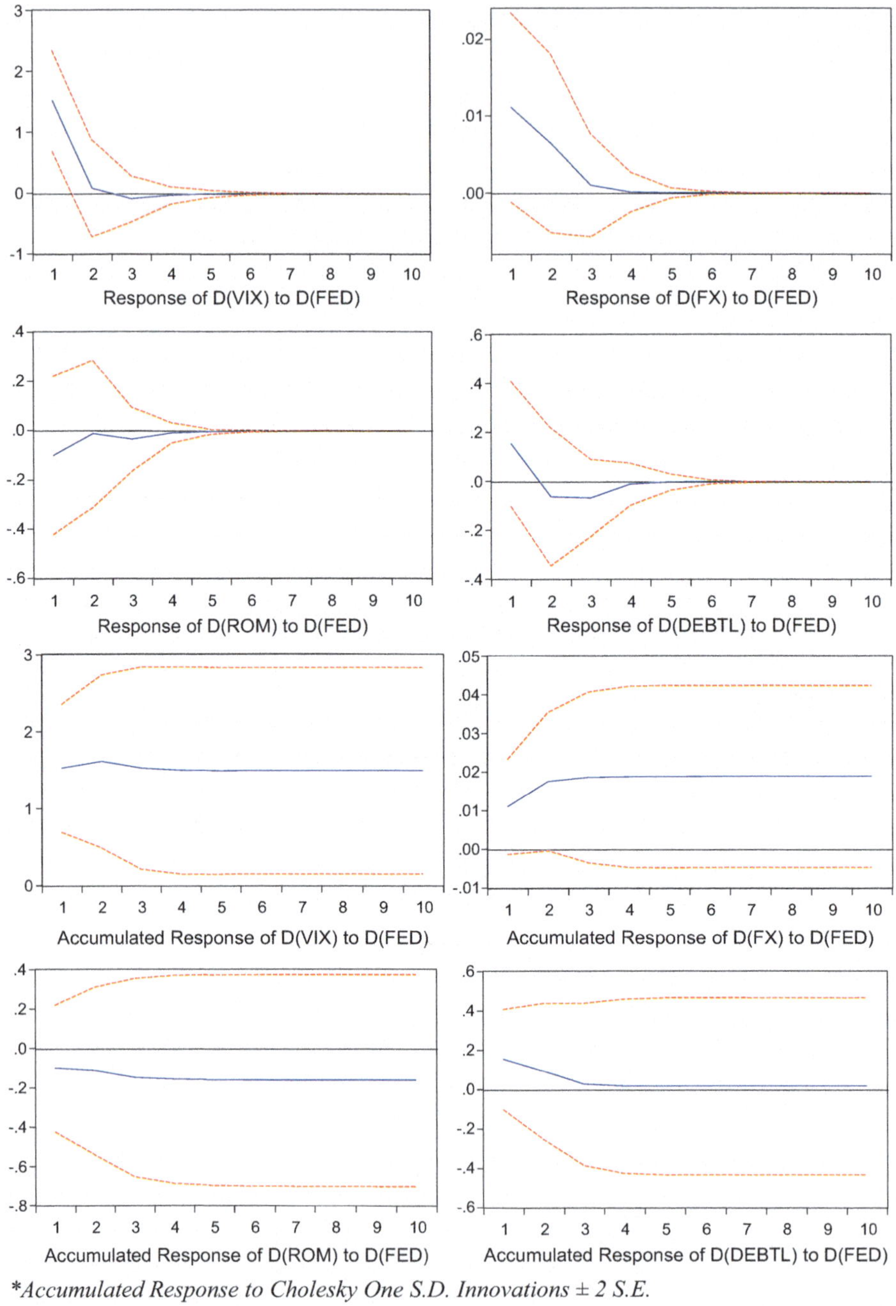

Fig. 6 Responses to FED's asset purchases

purchases. However, the effect fades away after 2 months and goes negative after third month. Similar to VIX, the USDTRY exchange rate increases and normalizes after fifth month in response to FED's asset purchases. However, the magnitude is smaller than that of VIX. As expected, the response of external borrowing level of Turkish banks to FED's asset purchases is positive at first month, but later decreases and hits below zero at the second month. As a whole, responses of the selected endogenous variables to the FED's asset purchases are high and positive at the first moths.

All the impulse response functions demonstrate that both FED's balance sheet and ROM facility have strong and positive effects on the external borrowings of Turkish banks. A shock in FED's balance sheet or CBRT's ROM leads banks to increase their external borrowings. On the other hand, the effects of ROM policy last longer than that of FED.

4.3.3 Variance Decomposition

The VAR system presented in this section gives the opportunity to decompose the forecast error variances into the contribution to the external borrowings of Turkish banks. The decomposition gives the overall magnitude role of these variables for measuring the subtleties of the endogenous variables. The variance decomposition results of external borrowing of Turkish banks are presented at the Fig. 7.

The variance decomposition results indicate that both FED's balance sheet and CBRT's ROM facility have limited effect on variance of the external borrowings of Turkish banks. On the other hand, USDTRY exchange rates has small effect on the first month while the effect increases in the following months. External borrowings of Turkish banks respond to CBRT's ROM facility very high after 2nd month and continue until 10th month. The results are similar to the regression model's results. On the other hand, the external borrowings of Turkish banks do not respond to the FED's large-scale asset purchases as expected.

4.3.4 Main Findings

In general, the VAR system explains whether external borrowings of Turkish banks are affected in a system of endogenous variables. According to the system, both FED's balance sheet and ROM facility have positive effects on external borrowings of Turkish banks. On the other hand, the ROM's effect is higher and lasts longer compared to that of the FED's unconventional monetary policy.

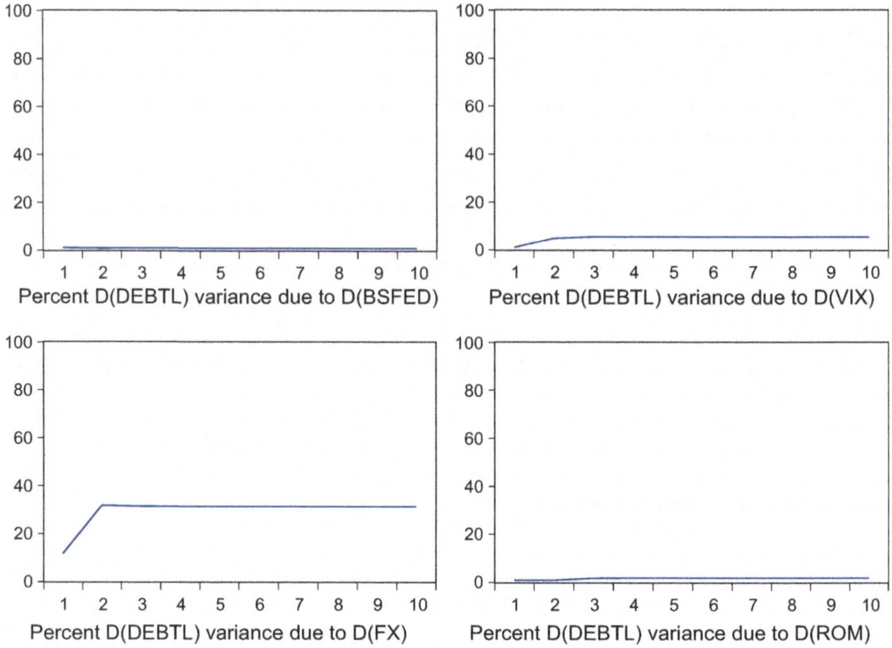

Fig. 7 Variance decomposition of external borrowing of Turkish Banks

5 Conclusion

At the end of 2008, the house market collapse in the US forced FED to reduce its policy rates to near zero levels. However, the impacts of the collapse could not be mitigated only by conventional monetary policies of FED. At this stage, FED announced to purchase direct obligations and MBS of mortgage related Government Sponsored Enterprises to rise stimulate again the economy. As the first stimulus package was not enough to heal the economy, FED expanded its purchases to include also long-term Treasury securities. As a result of these large-scale asset purchases, the balance sheet of the FED increased from 0.9 trillion US dollar to 4.5 trillion US dollar. The final and desired result of the large-scale asset purchases in the secondary market was to increase investment and purchases of consumer durables, to appreciate the domestic currency and to increase in the prices of more risky assets. In this framework, purchasing large scale securities at the secondary market when policy rates are near zero level is generally called unconventional monetary policy.

On the other hand, the abundant amount of US dollar liquidity due to FED's unconventional policy had some spillover effects especially on the emerging countries due to their positive interest rate difference with US. Having easier access to the global fund market compared to real sector, financial institutions of emerging countries borrowed large portion of these funds especially during the second stage of QE. As financial institutions provided these funds to domestic corporates in their countries, their balance sheets also expanded.

During FED's unconventional monetary policy period, banks in Turkey became able to use foreign exchange for their Turkish lira reserve requirements with certain limits at the end of 2011, which was called ROM. As the cost of funding for Turkish lira was higher compared to US dollar, the difference between the costs of funding encouraged banks to utilize ROM facility. Therefore, similar to FED's unconventional monetary policy, CBRT's ROM facility also indirectly affected banks' balance sheets.

The aim of this study is to demonstrate whether or not FED's unconventional monetary policy and CBRT's ROM policy affected external borrowings of Turkish banks. The effects of FED's unconventional monetary policy started in 2008 on other countries have been a topic for researchers since 2012 by using mainly event study, regression analysis and VAR. In this study, all of these three methods employed to demonstrate the impacts of FED's and CBRT's monetary policy actions on external borrowings of Turkish banks.

The event study results demonstrate that FED's unconventional monetary policy announcements significantly affected Turkish banks' external borrowing levels and leverage ratios. On the other hand, these effects' extent differentiated depending on the phases of the quantitative easing. Turkish banks' external borrowing levels and leverage ratio were decreased during the first phase of FED's quantitative easing. On the other hand, external borrowing levels and leverage ratio of Turkish banks were increased during second phase of FED's quantitative easing. The results are in line with the results of other researches such as Chen et al. (2011).

In the regression analysis, FED's balance sheet and utilization of CBRT's ROM facility are assumed to be as the main determinants of the Turkish banks' external borrowing levels. In this respect, explaining external borrowing level of the Turkish banks by using FED's balance sheet and CBRT's ROM facility is the main contribution of this study. According to the results, although expansion in FED's balance sheet leads Turkish banks to increase their external borrowings, the effect is not statistically significant. On the other hand, the model indicates that there are positive relationship between ROM facility and Turkish banks' external borrowings. Among the control variables, investment grade criterion is the most effective factor impacting external borrowings of Turkish banks.

In the VAR system, when FED decreases its policy rates and injects liquidity to the market via large scale asset purchases at the same time; the cost of borrowing decreases, available liquidity and risk appetite increases in the market. As a result of abundant liquidity and low yields in the US, the investors in the US start to search for assets with higher yields. When asset yields in Turkey are higher, some part of the liquidity is expected to head to assets in Turkey. As banks are assumed to have easier access to international fund markets, Turkish banks increase their external borrowings. In addition, the ROM facility is assumed to be another factor that may affect Turkish banks' external borrowings. In general, the VAR system explains how the external borrowings of the Turkish banks is determined in a system of endogenous variables. According to the system, both FED's balance sheet and ROM facility have positive effects on the external borrowing level of Turkish banks. On the other hand, the ROM's effect lasts longer compare to that of the FED's.

As a result of the study, it can be said that Turkish banks external borrowings are affected by FED's unconventional monetary policy. On the other hand, the magnitude and the direction of the effect differentiates according to the phases of FED's quantitative easing. As supported by the models, second phase of the quantitative easing encouraged Turkish banks to borrow abroad. Moreover, Turkish banks external borrowing levels are affected by the CBRT's ROM facility. In this respect, there are several contributions of the study.

There are several contributions of the study. Using both FED's balance sheet and CBRT's ROM facility in a VAR system; including an investment grade criterion in a regression model; and explaining external borrowing levels and leverage ratios of Turkish banks with FED's balance sheet and CBTR's ROM are considered as the main contributions.

References

Ahmed, S., & Zlate, A. (2014). Capital flows to emerging market economies: A brave new world? *Journal of International Money and Finance, 48*, 221–248.

Aït-Sahalia, Y., Andritzky, J., Jobst, A., Nowak, S., & Tamirisa, N. (2012). Market response to policy initiatives during the global financial crisis. *Journal of International Economics, 87*, 162–177.

Barroso, J. B. R. B., Silva, L. A. P., & Sales, A. S. (2016). Quantitative easing and related capital flows into Brazil: Measuring its effects and transmission channels through a rigorous counterfactual evaluation. *Journal of International Money and Finance, 67*, 102–122.

Bauer, M. D., & Neely, C. J. (2014). International channels of the FED's unconventional monetary policy. *Journal of International Money and Finance, 44*, 24–46.

Belke, A., & Dubova, I. (2018a). International spillovers in global asset markets. *Economic Systems, 42*(1), 3–17.

Belke, A., & Dubova, I. (2018b). On the role of international spillovers from the European Central Bank's unconventional monetary policy. *Credit and Capital Markets, 51*(1), 151–170.

Belke, A., & Fahrholz, C. (2018). Emerging and small open economies, unconventional monetary policy and exchange rates–a survey. *International Economics and Economic Policy, 15*(2), 331–352.

Bhattarai, S., Chatterjee, A., & Park, W. Y. (2015). Effects of US quantitative easing on emerging market countries. *Federal Reserve Bank of dallas globalization and monetary policy institute Working Paper*, No: 255.

Bowman, D., Londono, J. M., & Sapriza, H. (2015). U.S. unconventional monetary policy and transmission to emerging market economies. *Journal of International Money and Finance, 55*, 27–59.

Brown, S. J., & Warner, J. B. (1980). Measuring security price performance. *Journal of Financial Economics, 8*, 205–258.

Brown, S. J., & Warner, J. B. (1985). Using daily stock returns: The case of event studies. *Journal of Financial Economics, 14*(1), 205–258.

Bruno, V., & Shin, H. S. (2013). Capital flows and the risk-taking channel of monetary policy. *NBER Working Paper*, 18942.

Cerutti, E., Claessens, S. & Ratnovski, L. (2014). Global liquidity and drivers of cross-border bank flows. *IMF Working Paper*, WP/14/69.

Chen, Q., Filardo, A., He, D., & Zhu, F. (2011). International spillovers of central bank balance sheet policies. *BIS Papers.*

Chen, J., Mancini-Griffoli, T., & Sahay, R. (2014). Spillovers from United States monetary policy on emerging markets: Different this time. *IMF Working Paper*, WP/14/240.

Chen, Q., Filardo, A., He, D., & Zhu, F. (2015). Financial crisis, US unconventional monetary policy and international spillovers, *BIS Papers*, 494.

Chodorow-Reich, G. (2014). Effects of unconventional monetary policy on financial institutions. *Brookings Papers on Economic Activity*, Spring, 155–204.

Chung, H., Herbst, E., & Kiley, M. (2014). Effective monetary policy strategies in new Keynesian models: a reconsideration. *Federal Reserve Board Working Paper.*

Fratzscher, M., Lo Duca, M., & Straub, R. (2016a). Capital flows, push versus pull factors and the global financial crisis. *Journal of International Economics, 88*, 341–356.

Fratzscher, M., Lo Duca, M., & Straub, R. (2016b). On the international spillovers of U.S. quantitative easing. *The Economic Journal, 128*(608), 330–377.

Gilchrist, S., Yue, V. Z., & Zakrajsek, E. (2014). U.S. monetary policy and foreign bond yields. *Federal Reserve Board of Governors*, Mimeo.

Glick, R., & Leduc, S. (2012). Central bank announcements of asset purchases and the impact on global financial and commodity markets. *Journal of International Money and Finance, 31*, 2078–2101.

Glick, R., & Leduc, S. (2013). The Effects of unconventional and conventional U.S. monetary policy on the dollar. *Federal Reserve Bank of San Francisco Working Papers*, 2013–11.

Hamilton, J. D. (2011). Evaluating quantitative easing using event studies, Retrieved from http://econbrowser.com/archives/2011/07/evaluating_quan.

Hausman, J., & Wongswan, J. (2011). Global asset prices and FOMC announcements. *Journal of International Money and Finance, 30*(3), 547–571.

Hayo, B., Kutan, A. M., & Neuenkirch, M. (2012). Federal reserve communications and emerging equity markets. *Southern Economic Journal, 78*(3), 1041–1056.

International Monetary Fund. (2013a). IMF multilateral policy issues report 2013 spillover report–analytical underpinnings and other background. *IMF Policy Papers*, August 2013.

International Monetary Fund. (2013b). Global impact and challenges of unconventional monetary policies. *IMF Policy Papers*, October 2013.

Korniyenko, Y., & Loukoianova, E. (2015). The impact of unconventional monetary policy measures by the systemic four on global liquidity and monetary conditions. *IMF Working Paper*, WP/15/287.

Lim, J. J., & Mohapatra, S. (2016). Quantitative easing and the post-crisis surge in financial flows to developing countries. *Journal of International Money and Finance, 68*, 331–357.

Lim, J. J., Mohapatra, S., & Stocker, M. (2014). Tinker, taper, QE, bye? The effect of quantitative easing on financial flows to developing countries. *The World Bank Policy Research Working Paper*, 6820.

Lo Duca, M., Nicoletti, G., & Vidal, A. (2016). Global corporate bond issuance: What role for US quantitative easing? *Journal of International Money and Finance, 60*(c), 114–150.

McKinlay, A. C. (1997). Event studies in economics and finance. *Journal of Economic Literature, 35*(1), 13–39.

Moore, J, Nam, S., Suh, M., & Tepper, A. (2013). Estimating the impact of U.S. LSAPs on emerging market economies' local currency bond markets. *Federal Reserve Bank of New York Staff Report*, 595.

Morgan, P. J. (2011). Impact of US quantitative easing policy on emerging Asia. *Asian Development Bank Institute, Working Paper*, 321.

Neely, C. J. (2010). Unconventional monetary policy had large international effects. *Federal Reserve Bank of St. Louis. Working Paper Series*, 2010-018E.

Rogers, J. H., Scotti, C., & Wright, J. H. (2014). Evaluating asset-market effects of unconventional monetary policy: A multi-country review. *Economic Policy, 29*(80), 749–799.

Tillmann, P. (2016). Unconventional monetary policy and the spillovers to emerging markets. *Journal of International Money and Finance, 66*, 136–156.

The Impact of Research and Development Expenditures on the Value Relevance of Accounting Items

Melik Ertuğrul

Abstract The literature extensively analyses research and development expenditures (RDE) from the valuation perspective and documents its direct value relevance (VR). In this paper, in addition to revealing VR of RDE, we shed light on the impact of RDE on VR of book value of equity (BV) and earnings figures; hence, we analyze the indirect impact of RDE on VR of accounting items. By examining listed firms on the Borsa Istanbul between 2009 and 2018, we document that the impact of RDE on market values is significantly positive. Moreover, we report that the impact of BV (earnings) on market values becomes negative (more positive) RDE increase which should be read as evidence for the shifted attention of the market from the balance sheet to the income statement with increasing RDE. As losses convey more information than profits (Hayn, C., *Journal of Accounting and Economics 20*:125-153, 1995), we further extend our analyses by considering profit and loss firms. For loss recording firms, RDE significantly and negatively affect market values although this effect becomes insignificant for observations with RDE. Furthermore, as RDE increase, for loss firms, the impact of BV on market values significantly becomes negative while the impact of earnings on market values remains statistically unaffected. When analyses are reperformed for observations with RDE, all these statistically significant outcomes disappear which may indicate that our main outcomes may be driven by firms with no RDE.

1 Introduction

According to the literature, there is a move in the US economy from tangibility to intangibility (Ciftci et al. 2014). This shift is obvious for Turkish economy as well: research and development expenditures (RDE) to Gross Domestic Product ratio jumps from is 0.47% in 2003 to 0.96% in 2017 according to TURKSTAT's

M. Ertuğrul (✉)
Department of Economics, Istinye University, İstanbul, Turkey
e-mail: melik.ertugrul@istinye.edu.tr

H. Dincer, S. Yüksel (eds.), *Strategic Priorities in Competitive Environments*, Contributions to Management Science, https://doi.org/10.1007/978-3-030-45023-6_3

statistics.[1] Hence, at the global level, research and development (R&D) related issues are on the spotlight. Expectedly, R&D accounting has been at the center not only of most academic discussions (Abrahams and Sidhu 1998) but also of concerns of standard setters (Jones 2018).

RDE may be considered a form of investment which is expected to generate economic benefits in the future (Abrahams and Sidhu 1998). Future carries uncertainty. Paul et al.'s (2010) outcomes clearly show this uncertainty by analyzing the R&D productivity of the pharmaceutical industry: the final success rate for a drug is approximately 4%. In other words, RDE should be considered inputs (Hirschey et al. 2001; Hirshleifer et al. 2017) and large RDE have to be incurred to create untested, unguaranteed and unpredictable new outputs (Chan et al. 2001). Hence, the efficiency of R&D costs has been questioned whether R&D costs yield in (sustainable) new outputs which will eventually contribute to the firm value by creating profits. Moreover, although the potential new product is expected to be new at the investment decision date, the successful commercialization of the new output created by the completion of R&D activities heavily depends on the release date (Chen and Ramaboa 2017). It puts also another ambiguity on the impact R&D activities on the valuation and performance.

Most literature analyses VR (VR) of R&D by focusing on the following five streams. First, certain studies analyze the direct impact of RDE on stock markets (stock prices/market values and/or stock returns); and almost commonly report this impact is significantly positive at conventional levels. Beginning discussions of the first stream lead the way to the second stream which extensively dominates the literature as capitalization of R&D costs has been a very debatable issue for the world of accounting (Napoli 2015). The second stream deeply analyses the treatment of R&D costs: Should they be capitalized or expensed? This stream is mainly interested in whether capitalization or expensing R&D costs provide most value relevant information. These studies mostly discuss the convenience of recording R&D costs under intangible assets instead of immediate expensing since usefulness (and relevance) of financial statement information declines as an aftermath of the insufficiency of accounting practices to recognize several innovative activities including R&D costs under intangible assets (Lev and Zarowin 1999). The third stream aims to reveal which accounting regime provides more relevant R&D measurement by examining the impact of different accounting standards on VR of RDE. The fourth stream analyses VR of RDE for different sub-groups based on certain criteria including size and loss. The last stream studies VR of accounting items (AI) such as earnings and book value of equity (BV) in R&D intensive industries. The topic of our study falls under first, fourth and fifth streams of this classification.

To the best of our knowledge, although the literature documents ample evidence for the direct VR of RDE by analyzing its impact on market values or stock returns,

[1]TURKSTAT is the official governmental agency responsible for collecting data and publishing statistics. All these statistics are available at http://www.tuik.gov.tr (Accession Date: Aug 4, 2019)

there is no study on the indirect VR of RDE by analyzing its impact on VR of AI. Therefore, in this study, we aim to contribute to the extant literature by examining how RDE affects VR of major ingredients of the linear model of Ohlson (1995): BV and earnings. Among all studies, the research of Ciftci and Darrough (2015) may seem very close to our study. Ciftci and Darrough (2015) report VR of AI by dividing their sample into quintiles based on RDE and profit/loss. Although Ciftci and Darrough (2015) only present findings by considering the explanatory power of regressions which is a commonly used indicator of VR (Holthausen and Watts 2001), they do not provide outcomes for how RDE affect VR of earnings and BV.[2] This is the main contribution of our study to the extant literature. Furthermore, as losses convey more information than profits (Hayn 1995), we extend our research to profit and loss firms, and reveal significant findings which should be considered our ancillary contribution. VR literature overwhelmingly provides outcomes belonging to developed countries and it has very limited evidence for emerging economy. Our last contribution to the literature is documenting evidence for an emerging economy, Turkey.

By analyzing listed firms on the Borsa Istanbul between 2009 and 2018 and employing a modified linear model very similar to Ohlson (1995), we document the following outcomes. We reveal that RDE are not considered real expenditures by the market. On the contrary, the market considers RDE a kind of revenue: an increase in RDE lead to a significant increase in the market values of a firm. Hence, we report that RDE are significantly and positively value relevant. As the literature extensively reports the positive impact of RDE on the stock market (Jones 2018), this finding is very consistent with the literature. Moreover, by analyzing the impact of RDE on VR of AI, we document two more significant findings. First, the impact of RDE on VR of BV is significantly negative: an increase in RDE significantly reduces the effect of BV on market values. Second, the impact of RDE on VR of earnings is significantly positive: an increase in RDE significantly improves the effect of earnings on market values. In other words, the market gives more (less) importance to earnings (BV) figures as RDE increase which should be read as the shift from the balance sheet to the income statement as RDE increase.

We also distinguish between loss and profit firms by employing loss dummies and related interactions. Our outcomes reveal that, contrary to most literature, RDE negatively affect market values at conventional significance levels if a firm records loss. However, when we extend the analyses to only observations with R&D observations, we conclude that the valuation of RDE is independent of whether a firm records profit or loss. Besides, for loss firms, we find that the impact of earnings on market values does not significantly change and the impact of BV on market values significantly becomes negative as RDE increase. Although our robustness

---

[2]Ciftci and Darrough (2015) employ a separate regression for each sub-sample. Gujarati (1970b) reveals several weaknesses a separate regression for each sub-sample. The reader is referred to Gujarati (1970b, 1970a) for a very detailed discussion.

analyses confirm all these outcomes, the latter significantly negative effect becomes statistically insignificant for observations with RDE.

Preparing and releasing financial statements has become mandatory for all listed firms on the Borsa Istanbul since 2005, and the IFRS-based financial reporting regime has been in practice for 15 years in Turkey. Since the sample employed in this study belongs to the period 2009–2018, our outcomes are not affected by any change or shift in accounting standards. As shown by Kaytmaz Balsarı and Özkan (2009) and Dinçergök (2013), local economic turbulences severely affect VR of AI in Turkey. The analyzed period does include neither any local nor any global financial crises. These two factors make our sample convenient for our analyses. Furthermore, all new standards, as well as IFRS or IAS revisions, have been directly put into practice by responsible bodies in Turkey (Gür 2016). This unique characteristic of the Turkish accounting regime mitigates the potential treat of noise in accounting quality, which may distort VR and lead to incorrect inferences, exerted by local regulatory intervention (Ertuğrul and Demir 2018). Therefore, our sample provides a good research framework for our hypotheses.

This study has the following 5 main sections. Section 2 presents a brief summary of the VR concept and a review of the selected literature. Discussions on hypotheses development are available in Sect. 3. Section 4 describes data and sample selection, model and variables, and research method. Results including descriptive statistics and correlation matrices, as well as multivariate and robustness analyses, are discussed in Sect. 5. Section 6 concludes.

2 A Brief Summary of Value Relevance Concept and Selected Literature

2.1 A Brief Summary of Value Relevance Concept

VR literature begins with the pioneering three papers: Miller and Modigliani (1966), Ball and Brown (1968) and Beaver (1968) (Ertuğrul 2018). In general, the seminal research of Ball and Brown (1968) is deemed as the reference point of this literature. Beginning from these studies, the concept of VR is defined and interpreted in certain ways which bring us to one common ground: the statistically significant impact of financial reporting information on stock prices and/or returns is the definition or interpretation of VR (Ertuğrul 2019).[3] Since the VR concept provides a convenient framework for testing not only reliability but also relevance criteria of accounting information (Barth et al. 2001), it is still one of the widely used accounting quality metrics.

VR is measured by considering two perspectives: the market's reaction towards an announcement is studied by the signaling perspective and the association between

[3]The reader is referred to Ertuğrul (2019) for a theoretical discussion related to VR concept,

financial reporting (or accounting) information and stock market figures is studied by the measurement perspective (Hellström 2006). The first perspective generally employs the Return Model which reveals the impact of the change in an income statement figure as well as its level (or reported) version on stock returns. The second perspective generally employs the Price Model of Ohlson (1995) which shows the impact of income figures as well as balance sheet items on market values or stock prices. Both Models are criticized by the literature from different econometric concerns, as summarized by Ertuğrul (2019). As underscored by Mestelman et al. (2015), analyzing balance sheet items as well as other reconciliation figures is not convenient in the Return Model. As our study aims to shed light not only on VR of earnings but also VR of BV by considering RDE, we use a modified linear model very similar to Ohlson (1995) which provides a convenient setting for our research.

The extant VR literature is categorized under three fundamental branches by (Holthausen and Watts 2001). The first branch is named relative association studies which consider the explanatory power of a regression an indicator of VR. The second branch is named incremental association studies which directly consider the statistical significance of the regression coefficients of AI indicators of VR. The last branch is marginal information content studies which consider AI value relevant if they significantly contribute to the available information set. Among all, we see that the first two streams, association studies, dominate the literature review of Holthausen and Watts (2001). In a very recent literature review, Ertuğrul (2019) also confirms this dominance. In our literature review, we realize that the literature majorly analyses VR of RDE from the perspective of incremental association studies.

2.2 *Selected Literature*

2.2.1 Value Relevance of R&D Expenditures

This stream overwhelmingly documents evidence for the significantly positive association between RDE and stock market figures. By employing a dataset belonging to high-tech US companies between 1988 and 1990, Chauvin and Hirschey (1993) report that RDE have a significantly positive impact on market values. By employing a dataset belonging to US companies between 1975 and 1985, Sougiannis (1994) documents that RDE significantly affect stock prices and he further concludes that this outcome is valid for each year. By employing a dataset belonging to US companies between 1975 and 1999, Core et al. (2003) find that RDE have a statistically significant and positive impact on market values. Core et al. (2003) further confirm the same outcome for high-tech firms, young firms, and the rest. Guo et al. (2005) analyze the impact of RDE on market values of US biotech firms at the time of their initial public offering between 1991 and 2000. Guo et al.'s (2005) outcomes reveal that the only item -among all AI- reported as value relevant is RDE which have a statistically significant and positive impact on market values.

By employing a dataset belonging to US biotech companies between 1998 and 2004, Xu et al. (2007) conclude that RDE have a significantly positive impact on market values. Moreover, they extend their analysis by dividing their sample into two based on the relationship between sales and R&D activities, and they show that i) their outcome regarding the whole sample is valid for both sub-samples, ii) there is no statistically significant difference between VR of RDE for both sub-samples.[4] By employing a dataset belonging to US companies with RDE between 1973 and 2008, Donelson and Resutek (2012) conclude that not only RDE but also the change in RDE has a significantly positive effect on stock returns. Donelson and Resutek (2012) further document the same outcome when they eliminate tiny stocks, prices of which are less than $5. By employing a dataset belonging to high-tech US companies between 1990 and 2012, Xu and Cai (2016) report that RDE significantly and positively affect stock prices and this effect becomes more obvious in their second sub-period between 2000 and 2012.

2.2.2 Value Relevance of R&D Expenditures for Different Sub-Groups

This stream documents VR of RDE by dividing the whole sample into different sub-groups. During our literature research, we realize that this stream majorly concentrates on size-based and loss-based sub-groups. This stream also directly presents outcomes belonging to a specific sub-group without analyzing the others.

In this paragraph, the major outcomes of studies considering size-based sub--groups are presented. In the first section of this literature review, we discuss the major finding of Chauvin and Hirschey (1993): RDE have significantly positive impact on market values. They further extend their analyses by dividing their whole sample into three based on firm sizes.[5] For the whole sample as well as the sample including only manufacturing firms, Chauvin and Hirschey (1993) show that their general finding is more (less) obvious for large (middle) firms. However, for non-manufacturing firms, they conclude that their general finding is valid for large and small firms while RDE have no statistically significant impact on market values of small firms. By employing a dataset belonging to US pharmaceutical companies between 1985 and 1996 and dividing her sample into two based on firm sizes, Shortridge (2004) documents that the impact of RDE on stock prices is statistically significant and positive (negative) for large (small) firms.[6] Tsoligkas and Tsalavoutas (2011) employ a dataset consisting UK firms with R&D Scoreboard values between 2006 and 2008 and document outcomes by dividing their sample into two based on market values. They reveal that RDE have a significant and negative impact on market values for the sample of large firms while no statistically

---

[4]These findings belong to Xu et al.'s (2007) Panel A of Table 2. They repeat their analyses for different business cycles and conclude different outcomes.

[5]Chauvin and Hirschey (1993) calculate firm sizes based on sales revenues.

[6]Shortridge (2004) calculates firm sizes based on sales revenues.

significant effect is reported for the other sample. By employing a dataset belonging to UK companies between 2001 and 2011 and dividing their sample into two based on market values, Shah et al. (2013) conclude that RDE do not have any significant impact on stock prices of large firms while it has a significantly negative impact on stock prices of small firms.

In this paragraph, the major outcomes of studies considering loss-based sub--groups are presented. By employing a dataset belonging to US companies recording losses between 1971 and 2000, Joos and Plesko (2005) document that RDE positively contribute to stock returns at conventional significance levels. By employing a dataset belonging to US companies recording losses in 2003, Darrough and Ye (2007) conclude that RDE significantly and positively affect market values independent of the BV level of a firm. By employing a dataset belonging to US biotech companies between 1990 and 2001, Tan and Lim (2007) report that RDE do not play a significant role in market values of profit firms while their impact on market values of loss firms is reported as statistically significant and positive. This finding belongs to the extended version of Tan and Lim's (2007) Model 5 which presents outcomes for a smaller sample. Their outcomes reported for a larger sample reveal that RDE significantly and positively (negatively) affect market values of loss (profit) firms. By employing a dataset belonging to US companies with RDE between 1982 and 2002, Franzen and Radhakrishnan (2009) show that RDE significantly and positively (negatively) affect stock prices of loss (profit) firms. They also present their regression outcomes for each year and report that all regression coefficients of RDE for profit observations are always negative with one exception and all regression coefficients of RDE for loss observations are always positive. Franzen and Radhakrishnan (2009) further analyze the impact of RDE on stock prices by dividing their sample into three based on R&D intensity levels and confirm their general findings for each sub-group. By employing a dataset belonging to Australian companies recording losses between 1993 and 2006, Wu et al. (2010) document that RDE significantly and positively affect market values. They further extend their analyses by dividing their sample into two based on market values of equity and confirm their general findings for small and large firms. Besides, the impact of RDE on market values of large firms is more than two times the impact of RDE on stock prices of small firms. By employing a dataset belonging to UK companies recording losses between 1991 and 2010, Jiang and Stark (2013) report that RDE significantly and positively contribute to market values. In the first section of this literature review, we discuss the major finding of Xu and Cai (2016): RDE significantly and positively affect stock prices. Xu and Cai (2016) also document the following outcomes for loss and profit firms: the impact of RDE on stock prices is significantly positive for both profit and loss firms, and this impact is more apparent for the sample of profit observations especially in their first sub-period. By employing a dataset belonging to US companies with RDE between 1983 and 2011, Jones (2018) finds that RDE significantly and positively (negatively) affect stock prices of loss (profit) firms. Moreover, she divides loss and profit samples into two based on sales growth rate and she documents that i) independent of the growth level, the impact of RDE on stock prices is significantly positive for all loss firms, and ii) the impact of

RDE on stock prices is significantly positive (negative) for profit firms with the high (low) growth level.

2.2.3 Value Relevance of Accounting Items in R&D Intensive Industries

This stream documents VR of AI in R&D intensive industries and provides mixed outcomes. Among all studies, Amir and Lev's (1996) seminal research plays a significant role in this stream and related discussions. By employing a dataset belonging to US cellular companies between 1984 and 1993, Amir and Lev (1996) report that earnings, operating cash flows and BV figures have no statistically significant impact on neither stock prices nor quarterly stock returns. By employing a dataset belonging to high-tech US companies between 1989 and 1995, Hirschey et al. (2001) document that both earnings and BV figures significantly and positively contribute to market values. In the first section of this literature review, we discuss major findings of Core et al. (2003). They also reveal that both earnings and BV figures positively contribute to market values at conventional significance levels, and this outcome is also valid for high-tech firms, young firms, and the rest.

This paragraph presents the major findings of most studies, some of which are discussed in previous sections of our literature review. Chauvin and Hirschey (1993) reveal that cash flows have a statistically significant and positive impact on market values while Guo et al. (2005) report that operating cash flows have no statistically significant impact on market values. Callimaci and Landry (2004), Shortridge (2004), Xu et al. (2007), Tan and Lim (2007), Mitrione et al. (2014) and Napoli (2015) conclude that BV has a significantly positive association with stock market figures while Xu and Cai (2016) exhibit a reverse outcome for the sample of loss firms. Callimaci and Landry (2004), Shortridge (2004), Ke et al. (2004), Mitrione et al. (2014) and Xu and Cai (2016) document evidence for the significantly positive effect of earnings on stock market figures while Tan and Lim (2007) conclude a significantly negative association. Ciftci and Darrough (2015) analyze the combined VR of earnings and BV between profit and loss firms by dividing their sample into 6 based on R&D intensity levels. Their outcomes indicate that VR of accounting information for profit (loss) firms are significantly greater (less) than VR of accounting information for loss (profit) firms for the highest (lowest) two levels of R&D intensity levels. Note that Ciftci and Darrough (2015) document their outcomes by presenting the explanatory power of regressions which may be considered a form of total VR indicator instead of providing separate impacts of earnings and BV on market values.

To recap, this part of our literature review presents mixed outcomes regarding VR of earnings and BV figures.

3 Hypotheses Development

Immediate expensing of R&D costs may be considered a strong kind of conservatism (Ahmed and Falk 2006) which is defined by Riahi-Belkaoui (2004) as a pessimistic kind of reporting: financial statements should reflect "*the lowest values of assets and revenues and the highest values of liabilities and expenses*" (Riahi-Belkaoui 2004). The proponents of VR have criticized conservatism as financial reporting information should be neutral instead of being pessimistic (Mora and Walker 2015).

This discussion leads the way from expensing to capitalization. Code-Law countries generally have conservatism-based accounting systems and standards (Hellman 2008). Although the US is a part of the Common-Law family, its attitude towards R&D capitalization is like a Code-Law country: it does require immediately expensing all R&D costs.[7] As there is a switch from domestic accounting standards to IFRS especially after 2005 in most jurisdictions, the IFRS-based intangibles standard (IAS 38) provides a convenient framework to capitalize development costs if six criteria clearly stated in Paragraph 57 of IAS 38 are all met: If development costs meet all those criteria, it should be capitalized; in other words, there is no option for expensing. IAS 38 further requires expensing all research costs. However, as those criteria are very restrictive and rigid, expensing R&D costs is still a common practice (Bhana 2013). Furthermore, conservatism is still a part of discussions related to accounting treatment practices in certain Code-Law countries (Hellman 2008). and it may be a reason for the common practice of expensing R&D costs. Another reason may be the strong dependence on tangible assets (Chen and Ramaboa 2017).

As highlighted by Bhana (2013), expensing R&D costs is still a common treatment method; and hence, RDE are expected to reflect future economic benefits especially in Code-Law countries such as Turkey. Therefore, consistent with the literature documenting evidence for a significantly positive association between RDE and stock market figures (see, among others, Chauvin and Hirschey 1993; Core et al. 2003; Donelson and Resutek 2012; Guo et al. 2005; Sougiannis 1994; Xu et al. 2007; Xu and Cai 2016), we expect to see a significantly positive impact of RDE on market values, and we put forward our first hypothesis:

Hypothesis 1: RDE are positively value relevant.

Expensing R&D costs trigger the discussion of VR of other AI including earnings and BV. Contrary to Amir and Lev (1996) who report the value irrelevance of AI for intangible intensive firms, Collins et al. (1997) and Francis and Schipper (1999) find that VR of accounting information belonging to intangible intensive firms is not inferior to VR of accounting information belonging to non-intangible intensive firms. After Collins et al. (1997) and Francis and Schipper (1999), this discussion

[7]For detailed information, the reader is referred to the following link: https://advisory.kpmg.us/articles/2017/ifrs-vs-us-gaap-rd-costs.html (Accession Date: Aug 4, 2019)

continues with certain econometric concerns; and several researchers including Brown et al. (1999) show an econometrically correct way to perform these analyses. After performing the correct econometric method, VR of other AI belonging to intangible-intensive firms has echoed enough sound in academia.

A great number of studies analyses VR of accounting information by taking different R&D levels into account and they provide mixed outcomes, as discussed in the last section of our literature review. This study is the first one examining the indirect VR of RDE to our knowledge by revealing the effect of RDE on VR of two major AI: earnings and BV. By analyzing this, we reveal the indirect VR of RDE. Ciftci and Darrough (2015) provide outcomes for the total VR of AI (by obtaining and comparing explanatory powers of different regressions) for different RDE levels. However, they do not document evidence for the impact of RDE on VR of earnings and BV, separately.

Ciftci and Darrough (2015) underscored that RDE may lead losses which do not reflect financial distress indeed. Furthermore, RDE may get operating performance better in the future (Chen and Ramaboa 2017). Jiang and Stark (2013) also highlight that RDE may be an indicator of future earnings. Therefore, we expect to see that the market values earnings more positively when RDE increases, and we put forward our second hypothesis. If RDE carry information related to future improved operating performance (Chen and Ramaboa 2017) and they are a signal of future earnings (Jiang and Stark 2013), it implicitly means that RDE shift the market's attention from the balance sheet to the income statement. Hence, we expect to see that the market values BV (which is a balance sheet item) negatively when RDE increase, and we put forward our third hypothesis.

Hypothesis 2: Earnings have a more positive impact on market values when RDE increase.

Hypothesis 3: BV has a negative impact on market values when RDE increase.

Burgstahler and Dichev (1997) reveal that the firm value is determined by recursion value and adaptation value. Recursion (Adaptation) value becomes dominant when current operating performance is (not) favorable. Hence, as per recursion (adaptation) value, earnings (BV) are more significant determinants of the firm value. Only future earnings may help a loss firm to turn its earnings from red to black as its assets currently generate negative profits (Jones 2018). RDE may be a signal of future earnings (Jiang and Stark 2013). Therefore, consistent with the literature documenting evidence for a significantly positive association between RDE and stock market figures of loss firms (see, among others, Darrough and Ye 2007; Franzen and Radhakrishnan 2009; Jiang and Stark 2013; Jones 2018; Joos and Plesko 2005; Tan and Lim 2007; Wu et al. 2010), we expect to see the market values RDE of loss firms more positively, and we put forward our fourth hypothesis:

Hypothesis 4: RDE of loss firms have a more positive impact on market values.

High RDE leads losses which are not real indeed. Therefore, loss firms with high level of RDE may not be valued in accordance with adaptation value as they may convey more information via RDE (Ciftci and Darrough 2015). Therefore, we expect to see that the market values loss figures of loss firms positively when RDE increases, and we put forward our fifth hypothesis. However, loss firms with low level of RDE should be valued according to adaptation value as they do not have any informative tool other than BV (Ciftci and Darrough 2015). For instance, Jiang and Stark (2013) find that the impact of BV on market values becomes significantly negative for loss firms with high RDE. Therefore, we expect to see that the market values BV of loss firms negatively when RDE increase, and we put forward our sixth hypothesis.

Hypothesis 5: Loss figures have a positive impact on market values of loss firms when RDE increase.

Hypothesis 6: BV has a negative impact on market values of loss firms when RDE increase.

4 Data & Sample Selection, Model & Variables, and Research Method

4.1 Data & Sample Selection

This study employs a sample of listed firms on the Borsa Istanbul. Price data are retrieved from the database of the Borsa Istanbul which provides monthly market data for the ending day of each month since 2009. As we do not have monthly market data before 2009, it constraints our period of analyses: Price items used by this study belong to the period 2009–2019. Financial institutions, holdings, and utilities are excluded from the sample since their financial reporting practices and regulations are distinctively different. Furthermore, firms listed on the watchlist market are also excluded. Firms on the Borsa Istanbul may issue different classes of common stocks. C and D class stocks are used in this study as they are most frequently traded. By performing these filters, we finalize our price data.

Next, we collect financial statement information of each observation existing in the above described price data. The Public Disclosure Platform, which provides accounting information data beginning from 2009, includes financial statements of listed companies on separate MS Excel files. Therefore, all accounting data belonging to the period 2009–2018 are manually collected from this data source. After completing this step, all data are controlled twice by different two persons to prevent possible data errors. Finally, only observations with positive BV figures are included in the final sample due to going concern related issues of firms negative equity as highlighted by Gordon et al. (2010). Note that only firms with the fiscal year end of December are included to maintain the reporting homogeneity in the final sample. The final sample consists of 2226 observations belonging to 287 firms.

4.2 *Model & Variables*

Since our study majorly aims to shed light on the impact of RDE on VR of AI, it falls under the measurement perspective of Hellström (2006) which extensively utilizes the Price Model of Ohlson (1995) as discussed earlier. In order to test our hypotheses, we modify the linear model of Ohlson (1995) and employ Eqs. (1) to (4). We utilize the first equation to test our first hypothesis which is confirmed by a statistically significant and positive regression coefficient of β_3. The second equation tests our second (third) hypothesis which is confirmed by a statistically significant and positive (negative) regression coefficient of β_5 (β_4) respectively. Our fourth hypothesis is tested by the third equation: if β_5 is reported as statistically significant and positive, the hypothesis is confirmed. The last equation tests our last two hypotheses: if β_6 (β_5) is reported as statistically significant and positive (negative), the fifth (sixth) hypothesis is confirmed.

$$MV_{i,t+1} = \beta_0 + \beta_1 x\ BV_{i,t} + \beta_2 x\ E_{i,t} + \beta_3 x\ RDE_{i,t} \tag{1}$$

$$\begin{aligned} MV_{i,t+1} = {} & \beta_0 + \beta_1 x\ BV_{i,t} + \beta_2 x\ E_{i,t} + \beta_3 x\ RDE_{i,t} + \beta_4 x\ BV_{i,t} x\ RDE_{i,t} \\ & + \beta_5 x\ E_{i,t} x\ RDE_{i,t} \end{aligned} \tag{2}$$

$$\begin{aligned} MV_{i,t+1} = {} & \beta_0 + \beta_1 x\ BV_{i,t} + \beta_2 x\ E_{i,t} + \beta_3 x\ RDE_{i,t} + \beta_4 x\ L_{i,t} \\ & + \beta_5 x\ RDE_{i,t} x\ L_{i,t} \end{aligned} \tag{3}$$

$$\begin{aligned} MV_{i,t+1} = {} & \beta_0 + \beta_1 x\ BV_{i,t} + \beta_2 x\ E_{i,t} + \beta_3 x\ RDE_{i,t} + \beta_4 x\ L_{i,t} \\ & + \beta_5 x\ BV_{i,t} x\ RDE_{i,t} x\ L_{i,t} + \beta_6 x\ E_{i,t} x\ RDE_{i,t} x\ L_{i,t} \end{aligned} \tag{4}$$

where i and t stand for firm and year while MV, BV, E, RDE, and L represent market values measured after 3 months from the fiscal year end, book value of equity, earnings, research and development expenditures, and loss dummy, respectively. BV figures are calculated by subtracting liabilities and earnings from total assets. The term earnings is the bottom-line net income figure. L is a dummy variable standing for loss which is equal to one if a firm's earnings figure is below zero, and zero otherwise.

The extant literature discusses several weaknesses of the Price Model by documenting evidence for two major problems, named the scale effect problem and the stale information effect problem. Prior to analyses, these two problems should be eliminated. The most prevalent approach of mitigating these effects is dividing both dependent and independent variables by a common item. Among several deflator types, Goncharov and Veenman (2014) document concrete evidence for the convenience of using the previous market values. In this study, we use the previous market values as a deflator by following Goncharov and Veenman's (2014) convincing outcomes. Hence, each variable except loss dummy in Eqs. 1 to 4 is deflated by the previous market values.

4.3 Research Method

Extreme observations and data errors may significantly affect regression outcomes. Hence, such problems have to be controlled prior to analyses. As a solution, winsorization at the first and 99th percentiles are applied to all non-dummy variables before performing analyses.

Prior to analyses, we use all independent variables listed in Eqs. (1) to (4) in a single regression. Then, we run an ordinary OLS regression (with no fixed effects and year dummies) and perform the Variance Inflation Factor (VIF, henceforth) analysis in order to check whether multicollinearity creates a significant problem. In that unreported research setting, almost half of individual VIF figures, as well as the mean VIF figure, are reported as more than 5. Although the critical VIF figure is stated as 10 (as a rule of thumb), the VIF greater than 3 exerts uncertainty in parameters of interests (Sarabia and Ortiz 2009). In order to deal with the multicollinearity problem, we have two options: (i) performing a single regression to the whole sample by employing dummies, and (ii) performing several regressions by dividing the whole sample into sub-samples. Gujarati (1970a, b) documents evidence in favor of the former option while he reveals several weaknesses of the latter option. Among all weaknesses, we underline the following two: (i) the explanatory power comparison does not indicate the source of this power (from the intercept, the slope, or both), and (ii) it reduces the degrees of freedom Misund et al. 2008.

As per suggestions of Gujarati (1970a, b), we decide to keep the integrity (completeness) of the final dataset instead of dividing it into several sub-groups.[8] Therefore, we separate this equation into 4 sub-equations (by preserving the completeness of the final dataset) in order to mitigate mechanical interdependencies between our independent variables. For each of these sub-equations, we run an ordinary OLS regression (with no fixed effects and year dummies) and perform the VIF analysis. The maximum and mean VIF figures are reported as (i) 1.03 and 1.02 for Eq. (1), (ii) 3.27 and 1.97 for Eq. (2),[9] (iii) 1.89 and 1.53 for Eq. (3), and (iv) 2.13 and 1.71 for Eq. (4). All these VIF figures indicate that the multicollinearity problem does not significantly affect our models and regression outcomes.

Ertuğrul and Demir (2018) and Onali et al. (2017) highlight the importance of employing correct regression methods for VR analyses. By following concrete evidence of these studies, we first perform the Hausman Test in order to determine whether the fixed effects method or the random effects method is convenient. The null hypothesis which prefers the random effects method is rejected by the outcome of the Hausman Test obtained for each Equation. Hence, in this study, we use the

[8]By following this approach, we inherently do not allow both firm and year fixed effects to vary between different sub-groups which is a more convenient approach as per definition of fixed effects. For detailed discussion, the reader is referred to Ertuğrul and Demir (2018).

[9]We exclude RD from Equation (2) to reduce the mean VIF level below 3 and reperform all analyses. Outcomes remain unchanged.

fixed effects method which controls for individual-level endogeneity. Furthermore, another source of endogeneity is at time-level (Ertuğrul and Demir 2018). Therefore, in order to control for year-level endogeneity, we add year dummies into Eqs. (1) to (4). As a result, we obtain almost unbiased regression coefficients as stated by Allison (2006).

OLS regression residuals may be not only serially but also cross-sectionally correlated which may result in biased standard errors (Gow et al. 2010; Petersen 2009) and may lead to incorrect inferences. In order to get unbiased regression outcomes, these serial and cross-sectional correlations should be mitigated. As a solution, standard errors are clustered at the firm level and the year level in order to correct for serial correlation and cross-sectional correlation in standard errors as suggested by Gow et al. (2010) and Petersen (2009). Heteroscedasticity also springs from employing level variables (Goncharov and Veenman 2014; Kothari and Zimmerman 1995) and this potential problem is also mitigated because each variable except loss dummy in Eqs. (1) to (4) is scaled by a common deflator.

5 Results

5.1 Descriptive Statistics and Correlation Matrices

The first two Panels of Table 1 show descriptive statistics. First, firms are not face to face with a shrinking market values problem as indicated by both mean and median statistics belonging to market values. Hence, an expected outcome is reported by mean and median BV figures: firms do trade at a premium to BV. Additionally, the mean (and also median) earnings figure indicates that firms do not have profitability-related concerns on the average. Panel C reveals the annual bottom line loss and profit distribution: almost 43% of our total sample suffer from the profitability problem. The maximum percentage (25.5% of total observations) of loss firms are observed in 2015 while the minimum (37.8% of total observations) percentage of loss firms are observed in 2009. Mean and median RDE statistics reveal that Turkish listed firms do not engage in R&D intensive activities. If we would follow the approach of Dugan et al. (2016) and Lev and Sougiannis (1996) by analyzing only firms with RDE to sales ratio greater than 2%, we had to analyze only 146 observations which yield around 6.6% of our current sample. Our unreported statistics show that mean RDE to sales ratio is 0.48% while its median is zero.[10] Almost 60% of firms in our sample do not spend any Turkish Liras for RDE. Moreover, the annual distribution of firms with and without RDE reveals that approximately 45% of firms

[10]These lower values are also reported by the literature. For instance, the median R&D expenditures to market value ratio of Jiang and Stark (2013) is zero, and Ciftci et al. (2014) report the same outcome for non-intangible intensive industries.

Table 1 Descriptive statistics and correlation matrices

PANEL A

	N	MEAN	P50	SD	MIN	MAX
MV	2226	1.269	1.055	0.726	0.348	4.574
BV	2226	0.956	0.725	0.821	0.066	4.642
E	2226	0.031	0.045	0.212	−0.813	0.731
RDE	2226	0.006	0	0.016	0	0.095

PANEL B

Year	N	With R&D	Without R&D	Profit	Loss
2009	188	86	102	117	71
2010	192	87	105	137	55
2011	206	89	117	147	59
2012	221	89	132	159	62
2013	232	92	140	153	79
2014	233	85	148	172	61
2015	235	88	147	175	60
2016	244	93	151	158	86
2017	237	97	140	176	61
2018	238	100	138	164	74

PANEL C

	MV	BV	E	RDE
MV	1			
BV	0.2810*	1		
E	0.1747*	−0.0237	1	
RDE	0.1509*	0.1438*	0.1044*	1

PANEL D

	MV	BV	E	RDE
MV	1			
BV	0.2947*	1		
E	0.3502*	0.5172*	1	
RDE	0.1760*	0.1802*	0.1856*	1

PANEL E

	MV	BV	E	RDE

(continued)

Table 1 (continued)

MV	1									
BV	0.3052*	1								
E	−0.1065*	−0.4147*	1							
RDE	0.0844*	0.0961*	−0.0185	1						

Table 2 Regression outcomes

	Equation 1	Equation 2	Equation 3	Equation 4
BV	0.4186***	0.4585***	0.4174***	0.4236***
	(0.0603)	(0.0637)	(0.0614)	(0.0609)
E	0.8151***	0.6813***	0.6454***	0.6380***
	(0.1335)	(0.1426)	(0.1714)	(0.1685)
RDE	3.9050*	11.6718***	6.0348**	6.3667**
	(1.8887)	(2.7917)	(2.4010)	(2.1625)
BV × RDE		−5.2299***		
		(1.1666)		
E × RDE		19.2687***		
		(3.6925)		
L			−0.0958*	−0.1026*
			(0.0440)	(0.0456)
RDE × L			−4.6954**	
			(2.0540)	
BV × RDE × L				−3.4479***
				(0.7610)
E × RDE × L				−3.8365
				(5.8946)
Constant	0.8198***	0.7680***	0.8491***	0.8424***
	(0.0527)	(0.0570)	(0.0465)	(0.0463)
Number of Obs.	2226	2226	2226	2226
R^2	0.477	0.489	0.481	0.482
Firm FE	YES	YES	YES	YES
Year FE	YES	YES	YES	YES

This Table shows outcomes belonging to the dependent variable measured after 3 months from the fiscal year end. BV, E, RDE, and L respectively refer to book value of equity, earnings, R&D expenditures, and loss dummy which is equal to 1 if the earnings figure is less than 0. All variables are deflated by the previous market value. Regression outcomes are obtained by the fixed effects methodology. Year fixed effects are also controlled. Standard errors in parentheses are clustered at both the firm level and the year level

* $p < 0.1$

** $p < 0.05$

*** $p < 0.01$

in 2009 and 2010 record RDE while 36% of firms in 2014 record RDE. These are respectively maximum and minimum percentages.

The last three Panels of Table 1 provide several correlation matrices reported for the whole sample as well as the sample of profit observations and the sample of loss observations. Note that as a correlation matrix gives the direct relationship between two variables by not taking the others into account, it provides a limited framework to interpret hypotheses. For the whole sample, associations between the dependent variable (market values) and all independent variables (BV, earnings, and RDE) are found as significantly positive. These findings reported for the whole sample are also valid for the sample of profit firms. Expectedly, for loss firms, there is a significantly negative (positive) association between market values and earnings (BV) and there is a significantly positive association between market values and RDE. Furthermore, for loss firms, the association between RDE and earnings is not reported as statistically significant. Since correlation coefficients are not reported as very large, it indicates that the multicollinearity problem may not exist. In order to statistically detect the multicollinearity problem if any, we perform the VIF analysis as discussed previously in detail. All VIF values strongly reveal that the multicollinearity problem does not significantly affect our regression outcomes.

Panel A shows descriptive statistics and Panels C, D and E present correlation matrices. MV, BV, E and RDE respectively refer to market value measured after 3 months from the fiscal year end, book value of equity, earnings, and R&D expenditures. All variables in these Panels are deflated by the previous market value. Panel C (D) [E] is the correlation matrix belonging to the whole (profit) [loss] sample. Panel B reveals annual distribution of data and observations with and without R&D expenditures as well as profit and loss observations. Loss observations consist firms with below-zero earnings figures. N, MEAN, P50, SD, MIN, and MAX refer to the number of observations, mean, median, standard deviation, minimum, and maximum. $*$ indicates the significance level at 5%

5.2 *Multivariate Analyses*

Table 2 reveals regression outcomes belonging to the dependent variable measured after 3 months from the fiscal year end. First, each column clearly presents that the impacts of BV and earnings on market values are significantly positive. In other words, these AI are reported as value relevant. This general finding is very consistent with the literature (see, among others, Bilgic et al. 2018; Ertuğrul 2020; Ertuğrul and Demir 2018; Kargin 2013; Suadiye 2012; Türel 2009) documenting evidence for VR of Turkish firms after IFRS adoption.

The regression coefficient of RDE is reported as statistically significant and positive which means that this item is positively value relevant. To illustrate, the market significantly values RDE, and an increase in RDE leads to a significant increase in market values. This outcome may be interpreted as the significance of RDE for reflecting future economic benefits, and it is consistent with the most literature (see, among others, Chauvin and Hirschey 1993; Core et al. 2003; Donelson and Resutek 2012; Guo et al. 2005; Sougiannis 1994; Xu et al. 2007; Xu and Cai 2016). All in all, our first hypothesis is confirmed.

The interaction term between RDE and earnings is reported as significantly positive. In other words, as RDE increase, the impact of earnings on market values becomes more positive. As an economic interpretation, future operating performance may be improved by today's RDE (Chen and Ramaboa 2017; Jiang and Stark 2013) and we confirm our second hypothesis. Since the interaction term between RDE and BV is reported as significantly negative, the impact of BV on market values becomes negative as RDE increase. This significantly negative interaction term confirms our third hypothesis which states the market's shifted attention from the balance sheet.

The interaction term between loss dummy and RDE is reported as significantly. We hypothesize -in accordance with the literature- that a loss firm may convert its existing situation by investing more in activities generating future earnings (Jones 2018) which are signaled by RDE (Jiang and Stark 2013). However, this interaction term directly rejects our fourth hypothesis and it does not in line with the literature (see, among others, Darrough and Ye 2007; Franzen and Radhakrishnan 2009; Jiang and Stark 2013; Jones 2018; Joos and Plesko 2005; Tan and Lim 2007; Wu et al. 2010). This unexpected and contrary outcome may indicate the following interpretation: for loss firms, the market does not consider that such activities will eventually result in improved performance and it negatively reacts to RDE. In other words, current RDE of loss firms do facilitate additional significant information to the market, but in the negative way.

The interaction term between loss dummy, RDE and earnings is not reported as statistically significant. As highlighted by Ciftci and Darrough (2015), loss firms may convey more information through RDE to the market. Hence, we hypothesize that loss figures have a positive impact on market values of loss firms when RDE increase. As per this hypothesis, we expect to report a statistically significant and positive interaction term. However, this interaction term is not significantly meaningful at conventional significance levels; therefore, it rejects our fifth hypothesis. Last, the interaction term between loss dummy, RDE and BV is reported as statistically significant and negative. Ciftci and Darrough (2015) explain that BV should play a more important role in the valuation of loss firms with low R&D intensity, as per adaptation value. Correspondingly, for loss firms with high R&D intensity, Jiang and Stark (2013) conclude the significantly negative effect of BV on market values. This significantly negative interaction term is in line with Ciftci and Darrough (2015) and Jiang and Stark (2013), and it confirms our sixth hypothesis.

All in all, our outcomes reveal that although the effect of RDE on market values is significantly positive, it turns to be significantly negative for loss firms. Furthermore, the effect of RDE on VR of earnings is significantly positive while it turns to be insignificant for loss firms. Last, the effect of RDE on VR of BV is significantly negative independent of reporting loss or profit.

5.3 Robustness Analyses

In order to increase the robustness of our outcomes, we perform two-way fixed effects and two-way clustering approaches. To get approximately unbiased regression coefficients, by following Ertuğrul and Demir (2018) and Onali et al. (2017), we present all regression outcomes provided in Tables 3 by taking firm fixed effects and year fixed effects into account. To get approximately unbiased standard errors, by following Gow et al. (2010) and Petersen (2009), serial correlation and cross-sectional correlation in standard errors are corrected by performing two-way

Table 3 Robustness analyses

PANEL A					PANEL B				
	Equation 1	Equation 2	Equation 3	Equation 4		Equation 1	Equation 2	Equation 3	Equation 4
BV	0.4035***	0.4415***	0.4028***	0.4080***	BV	0.3350***	0.4288***	0.3340***	0.3398***
	(0.0693)	(0.0700)	(0.0701)	(0.0695)		(0.0727)	(0.0812)	(0.0737)	(0.0744)
E	0.7534***	0.6476***	0.5733***	0.5612**	E	1.6551***	1.4260***	1.5841***	1.6625***
	(0.1392)	(0.1537)	(0.1709)	(0.1740)		(0.2259)	(0.2918)	(0.3044)	(0.3192)
RDE	3.8432**	12.8404***	5.8623**	6.4959***	RDE	4.0228***	8.9868***	4.6529***	4.1251***
	(1.4934)	(3.1743)	(1.8398)	(1.7510)		(0.6023)	(1.8097)	(1.0267)	(0.9677)
BV × RDE		−6.3281***			BV x RDE		−3.4901***		
		(1.5793)					(0.9987)		
E × RDE		17.8682***			E x RDE		8.8463***		
		(4.3076)					(2.5494)		
L			−0.1111**	−0.1125**	L			0.0044	−0.0066
			(0.0443)	(0.0472)				(0.0885)	(0.0970)
RDE × L			−3.8455*		RDE x L			−1.7199	
			(1.8188)					(1.8670)	
BV × RDE × L				−3.4813***	BV x RDE x L				−1.5896
				(0.4530)					(0.8896)
E × RDE × L				−1.0805	E x RDE x L				−11.8674
				(5.7131)					(8.0922)
Constant	0.8319***	0.7811***	0.8643***	0.8571***	Constant	0.8133***	0.7185***	0.8154***	0.8080***
	(0.0614)	(0.0603)	(0.0544)	(0.0524)		(0.0643)	(0.0801)	(0.0666)	(0.0680)
Number of Obs.	2226	2226	2226	2226	Number of Obs.	906	906	906	906
R^2	0.446	0.458	0.450	0.451	R^2	0.572	0.583	0.573	0.574
Firm FE	YES	YES	YES	YES	Firm FE	YES	YES	YES	YES
Year FE	YES	YES	YES	YES	Year FE	YES	YES	YES	YES

Panel A (B) shows outcomes belonging to the dependent variable measured after 4 (3) months from the fiscal year end. Panel A and B present outcomes for the whole sample and only observations with R&D expenditures. All variables in each Panel are deflated by the previous corresponding market value. BV, E, RDE, and L respectively refer to book value of equity, earnings, R&D expenditures, and loss dummy which is equal to 1 if the earnings figure is less than 0. Regression outcomes are obtained by the fixed effects methodology. Year fixed effects are also controlled. Standard errors in parentheses are clustered at both the firm level and the year level

* $p < 0.1$

** $p < 0.05$

*** $p < 0.01$

clustering (at both the firm level and the time level). In this part of our study, two robustness checks are discussed.

First, Ertuğrul (2019) reveals that employing the dependent variable measured for different months as a robustness check is a very preferred practice in most VR research. Although a rich body of VR research employs the dependent variable measured after 6 months from the fiscal year end, we do not prefer this measurement since more than half of the sample release financial reports of the first quarter in the fifth month which directly influences market values of June. Ertuğrul (2019) shows that there are also a great number of studies measuring the dependent variable after 4 months from the fiscal year end. As the first robustness check, we measure the dependent variable after 4 months from the fiscal year end and reperform all analyses. Outcomes reported in Panel A of Table 3 purely confirm findings presented in Table 2.

Second, by following the existing approach in the literature (see, among others, Cazavan-Jeny and Jeanjean 2006; Donelson and Resutek 2012; Han and Manry 2004; Shah et al. 2013), we reperform all analyses by employing a sample with RDE. Outcomes reported in Panel B of Table 3 are partially in line with our findings reported for the whole sample: (i) the regression coefficient of RDE is significantly positive which confirms our first hypothesis, (ii) the interaction term between RDE and earnings (BV) is reported as significantly positive (negative) which confirms our second (third) hypothesis. In other words, RDE are positively value relevant and earnings (BV) have a more positive (negative) impact on market values when RDE increase. On the other hand, the interaction term between loss dummy and RDE is not reported as statistically significant contrary to the significantly negative regression coefficient reported in Table 2. In any case, this outcome does not confirm our fourth hypothesis similar to the outcome reported in Table 2. The market does not distinguish between RDE of profit and loss firms reporting RDE. This outcome may indicate that the significantly negative interaction term between loss dummy and RDE reported in Table 2 is majorly driven by firms with no RDE. Furthermore, neither the interaction term between loss dummy, RDE and earnings nor the interaction term between loss dummy, RDE and BV is reported as statistically significant. While the former does not in line with the outcome reported in Table 2, the latter does; and these outcomes do not support our last two hypotheses. All in all, although this robustness analysis provides four outcomes in line with outcomes reported in Table 2, it yields in the same hypotheses confirmation with one exception which is our fifth hypothesis.

As underlined and deeply discussed by Correia (2015), singleton observations may be detrimental to regression coefficients by being inefficient and overstating significance levels. Hence, excluding such observations is convenient for obtaining correct inferences. By following explanations of Correia (2015), we also perform one more robustness check; however, outcomes belonging to those analyses are not provided for the sake of brevity.[11] We reperform all analyses by excluding singleton observations and our untabulated outcomes confirm our findings reported in Table 2.

6 Conclusion

By analyzing listed firms on the Borsa Istanbul from 2009 to 2018, we analyze both direct VR of RDE by analyzing the impact of RDE on market values and indirect VR of RDE by analyzing the impact of RDE on VR of earnings and BV. We also document evidence by extending our analyses to profit and loss firms. We use a modified linear Price Model very similar to Ohlson (1995) and present our outcomes.

Consistent with the existing literature, we report that the impact of RDE on market values is statistically significant. As stated by Jiang and Stark (2013) and Chen and Ramaboa (2017), future operating performance may be improved by current RDE. Hence, the market's attention is expected to shift from the balance sheet to the income statement. From this perspective, we confirm this shift by documenting following outcomes: as RDE increase, the impact of earnings on market values becomes more positive and the impact of BV on market values becomes negative.

As stated by Jones (2018), current RDE may help loss firms recording profits in the future while earnings figures are dominant in the valuation of profit firms in line with recursion value (Burgstahler and Dichev 1997). Hence, current RDE of loss firms may facilitate additional information to the market. From that perspective, in line with the literature, we hypothesize that RDE of loss firms have a more positive impact on market values. However, contrary to the literature, we do not find any evidence for this hypothesis. Moreover, we document that the impact of earnings of loss firms on market values does not significantly change as RDE increase. Lastly, we conclude that the impact of BV of loss firms on market values does significantly become negative as RDE increase. However, one of our robustness analyses reveals that this significantly negative impact disappears when the analysis is reperformed for observations with RDE.

By documenting the aforementioned findings, we contribute to the existing literature in threefold. First, we report not only the impact of RDE on market values (or direct VR of RDE) but also the impact of RDE on VR of AI or indirect VR of RDE). Second, we extend our analyses to profit and loss firms, and document that RDE do not carry additional significance information for loss firms from the market's valuation perspective. We also present outcomes belonging to an emerging economy, Turkey, which has very few evidence in the accounting quality literature. As this study analyses the period over 2009–2018, it covers the latest data and presents a more recent picture of VR in Turkey.

[11]Outcomes are available from the authors upon request.

Our study provides certain insights for regulatory authorities as it reveals that the market still perceives RDE as not real expenditures. Although R&D capitalization under IAS 38 is allowed, capitalization criteria are very rigid which may be a reason for expensing R&D (Bhana 2013). Regulatory authorities may reconsider relaxing criteria to record R&D costs as intangibles. Therefore, the real expense part of R&D costs may be obtained, and the financial reporting quality may be improved. Moreover, the market values BV less while it values earnings more as RDE increase. By considering these outcomes, we suggest regulatory authorities designing certain rules to improve VR of BV. Our findings should also be of interest to equity analysts who use accounting-based valuation models since RDE significantly change VR of accounting information which are ingredients of such valuation models.

Although this study has several contributions to the literature, it has certain limitations. First, using data belonging to one country restricts the generalizability of our outcomes. A larger dataset including many countries may be used by future research to report generalizable findings. Second, the database of the Borsa Istanbul does not provide market values figures adjusted for dividends. Future research may use dividend-adjusted price figures which directly make the Return Model appropriate. In any case, the Return Model does not give a solid and proper ground to analyze the impact of RDE on VR of balance sheet items and it is not convenient for our analyses, as highlighted by Mestelman et al. (2015). Last, financial statement information available at the Public Disclosure Platform provides very few firms filling capitalized R&D costs sections of MS Excel files. For instance, in their MS Excel files, almost 5% of total firms report capitalized R&D figures for the fiscal year 2018. It may spring from the fact that either they do not have any R&D costs to capitalize or they do not prefer disclosing this item on their MS Excel files. In any case, we consider such small numbers inconvenient for analyses. Future research may extend our outcomes by obtaining a sufficient number of observations with capitalized R&D costs to properly perform analyses by retrieving those data from corresponding footnotes of annual reports. We hope our findings provide beneficial insights for researchers in spite of aforementioned caveats.

References

Abrahams, T., & Sidhu, B. K. (1998). The role of R&D capitalisations in firm valuation and performance measurement. *Australian Journal of Management, 23*(2), 169–183.

Ahmed, K., & Falk, H. (2006). The value relevance of management's research and development reporting choice: Evidence from Australia. *Journal of Accounting and Public Policy, 25*(3), 231–264.

Allison, P. D. (2006). Fixed effects regression methods. In SAS®. *SUGI 31 Proceedings*, 1–20.

Amir, E., & Lev, B. (1996). Value-relevance of nonfinancial information: The wireless communications industry. *Journal of Accounting and Economics, 22*(1–3), 3–30.

Ball, R., & Brown, P. (1968). An empirical evaluation of accounting income numbers. *Journal of Accounting Research, 6*(2), 159–178.

Barth, M. E., Beaver, W. H., & Landsman, W. R. (2001). The relevance of the value relevance literature for financial accounting standard setting. *Journal of Accounting and Economics, 31* (1–3), 77–104.

Beaver, W. H. (1968). The information content of annual announcements earnings. *Journal of Accounting Research, 6*(3), 67–92.

Bhana, N. (2013). The valuation of research and development expenditures: The case for companies listed on the Johannesburg stock exchange. *International Journal of Finance and Policy Analysis, 5*(2), 3–15.

Bilgic, F. A., Ho, S., Hodgson, A., & Xiong, Z. (2018). Do macro-economic crises determine accounting value relevance? *Accounting in Europe, 15*(3), 402–422.

Brown, S., Lo, K., & Lys, T. (1999). Use of R2 in accounting research: Measuring changes in value relevance over the last four decades. *Journal of Accounting and Economics, 28*(2), 83–115.

Burgstahler, D. C., & Dichev, I. D. (1997). Earnings, adaptation and equity value. *The Accounting Review, 72*(2), 187–215.

Callimaci, A., & Landry, S. (2004). Market valuation of research and development spending under Canadian GAAP. *Canadian Accounting Perspectives, 3*(1), 33–53.

Cazavan-Jeny, A., & Jeanjean, T. (2006). The negative impact of R&D capitalization: A value relevance approach. *European Accounting Review, 15*(1), 37–61.

Chan, L. K. C., Lakonishok, J., & Sougiannis, T. (2001). The stock market valuation of research. *Journal of Finance, 56*(6), 2431–2456.

Chauvin, K. W., & Hirschey, M. (1993). Advertising, R&D expenditures and the market value of the firm. *Financial Management, 22*(4), 128–140.

Chen, T.-L. G., & Ramaboa, K. K. K. M. (2017). Evidence of mispricing for south African listed R&D firms contributed by accounting conservatism. *Intangible Capital, 13*(2), 411–429.

Ciftci, M., & Darrough, M. (2015). What explains the valuation difference between intangible-intensive profit and loss firms? *Journal of Business Finance and Accounting, 42*(1–2), 138–166.

Ciftci, M., Darrough, M., & Mashruwala, R. (2014). Value relevance of accounting information for intangible-intensive industries and the impact of scale: The US evidence. *European Accounting Review, 23*(2), 199–226.

Collins, D. W., Maydew, E. L., & Weiss, I. S. (1997). Changes in the value-relevance of earnings and book values over the past forty years. *Journal of Accounting and Economics, 24*, 39–67.

Core, J. E., Guay, W. R., & Van Buskirk, A. (2003). Market valuations in the new economy: An investigation of what has changed. *Journal of Accounting and Economics, 34*(1–3), 43–67.

Correia, S. (2015). *Singletons, cluster-robust standard errors and fixed effects: A bad mix.* Technical Note, Duke University.

Darrough, M., & Ye, J. (2007). Valuation of loss firms in a knowledge-based economy. *Review of Accounting Studies, 12*(1), 61–93. https://doi.org/10.1007/s11142-006-9022-z.

Dinçergök, B. (2013). Value relevance of earnings and BV in Turkey: The 2003-2009 period. *İktisat, İşletme ve Finans, 28*(332), 47–66.

Donelson, D. C., & Resutek, R. J. (2012). The effect of R&D on future returns and earnings forecasts. *Review of Accounting Studies, 17*(4), 848–876.

Dugan, M. T., McEldowney, J. E., Turner, E. H., & Wheatley, C. M. (2016). The impact of different accounting reporting methods on the informativeness of research and development costs: IFRS compared to U.S. GAAP. *Review of Pacific Basin Financial Markets and Policies, 19*(04), 1650025.

Ertuğrul, M. (2018). *Muhasebe Verilerinin Değer İlişkisi* (1st ed.). Ankara: Nobel Bilimsel Eserler.

Ertuğrul, M. (2019). A review of the literature on IFRS adoption from the perspective of the value relevance. In H. Dincer & S. Yüksel (Eds.), *Handbook of research on global issues in financial communication and investment decision making* (pp. 367–394). Hershey: IGI Global.

Ertuğrul, M. (2020). Maddi Olmayan Duran Varlıkların Değer İlişkisi. *Muhasebe ve Denetime Bakış, 59*, 213–233.

Ertuğrul, M., & Demir, V. (2018). How does unobserved heterogeneity affect value relevance? *Australian Accounting Review, 28*(2), 288–301.

Francis, J., & Schipper, K. (1999). Have financial statements lost their relevance? *Journal of Accounting Research, 37*(2), 319–352.
Franzen, L., & Radhakrishnan, S. (2009). The value relevance of R&D across profit and loss firms. *Journal of Accounting and Public Policy, 28*(1), 16–32.
Goncharov, I., & Veenman, D. (2014). Stale and scale effects in markets-based accounting research: Evidence from the valuation of dividends. *European Accounting Review, 23*(1), 25–55.
Gordon, L. A., Loeb, M. P., & Sohail, T. (2010). Market value of voluntary disclosure concerning information security. *MIS Quarterly, 34*(3), 567–594.
Gow, I. D., Ormazabal, G., & Taylor, D. J. (2010). Correcting for cross-sectional and time-series dependence in accounting research. *Accounting Review, 85*(2), 483–512.
Gujarati, D. (1970a). Use of dummy variables in testing for equality between sets of coefficients in linear regressions: A generalization. *American Statistician, 24*(5), 18–22.
Gujarati, D. (1970b). Use of dummy variables in testing for equality between sets of coefficients in two linear regressions: A note. *American Statistician, 24*(1), 50–52.
Guo, R. J., Lev, B., & Zhou, N. (2005). The valuation of biotech IPOs. *Journal of Accounting, Auditing and Finance, 20*(4), 423–459.
Gür, E. (2016). *Do improvements in IFRS mitigate earnings management in the post-adoption period? Evidence from Turkey*. Unpublished Master's Thesis, Tilburg University.
Han, B. H., & Manry, D. (2004). The value-relevance of R&D and advertising expenditures: Evidence from Korea. *International Journal of Accounting, 39*(2), 155–173.
Hayn, C. (1995). The information content of losses. *Journal of Accounting and Economics, 20*, 125–153.
Hellman, N. (2008). Accounting conservatism under IFRS. *Accounting in Europe, 5*(2), 71–100.
Hellström, K. (2006). The value relevance of financial accounting information in a transition economy: The case of the Czech Republic. *European Accounting Review, 15*(3), 325–349.
Hirschey, M., Richardson, V. J., & Scholz, S. (2001). Value relevance of nonfinancial information: The case of patent data. *Review of Quantitative Finance and Accounting, 17*(3), 223–235.
Hirshleifer, D., Hsu, P.-H., & Li, D. (2017). *Innovative Originality, Profitability, and Stock Returns* (No. 23432).
Holthausen, R. W., & Watts, R. L. (2001). The relevance of the value-relevance literature for financial accounting standard setting. *Journal of Accounting and Economics, 31*(1–3), 3–75.
Jiang, W., & Stark, A. W. (2013). Dividends, research and development expenditures, and the value relevance of book value for UK loss-making firms. *British Accounting Review, 45*(2), 112–124.
Jones, D. A. (2018). Using real options theory to explain patterns in the valuation of research and development expenditures. *Review of Quantitative Finance and Accounting, 51*(3), 575–593.
Joos, P., & Plesko, G. A. (2005). Valuing loss firms. *Accounting Review, 80*(3), 847–870.
Kargin, S. (2013). The impact of IFRS on the value relevance of accounting information: Evidence from Turkish firms. *International Journal of Economics and Finance, 5*(4), 71–80.
Kaytmaz Balsarı, Ç., & Özkan, S. (2009). Impact of financial crises on the value relevance of earnings and book value: 1994 and 2001 crises in Turkey. *EconAnadolu 2009: Anadolu International Conference in Economics*. Eskişehir, Turkey.
Ke, F. Y., Pham, T., & Fargher, N. (2004). The relevance to firm valuation of capitalized Research and Development expenditures. *Australian Accounting Review, 14*(3), 72–76.
Kothari, S. P., & Zimmerman, J. L. (1995). Price and return models. *Journal of Accounting and Economics, 20*(2), 155–192.
Lev, B., & Sougiannis, T. (1996). The capitalization, amortization, and value-relevance of R&D. *Journal of Accounting and Economics, 21*, 107–138.
Lev, B., & Zarowin, P. (1999). The boundaries of financial reporting and how to extend them. *Journal of Accounting Research, 37*(2), 353–385.
Mestelman, S., Mohammad, E., & Shehata, M. (2015). The convergence of IFRS and U.S. GAAP: Evidence from the SEC's removal of form 20-F reconciliations. *Accounting Perspectives, 14*(3), 190–211.

Miller, M. H., & Modigliani, F. (1966). Some estimates of the cost of capital to the electric utility industry, 1954-1957. *The American Economic Review, 56*(3), 333–391.

Misund, B., Asche, F., & Osmundsen, P. (2008). Industry upheaval and valuation: Empirical evidence from the international oil and gas industry. *International Journal of Accounting, 43*(4), 398–424.

Mitrione, L., Tanewski, G., & Birt, J. (2014). The relevance to firm valuation of research and development expenditure in the Australian health-care industry. *Australian Journal of Management, 39*(3), 425–452.

Mora, A., & Walker, M. (2015). The implications of research on accounting conservatism for accounting standard setting. *Accounting and Business Research, 45*(5), 620–650.

Napoli, F. (2015). The value relevance of R&D expenditure after the adoption of the international accounting standards by Italian publicly listed companies. *Problems and Perspectives in Management, 13*(2), 91–101.

Ohlson, J. A. (1995). Earnings, book values, and dividends in equity valuation. *Contemporary Accounting Research, 11*(2), 661–687.

Onali, E., Ginesti, G., & Vasilakis, C. (2017). How should we estimate value-relevance models? Insights from European data. *British Accounting Review, 49*(5), 460–473.

Paul, S. M., Mytelka, D. S., Dunwiddie, C. T., Persinger, C. C., Munos, B. H., Lindborg, S. R., & Schacht, A. L. (2010). How to improve RD productivity: The pharmaceutical industry's grand challenge. *Nature Reviews Drug Discovery, 9*(3), 203–214.

Petersen, M. A. (2009). Estimating standard errors in finance panel data sets: Comparing approaches. *Review of Financial Studies, 22*(1), 435–480.

Riahi-Belkaoui, A. (2004). *Accounting theory* (5th ed.). London: Cengage Learning EMEA.

Sarabia, L. A., & Ortiz, M. C. (2009). Response surface methodology. *Comprehensive Chemometrics*, 345–390.

Shah, S. Z. A., Liang, S., & Akbar, S. (2013). International financial reporting standards and the value relevance of R&D expenditures: Pre and post IFRS analysis. *International Review of Financial Analysis, 30*, 158–169.

Shortridge, R. T. (2004). Market valuation of successful versus non-successful R&D efforts in the pharmaceutical industry. *Journal of Business Finance and Accounting, 31*(9–10), 1301–1325.

Sougiannis, T. (1994). The accounting based valuation of corporate R&D. *Accounting Review, 69*(1), 44–68.

Suadiye, G. (2012). Value relevance of book value & earnings under the local GAAP and IFRS: Evidence from Turkey. *Ege Akademik Bakış, 12*(3), 301–310.

Tan, P. M.-S., & Lim, C. Y. (2007). The value relevance of accounting variables and analysts' forecasts: The case of biotechnology firms. *Review of Accounting and Finance, 6*(3), 233–253.

Tsoligkas, F., & Tsalavoutas, I. (2011). Value relevance of R&D in the UK after IFRS mandatory implementation. *Applied Financial Economics, 21*(13), 957–967.

Türel, A. (2009). The value relevance of IFRS: The case of Turkey. *Acta Universitatis Danubius. Œconomica, 5*(1), 119–128.

Wu, H., Fargher, N., & Wright, S. (2010). Accounting for investments and the relevance of losses to firm value. *International Journal of Accounting, 45*(1), 104–127.

Xu, L., & Cai, F. (2016). Value relevance of earnings, book value, revenue, and R&D. *Business Review, 24*(1), 91–97.

Xu, B., Magnan, M. L., & André, P. E. (2007). The stock market valuation of R&D information in biotech firms. *Contemporary Accounting Research, 24*(4), 1291–1318.

Factors Influencing the Consumers' Expenditure on Wine According to their Own Expectations in a Tourism Perspective: A Statistical Analysis

Marco Remondino and Enrico Ivaldi

Abstract The work deals with the theme of consumer behavior and preferences in the wine sector in a tourism perspective. In particular, it aims to analyze the consumer's propensity to spend a certain amount of money on the purchase of wine, based on a set of variables arising from the administration of a questionnaire. A sample with different characteristics has been analyzed, coming from different sources: some subjects were reached through specialized wine blogs, others in physical wine shops, others through non-specialized social networks. Each subject was asked to indicate the specific importance she attributes to different factors in the choice of a wine (i.e.: suggestions from friends, reviews in magazines, advice from specialized blogs, price, brand, previous experience). Each of these attributes is here considered as a possible RRS, leading to a satisfaction of consumer's personal expectations. Two statistical techniques have been used to analyze data: the logistic regression and the classification tree. The results show clear correlations between the propensity to spend a high figure with some categorical data, in particular the gender and the source of the respondent. In addition, the experience variable has a positive correlation with expenditure, while the variables related to the impact of advice received from friends and price have a negative correlation. The work, through a statistical approach, links consumers' behavior, preferences and expectations with expenditure propensity in the wine sector. Hence, it includes practical implications for companies to better understand the drivers of consumers' choices and their propensity to spend in wine to meet their expectations.

M. Remondino (✉) · E. Ivaldi
Department of Economics (DIEC), University of Genova, Genoa, GE, Italy

Political Science Department (DISPO), University of Genova, Genoa, GE, Italy
e-mail: marco.remondino@economia.unige.it; enrico.ivaldi@unige.it

H. Dincer, S. Yüksel (eds.), *Strategic Priorities in Competitive Environments*, Contributions to Management Science, https://doi.org/10.1007/978-3-030-45023-6_4

1 Introduction

In the wine market, the complexity and the wide range of products on the market contribute to a high degree of uncertainty, regarding the possibly negative consequences of the choice made; this leads buyers to execute the so-called risk-reduction strategies (RRS), i.e. mechanisms aimed at reducing uncertainty even when the information available is inadequate and the consequences of the purchase are unpredictable. This is especially true since most consumers do not have the knowledge to make informed buying decisions about wine, but do not want to appear totally incompetent and, above all, have high expectations towards the specific product. In the choice of wine, the consumer perceives three types of risk that would deny her expectations: the functional risk, in relation to the potential bad taste of the chosen bottle; the social risk, for a lack of approval of the wine by family and friends; the financial risk, due to a low connection between the total sum of costs incurred and the perceived quality. When a specific product is unknown (e.g. brand and/or type), the most common RRS are: tasting wine before buying or following personal recommendations from more acknowledgeable persons, but there are other drivers that could lead consumer's choice towards their personal expectations.

For this reason, in the present research, each subject was asked to indicate the specific importance she attributes to different factors in the choice of a wine (i.e.: suggestions from friends, reviews in magazines, advice from specialized blogs, price, brand, previous experience). Each of these attributes is here considered as a possible RRS, leading to a satisfaction of consumer's personal expectations.

The total sample is composed of 460 respondents and comprises mainly Italian people. Future works will address this geographical limitation. The questionnaire is deliberately short and concise, with the aim of encouraging the respondent. The most interesting aspect, in order to evaluate the propensity to spend and consumption habits, is the channel through which the questionnaires were collected. In particular, a part of them (267 out of 460) comes from specialized blogs, which kindly inserted the link to the questionnaire, explaining its aims and motivations. Other 71 questionnaires were collected in physical wine shops, by filling in a form specifically prepared and submitted by the shop owner to his customers. Other 122 were collected through e-mail and social media and then submitted, therefore, through channels that have nothing to do, directly, with wine.

Two statistical techniques have been used to analyze data: the logistic regression and the classification tree. In particular, in order to evaluate the impact of these variables on the consumer's propensity to spend a certain amount of money on the purchase of wine, a logistical regression analysis was carried out to assess the role played by several independent variables (predictors) with respect to the probability that the dependent variable has one of its two values. The second method used to validate the results, in order to identify population characteristics that were predicted, is the classification tree methodology. This method is a data mining technique that organizes the data in a hierarchical structure composed of nodes, branches and leaves.

The results show clear correlations between the propensity to spend a high figure with some categorical data, in particular the gender and the source of the respondent. In addition, the experience variable has a positive correlation with expenditure, while the variables related to the impact of advice received from friends and price have a negative correlation.

Furthermore, the particularly relevant aspect is the identification of the respondent's provenance (source of the questionnaire), which defines, by extension, the level of consumers' expectations and interest in the wine product. If in fact about 73.5% of the responses were collected on wine channels (blogs and specialized forums and physical wine shops), the remaining 26.5% was obtained on generic channels (e-mail and social networks). From a statistical point of view, as can be seen from the results, this weighs significantly on the propensity to spend in wine, so that the first category of respondents has a definitely higher propensity than the second. Other important factors are the sexual gender (with the category of males with a statistically higher propensity to spend) and a series of preliminary categorizations derived from the answers given, the most important of which is the dichotomy between experience and advice from friends as a factor that influences the choice of wine. The respondents who have indicated personal and direct experience as the primary criterion of choice have in fact a propensity to spend, on average, higher sums, while those who have indicated as primary meter the suggestion from friends have a propensity to spend lower sums. This also seems to confirm the specific attitude of the wine connoisseurs, seen as an expert and passionate, able to direct their choices in a conscious way and more likely to spend high amounts on their "hobby".

The work, through a statistical approach, links consumers' behavior, preferences and expectations with expenditure propensity in the wine sector. Hence, it includes practical implications for companies to better understand the drivers of consumers' choices (RRS) and their propensity to spend in wine to meet their expectations. In fact, it is useful to understand the key factors influencing specific choices, in order to better address which factors affect the propensity of a certain expenditure, starting from certain specific expectations.

As wine plays an important role in people's lifestyles, there has been growing interest in visiting places of production, with a rapid growth in the popularity of wine regions around the world (Molina et al. 2015). Wine is considered a central element in the development and promotion of tourism and can contribute to the creation of wealth at national, regional and local levels (O'Neill and Charters 2000).

Italy is one of the leading countries in the production of wines and is recognized worldwide for the quality of its products. In the last decades the simple wine production has been enriched with the development of a new form of tourism: wine tourism. Tourists, in fact, visit Italy not only for its coastline, historical heritage, geographical attractions or traditional cities, but also to embrace the Italian wine tradition with tasting activities, visits to wineries and vineyards or other events related to wine.

The success of the Italian wine sector, together with the worldwide popularity of Italian cuisine on the demand side, and the policy of diversification of tourist products on the supply side, have led to a serious and coordinated approach to the development of wine tourism in Italy (Romano and Natilli 2009). In recent years, wine tourism has changed in Italian wineries and consequently the entire economy of wine-growing areas. Foreign visitors to Italian wineries are estimated at between 4 and 6 million per year with an annual increase of 3.6%, well above the general Italian tourism that is going through a difficult time (Colombini 2015). Moreover, while wine tourism allows visitors to experience a distinctive product, it also promotes regional economic growth and offers local wineries the opportunity to increase sales and develop tourism-related activities (Canovi and Pucciarelli 2019).

Despite the growing popularity of wine tourism in general, research on wine tourism is slowly emerging: there is a growing need for knowledge of the size of the sector, estimates and monitoring data (Antonioli Corigliano and Viganò 2004; Marangon et al. 2013; Romano and Natilli 2009; Colombini 2015; Canovi and Pucciarelli 2019).

The Italian wine tourist is generally male (61.3%) and aged between 30 and 50 years. He travels as a couple or with a group of friends (Istituto Nazionale Ricerche Turistiche 2015). CENSIS estimates that every 10 euros spent in the vineyard generates 50 euros of revenue for the local economy (2006), and that about 5 million people contribute with about 2.5 billion euros to the wine territories. As always, the rapid growth has its pros and cons, and in fact, the number of wineries equipped to accommodate people is low. Of the 21,000 wineries with shops, only 1000 have qualified multilingual staff, rest rooms, a tasting room, a recreational information activity and a well-equipped commercial area. (Colombini 2015).

Dodd and Gustafson (1997) suggest considering four groups of variables for the evaluation of the wine tourism experience: service, wine characteristics, cellar environment and price of the experience. Today, the advent of social media has radically changed the wine tourism industry, allowing both travelers and tour operators to become the "media" themselves to communicate, collaborate and share tourist information (Hudson et al. 2015; Leung et al. 2013).

The present work aims at contributing to the extant literature about wine tourism, from a specific perspective. In particular, it analyzes a generic touristic trip taken by a potential wine consumer, and tries to explore the potential correlations among her expenditure in wine (during the trip) and other factors.

This is strictly connected with the perspective that most adults consume wine (e.g. "The Harris Poll" of 2,056 adults surveyed online between February 6 and 13, 2012 by Harris Interactive, revealed that 62% of US adults purchase wine) regularly or at least occasionally.

2 Wine Consumers' Choice

The complexity and the wide range of products on offer contribute to a high risk perceived by the consumer or to a high degree of uncertainty regarding the negative consequences of the choice made; this leads buyers to put in place the so-called risk-reduction strategies (RRS), i.e. mechanisms aimed at reducing uncertainty even when the information available is inadequate and the consequences of the purchase are unpredictable.

More scholars have tried to categorize the different types of risk that the consumer has to bear in the consideration phase of the consumer journey, in this context will be taken into account the subdivision into 6 types of risk created by Jacoby and Kaplan in 1972: functional risk, inherent in the inadequacy of the product understood as a set of tangible and intangible attributes to achieve the objectives of the consumer, financial risk, inherent in the total costs incurred by the consumer, risk loss of time, inherent in the time for maintenance or to learn how to use the good, physical risk, closely related to the potential damage caused by the product to the health of the user or the environment, psychological risk regarding the psychological consequences of an incorrect choice and finally the social risk inherent in the inconsistency between the image of the product perceived by society and the personality of the buyer.

The perception of risk is influenced by external factors and also by specific variables of the individual, the propensity to risk is in fact a subjective variable, as well as experience; according to the literature, for example, uncertainty is reduced to increasing the experience gained in a specific field (Lacey et al. 2009). Despite this, it is possible to identify various generic risk reduction strategies such as: searching for information, being faithful to a brand, buying the product of a seller who enjoys a high reputation, relying on the price of the asset, looking for guarantees and assurances.

These notions have been applied to the wine market, starting from the assumption that the decision to purchase this drink is dominated by fear and anxiety because: most consumers do not have the knowledge to make informed decisions, but do not want to appear totally incompetent (Gluckman 1986).

Lacey et al. (2009) state that in the choice of wine the consumer perceives four of the previous types of risk: the functional risk in relation to the potential bad taste of the chosen bottle, the social risk for a lack of approval of the wine by family and friends, the financial risk due to a very bad relationship between the total sum of costs incurred and the perceived quality and finally the physical risk related to the state of drunkenness.

In the same way, a series of specific Risk Reduction Strategies can be identified for this market, the same authors outline two in particular: the opportunity to taste the wine before buying through free samples or through a tasting at the point of sale and personal recommendations.

According to Spawton (1991), however, all the mechanisms mentioned above are adaptable to the choice of wine, the consumer tends to buy products of brands of which he has already had experience, tends to acquire information from others and the sales staff, is often based on price and format of packaging and label.

Hence wine is an experience and cognitive product: to deepen the process of buying this good, it is useful to distinguish the intrinsic attributes from the extrinsic attributes.

The first are physical characteristics of the product that cannot be modified without totally altering the nature of the product itself, they are therefore specific to each output; in the case of wine they fall into this category: taste and the consequent aromas. The consumer-purchaser of wine has difficulty in finding information about these attributes in the phase prior to the purchase, except for repeated purchases or for products that have already been consumed previously. Despite this, according to a study conducted in Italy by researchers Hertzberg and Malorgio (2008), taste is the attribute that most affects consumer choice along with the opinions of friends. 65% of the respondents to the research indicate: opinions of friends and preliminary tasting as the most effective methods to promote and encourage the purchase of a bottle of wine.

Extrinsic attributes also refer to a specific product, but unlike the previous ones they do not belong to it in the strict sense, this category includes external factors such as: producer's brand, certifications of origin, price and label.

The blog "I numeri del vino" provides a ranking of these attributes in relation to the importance they play in the choice of wine for consumption outside the home.

At the top of the ranking there is the brand of the producer, this element performs three main functions for the consumer, especially in situations of risk or asymmetry of information (such as that described so far): orientation, reassurance and warranty. The brand distinguishes the product of a specific company from those of its competitors and communicates to the consumer the presence of specific attributes, the brand also reassures the consumer about the level of quality found in the specific product; the producer therefore assumes a responsibility towards his customer, disappointing him means determining strong negative consequences on his reputation. The brand's reputation plays an extremely important role in a very fragmented market such as that of wine, which is why companies must monitor customer feedback, wine guides and the specialized press.

Immediately after the brand, it is the origin of the wine that plays a key role in consumer choice. The latter, in relation to complex decisions such as this, tends to adopt a heterogeneous attitude towards different outputs by basing its perception of attributes and consequent preferences on the basis of the country or region in which they were produced, this phenomenon is called the "country effect".

The place of origin therefore acts as a cognitive or heuristic shortcut, this effect can occur both in "halo" and in "synthesis" form. In the first case, the purchaser, although not having had direct experience with the country in question or with the product, evaluates its purchasing decision on the basis of the image it has of the territory of origin; in the case of a synthetic country effect, on the other hand, the consumer has direct experience with the good and the territory and tends to generalize.

The position of the origin of the wine in the above mentioned ranking is therefore consistent with the importance of the country effect in the agri-food sector, this is in fact composed of goods that have a strong link with their land in relation to both natural resources and lifestyles. The region where the wine is produced involves for the buyer a set of tangible elements such as the type of grape used, the type of soil and climate and intangible elements such as the different practices and specific knowledge of local producers.

For this reason, Designations of Origin have been created, these occupy third place in the ranking and offer consumers a tool to identify a specific type, ensuring a higher or lower quality threshold depending on the certification. Currently, wines are divided into two main categories: wines with a geographical origin and wines without a geographical origin. The former has a link with the territory in which they were produced and must respect specific disciplines of different rigidity. The least rigid concerns the Typical Geographical Indication (IGT) which, following the new regulations that came into force in Italy in 2010, has been included in the Community category PGI (Protected Geographical Indication).

The discipline is rigid in order to obtain the DOC (*Denominazione di Origine Controllata*—Controlled Designation of Origin) certification; in fact, a chemical analysis and an organoleptic examination are required to guarantee a high quality standard. The latter denomination, in addition to the more restrictive DOCG (*Denominazione di Origine Controllata e Garantita*—Controlled and Guaranteed Denomination of Origin), has been reduced, following the same regulations, to the broader DOP (*Denominazione di Origine Protetta*—Protected Designation of Origin) denomination.

Another extrinsic attribute, the price, takes on a less important role. The monetary value of the bottle of wine is also considered as a cognitive shortcut and is part of the Risk Reduction Strategies mentioned above, is in fact used as a quality signal by less experienced consumers, the latter tend to protect themselves from poor quality by buying more expensive bottles. Price is therefore the fifth position in the ranking, being an attribute considered only by a portion of wine drinkers; in fact, those who have more experience can base their choices on other quality indicators.

Overall, however, buyers tend to know in the phase prior to purchase the price range in which the bottle should be placed, an interval that can obviously vary depending on the occasion of consumption.

The relationship between quantity requested and price is called Elasticity, a research presented on the already mentioned blog "I numeri del vino", shows how this is negative.

This means that as the price of the good increases, the quantity requested drops. The price of wine has a lower impact than that of liqueurs, but the elasticity is still higher than that of beer at a value of (−0.65).

Finally, the last extrinsic attribute mentioned is the label, the latter represents both an important tool to reduce the information asymmetry between consumer and producer and an important factor of differentiation of the bottle from the aesthetic point of view.

The information contained in the label serves in fact as a fundamental support in the decision for those who have less experience, for this reason the European legislation indicates some mandatory notions for wines of geographical origin: designation of origin or geographical indication, alcohol content, indication of origin, indication of the bottler, presence of allergens, vintage of the grapes and quantity. In addition to this, producers may provide other optional information such as: the name of the grape variety, names and symbols concerning the producer and any indications on production methods.

From the design point of view, the label occupies the tenth position in the ranking and it has been demonstrated that the color, images and logos on the label have a greater impact on women than on men (Thomas and Pickering 2003).

3 The Questionnaire

The basic tool used to carry on the analysis about consumers' choices and preferences is a questionnaire, aiming to explore the average expenditure of potential customers towards wine, along with a series of attributes (some of which demographical, others based on preferences and experiences). The final goal is to understand whether the expenditure can be linked to some of those and why.

The sampling and data collection procedure consisted of four steps, namely the selection of motivation elements, the development of questionnaires, the pilot test and the data collection.

During the implementation of the three phases, a study was carried out in order to determine the a priori sample size: a stratified probabilistic sampling was carried out, dividing the sample obtained from the reference population as homogeneously as possible with respect to the variable whose value was to be estimated. The sample was then stratified on the basis of age, gender and education (this is not true but it is plausible).

The questionnaire was designed based on the extant literature on wine tourism and on the aforementioned literature review (Antonioli Corigliano and Viganò 2004; Marangon et al. 2013; Romano and Natilli 2009; Colombini 2015; Canovi and Pucciarelli 2019) and asks to evaluate a set of heuristics (Remondino 2018).

The questionnaire is deliberately short and concise, with the aim of encouraging the respondent. The most interesting aspect in order to evaluate the propensity to spend and consumption habits is the channel through which the questionnaires were collected. In particular, a part of them (267 out of 460) comes from specialized blogs, which kindly inserted the link to the questionnaire, explaining its aims and motivations. Another 71 questionnaires were collected in physical wine shops, by filling in a form specially prepared and submitted by the shop owner to his customers. Another 122 were collected through email and social media and then submitted, therefore, through channels that have nothing to do, directly, with wine.

The following were the question asked to the respondents, while the provenience was recorded directly—specialized blog, wine shop, social or generic channel—(Table 1).

The questionnaire aims to investigate the propensity to spend in wine made during a generic trip lasting about a week. The relevant aspect is the non-specificity of the questionnaire, which can therefore be addressed to experienced and regular wine consumers, but also to occasional consumers. Another

Table 1 Questions asked in the survey

Age [open]
Gender [M, F]
Region [Italian regions]
Education [elementary/medium, higher]
Average expenditure during a touristic trip of about 1 week [open]
Relative importance of:
Brand [1...7]
Price [1...7]
Specialized magazines or other traditional media [1...7]
Specialized blogs or other new media [1...7]
Friends' advice [1...7]
Previous personal experience [1...7]

peculiar aspect is the brevity of the questionnaire itself, which allowed to propose it also in physical places (wine shops) obtaining a fair redemption rate.

The demographic part of the questionnaire aims to identify the respondent by means of usual and generic parameters, such as age, gender, region of residence (in Italy), level of education. The part relating to the criteria for choosing wine uses a Likert scale with the attribution of a weight (from 1 to 7) to different specific parameters: the brand of the wine, the price, the attention to the reviews published in physical journals of the sector, the attention to the reviews published on blogs and other new media specific to the sector, suggestions from friends or acquaintances and, finally, personal experience. It is required the average expected expenditure in wine to be made during a tourist trip of about 1 week, while the channel of origin of the questionnaire (blog/specialized forum, wine shop, generic social network, e-mail) is recorded at the time of response.

4 Methodology

Two statistical techniques have been used: the logistic regression and the classification tree. In order to evaluate the impact of these variables on the consumer's propensity to spend a certain amount of money on the purchase of wine, a logistical regression analysis was carried out to assess the role played by several independent variables (predictors) with respect to the probability that the dependent variable has one of its two values. The general formula for the model is:

$$Logit(\mathbb{P}(Y=1)) = ln\left(\frac{\mathbb{P}(Y=1) \mid X}{1-(\mathbb{P}(Y=1)|X)}\right) = \alpha + \sum_i \beta_i(X_i) + \varepsilon$$

The estimates of the β parameters (which are represented in the values of the first column (B)), are linearly linked to the variation of the logit but are not linearly linked to the variation of the probability of the dependent variable, so their interpretation is not immediate.

The model was applied to test the research hypothesis that some independent variables influence the probability that an individual spends more than 50 euros to buy a bottle of wine. The analysis was conducted using the Odds Ratios (Exp (B)), which evaluates the direction and intensity of the association between the variables and approximates the so-called relative risk. It is defined as the ratio between the probabilities of the event (i.e. the probability of the event divided by its complement) in the presence and absence of a certain condition X (independent variable) or, in the case of independent variables that are not dichotomous, in the presence of a unitary variation of this condition.

The second method used to validate the results, in order to identify population characteristics that were predicted, is the classification tree methodology.

This method is a data mining technique that organizes the data in a hierarchical structure composed of nodes, branches and leaves. The first node is called the root node, and it is the node where all the cases under consideration are present and from which the whole structure originates. The root node is recursively divided into a number of branches, creating a kind of path from the root node to the leaves that are the last and the closure of the nodes. The algorithms aim to create increasingly homogeneous nodes with respect to the dependent variable, so that the first node is the most heterogeneous node, while the leaves are the most homogeneous node method with respect to waiting times. The subdivisions are based on different criteria.

This work used the non-parametric algorithm CHAID (Chi-squared Automatic Interaction Detection) based on the Chi-square test. It maximizes the meaning of a chi-squared statistic to each partition. The CHAIN was chosen because it is suitable for working with many categorical variables and because of its algorithm's simultaneous ability to merge the attributes of the original variables into a smaller number of combined categories (if they do not differ statistically in their forecast of dependent production).

CHAID proceeds step by step. First, the best partition for each predictor is determined. Then, the predictors are and you choose the best. The data is divided according to the chosen predictor. Each of these subgroups are reanalyzed independently to produce further subdivisions for analysis (Siciliani 2015; Landi et al. 2018). In this way, CHAID divides the data into mutually exclusive and exhaustive subsets, which implies that the segments do not overlap and that each case/individual is included in a segment (Kass 1980).

Note that variables showing a stronger association with waiting time are chosen first (Testi et al. 2010). All the cases indicated in the leaf node belong to an established classification rule. A classification rule is defined by the series of steps starting from the root node and descending towards the leaf node.

5 Results

In order to evaluate the impact of these variables on wine expenditure (considered dichotomous up to 50 euro and over 50 euro), a logistic regression analysis was then carried out to possibly link the role of several independent variables (predictors) with respect to the probability that the dependent variable has one of its two values. The analysis was carried out through the study of the Odds Ratios (Exp (B)) that assess the direction and intensity of the association between the variables and approximate the so-called relative risk.

The model correctly classified 63.1% of the cases (Table 2).

Of all the predictors considered, only five were statistically significant: gender, origin, price, friends, as shown in Table 3.

As far as the categorical data are concerned, the gender and the origin were significant.

Women appear to have a propensity to spend less than 50 euros less than men by about half (exp (β) = 0.512) As for the origin, people who are part of the sample because they belong to a blog have a relative propensity exp (β) = 1.775 times more to spend more than 50 euro than those who are part of the sample from the email. The

Table 2 Percentages of correct classification logistics analysis

Classification table[a]					
			Forecast		
			Expenditure		
	Observed		Up to 50	Over 50	Correct percentage
Step 1	Expenditure	Up to 50	192	63	75.3
		Over 50	104	93	47.2
	Global percentage				63.1

[a]Reference value is 0.500

Table 3 Results of logistic regression

Variables in the equation									
								95% CI per Exp(B)	
		B	E.S.	Wald	df	Sig.	Exp(B)	Inferior	Superior
Step 1[a]	Gender (1)	−0.669	0.236	8.040	1	0.005	0.512	0.323	0.813
	Origin			5.712	2	0.057			
	Origin (blog)	0.574	0.240	5.700	1	0.017	1.775	1.108	2.843
	Origin (wine shop)	0.369	0.325	1.294	1	0.255	1.447	0.766	2.733
	Price	−0.240	0.071	11.328	1	0.001	0.787	0.684	0.905
	Friends	−0.195	0.068	8.170	1	0.004	0.823	0.720	0.941
	Experience	0.284	0.090	10.060	1	0.002	1.329	1.115	1.584
	Constant	−0.202	0.599	0.114	1	0.736	0.817		

[a]Variables entered in step 1: Gender, Origin, Price, Friends, Experience

Table 4 Percentages of correct classification logistics analysis classification tree

Classification			
	Previsto		
Observed	Up to 50	Over 50	Correct percentage
Up to 50	131	124	51.4
Over 50	67	130	66.0
Global percentage	43.8	56.2	57.7

Expansion Method: CHAID
Dependent variable: expenditure

origin of the wine shop, although it has a odds ratio higher than 1, therefore potentially with a propensity of exp (β) = 1.447 times higher than those who are part of the sample coming from the mail are not significant, however, being the value of 1 included in the confidence interval of the ODDS ratio.

The other variable that shows a positive relative propensity for expenditure over 50 euro is the variable Experience: it is observed that this has a propensity of exp (β) = 1.329 times higher than an expenditure over 50 euro.

The variable recommendations of Friends and Price, on the other hand, lead to a lower propensity to spend more than 50 euros on wine, respectively exp (β) = 0.823 and exp (β) = 0.787.

An interesting comparison can be made through the classification tree method that partially confirm the results of logistic regression. In this case the model correctly classifies 57.7% of the data (Table 4).

As it can be seen in Fig. 1, the analysis shows that the expenditure on wine, for which the initial data report 43.6% of the sample that spends more than 50 euros, depends primarily on the origin of the respondent. In the first level, in fact, the node classifies on the one hand those who come from the email, of which only 33.1% spends more than 50 euros while those who come from the blog or wine shop for 47.4% of cases spend more than 50 euros.

The second node that the tree classifies is a subdivision of those who come from blogs and wine shops and subdivides according to the variable gender. 51.2% of males spend more than 50 euros while only 35.1% of females spend more than 50 euros.

6 Conclusions, Limitations and Future Directions

The interrelationship between wine and tourism in terms of space and regional identity is something important and lies at the heart of the contemporary economic and cultural debate on the processes of globalization and localization (Hall 1996). At a time of profound restructuring in many of the country's rural regions, policy responses require the encouragement of greater links between industry and a greater capacity to promote places to attract investment and visitors and encourage

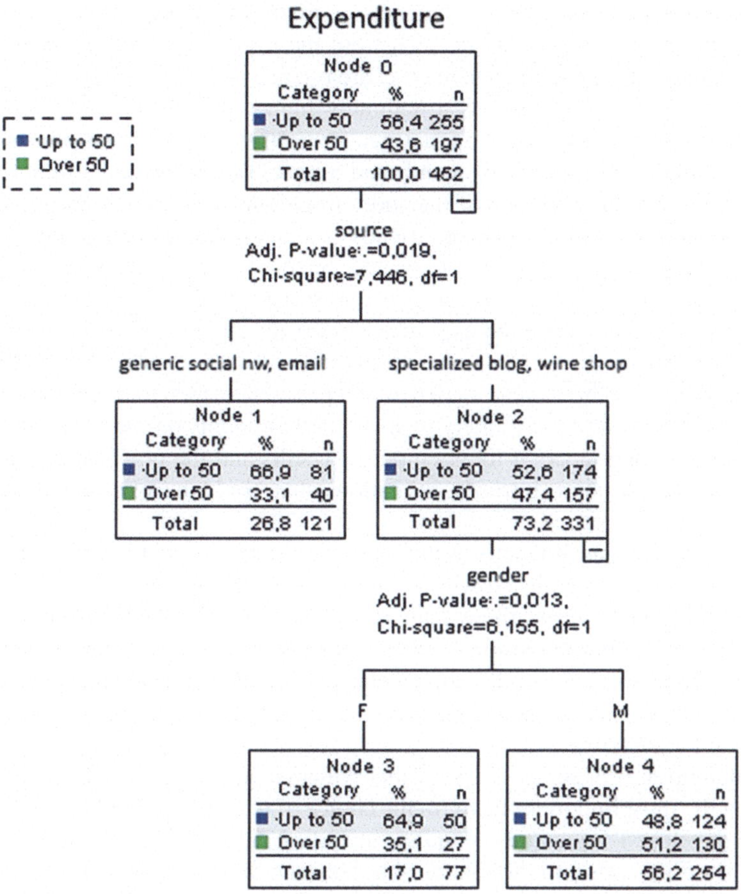

Fig. 1 Classification tree

employment. Unfortunately, the greatest obstacle to such developments remains the inability of the wine and tourism industry to understand and work together. Wine tourism offers precisely this opportunity.

The work appears to be in line with the work of the National Research Institute (CENSIS).

This study serves as a first step to better understand the expenditure of a tourist in wine during a trip lasting about 1 week. This is useful to understand the key factors influencing specific choices, but also to better understand which factors affect the propensity of a certain expenditure (greater or less than a certain threshold, here set at 50 euros on the duration of the entire trip).

Furthermore, the particularly relevant aspect is the identification of the respondent's provenance, which defines, by extension, the level of consumer interest in the wine product. If in fact about 73.5% of the responses were collected on wine channels (blogs and specialized forums and physical wine shops), the remaining

26.5% was obtained on generic channels (e-mail and social networks). From a statistical point of view, as can be seen from the results, this weighs significantly on the propensity to spend in wine in other areas (such as, in fact, tourism), where the first category of respondents has a definitely higher propensity than the second. Other important factors are the sexual gender (with the category of males with a statistically higher propensity to spend) and a series of preliminary categorizations derived from the answers given, the most important of which is the dichotomy between experience and advice from friends as a factor that influences the choice of wine. The respondents who have indicated personal and direct experience as the primary criterion of choice have in fact a propensity to spend on average higher, while those who have indicated as primary meter the suggestion from friends has a propensity to spend lower. This also seems to confirm the specific attitude of the wine connoisseur, to be seen as an expert and passionate, able to direct their choices in a conscious way and more likely to spend high amounts on their "hobby".

Despite the importance of these empirical results and the practical implications, this document has some intrinsic limitations that could be questioned in future research.

First of all, the questionnaire was mainly addressed to people living in Italy, a country with a well-established wine tradition. In future studies, the sample will be expanded in order to verify these same results and possibly introduce new parameters to reflect on. Further studies are therefore necessary to extend the sample to include different areas. Secondly, the number of variables to which the questionnaire refers could be expanded by adding factors to better understand the impact of wine tourism on the income.

The definition of a series of issues that wineries and wine tourists must address regarding the most important factor in the choice of wine is another key issue, which must be developed from further studies, including anthropological and psychological studies. Research into the relationship between involvement and the search for sensations is in fact necessary to determine whether the search for sensations causes involvement and what is the relationship between involvement and types of wine tourism behavior.

Further work is needed on the segmentation of the wine tourism market. Even at the widest levels, it was not clear how to distinguish between "specialized" and "generalist" wine tourists. For this reason, the path taken has been to identify channels usually followed by those who look for "wine" in everyday life (blogs and specialized forums and wine shops) and those who do not necessarily look for it (generic social networks and e-mails). The question to be answered is whether this distinction should be made only for motivational reasons, for effective and measurable behavior related to wine or for both. Another interesting aspect to be investigated is that of the corporate reputation (Remondino and Boella 2010) so to link this with the expenditure of a potential client towards a specific wine type or brand.

Finally, since the questions refer to a generic trip (and not to a specific wine tourism trip) it is necessary to establish to what extent a visit to the winery acts as a multiplier of the tourist's (in general) wine expenditure and future wine sales of the winery in the retail trade and on what wine tourism factors the strength of this multiplier effect depends.

References

Antonioli Corigliano, M., & Viganò, G. (2004). *Turisti per gusto. Enogastronomia, territorio, sostenibilità*. Novara: De Agostini Editore.

Canovi, M., & Pucciarelli, F. (2019). Social media marketing in wine tourism: Winery owners' perceptions. *Journal of Travel & Tourism Marketing, 36*(6), 653–664. https://doi.org/10.1080/10548408.2019.1624241.

Colombini, D. C. (2015). Wine tourism in Italy. *International Journal of Wine Research, 7*, 29–35. https://doi.org/10.2147/IJWR.S82688.

DODD, T., & GUSTAFSON, A. W. (1997). Product, environment and service attributes that influence customers' attitudes and purchases at wineries. *Journal of Food Products Marketing, 4*(3), 41–59.

Gluckman, R. (1986). A consumer approach to branded wines. *European Journal of Marketing, 20* (6), 27–46.

Hall, C. M. (1996). Geography, marketing and the selling of places. *Journal of Travel and Tourism Marketing, 6*(3/4), 61–84.

Hertzberg, A., & Malorgio, G. (2008). Wine demand in Italy: An analysis of consumer preferences. *New Medit, 4*(2008), 40–46.

Hudson, S., Roth, M. S., Madden, T. J., & Hudson, R. (2015). The effects of social media on emotions, brand relationship quality, and word of mouth: An empirical study of music festival attendees. *Tourism Management, 47*, 68–76.

Istituto Nazionale Ricerche Turistiche. (2015). Accessed April 2, 2015, from http://isnart.it/rassegnaStampa_elenco.php?totrec=3978&startRec=1970&PHPSESSID=

Kass, G. V. (1980). An exploratory technique for investigating large quantities of categorical data. *Applied Statistics, 29*(2), 119–127.

Lacey, S., Bruwer, J., & Li, E. (2009). The role of perceived risk in wine purchase decisions in restaurants. *International Journal of Wine Business Research, 21*(2), 99–117.

Landi, S., Ivaldi, E., & Testi, A. (2018). Socioeconomic status and waiting times for health services: An international literature review and evidence from the Italian National Health System. *Health Policy, 122*, 334–351. https://doi.org/10.1016/j.healthpol.2018.01.003.

Leung, D., Law, R., Van Hoof, H., & Buhalis, D. (2013). Social media in tourism and hospitality: A literature review. *Journal of Travel & Tourism Marketing, 30*(1–2), 3–22.

Marangon, F., Troiano, S., Tempesta, T., & Vecchiato, D. (2013). *Consumer behaviour in rural tourism*. Conjoint analysis of choice attributes in the Italian-Slovenian cross-boundary area (no. 171-2016-2082).

Molina, A., Gómez, M., González-Díaz, B., & Esteban, Á. (2015). Market segmentation in wine tourism: Strategies for wineries and destinations in Spain. *Journal of Wine Research, 26*(3), 192–224.

O'Neill, M., & Charters, S. (2000). Service quality at the cellar door: Implications for Western Australia's developing wine tourism industry. *Managing Service Quality: An International Journal, 10*(2), 112–122.

Remondino, M. (2018). Information technology in healthcare: HHC-MOTES, a novel set of metrics to analyse IT sustainability in different areas. *Sustainability, 10*(8), 2721.

Remondino, M., & Boella, G. (2010). How users' participation affects reputation management systems: The case of P2P networks. *Simulation Modelling Practice and Theory, 18*(10), 1493–1505.

Romano, M. F., & Natilli, M. (2009). Wine tourism in Italy: New profi les, styles of consumption, ways of touring. *Tourism, 57*(4), 463–475.
Siciliani, L. (2015). Waiting times: Evidence of social inequalities in access for care. In B. Sobolev, A. Levy, & S. Goring (Eds.), *Data and measures in health services research. Health services research*. Boston, MA: Springer.
Spawton, A. L. (1991). Grapes and wine seminar–prospering in the 1990s: Changing your view of the consumer. *International Marketing Review, 8*(4), 32.
Testi, A., Ivaldi, E., & Cislaghi, C. (2010). Primi elementi per la costruzione di una tariffa nelle RSA:i predittori della complessità assistenziale. *Tendenze nuove, 1*, 9, 28.
Thomas, A., & Pickering, G. (2003). The importance of wine label information. *International Journal of Wine Marketing, 15*(2), 58–74.

Benchmarking Competitive Market Environment Using Market-Based Database

İpek Gürsel Tapkı

Abstract The aim of this study is to provide a review of the literature on benchmarking in competitive markets. The first two sections cover the general information about benchmarking, its types and how it is done. Next section relates benchmarking to other business approaches that are used to improve performance of organizations. The remainder of the chapter focuses on the applications of competitive benchmarking in different sectors.

1 Introduction

Benchmarking is a widely used technique in many disciplines including business. In general, it is defined as the procedure to compare and evaluate a company's product, strategy, process, and service performance both within its own organization and with those of the leading companies in the market (Watson 1992, 1993; Camp 1989; Meybodi 2005; Maire 2002; Hong et al. 2012).

It is very important for managers to know the competition conditions and competitors well in order to exist in the market. Providing managers with the right information helps them make the right decisions. At this point, benchmarking comes into play (Jetmarová 2011). Benchmarking gives companies the opportunity to measure and evaluate their performance and processes by looking at the leading companies (Benson 1994). Therefore, it is an opportunity for continuous improvement. It allows companies to bypass the trial process and improve themselves directly. This enables them to develop more quickly and this fast improvement is very important especially in competitive environments (Lankford 2000).

The first benchmarking process was carried out in the late 1970s by the American company Xerox, one of the world's largest manufacturer of copiers. During this period, Japanese manufacturers started to make profit by selling the same product at

İ. G. Tapkı (✉)
Department of Economics, Gebze Technical University, Gebze/Kocaeli, Turkey
e-mail: ipek.tapki@gtu.edu.tr

H. Dincer, S. Yüksel (eds.), *Strategic Priorities in Competitive Environments*, Contributions to Management Science, https://doi.org/10.1007/978-3-030-45023-6_5

a much cheaper price. First, Xerox began benchmarking process by comparing its copiers with its Japan affiliate Fuji-Xerox's machines. Then, the comparison was made with Japanese machines. By evaluating the results of benchmarking and developing appropriate strategies, Xerox reestablished its leading position in the market (Camp 1989).

After Xerox, many large companies have performed benchmarking applications. In 1991, Motorola executives used benchmarking to plan the company's future software management and technology. The purpose of this benchmarking exercise was to identify and continuously monitor best practices in the United States, Asia and Europe. Fritsch discussed this benchmarking application and its results (Fritsch 1993).

Although the first benchmarking applications were in the United States, they have been implemented in Europe and Asia-Pacific countries. In addition, it has found application in many different sectors such as construction, health, education and transportation (Ralston et al. 2001).

Benchmarking, which has applications in many countries and sectors, has attracted the attention of many researchers. There are many studies that provide general information about benchmarking and also its various applications. There are also some literature surveys. Dattakumar and Jagadeesh compared the previous literature surveys and classified them according to their objectives, number of articles covered and review methodologies (Dattakumar and Jagadeesh 2003). However, this study does not cover the studies carried out in 2003 and beyond. Francis and Holloway presented a literature review by separating the benchmarking literature into four main themes: nature of benchmarking, criticisms of benchmarking, effectiveness of benchmarking and the notion of best practice (Francis and Holloway 2007). Hong and others provided another literature review covering academic studies on benchmarking between 2001 and 2010 (Hong et al. 2012).

This chapter focuses on competitive benchmarking. It provides a literature review of not only benchmarking studies and applications using market based data in a competitive environment but also links between competitive benchmarking and other business approaches in the presence of competition. It is organized as follows: In the following two sections, general information about benchmarking, its types and steps, will be given. The fourth section relates benchmarking to other business approaches including organizational learning, total quality management, quality function deployment, business excellence and market orientation. Last section provides competitive benchmarking applications from different sectors.

2 Types of Benchmarking

There are many different classifications for benchmarking. The most commonly used classification is based on who is compared to who. According to this classification, there are four types: internal benchmarking, competitive benchmarking,

Table 1 Four types of benchmarking according to the classification "who is compared to who"

Internal benchmarking	Determination of the best methodology or practice within the company
Competitive benchmarking	Comparison of companies that have competing products, services or work processes
Functional or industry benchmarking	Functional comparison of industry leaders having similar characteristics
Generic benchmarking	Comparison of the operations and performances of different companies in different sectors

functional or industry benchmarking, and generic benchmarking (Camp 1989; Zairi 1992; Watson 1993).

Internal benchmarking is a particular benchmarking that a company does to determine the best methodology or practice within the company to do a particular job. It includes performance comparison of different departments and determination of the best performance within the organization. Internal benchmarking is faster and easier to perform than other types. This type of benchmarking is used especially for the leading companies in the market or for the companies in the markets where there is not much competition.

Competitive benchmarking is done externally and it is the comparison of companies that have competing products, services or work processes (Elmuti and Kathawala 1997). It is based on the company's comparison of data from its direct competitors and analysis of these data with their own in order to improve the quality of a company. In markets where competition is intense, knowing the performance processes of competing firms and developing strategies and processes in line with it provides great advantages to companies.

Functional or *industry benchmarking* is also done externally and it is the functional comparison of industry leaders having similar characteristics. The difference from competitive benchmarking is that it does not need to be direct competitor to be benchmarked. For example, it is possible for managers from diversified sectors to come together and compare their similar information technologies. Since this type of benchmarking is not directly with competitors, companies are more willing to do this compared to competitive benchmarking.

Generic benchmarking is a comparison of the operations and performances of different companies in completely different sectors. Generic benchmarking is not intended to analyze a company's performance, but to gather information on more generally innovative and excellent business processes. These types are summarized in Table 1.

Another classification of benchmarking is based on what is benchmarked instead of who is benchmarked. According to this classification, there are three types: performance benchmarking, process benchmarking and strategic benchmarking (Andersen 1999).

Performance benchmarking is based on the comparison of the performance levels of the companies. It is not interested in how they achieve these levels of

Table 2 Three types of benchmarking according to "what is benchmarked"

Performance benchmarking	Comparison of the performance levels of the companies
Process benchmarking	Comparison of a particular process
Strategic benchmarking	Examines the strategic decisions of other companies and preparing long-term strategic plan

Table 3 Two types of benchmarking according to Zairi and Hutton (1995)

Results-driven benchmarking	Comparison of the performances of the companies that perform better
Process-driven benchmarking	Comparison of a poorly performing process

performance; it is completely focused on the result. The information obtained here is used to achieve better performance levels.

Process benchmarking is not a comparison of the whole company, but a comparison of a particular process. Although benchmarking is often a comparison of the overall performance of the two competitors, this type of benchmarking compares the processes leading to these performances. It is sometimes called *best practice benchmarking*. It allows the company to understand how other companies do business and to develop more efficient methods based on them. In particular, financial firms often use process benchmarking to survive in a rapidly changing global financial market (Ralston et al. 2001).

Strategic benchmarking examines the strategic decisions of other companies. It generally examines companies that have achieved a certain success in the industry and seeks to understand the underlying strategy of this success. According to the benchmarking result, companies prepare themselves a long-term strategic plan. Table 2 depicts these three types of benchmarking.

Apart from the aforementioned classifications, different authors have used different classifications. Zairi and Hutton defined these two different classifications as results-driven and process-driven benchmarking. Firms that are left behind in the competitive market compare their performances in the companies that perform better. This results-driven benchmarking is mainly based on reducing costs. However, with this approach, firms are not always able to keep up with the better performing firms and the gap between them continues. For a truly successful benchmarking, companies need to apply process-driven benchmarking. The aim should be to understand and improve the poorly performing process (Zairi and Hutton 1995). Table 3 summarizes this classification.

3 Benchmarking Model

Numerous models have been used for benchmarking. These models differ not only in terms of the number of steps, but also in terms of the content of these steps. Even if the steps are different, there are some key points that are important in every benchmarking application. What is done is to first determine what is to be benchmarked, collect data and then analyze the current situation and determine the future plan and strategy accordingly (Jetmarová 2011). In other words, a typical benchmarking includes four-stages: planning, data collection, data analysis and reporting and adaptation. Table 4 summarizes these stages.

The first stage, *planning* begins with the determination of the process to be benchmarked. This is one of the most important steps, because the wrong selection of the process will cause benchmarking not to produce the desired results. This decision should take into consideration the processes that are effective and important in the success of the company and also in the problematic areas considering the overall performance of the company (Andersen 1999). After deciding on the process, the second planning stage is to decide the organizations to be benchmarked. For this, the best companies in the selected process must be decided. Some of the issues to be considered in the decision stage are whether the structure of the selected firms is compatible with the firm to be benchmarked and whether they are willing to cooperate in data collection during the benchmarking phase. The final step in planning is to plan how to collect data from selected companies and what data to collect.

The second stage of benchmarking is the *data collection* phase. At this stage, visits to selected companies will be made and a report will be prepared with the collected data. It is important to collect the correct data for the planned process to be compared.

The third stage, *data analysis* is the part where the collected data is analyzed. At this stage, it is aimed to understand why the best firms are the best by looking at the differences between the data collected and the company's own data compared. The best practices that can be done under the constraints of the firm are decided to minimize the difference.

Table 4 Four stages in a typical benchmarking model

Planning	Determination of the process to be benchmarked
	Determination of the organizations to be benchmarked
	Planning of collection of data
Data collection	Visits to selected companies
	Collection of data
Data analysis	Analysis of collecting data
Adaptation	Determination of the best strategy
	Implementing the best strategy

In the final step, *adaptation* phase, the best strategy for the company is determined and implemented. In the long term, performance in the company is monitored and benchmarking is aimed to succeed.

Freytag and Hollensen named these stages as follows. The benchmarking phase is the stage in which a plan is made about with whom the benchmark is to be made and what is to be benchmarked. According to the authors, the planning and the data collection stages mentioned above are counted in the benchmarking phase. In addition, the authors called the data analysis stage as the benchlearning stage and the adaptation stage as the benchaction stage (Freytag and Hollensen 2001).

4 Relationship Between Benchmarking and Other Business Applications

Today, increasing competition with globalization has made businesses compulsory to improve themselves and make the necessary changes. Benchmarking offers companies the opportunity to get to know the leading companies in the industry, to learn the methods that are effective in their success and to improve themselves accordingly. There are also other managerial approaches that enable the development of the company in the competitive environment. Although the aims of these methods are similar, they are all different approaches. Although the aims of these methods are similar, they are all different approaches. Below are some studies on the relationship between benchmarking and some other approaches.

Pemberton and others examine the relationship between benchmarking and organizational learning. Although the two concepts seem very close to each other, they are actually different. The authors defined benchmarking as comparing the performance, product, and processes of the organization with other organizations and targeting organizational performance to achieve certain standards accordingly. On the other hand, organizational learning was defined as the acquisition and management of new organizational information to exist in a competitive environment. The authors surveyed a large number of firms from the manufacturing and service sectors in England to obtain the relationship between these two concepts. The authors showed that benchmarking was successful in improving the performance of the organization when supported by organizational learning (Pemberton et al. 2001).

Total quality management is a management approach that focuses on quality within an organization, based on the participation of all members of the organization, and aims for long-term success through customer satisfaction. In an increasingly competitive environment, total quality management is inevitable for companies. The main objective of total quality management is customer satisfaction and the strategies implemented for this purpose are completely market oriented. Benchmarking adds an external perspective to this total quality management. The purpose of it is to determine whether firms are on the right track to improve continuously and to achieve higher competitiveness (Zairi and Hutton 1995). Lema and Price analyzed the relationship between benchmarking and total quality management. They discussed this relationship in the construction sector, where labor productivity declined gradually in the 1970s and 1980s. As the authors stated many studies have revealed that serious reforms are needed in this sector and that companies must adopt total quality management. Benchmarking is based on continuous performance improvement as well as total quality management. The authors mentioned the benefits of benchmarking in the comparison of the experiences of total quality management in the construction sector with other competitors. Therefore, the authors argued that benchmarking is a practice that supports total quality management (Lema and Price 1995).

Business excellence is another management approach. Since it is based on the same values as total quality management, the two are similar concepts. It is defined as best practices in managing the organization and achieving results, depending on some values (Kanji 1998). It is an important application in terms of improving performance within the institution. McAdam and Kelly focused on generic benchmarking between small and medium-sized firms. They analyzed how generic benchmarking improves business excellence within the organization. The authors selected some small and medium-sized firms and examined the factors that affect the success of business excellence through benchmarking (McAdam and Kelly 2002). Monkhouse similarly studied benchmarking in small and medium-sized firms. The author emphasized the importance of benchmarking, especially non-financial performance benchmarking, in small and medium-sized enterprises.

Quality function deployment is another quality system to guarantee customer satisfaction within total quality management. It is one of the systems that can be used to create positive and new values by correctly understanding customer demands and needs, and thus to make customers more satisfied. Talebi and others proposed a model that facilitates competitive benchmarking by establishing a link between quality function deployment and benchmarking. In their empirical study, they examined the air transport industry in Iran. Firstly, they determined the expectations of airport customers and determined the service quality factors required to meet these expectations. Finally, they weighed these factors according to their importance and determined benchmarking factors. They showed that the convenience of transport facilities with outside and foreign countries, sufficiency of related institutions, and efficiency of passport and visa checks are the most important benchmarking factors (Talebi et al. 2014).

Drew emphasized the effects of benchmarking on competitive intelligence and strategy development. The author pointed out that benchmarking is crucial for strategic management because it has indirect effects as well as direct effects, such as improving the company's performance. If benchmarking enables the business to reach higher levels of thinking within itself, the desired success is achieved (Drew 1997).

One of the other important sources for companies in the competitive environment is knowledge. At this point, information management and sharing within the company gain importance. Dong and others emphasized how knowledge-intensive firms should design knowledge flow networks to facilitate the flow of information in different organizational environments. The authors argued that the proposed model and solution could be considered as an effective benchmarking for information flow management. In the competitive environment, it is important for managers to benchmark the flow of information in their own organizations with other organizations in terms of their performance (Dong et al. 2011, 2012).

Haverty and Gorton examined market orientation and its relationship with competitive benchmarking. Market orientation is a customer-oriented approach. In this approach, customer needs and expectations are at the forefront and the focus is how to meet them. According to the authors, there are some problems in measuring the market orientations of companies. In this study, they argued that it would be more accurate to measure according to customer evaluations than to measure according to the firms' evaluations. The authors also thought that it is necessary to look at the evaluations of the customers, not the firms, in determining the competitors in the competitive benchmarking application. The authors showed that when customer-oriented market orientation and competitive benchmarking applications are integrated, the performance measurements of the firms will be achieved more successfully (Haverty and Gorton 2006).

Strategic group is the group of companies with similar business models or similar strategies within an industry. The concept of the strategic group is an important concept for strategic management and a lot of work has been done on it. In his industry analysis, Hunt revealed that there is a high degree of competition than industry concentration ratio, and as a result, he suggested that there are sub-groups, called strategic groups, within the sectors and that the competition is more intense in these groups (Hunt 1972). Panagiotou examined competitive benchmarking in the presence of strategic groups. According to the author, companies in the same strategic group face similar challenges and implement similar strategies in a competitive environment. Their strategies based on the results of benchmarking applications among them become more and more similar over time. Thus, the differences between the companies in the same group are reduced even more with benchmarking. The author also stated that this may create some problems. For example, the gradual reduction of inter-firm differences makes them closed to innovations (Panagiotou 2007).

5 Competitive Benchmarking

Competitive benchmarking is one of the most beneficial benchmarking type. It allows firms to directly measure competitors' performance, understand customer expectations, and understand which strategies rival companies are applying to meet these customer expectations (Neely et al. 2005).

After 1980s, competitive benchmarking started to be applied in a variety of sectors such as production, health services, marketing, supply chain, human resources, insurance, education, government, airport services and accounting (Luu et al. 2008; Henderson-Smart et al. 2006; Graham 2005; Jarrar and Zairi 2001; Ball et al. 2000; Hong et al. 2012).

Regardless of the sector in which it is made, there are some stages of competitive benchmarking application. First of all, critical success factor should be determined for companies. Then, how customers perceive businesses according to this factor is examined. Competitors are determined according to the perceptions of the customers. Then, the performances of firms are measured compared to competitors, and their weak and strong sides are determined. Finally, a plan is made on how to eliminate the performance gap (Haverty and Gorton 2006).

One example for competitive benchmarking is benchmarking to fast food restaurants. Due to the change in lifestyle, the number of fast food restaurants has increased significantly in recent years. Therefore, competition between them has increased and it is important for these restaurants to know customer expectations in order to make profit in this competitive environment. Min and Min developed series of competitive benchmarking to determine the factors affecting the competitive performance of fast food restaurants in America. In their studies, they showed that taste of food is one of the most important factors affecting service performance. In addition to taste, the closeness and easy accessibility of the restaurants are also important factors (Min and Min 2011). In their other study, the authors examined the cross cultural competitive benchmarking of fast food restaurants. The authors performed competitive benchmarking between fast food restaurants in USA and Korea to understand which cross cultural differences for fast food restaurants are influencing the globalization process and how to increase their strength in foreign markets. They found differences between the two countries among the factors that customers attach great importance to. In America, customers pay more attention to taste, while in Korea they pay more attention to cleanness (Min and Min 2013).

Schuler and Buehlmann analyzed the U.S. wood furniture industry which has lost a significant portion of its market share to its competitors outside the country. They first discussed the benchmarking of this industry with the best wood industries in the world. Next, they mentioned the strategies that the U.S. wood furniture market should follow to avoid losing more market share in this competitive market environment. At this point, they argued that companies should take advantage of benchmarking, because it is important to know the strengths and weaknesses in the competitive market. They suggested that a new business model that should be developed based on mass customization and delivery speed in order to survive in the global market (Schuler and Buehlmann 2003).

Another example of competitive benchmarking is a benchmarking in the air cargo freight industry (Lobo and Zairi, Part I, II and III, 1999a, b, c). In these studies, the authors examined the benchmarking among nine competitors, which are considered leaders in the field of service excellence in the air cargo freight industry. In their first study, the authors gave general information about this sector, discussed the changes that have occurred in recent years and evaluated all competitors in general. In their second study, the authors performed qualitative benchmarking between companies in areas such as leadership, strategic quality planning, human resources management and development and process management. They discussed how each firm is doing in these areas. In their last study, the authors analyzed the benchmarking application they did in the second part. They looked at the gaps between competing companies and looked at the applications that provide this advantage to these companies.

Min and Min performed a competitive benchmarking application on Korean luxury hotels. With the 1988 Summer Olympics held in Korea, the demand for luxury hotels in Korea and the number of these hotels increased rapidly. Thus, the competition among the hotels increased and the hotels realized that the quality of service is important in obtaining competitive advantage. In order to exist in this competitive environment, it has become inevitable to follow the competitors and to be among the best in the market. The authors primarily focused on the determinants of the service quality of the hotels such as reliability, competence, communication, understanding the customer, and security. The authors also used analytic hierarchy process and competitive gap analysis to measure service quality (Min and Min 1996).

Benchmarking on hotel service is not limited to Min and Min (1996). Nassar studied benchmarking on the hotel industry in Egypt. In Egypt, the hotel industry has an important place in the national economy and the competitive environment between the hotels is increasing. The author stressed the importance of performing a quality assessment in order to gain power in a competitive environment and for this reason, it was argued that it is very important for companies to compare themselves with competing companies, namely benchmarking. With a questionnaire, the author showed that most hotels in Egypt would like to use benchmarking regardless of their size and location because it gives them competitive power (Nassar 2012).

Benchmarking in small and medium enterprises (SMEs) is quite important as in large enterprises. These businesses occupy an important place in the national economy with their business opportunities and support for large-scale firms by increasing competition (Gunasekaran 2003). Cassell and the others analyzed the use and the effectiveness of benchmarking in SMEs. The authors selected financial performance, customer satisfaction and product quality indices for benchmarking among these enterprises. They showed that benchmarking is effective in all these selected indices (Cassell et al. 2001).

Competitive benchmarking also helps small firms to have more strategic planning and market orientation. Regardless of which sector they are in, their locations, market type or customers, small firms generally act by thinking about the short run, do not act strategically and attach importance to sales growth rather than market orientation (Birley 1982; McNamee et al. 2000; Gray 1997). McNamee and the others developed a competitive analysis model that allows small firms to increase their performance with strategic market planning. The authors benchmarked client firms with leading firms in the sector and sub-sector, as well as firms of the same size in different sectors in Ireland (McNamee et al. 2000).

Meybodi argued that competitive benchmarking practices are beneficial, but the impact will be limited if a strategy is not followed that implements benchmarking results on all firm performance improvement processes. Therefore, before performing external benchmarking, the firm must determine its own strategy (Meybodi 2005). The fact that the benchmarking application is compatible with the structure, objectives and priorities of the company will bring long-term success (Day 1992).

Competition in the aviation industry has been intensifying in recent years, and this applies not only to the "air side" but also to the "ground side". As part of the "ground side", ramp handling has gained importance for airports, and with increasing competition pressure on them, the ramp handlers have had to compare their performance with their competitors and be more competitive, market-oriented and customer-driven (Müller et al. 2005; Chan et al. 2006). Schmidberger and the others developed a performance measurement system that will be the basis for competitive benchmarking for the ramp service at major airports in the European Union. The authors showed that factors that make a difference in hub airports are accessibility of employees, staff availability, overhead structure, quality and process quality (Schmidberger et al. 2009).

Another example of competitive benchmarking is applications in the healthcare industry. With the increasing competition in the health sector, the success of hospitals and medical clinics in the long term has become dependent on the quality of the service they provide (Min et al. 1997). Therefore, it has become important for health care providers to benchmark with their competitors to improve the quality of the service they offer. Min and the others developed a benchmarking model for healthcare quality in the healthcare market and built a comparative measure for service quality in Korean health care system (Min et al. 1997). Another study on the application of the benchmarking in the health care market is made by Gonzalez and the others. The authors developed an activity based costing model for hospitals with benchmarking and quality function deployment analysis in the Spanish health care system (González et al. 2005).

Not only in the private sector, but also in the public sector, benchmarking takes an important place. As in the private sector, in the public sector also, benchmarking is very useful for making the right decisions, making the right investments and making budget and cost calculations. An example of a public sector benchmarking is the North Carolina benchmarking project, which began in 1995. Ammons analyzed this benchmarking project and he mentioned how effective it is and the results obtained. In this project, municipalities had the opportunity to compare themselves with other municipalities (Ammons 2000). It also contributed to the performance measurement of the project and the determination of the factors affecting this measurement (Ammons and Rivenbark 2008).

6 Conclusion

In this study, with a literature survey, the importance of benchmarking in sectors where competition is intense is emphasized. It is argued that competitive benchmarking enables companies to know the market, to understand how leading firms achieve their competitive power, and to change and develop themselves accordingly. Also, competitive benchmarking is linked to other business approaches and it is shown that these approaches are successful if they are integrated with competitive benchmarking. Finally, applications of competitive benchmarking to different sectors are given.

References

Ammons, D. (2000). Benchmarking as a performance management tool: Experiences among municipalities in North Carolina. *Journal of Public Budgeting, Accounting & Financial Management, 12*(1), 106–124.

Ammons, D., & Rivenbark, W. (2008). Factors influencing the use of performance data to improve municipal services: Evidence from the North Carolina benchmarking project. *Public Administration Review, 68*, 304–318.

Andersen, B. (1999). Industrial benchmarking for competitive advantage. *Human Systems Management, 18*, 287–296.

Ball, A., Bowerman, M., & Hawksworth, S. (2000). Benchmarking in local government under a central government agenda. *Benchmarking: An International Journal, 7*(1), 20–34.

Benson, H. R. (1994). An introduction to benchmarking in healthcare. *Radiology Management, 16* (4), 35–39.

Birley, S. (1982). Corporate strategy and the small firm. *Journal of General Management., 8*(2), 82–86.

Camp, R. C. (1989). *Benchmarking: The search for industry best practices that lead to superior performance*. Milwaukee, WI: ASQ Quality Press.

Cassell, C., Nadin, S., & Older Gray, M. (2001). The use and effectiveness of benchmarking in SMEs. *Benchmarking: An International Journal, 8*(3), 212–222.

Chan, F., Chan, H., Lau, H., & Ip, R. (2006). An AHP approach in benchmarking logistics performance of postal industry. *Benchmarking: An International Journal, 13*(6), 636–661.

Dattakumar, R., & Jagadeesh, R. (2003). A review of literature on benchmarking. *Benchmarking: An International Journal, 10*(3), 176–209.

Day, C. R. (1992). Benchmarking's first law: Know thyself! *Industry Week, 241*(4), 70.

Dong, S., Johar, M. S., & Kumar, R. (2011). A benchmarking model for management of knowledge-intensive service delivery networks. *Journal of Management Information Systems, 28*(3), 127–160.

Dong, S., Johar, M., & Kumar, R. (2012). Understanding key issues in designing and using knowledge flow networks: An optimization-based managerial benchmarking approach. *Decision Support Systems, 53*, 646–659.

Drew, S. A. W. (1997). From knowledge to action: Impact of benchmarking on the organizational performance. *Long Range Planning, 30*(3), 427–441.

Elmuti, D., & Kathawala, Y. (1997). An overview of benchmarking process: A tool for continuous improvement and competitive advantage. *Benchmarking for Quality Management & Technology, 4*(4), 229–243.

Francis, G., & Holloway, J. (2007). What have we learned? Themes from the literature on best-practice benchmarking. *International Journal of Management Reviews, 9*(3), 171–189.

Freytag, P., & Hollensen, S. (2001). The process of benchmarking, benchlearning and benchaction. *The TQM Magazine, 13*(1), 25–34.

Fritsch, J. (1993). The Motorola software engineering benchmark program: Organization, directions, and results. In Proceedings of 1993 IEEE 17th International Computer Software and Applications Conference COMPSAC (pp. 284–290), Phoenix, AZ, USA.

González, M., Quesada, G., Mack, R., & Urrutia, I. (2005). Building an activity-based costing hospital model using quality function deployment and benchmarking. *Benchmarking: An International Journal, 12*(4), 310–329.

Graham, A. (2005). Airport benchmarking: A review of the current situation. *Benchmarking: An International Journal, 12*(2), 99–111.

Gray, C. (1997). Managing entrepreneurial growth: A question of control? In D. Deakins, P. Jennings, & C. Mason (Eds.), *Small firms: Entrepreneurship in the nineties* (pp. 18–28). London: Paul Chapman.

Gunasekaran, A. (2003). Benchmarking in small and medium enterprises. *Benchmarking: An International Journal, 10*(3), 287.

Haverty, M., & Gorton, M. (2006). Integrating market orientation and competitive benchmarking: A methodological framework and application. *Total Quality Management & Business Excellence, 17*(8), 1077–1091.

Henderson-Smart, C., Winning, T., Gerzina, T., King, S., & Hyde, S. (2006). Benchmarking learning and teaching: Developing a method. *Quality Assurance in Education, 14*(2), 143–155.

Hong, P., Hong, S., Roh, J., & Park, K. (2012). Evolving benchmarking practices: A review for research perspectives. *Benchmarking: An International Journal, 19*, 444–462.

Hunt, M. (1972). *Competition in the major home appliance industry*. Doctoral Dissertation, Harvard University.

Jarrar, Y. F., & Zairi, M. (2001). Future trends in benchmarking for competitive advantage: A global survey. In *Proceedings of the 6th TQM World Congress* (pp. 906–912), St Petersburg, Russia, 12, Routledge, London.

Jetmarová, B. (2011). Comparison of best practice benchmarking models. *Problems of Management in the 21st Century, 2*, 76–84.

Kanji, G. K. (1998). Measurement of business excellence. *Total Quality Management, 9*(7), 633–643.

Lankford, W. M. (2000). Benchmarking: Understanding the basics. *Coastal Business Journal, 1*(1), 57–62.

Lema, N. M., & Price, A. D. F. (1995). Benchmarking: Performance improvement toward competitive advantage. *Journal of Management in Engineering, 11*(1), 28–37.

Lobo, I., & Zairi, M. (1999a). Competitive benchmarking in the air cargo industry: Part I. *Benchmarking: An International Journal, 6*(2), 164–191.

Lobo, I., & Zairi, M. (1999b). Competitive benchmarking in the air cargo industry: Part II. *Benchmarking: An International Journal, 6*(3), 220–238.

Lobo, I., & Zairi, M. (1999c). Competitive benchmarking in the air cargo industry: Part III. *Benchmarking: An International Journal, 6*(4), 302–309.

Luu, V. T., Kim, S. Y., & Huynh, T. A. (2008). Improving project management performance of large contractors using benchmarking approach. *International Journal of Project Management, 26*(7), 758–769.

Maire, J. (2002). A model of characterization of the performance for a process of benchmarking. *Benchmarking: An International Journal, 9*(5), 506–520.

McAdam, R., & Kelly, M. (2002). A business excellence approach to generic benchmarking in SMEs. *Benchmarking: An International Journal, 9*(1), 7–27.

McNamee, P., Greenan, K., & McFerran, B. (2000). Shifting the predominant cultural paradigm in small businesses through active competitive benchmarking. *Journal of Strategic Marketing, 8*, 241–259.

Meybodi, M. Z. (2005). Strategic manufacturing benchmarking. *The TQM Magazine, 17*(3), 249–258.

Min, H., & Min, H. (1996). Competitive benchmarking of Korean luxury hotels using the analytic hierarchy process and competitive gap analysis. *Journal of Services Marketing, 10*(3), 58–72.

Min, H., & Min, H. (2011). Benchmarking the service quality of fast-food restaurant franchises in the USA: A longitudinal study. *Benchmarking: An International Journal, 18*(2), 282–300.

Min, H., & Min, H. (2013). Cross-cultural competitive benchmarking of fast-food restaurant services. *Benchmarking: An International Journal, 20*(2), 212–232.

Min, H., Mitra, A., & Oswald, S. (1997). Competitive benchmarking of health care quality using the analytic hierarchy process: An example from Korean Cancer clinics. *Socio-Economic Planning Sciences, 31*, 147–159.

Müller, J., Kamp, V., & Niemeier, H. (2005). *Can we learn from benchmarking studies of airports and where do we want to go from here?* Paper presented at the German Aviation Research Society Workshop on Benchmarking, Wien.

Nassar, M. (2012). Exploring current benchmarking practices in the Egyptian hotel sector. *Benchmarking: An International Journal, 19*(6), 730–742.

Neely, A., Gregory, M., & Platts, K. (2005). Performance measurement system design: A literature review and research agenda. *International Journal of Operations & Production Management, 25*, 1228–1263.

Panagiotou, G. (2007). Reference theory: Strategic groups and competitive benchmarking. *Management Decision, 45*(10), 1595–1621.

Pemberton, J. D., Stonehouse, G., & Yarrow, D. M. (2001). Benchmarking and the role of organizational learning in developing competitive advantage. *Knowledge and Process Management, 8*(2), 123–135.

Ralston, D., Wright, A., & Kumar, J. (2001). Process benchmarking as a market research tool for strategic planning. *Marketing Intelligence & Planning, 19*(4), 273–281.

Schmidberger, S., Bals, L., Hartmann, E., & Jahns, C. (2009). Ground handling services at European hub airports: Development of a performance measurement system for benchmarking. *International Journal of Production Economics, 117*, 104–116.

Schuler, A., & U. Buehlmann. (2003). *Identifying future competitive business strategies for the U.S. residential wood furniture industry: Benchmarking and paradigm shifts*. Technical report NE-304, United States Department of Agriculture, Forest Service, Northeastern Research Station, Newtown Square, PA.

Talebi, D., Farsijani, H., Sedighi, F., & Shafiei Nikabadi, M. (2014). The role of quality benchmarking deployment to world-class manufacturing. *Quality Engineering, 26*(2), 206–214.

Watson, G. H. (1992). *The benchmarking workbook: Adopting best practices for performance improvements*. Portland, OR: Productivity Press.

Watson, G. H. (1993). *Strategic benchmarking: How to rate your company's performance against the world's best*. London: Wiley.

Zairi, M. (1992). *Competitive benchmarking: An executive guide*. Letchworh: Technical Communications Ltd.

Zairi, M., & Hutton, R. (1995). Benchmarking: A process-driven tool for quality improvement. *The TQM Magazine, 7*(3), 35–40.

Examination of Effects of Competitiveness on Businesses and Countries

Zafer Adiguzel

Abstract "Innovations" in the changing world of competition together with the developing technology and globalizing markets have become the most important factor in the fact that businesses create difference. In the beginning, companies whose aim was offering maximum product/service to the market with the advantage of cost and make maximum profit have to offer different products or services at low cost in today's complicated and challenging circumstances. Technology and Innovation management should be placed within the culture of organization and this culture should be able to be experienced in each member from the employee to the senior management in scope of Industry 4.0. Innovation management has become a necessity beyond being a strategy for businesses that aim to grow by offering new products/services. While it is taken for the companies that produce and manage will create a difference in the competition market granted, it is known that the companies that are far from development, and change will be easily vanquished off the market. Within the scope of the study, competitiveness, competitiveness at institutionalization level, industry 4.0, technology based and international competitiveness are examined.

1 Introduction

The competitiveness of an economy, educational attainment, technology, property rights, political structure and legal order are evaluated under the institutional structure. Therefore, the variables discussed in economic growth and growth analyzes are expressed as components of institution and institutional structures (Biber 2010). In this context, the relationship between competition and competitiveness and growth as an indicator of the institutional structure has emerged as a question considered valuable to study. Competition is simply defined as debate and competition between

---

Z. Adiguzel (✉)
Medipol Business School, İstanbul Medipol University, Beykoz/İstanbul, Turkey
e-mail: zadiguzel@medipol.edu.tr

H. Dincer, S. Yüksel (eds.), *Strategic Priorities in Competitive Environments*,
Contributions to Management Science, https://doi.org/10.1007/978-3-030-45023-6_6

the parties with the same objectives (Francis 1989). Competitiveness can be said as the competence abilities of the parties to compete in the same field (Francis and Tharakan 1989). Economically, there are two different perspectives on competitiveness. These are micro-level perspectives on industry, firm or business basis and macro-level perspectives on country basis. The term competitiveness is used in different ways. In some cases, analysis of price and exchange rate fluctuations in the competition can be made entirely based on macroeconomic criteria. In some cases, a broader sense of competitiveness is brought by efficiency, skill and innovation. However, competitiveness includes reforms, existence of legal and economic conditions in countries and strategy (Ailenei and Mosora 2011).

The relationship between competition, competitiveness and economic growth has increased its importance in modern world where globalization and information age is experienced and has entered into a continuous renewal (Farinha et al. 2015). Prior to the industrial revolution, the competitiveness element which is especially important in gun technology, started to be shaped by the creation of added value and foreign trade with the industrial revolution. Therefore, as a result of rapid changes in information and communication technology, economic, social and political influence and competitiveness of countries have started to change continuously. Moreover, the desire and efforts of countries to achieve a better level of competitiveness can increase the productivity in economic life and affect the macroeconomic dynamics positively.

Institutionalization has been a topic that both practitioners and organizational theorists have focused on. As a matter of fact, as a result of many studies they carried out from the 1950s to the 2000s, theoreticians of the organization agreed on the main points that institutionalization provides the legitimacy, stability and continuity of the organizations (Farashahi et al. 2005). However, the reconciliation point of practitioners is that institutionalization enables firms to survive in a stable manner (Yazıcıoğlu and Hakan 2009). The emergence of the need for institutionalization, overgrowth of the company organization, changes in the partnership and management structure, norms and values of decision-makers, or the constraints of the corporate environment (Scott 1987). As a matter of fact, institutionalization occurs both by the individual efforts of strong managers as decision-makers or authorities in the firm and by the relative power, interests and coercion of institutional actors (state, public institutions, professional chambers, sectoral norms, social values, etc.). Although the findings revealed that the institutional environment makes the institutionalization practices similar to each other in the companies, the effect of the institutionalization level on the competitiveness of the companies was questioned in this study considering that there will be different practices due to the factors such as strengthening the culture of institution, creating professional organizations and socialization.

2 Literature Review

Competition is a term that is used frequently but there is not a full agreement on its definition and different meanings are imposed in different environments (Dunning 2013). So much so that, the reason why some companies are more successful in the competitive environment and why other companies operating in the same sector have failed has long been are important issues that have been tried to be answered. Competition benefits new entrepreneurs by providing consumers with the best possible use of resources and encouraging entrepreneurship by keeping prices low, quality high, allowing the economy to enter any business field with better ideas, prices or quality, and to compete with its predecessors. On the other hand, it is clear that it also partially pays dividends the producers. Undoubtfully, it encourages manufacturers to be more productive and efficient. But the benefits of this are not reflected as profits but only helps to survive. As a result, competition considers the benefit of the economy and the consumer as a whole. As part of the basic line of survival, competition alone is not enough to survive. There are many things that are necessary for a firm to survive, but not good enough alone (e.g. cost control). Therefore, in order to achieve success, it is necessary to be supercompetitive by passing over the competition (De Bono 1996).

Competition is the way to determine this in cases where it is not known who is good in social life (Doğan 2000). In other words, "it is the job of making choices in order to create different kinds of activities or to perform different activities from competitors in order to get a big share from the market". Briefly, the essence of competition is to create difference (Thompson and Strickland 1999). Hamel (1997) stated that from a different point of view, competition is in an industry, rather than dividing economic value, because the emerging areas of opportunity affect the market. According to Hamel (1997), a supermarket company is competing with both fast food stores and successful companies serving ready-made food to homes can be exemplified. According to Porter (2000), the firm must develop a defensive position in a sector to successfully cope with its five competitiveness (current competitors, possible competitors, suppliers, customers, substitutes) and it should create a difference compared to others with the competition strategy in order to achieve a great return on investment.

The concept of competitiveness is generally addressed in three different levels in the literature. These are businesses, industries and countries (Besler and Tonus 2004). Relatively, it can be defined as an industry's ability to generate higher income and employment than other countries' same industries (Demir 2002). Competitiveness which is a relative measure, serves to reveal the current situation of industries or countries. It is relatively easy to define competitiveness for businesses, but it is more difficult to define competitiveness of regions or countries. For example, it is difficult to compare an agricultural region with a financial center because they are not rivals. Competitiveness at the business level is the ability of any business to produce at lower cost compared to its competitors in national or global markets (price and cost competitiveness), to be in a position equal to or superior to its competitors in terms of the quality of the product, the service offered and the attractiveness of the product (quality competitiveness), and the ability to innovate and invent although the competitiveness criteria of businesses can be reduced and increased according to the field of activity of businesses.

Competitiveness of businesses can be summarized as a competitive advantage over other domestic or global competing firms operating in the same field (Balassa 1989). Porter (1990) analyzes various approaches in detail while explaining the reasons for the competitiveness of the national economies of different businesses and countries. Considering factors such as labor force, abundance of natural resources, national government protective policies and differences between firm management, Porter (1990) states that none of these factors alone can explain the reasons for successful or unsuccessful businesses in competition (Şağbanşua and Bişkek 2006). It is useful to state an important point at this stage. Competitiveness is not an inherent quality or inherent quality of business. In other words, the competitiveness of the businesses can only be determined when they are evaluated together with other businesses working in the same field or producing similar products or services.

Competitiveness is achieved by comparing with other businesses in the national and world markets (Boltho 1996). Therefore, the competitiveness of businesses is a relative concept: For example, the same company may have high competitiveness among the competitors in the local market and may not have any chance of competing in the international market. In this sense, it is difficult to establish a competitiveness value indicating the competitive advantages of businesses over other companies. In other words, it is possible to estimate the competitive advantage of one of the two companies serving in the same sector and meeting the similar needs of consumers. Therefore, both companies are approximately in the same life cycle. Otherwise, the comparison will not be correct (Porter 1993).

Competitive advantage arises from decreases in costs and differentiation of products. Differentiation is realized in the form of providing innovative and high quality products to consumers, meeting special customer requests and after-sales service (Porter 1985). Whether it's a reduction in costs or product differences, allows competitive advantage allows businesses to use resources more effectively than competitors. Companies capable of producing at low costs can reach higher profit levels with the effect of producing standard products with mass production.

3 Development of Competitiveness

Although competition has always existed throughout history, the countries have changed through different stages depending on the conditions. Along with the development of economic literature, there have been changes in approaches that explain competitiveness. In the 1960s, the fundamental element of production-dependent competition strategies within the framework of absolute superiorities, comparative superiorities and factor theories became producers. In the period based on production superiority, the product price gained importance and it was aimed to expand the product market by following policies based on low price practices. In the following years, the companies turned to new policies in order to maintain their market share and to gain superiority over their competitors. With the 1970s, the most important factor explaining the competitiveness was a production approach based on cost advantage. With the effect of increasing technology, firms that can achieve low cost outputs have gained an advantageous position in terms of competitiveness. After 1980, Michael E. Porter (1985) introduced a new and different theory of competitiveness of nations. This theory is aimed at transforming comparative advantages into competitive advantages. Along with this theory, the structure of comparative advantages changes. The new determinants of competitiveness are cost, quality, product differentiation, new product, technological differences, focus and market structures. Because the natural resources of the countries decrease in time.

International competitiveness is defined from two different perspectives as micro and macro. Competitiveness from the micro perspective, while examining the effects of the competition between the actors in the national market on the national or international market, competitiveness from the macro perspective refers to the position of international competition (Berger et al. 2016). The main purpose of the competitiveness at the macro level is to increase the real income and welfare per capita and to ensure a sustainable living under free market conditions (Witkowski 2017). There are two approaches about the competition. The first of these, whether dynamic or static, is based on the relative efficiency problem of competition. Accordingly, competition can be measured by looking at relative performance levels, such as productivity and productivity gains. The second of these, the competitiveness stems from the international trade performance in terms of the share of world export markets, the import rate or the comparative advantage index. According to this approach, the country with the highest productivity level may not have the highest share of trade. In cases where the share of trade is based on strategies in world markets, competitiveness is determined by the model that analyzes efficiency and market power together (Alçın 2016).

Economists comparing the competitiveness of the countries are the two most important indicators on total factor productivity and per capita income growth. Economists who make analyzes based on factor productivity, think that welfare will increase in the long term in economies with high factor productivity. According to another approach, in order to increase competitiveness, it is important to renew, develop and adapt to technological transformations of human resources, capital and natural resources (Chen 2012). In the case where competitiveness is defined as an increase in the general welfare level and standard of living, the increase in trade, investment and production activities is possible through coordination and specialization among the domestic institutions. In order to compete with other economies in the development, marketing and distribution of production capacity, country capabilities need to be developed and new potentials must be unveiled (Schwab 2017).

Competitiveness is the concept which is an extension of the concept of competition and gains more importance in practice. In general, competitiveness can be defined as the ability of a firm, an industry or a country to compete in the national or international market. But it would not be correct to say that there is only one generally accepted definition. There are several reasons for this. These are:

1. Competitiveness may vary according to the area addressed. For example, it can be handled by firm, sector or country. Competitiveness can be defined differently at each level from the point of view.
2. Different criteria can be used to determine competitiveness. For example, the competitiveness of the country can be determined only in terms of foreign trade. Or the country's competitiveness can be determined by using a large number of indicators.
3. Competitiveness can be defined differently from an economic point of view. For example, different definitions can be made by considering micro or macro aspects of competitiveness (Atik 2005).

First of all, it should be stated that competitiveness is a dynamic concept. The change in production technologies should be monitored and applied simultaneously with competing companies. In order to achieve and maintain competitiveness, an appropriate economic and political environment must be created. Increasing competitiveness leads to an increase in production and trade, simultaneous increase in profitability and investments and consequently increase in employment (Dong-sung and Hwy-Chang 2013).

3.1 Importance of Competitiveness

The circulation of labor and capital has become easier worldwide with the impact of globalization (Sirikrai and Tang 2006). This situation increased the importance of competitiveness for all countries. This is because now businesses have to compete not only with their competitors, but also with their global competitors. Increasing awareness of consumers, the necessity of complying with certain standards due to the economic associations to which they belong, the decreasing of resources and the necessity of using these resources more efficiently, and the fact that being sensitive to environmental pollution become a necessity are the factors that make competition in the world difficult. With the development of the IT sector, consumers have the chance to order products without having to physically see the products and to receive all kinds of information about the product. The change of marketing channels has abolished the concept of "stock" for many businesses. Competitive advantage is the most distinctive way for a business to be placed in a position to gain advantage over its competitors in the market. This advantage clarifies the sustainable level of profitability that the business creates and achieves above the sector average.

The sustainability of the competitive advantage is based on the ability of the organization to achieve economic value created by the same or different temporary skills of competitors (Fleisher and Bensoussan 2003). Competition rules valid for all businesses that are engaged in economic activity irrespective of the size of an entity. The existence of competing strategies of companies and their success in implementing these strategies can increase their competitiveness (Siggel 2006). In this case, it is necessary to determine the competition strategy correctly according to market conditions, consumer profile, basic skills, equity, number of labor force and quality. Strategies can be developed with the help of economic researches and consultant support to identify opportunities and threats. Implementing the strategy may not always be as planned. The consequences of conditions that may arise outside the will of the business may constitute an obstacle for the businesses (Türkkan 2001). According to Porter (1990), businesses need to produce higher quality and increase their productivity in order to provide competitive advantages (Porter 1990). At the core of the economic dimension of changing world conditions is technological development, productivity (Helms 1996) and competition. Today, countries need to base their competitive advantages on this idea.

3.1.1 Competitiveness at Firm Level

Competitiveness at the firm level refers that companies have the features that will create competitive advantage such as the ability to offer higher quality products at lower cost than the competing firms in the national and international arena, and the attractiveness of the products and services offered (Ada et al. 2008). Competitiveness at the firm level is based on R&D and innovation investments as determined by the company structure. At the firm level, competition is divided into two as input and output. Competitiveness at the firm level is expressed as the ability to produce high quality and low cost. In this sense, the ability of companies to increase their competitiveness passes through a production model that increases their productivity and product quality and reduces their costs. While quality, cost and price are the most important elements of competition at the firm level, efficiency, organizational chart and management structure, resource usage, innovation and creativity are also listed as internal factors (Chen et al. 2014).

Feurer and Chaharbaghi (1994), in the definition of competitiveness at the level of another firm by considering the expectations of customers and shareholders, is considered as a highly competitive company in the eyes of customers that produces and sells better products and services compared to competitors. Feurer and Chaharbaghi (1994) do not consider the company's competitiveness only in the eyes of customers. The company must also be competitive for the shareholders. This means that the firm provides a satisfactory return to shareholders (Feurer and Chaharbaghi 1994). Competitiveness is the ability to steadily increase revenues in domestic markets, as well as the ability to sell goods in international markets (Aiginger 1998). Firms can be directed to new organizational structures and ways of doing business in order to fulfill their goals of reducing production costs and developing technological innovations (Teece 2010). For example, focusing on the core capabilities of the firm can lead to the development of a structure and content within the firm that responds quickly to needs and organizes itself to adapt to new situations. Small and large companies give priority to a stable quality level, high reliability products, reliability and speed in delivery to increase of competitiveness. What big companies do beyond this is to create and grow a brand.

3.1.2 Competitiveness at Industry Level

In the economic literature, competition at the industrial level is recognized as the ability to make satisfactory gains in international markets (Davenport 2014). According to Porter and Van der Linde (1995), the average productivity level of the industry or the value of the generated value, the average value per employee and the capital investment per dollar constitute the definition of competitiveness at the industrial level (Porter and Van der Linde 1995; Rexhäuser and Rammer 2014). Sectoral growth and profitability, employment and productivity are among the most important indicators of competitiveness at the industrial level (Özdoğan 2017). Industry is simply the community of companies competing with each other in the production of a product or service. Markusen (1995), his definition of industrial competitiveness is the ability of any industry to outperform its competitors with high level of efficiency, maintain this level of productivity and produce and sell at a lower cost than its competitors.

The competitiveness of an industry means that it has strong and productive companies in its field of activity, region or internationally (Oral 1986). In this respect, competitiveness at the industry level can also be considered as the competitiveness of the big firms that the industry holds. For Porter (2011), the structure of the industry is an important element that determines the competitive structure. But industries show significant differences in their competitive structure, and as a result they do not offer equal opportunities for sustainable profitability. For example, while the average profitability in the cosmetics industry is extremely high; profitability in the iron and steel industry may not be as high as this level. Consequently, according to Porter (2011), the structure of industrial competition depends on these factors, whether an industry is national or international;

1. Threat from new entrants to the industry,
2. Threat from substitute goods or services,
3. The bargaining power of raw material or semi-finished goods suppliers,
4. Negotiating power of buyers,
5. Competition between existing competitors.

According to Porter (2011), the strength of these five elements varies for each industry and determines the profitability of the industry in the long term. These five factors will have a direct impact on the profitability of the industry, as they shape the prices that firms will collect, while at the same time determining the costs that firms must bear, and they are decisive on the necessary investments for competition in industry. If these elements are effective in an industry, firms in this industry gain significant advantages. However, only a few companies will be profitable in industries where only one or more of these elements are effective (Porter 2011).

3.1.3 Competitiveness at International Level

Competitiveness at the international level is the ability of a country to increase its income level in real terms by providing full competitive market conditions and to produce products or services that can compete in global markets (Ada et al. 2008). International competitiveness, are tried to be explained in the literature with Adam Smith's Absolute Superiority Theory (Smith 2010), David Ricardo's Comparative Superiority Theory (Ruffin 2002), Heckscher-Ohlin's Theorem (Bernhofen and Brown 2016), Paul Krugman's Approach (Martin and Sunley 2017), Porter (1990)'s Diamond Model. The basis of Smith (2010)'s Theory of Absolute Superiority lies in the fact that one country can produce and specialize in lower cost than any other commodity. Ricardo (1955)'s Theory of Comparative Advantage, on the other hand, is based on the idea that a country specializes in the production of products produced with higher efficiency than other goods and exports them. The Heckscher and Ohlin (1991) is expressed as the production and export of products that are equipped by the production factor that countries have intensively. On the other hand, Krugman (1994) considers competitiveness as a different explanation of productivity, which makes no sense when used at country level (Krugman 1994). It is important that a country's competitiveness is not only to sell products at an affordable price but also to increase the level of employment in the country and to provide acceptable and sustained increases in quality of life. First of all, in order for a country to increase its competitiveness, citizens' welfare must be high. The most important indicator of this is real GDP per capita. In addition, the high quality of life of all citizens living in the country is an indicator of prosperity. As a result, it will be inevitable that countries with high welfare, citizens and institutions will be more productive and have higher competitiveness.

3.1.4 Relationship Between Institutionalization and Competitiveness

It is generally accepted by both researchers and practitioners that the institutionalization has a significant contribution to the survival of firms for many years (Farashahi et al. 2005; Ulukan 2004). Ararat (2005) who put forward the positive relationship between institutionalization and competition, stated that the competition strategy of a firm in the institutionalization process should be answered consistently by the decision makers and those who implement these decisions. As a matter of fact, it can be stated that in companies with high level of institutionalization due to their formal structure, professional management, strong culture and internal harmony, these common answers can be obtained better than others (Welford et al. 2003). As a result, the common competition strategy advocated and believed will help to increase the competitiveness of the firm by uncovering common reason and effort.

According to Oliver (1997), a sustainable competitive advantage can be achieved by combining resource-based determinants (economic rationality, strategic factors, market imperfections) and institutional determinants (normative rationality, institutional factors, uniformity pressures). Because, the rational decisions of the managers in the competition process are limited due to social judgments, historical limitations and habits according to the assumptions of institutional theorists, and uncertainty, limited knowledge and prejudices according to the assumptions of resource based theorists. In addition, due to regular pressures, strategic alliances, transfer of human capital, social and professional relations, competence replication, firms can become homogenized in competition. Therefore, firms need both resource and institutional capital to gain and maintain long-term competitive advantage.

Cho and Tansuhaj (2003) emphasized that the corporate environment is a very important factor affecting the competitive advantages of firms. There are also studies showing the relationship between institutionalization and financial competitiveness. As a matter of fact, Baraz (2006) states that institutionalization facilitates finding foreign partners and cheap funds. While there are studies indicating that the competitiveness of the firm increases as the level of institutionalization increases, there are studies that claim the opposite. But these are only a few elements of institutionalization. For example, it can be stated that the competitiveness of firms can be limited by restrictions (changing social norms, habits and traditions) from the corporate environment (Gül et al. 2009). At the same time, it is stated that the competitiveness of excessive corporate firms may be affected negatively (Ararat 2005). But these studies are stuck in only a few elements of institutionalization. Therefore, it is very difficult to spread these findings throughout the institutionalization. Because with a limited number of findings, it cannot be made clear that the institutionalization level has a negative effect on competitiveness.

4 Effect of Competitiveness on Economic Growth

In highly competitive countries, the employment rate, foreign trade income and per capita income are high and the inflation rate is low. On the contrary, employment rate, foreign trade income and per capita income are relatively low and inflation rate is high in low-competitive countries. Gross domestic product (GDP) is the currency value of all products and services produced for a year within the boundaries of a country. The general opinion is that there is a positive relationship between the two in terms of competitiveness and GDP ratios. In other words, in developed countries with high competitiveness, GDP rates are high and in countries with low competitiveness, GDP ratios are relatively low. First of all, GDP most affected by the quantity of products and services produced in a country. Countries that are able to produce high value products and services in international markets will automatically increase their GDP and grow economically. In this respect, especially the countries with firm-based competitiveness will enter the economic growth process. For the sustainability of economic growth, countries must take the necessary steps in terms of social and democratization besides providing commercial adequacy. For example, the macroeconomic environment, infrastructure, the state of the business world, the effectiveness of public institutions and organizations are common issues in these reports. The development of countries on these issues is important for increasing their competitiveness. As a result, it is very important for countries to have international competitiveness for both economic growth and sustainability of this growth and to follow the necessary policies to increase this power.

4.1 Impact of Industry 4.0 on Competitiveness

Today's industrial production model is based on the principle of increasing production capacity with the understanding of more production and less unit costs and simultaneously reducing production costs. As a result, the priority of the industry is based on optimization of the product cost and prices and the level of capital required. However, this industrial paradigm has recently been questioned (Ganz 2018). Because, by providing a new model in production, Industry 4.0, which enables all the components to be connected to each other and independent computers via the Internet, will increase the competitiveness by decreasing the costs and speed as well as the flexibility in production. In the Industry 4.0 process, intelligent machines are expected to be in constant communication with each other, leading to an increase in mass production and consequently to personalized production. On the other hand, since production and delivery processes will be controlled from a single point, it is possible to reach maximum efficiency in production with new data analysis methods (Oks et al. 2017).

McKinsey & Company approach that called "Digital Compass" in which producers explore the driving forces of their activities to improve their performance under eight main headings such as asset utilization, labor productivity, inventory management, quality improvement, supply-demand matching, fast marketing and after-sales services is also explanatory in determining the possible effects of Industry 4.0 on competitiveness. Accordingly, the possible effects of each heading on the competitiveness of Industry 4.0 are as follows (Çelen 2017):

- Resource Usage and Optimization: Industry 4.0 which ensures lesser loss in usage of raw material by improving production processes, allows real time observation of processes by the help of cyber-physical systems, thus leads to fast and error-free manufacturing of products and reduced raw material costs. This paves the way for automatic and rapid response to problems in the production network and thus improves production processes and offers a productivity increase of 3–5%.
- Asset Usage: The use of assets which expresses the anticipation and realization of the maintenance required to get the best performance from the machines in the factories by means of smart systems, provides an increase in productivity in order to prevent problems that may hinder production.
- Labor Productivity: Industry 4.0 reduces the waiting time between the different stages of the production process, accelerates R&D activities and the

implementation of human-robot cooperation and division of labor leads to an increase in labor productivity (Kergroach 2017).

- Stock Management: In modern day, where wrong inventory management leads to huge capital losses, Industry 4.0 allows for a 20–50% reduction in inventory costs through systems such as accurate production planning and real-time supply chain optimization (Gilchrist 2016).
- Quality Improvement: Thanks to its advanced process control capabilities with real-time problem solving and debugging methods, Industry 4.0 applications prevent unstable production, reprocessing and the associated extra costs, leading to improved product and manufacturing quality. This allows cost savings of 10–20% (Rüßmann et al. 2015).
- Supply-Demand Matching: Industry 4.0 applications, which are used to prevent unnecessary inventory and storage costs, help to better understand customer demands and help increase demand forecast accuracy above 85%.
- Fast Marketing: Designing and introducing new products to the market as quickly as possible with Industry 4.0 applications allows for revenue growth and competitive advantage (Ungerman et al. 2018).
- After Sales Services: Remote maintenance or guided self-service applications for product repair are expected to reduce average maintenance costs by 10–40%.

Although it has the potential to have a positive impact on economic growth, it is likely that the technology will have negative impacts on labor markets due to its destructive and transformative characteristics in the short term. Even though the technical advances have made production intelligent and the use of autonomous robots and machines create employment problems, they also have the potential to create new opportunities or areas (Tolbert and Zucker 1999). Researchers with different expectations for short-term, medium-term and long-term employment, stated that the impact of Industry 4.0 on the labor market cannot be fully predicted, but even if some lines of business are lost, new products will be born, new products will be developed with the change of needs, labor supply and demand and wages and prices will reach a balance (Lasi et al. 2014).

Due to the criteria of qualified personnel required by Industry 4.0, there are also researchers who expect that it will negatively affect employment in the short term. According to them, Industry 4.0, which also means a decrease in labor demand, increases the amount of production and quality in the industry and helps to reduce raw material waste, to use energy resources effectively and to take measures for environmental pollution. The biggest obstacle to Industry 4.0, which requires a workforce capable of using intelligent machines and data analysis with advanced IT capabilities, is the lack of qualified labor. In the last years of the twentieth century and in the first years of the twenty-first century, each unit of wealth was produced with more labor force, but today it is obtained with fewer workers (Rodič 2017). For instance, the biggest companies who carry out business in silicon valley had 36 billion dollars market value in 1990 with total of one million 200 thousand employees, while their total income is 250 billion dollars, they produced 250 billion dollars with 137 thousand employees in 2014, however their market value increased to 1,9 trillion dollars. This is accepted as an indication that technological development and employment have negative correlation (Hermann et al. 2016).

4.2 Technology Based Competition Concept

Nowadays, in the competitive environment created by new technologies and globalization, the ability to reach international competitiveness is in fact dependent on competence in technological innovation (Soylu and Göl 2010). Therefore, it is accepted that technological innovation is one of the most important determinants of gaining international competitiveness in addition to rapid production (Ansal 2004). In this regard, Schumpeter (1934) was the first economist to emphasize that processes such as developing new products, manufacturing, management, etc. have more meaningful effects on competition than price changes in products, and in this sense, technological developments will have positive effects on economic growth (Bozkurt 2007). In this context, no country or society, whether developed or developing, can remain to indifferent to this process of change. In this new production system which enables businesses to operate with zero error and zero stock with the advanced and flexible manufacturing technologies developed, competition is called "technology-based competition" (Çetin 2000).

According to Porter (1990), "The only concept that makes sense about competitiveness at national level is national productivity. An gradually increasing standard of living depends on a nation's business achieving high levels of productivity and increasing productivity over time". In this sense, Porter (1990) connects the sustainability of productivity growth to a continuously developing economy and emphasizes the importance of increasing product quality and providing additional features to the product, meaning that the technological innovations and the developments in product technology are important in gaining international competitive power today (Ansal 2004).

A company with large R&D investments, with strong strategies in marketing and protection of intellectual property rights, may choose to be a pioneer in technology or wait for others to develop a new product or production process and become a follower of them. Small businesses may choose to specialize in one area or to follow a path in line with customers technological strategies. Errors in strategy selection are often due to the fact that businesses overestimate their capabilities and choose strategies they cannot support. Technological superiority can be achieved through communication, participation and commitment between organizational units. Because it is obvious that innovations are successful when they are compatible with technological superiority fields (Bayhan 2004). Business which are facing new competitors and declining profits, can try to reduce their prices by using a new production process. In order to do this, technological level must be raised.

4.3 Technological Change and Competitiveness

In many studies in the literature, it is emphasized that as a result of globalization, competition strategies have changed dimension and technological change is the main source of competitiveness both on company and country basis, and there is a positive and strong relationship between technological change and competitiveness. In this regard, Schumpeter (1934) stated that developing new products, production, management and similar processes have more significant effects on competitiveness than price changes in goods, and technological developments will have positive effects on economic growth (Bozkurt 2007). Furthermore, according to Schumpeter (2017), the process of technological change is the most important driving force in the functioning and development of market economies, and technological change is the most important means of competition in market economies (Schumpeter 2017). The effect of technological change on competitiveness can take different forms. The first is the reduction of labor costs. The most common result of using new technology is the reduction of labor cost per unit output. While this situation enables the production to increase rapidly with the use of advanced technologies, it does not cause any decrease in the total number of employees. The labor force that technology replaces is again employed by technology in a new field of business. For example, with the widespread use of computers in production, many new business lines such as computer engineering, programming and technical service were born and new business opportunities were created (Simpson et al. 1987). The issue that needs to be considered is the increase in the need for qualified labor while decreasing labor cost with technological change (Dönek 1995). This is because qualified labor is required to produce advanced technology products and use them in the most effective way.

Another effect of technological change on competitiveness is the reduction of capital costs. In the absence of advanced technological developments, companies had to keep stocks of raw materials, semi-finished and finished goods. As the working capital needs of the firms with high stocks increased, total costs were increasing, especially in periods of high interest rates. Another effect of technological change on the competitiveness of the product and service quality is manifested in the form of increasing. Especially with the use of new technologies in the engineering fields and the adoption of total quality management principle, product quality has increased and it has become possible to produce in different shapes, sizes and designs. In addition, new technologies enable diversification of products and services to meet changing and evolving consumer needs. Providing a wider range of products and services to consumers than ever before gives companies a competitive edge. In this way, companies can respond to customer needs in a shorter time and offer new products to the customers that were not included in the production processes before. A company that has started to gain competitiveness in the market positively affects the technological change process as the resource to be transferred to R&D activities starts to increase and it wants to increase its competitiveness with this resource. However, as the competitiveness of the firm gradually increases towards monopolization, the companies do not want to increase their costs by performing R&D activities since they can have high profitability without making any innovation. Therefore, it can be said that competitiveness will affect technological change positively up to a certain level, and after a certain level, this positive effect will decrease and even negative effect will begin.

4.4 Technological Developments and Changing Business Structures

The effect of technological developments has become more noticeable especially with the globalization factor. Developments in the IT sector have enabled businesses to research, develop and sell in different markets, and at the same time, developments in IT have enabled the financial markets to integrate with global markets. Today, thanks to the fast and effective international marketing and interaction technology offers, it is much more possible for a business to see itself globally. Of course, it is important to remember that globalization is the most effective factor in the spread of technology. Thanks to globalization, the existing national technological competencies are opened to international use, organizations can have the chance to develop their innovations in more than one country, and a wide variety of global technological cooperation can be provided between countries (Zerenler et al. 2007).

At the beginning of the opportunities offered by the global markets to businesses is to supply their inputs at a higher quality and cheaper than international markets rather than national ones. In other words, the fact that the valuable resources available in the world can be reached pushes businesses to global markets. At the same time, businesses want to deliver their products or services to a greater number of consumers and expand their market share. This will only be possible by reaching international markets. It will not be difficult for businesses that think and apply this way to take their shares of traditional thinkers in their local markets.

With the change of businesses in world across activities with globalization, experts classify organizations in today as local, international (exporter) multinational and global businesses with the changes in marketing, sales, distribution and economic policies. Businesses keep pace with the global world with innovative steps and innovations in technology, and they deem this as a necessity to continue their lives successfully. Thus, global businesses develop their products or services to meet the needs of customers around the world. Instead of replicating the same business in different countries, global businesses use global resources to deliver the highest quality products/services to different markets at the lowest cost.

5 International Competitiveness

Competitiveness serves to demonstrate the current situation of sectors or countries. Rather than revealing the reasons for creating competitive advantage, it allows to measure the resulting competitive power (White 1991). There are also important trends affecting competitiveness. These include global trade; customs tariff rates, reduction of non-tariff barriers, rapid dissemination and advancement of information and technology. As a result of this, competition pressure has increased on firms (Fagerberg 1988). International competitiveness: The fact that a domestic firm has international competitiveness in the foreign market or in the domestic market means that it is currently or in the same situation or superior in terms of non-price factors such as punctuality in product price or product quality delivery and after-sales service compared to competing domestic and foreign firms (Ghose and Kharas 1993). Today, definitions of international competitiveness at country level are made. Competitiveness at the international level is "the ability of a country to produce goods and services in line with the conditions and standards of international markets, while increasing the real income of its people in the long term, under free and fair market conditions" (Maskell and Malmberg 1999). In other words, international competitiveness is defined as "the competitiveness of manufactured goods and services in international markets with the goods and services of other countries".

The concept of competitiveness or economic development of an economic system means the development of the productive sectors of the country dynamically and achieving competitiveness in the coming years and increasing the standard of living and real wages in the economy as a whole (Summers 1988). Nations are successful in the branches where their own domestic advantages are also valuable to other countries and their innovations and developments outshine international needs (Porter 1994). The concept of international competitiveness is often used to measure the macroeconomic power of countries. International competitiveness is the comparison of the specific economic characteristics of a country with its trading partners with respect to international trade trends. Competitiveness, on the other hand, is not only the ability to sell products abroad and maintain the balance of foreign trade, but also the ability of countries to increase their income and employment levels, and to provide continuous increases in quality of life such as improvements in science, technology and education quality, infrastructure problems and increase their share in international markets. Therefore, international competitiveness indicators do not consist only of foreign trade data. GNP per capita, competitiveness index, foreign trade balance, foreign capital investments are some of the criteria used to determine international competitiveness.

5.1 Globalization and Its Consequences

Businesses are the institutions that constitute the basis of economic systems and are most affected by the changes in technology in the international economy (Schwab and Porter 2007). Today, they are at great risk of adapting to these frequent changes and developments due to technology or markets. They must be on the side that is flexible and easy to adapt to change and even initiates change. Globalization which showed its first signs in twentieth century and accelerated with technological developments is also the source of many economic, political and sociocultural changes in society. Globalization, which includes integration and interdependence and is also referred to as the new world order, is one of the fundamental trends of the last century. The rapid developments after the 1980s have led to economic and social activities becoming international rather than international (Güleş and Bülbül 2003).

Although the effects of globalization seem to be more intense in recent years, it is not a new concept. The goals that globalization wants to achieve can be listed as the removal of barriers to flow of goods, service sales, money flow and human mobility. When we look at the recent developments, we can say that these goals have been reached to a great extent. World trade grew by an average of 6.6% per year (1948–1966), especially when the effects of globalization were felt intensely. During the Second World War, the exports of developed countries have changed from basic goods to manufacturing and from manufacturing to services. In other words, service trade has increased its importance, and since the end of 1980s, it has shown a rapid development and grew by 8.8% annually between 1980 and 1993. In the same period, goods trade remained at 5% (Bhalla 1998). Globalization and developments in world trade and money flow have led to changes in national economies. While the growth rates of developed countries experienced a slowdown, it was observed that the growth rates of newly industrialized countries varied between 5 and 11%. As can be seen from all of these, with the addition of new technological developments to globalization, economic balances have started to change in the world and the necessity of questioning the concepts has emerged again.

5.2 New Competition World

As a result of globalization and developing technology, direct capital investment flow increased in financial and capital markets, information dissipation accelerated and marketing-distribution and sales channels of products and services produced diversified (Porter et al. 2009). Global production has increased competition between manufacturers and suppliers. The fact that businesses give services in these markets in international, they find less balanced and stable place. For this reason, businesses should react more quickly to external changes and threats (Porter and Kramer 2002). The competitive elements in today's world are to improve the quality of products and services, respond to customer needs more quickly and enter the market faster. When doing this, it is necessary not to ignore the low cost and different product and service options that are required for operation. Because in these new markets, businesses with fast technology and performance determine the rules in advance and these rules become the standard for all other followers. Thus, companies with strong performance can easily delete others from the market.

Many factors such as globalization, change, knowledge, speed, technology and so on have affected the definition, form and rules of competition (Amendola et al. 1993). This rapid change in globalization and information communication technologies has led to the formation of an information-based economic structure (Brown 2000). In today's economic structure called knowledge economy, the phenomenon of competition forces businesses to learn, acquire information and try to maintain change (David and David 2013). In the new world of competition, businesses have to be in close relationship with their customers, work with their suppliers, form teams, and perhaps go to strategic partnerships with their competitors from time to time. This environment forces them to cooperate in forming the cake and to compete in the split. In other words, businesses are expected to realize two opposing ideas, both cooperation and competition at the same time (Brandenburger Adam and Nalebuff 1998). We can easily say that the development and diffusion of new technologies has increased the importance of innovation for businesses that want to be competitive. Traditional competition has now been replaced by the benefits of this era. In the past, industry limits were known in competition, but now it is not even known who is competing and who is a customer.

6 Discussion

Companies should innovate to maintain their presence and increase their competitiveness (Göker 2000). For this purpose, it is essential to reduce costs, to diversify products and services on the one hand, and to improve the quality of products/services on the other hand. It is from these obligations that the elements that bring out the ideas of innovation. Only in this way can it be possible to enter new markets and increase the existing market share. Innovation is the key to economic growth, increased employment and quality of life. Taking into account the rapid change in consumers' tastes, technology and competition, it is understood that companies should constantly offer new products and services. The reason for the new product development is to encourage the growth of the company, to respond to competition, to evaluate the excess capacity and cash flow in the firm and to adapt to the changing environment (Barney and Hesterly 2009).

Porter (1985) states that in order to create and develop competitive advantage in a given industry, companies should choose one of the general competition strategies called cost leadership, differentiation, cost focus and focus on differentiation. Innovation at this point gives a business the chance to gain a competitive advantage through a relative difference compared to its competitors, a relative low cost, or both at a certain level (Porter 1985). In other words, innovations are one of the rare sources that enable businesses to differentiate against their competitors and apply cost strategies together. Competition is the most effective method for the mutual coordination of the individual activities of the firms in the market without the need for a central intervention. In addition to advantages such as reducing production costs and improving the quality of products and services, competition can lead to a decrease in the profitability of companies and even endanger their assets in the market.

If point out the importance of innovation for communities with s quote of Professor Peter Drucker which is published in Harvard Business Review in 1998, "...Today, it is accepted that innovation is very important for the development of countries. It will be possible to state that the conditions of intense competition and the rapidly changing market conditions and the developments in technology are effective in accepting this situation. In this context, how innovation is to be done is the key question" (Drucker 1998). Innovation covers all processes to develop and commercialize new or improved products, services or production methods. Since innovation is a continuous activity, these ideas and their results, which are developed, developed and marketed in a way that gives the company competitive power, should be re-evaluated continuously and disseminated for new returns. Today's competitiveness is based on innovative products, just in time, quality and price.

The adoption and diffusion of innovation increases the knowledge of a society, thus supporting the development of markets, increasing welfare in the long term and higher living standards (Cantwell 2005). With the new products and services it develops, good financial results will not be surprising for a business that rises in competition. The increasing number of customers and subscribers will increase sales revenues in the company's financial statements, and increase in sales may directly affect the profit together with other factors. The increase in profits will attract the attention of investors and increase the interest and attractiveness of the firm in the market. Perhaps with increasing profits, the firm will provide added value by distributing more dividends to its investors. Or the business will re-use this profitability in production and innovation to maintain growth and market dominance. This will again increase the firm's preferability and all these developments will be interactions to increase the value of the company in the market. With effective and robust financial indicators and high profits announced, firms will gain value in terms of investors.

7 Future Studies Suggestions

It is evident that competitiveness in countries positively affects economic growth (Kuczmarski 1996). Given the theoretical and practical situation, it is a known fact that countries that increase their competitiveness in the world constantly improve their position. In the development of competitiveness, some countries develop only their economic performance or infrastructure arrangements, business world activities and public activities, while others improve in several or all of these sub-indices (Grandori 1999). The steps to increase the competitiveness that started under the leadership of the private sector, especially in developing countries, will strengthen the economic performance and infrastructure indices, which are expected to yield long-term results with the support provided by the public sector. Eliminating the weaknesses in these indices is expected to provide a great advantage for middle income countries in their transition to upper income group. Otherwise, it can be argued that they will be considered in place and cannot escape the middle income trap with the definition of the latest fashion.

Having a solid infrastructure means that a country is fast in both transportation and communication, which is an important factor in increasing competitiveness. In this sense, both the quality of roads and railways in transportation infrastructure, the quality of port infrastructure and the quality of air transportation and the quality of electricity and telephone infrastructure in communication infrastructure can be listed as topics to be considered. It should be emphasized that the steps taken by the countries in the field of health, the innovations they will bring and the investments they will make will contribute to the competitiveness and thus economic growth of the countries. At the same time, basic education, which we call primary education, and increasing the level of vocational and higher education are extremely important issues. The investments and the steps taken by the governments will take the countries one step further.

One of the most important factors for economic growth is technology (Kim and Mauborgne 1999). Technology is one of the most important factors for developing countries, especially for developing countries that have fulfilled the basic requirements (Güleş and Bülbül 2004). At the same time, it is necessary to adopt technology and increase the use of information and communication technologies in order to increase the level of technology which is a sine qua non of competition. Therefore, it is of utmost importance that both companies and countries increase their technology investments. The level of innovation used as a term in terms of innovation in the recent fashion is generally measured in accordance with the scientific studies and R&D expenditures made in the country. It is innovation that will take countries one step forward for development. Both the existing technology and the level of production will not bring growth after a certain level. Therefore, the countries that reach the optimum level should increase their innovation capacity, develop scientific research institutions and bring advanced technology to the country, especially with the policies they will apply at the state level. In addition to this, companies should cooperate with universities by giving importance to R&D investments and keep their doors open to more innovative ideas.

8 Conclusion

As a result of the integration of information technologies with industry, production processes are restructured. Based on real-time communication and interaction of people, machinery and products, Industry 4.0 enables faster and error-free response to both production and consumption needs. Industry 4.0, unlike the previous revolutions, does not actually emerge with a new technology, it means the organization of existing technologies together in a new and integrated model. Mechanical systems of the First Industrial Revolution, electricity of the Second Industrial Revolution, and information and communication technologies of the Third Industrial Revolution are used collectively and integrally in Industry 4.0.

Especially the productivity and sustainable growth performance created by the Industrial Revolution has increased the interest in the concept of technological change all over the world. Technological change, technical progress, technological progress and technological innovation and similar concepts, although there are very little differences between them are often used synonymously today. Technological change is expressed in a broad sense as "the change in technological knowledge with the organizational styles and operational methods used to convert inputs to outputs". The concept of technological change has been discussed in many economic theories, especially Classical, Neoclassical, Marxist, Schumpeter/Evolutionist (Neo-Schumpeterian) and Development Economics. While some of these economic thought currents ignore the technological change and its impact on the economy, they see technology as an external variable, while others are not insensitive to the effects of technological change and internalize technology in the economic models they create.

Increasing productivity by digitizing the production processes of Industry 4.0 brings competition to a new dimension. Considering that all countries are trying to gain competitive advantage in today's world, it is very important that they realize digital transformation in industry. Competitiveness is discussed in the literature at firm, industry and international level. Competition at company level is directly proportional to the success of companies in R&D and innovation. At the industrial level, competition is explained by sectoral growth, employment and profitability. International competitiveness means that countries produce and export high value-added products by using their production factors.

Today, the use of technology and the pursuit of technological development has become a necessity for countries and companies. Developing countries need to develop their technological capabilities in order to gain and maintain international competitiveness. The concept of Technological Capabilities can be examined at the country level as well as at the firm, region and sector level. Technological Capabilities at company level can be defined as the knowledge and skills necessary for companies to select, install, operate, maintain, adapt, improve and develop technologies. The company possesses technological capabilities and can adapt rapidly to changing conditions, gain competitiveness and maintain competitiveness. The final stage of technological capabilities is innovation. The concept of innovation can be defined as the transformation of science and technology into economic or social benefit. Technological Innovation consists of Product and Process Innovation. Product Innovation involves the development of new or improved products, while Process Innovation is the technical improvement that reduces the cost of the existing product. Innovations lead the company to offer a cheaper and better quality product than the products on the market or to provide a competitive advantage over its competitors as a result of developing a production process that will significantly reduce production costs.

While the innovative policies of the companies lead to the competitive power in the market, this will affect the assets and profitability of the company, and the positive impact that will be positively reflected to the business shareholders will increase the market value. One of the sectors most affected by technological developments is the telecommunications sector. The fact that the sector is very active and the rapid changes are felt can be a threat for the businesses operating in this sector, while it can be a triggering factor. Management of innovation is particularly important for companies in this sector.

References

Ada, E., Ventura, K., Aracioglu, B., Savasci, I., & Kazancoglu, Y. (2008). KOBI'lerin Rekabet Gucu ve E-Ticarete Gecis Sureci: Bir Model Onerisi. *Ege Academic Review, 8*(1), 53–68.

Aiginger, K. (1998). A framework for evaluating the dynamic competitiveness of countries. *Structural Change and Economic Dynamics, 9*(2), 159–188.

Ailenei, D., & Mosora, L. C. (2011). Economics of sustainable development. Competitiveness and economic growth. *Theoretical and Applied Economics, 2*(2), 5.

Alçın, S. (2016). Üretim için yeni bir izlek: sanayi 4.0. *Journal of Life Economics, 3*(2), 19–30.

Amendola, G., Dosi, G., & Papagni, E. (1993). The dynamics of international competitiveness. *Weltwirtschaftliches Archiv, 129*(3), 451–471.

Ansal, H. (2004). Geçmiş ve gelecekte ekonomik gelişmede teknolojinin rolü. TMMOB (derl.) Teknoloji, (Ankara: TMMOB Yayınları), 35–58.

Ararat, M. (2005). Turkey. In *Corporate social responsibility across Europe* (pp. 247–259). Berlin: Springer.

Atik, H. (2005). *Yenilik ve ulusal rekabet gücü.* Ankara: Detay Yayıncılık.

Balassa, B. A. (1989). *Comparative advantage, trade policy and economic development.* New York: Harvester Wheatsheaf.

Baraz, B. (2006). Aile İşletmelerinde Kurumsallaşma Ölçütleri. 2. Aile, 14–15.

Barney, J. B., & Hesterly, W. S. (2009). *Strategic management and competitive advantage.* Upper Saddle River, NJ: Pearson Education.

Bayhan, B. D. (2004). *Teknoloji ve inovasyon yönetimi* (pp. 283–308). Ankara: Türk Mühendis ve Mimar Odaları Birliği Yayını.

Berger, C., Hees, A., Braunreuther, S., & Reinhart, G. (2016). Characterization of cyber-physical sensor systems. *Procedia CIRP, 41*, 638–643.

Bernhofen, D. M., & Brown, J. C. (2016). Testing the general validity of the Heckscher-Ohlin theorem. *American Economic Journal: Microeconomics, 8*(4), 54–90.

Besler, S., & Tonus, H. (2004). *KOBİ'lerin Uluslararası Düzeyde Rekabet Gücü.*

Bhalla, A. S. (1998). *Globalization, growth and marginalization.* Cham: Springer.

Biber, A. E. (2010). İktisadi Büyümede Kurumsal Faktörler ve Kurumsal Değişim. *Akademik Bakış Dergisi, 19*(1), 1–24.

Boltho, A. (1996). The assessment: International competitiveness. *Oxford Review of Economic Policy, 12*(3), 1–16.

Bozkurt, K. (2007). İçsel Büyüme Modelleri Bağlamında Türk İmalat Sanayinde Teknolojik Gelişme ve Ekonomik Büyüme. *Finans Politik & Ekonomik Yorumlar, 44*(513), 64–74.

Brandenburger Adam, M., & Nalebuff, B. J. (1998). *Ortaklaşa Rekabet, (Çev. Levent Cinemre).* İstanbul: Scala Yayıncılık ve Tanıtım.

Brown, P. (2000). The globalisation of positional competition? *Sociology, 34*(4), 633–653.

Cantwell, J. (2005). Innovation and competitiveness. In *The Oxford Handbook of Innovation* (pp. 543–567). Oxford: Oxford University Press.

Çelen, S. (2017). Sanayi 4.0 ve Simülasyon. *International Journal of 3D Printing Technologies and Digital Industry, 1*(1), 9–26.

Çetin, M. (2000). Avrupa Birliği'nde KOBİ'lere Yönelik Teknoloji Politikaları. *Dış Ticaret Dergisi, Yıl, 5*, 1–15.

Chen, Y. K. (2012). Challenges and opportunities of internet of things. In *17th Asia and South Pacific design automation conference* (pp. 383–388). Piscataway, NJ: IEEE.

Chen, M., Mao, S., & Liu, Y. (2014). Big data: A survey. *Mobile Networks and Applications, 19*(2), 171–209.

Cho, H., & Tansuhaj, P. (2003). Examining LDC firms' competitive advantage from the resource-based and institutional perspectives. Washington State University, USA. Paper for the Seventh International Conference on Global Business and Economic Development.

Davenport, T. (2014). *Big data at work: Dispelling the myths, uncovering the opportunities.* Boston: Harvard Business Review Press.

David, F. R., & David, F. R. (2013). *Strategic management: Concepts and cases: A competitive advantage approach*. Upper Saddle River: Pearson.

De Bono, E. (1996). *Rekabet Üstü (Çev: Oya Özel)(Elektronik Sürüm)*. İstanbul: Remzi Kitapevi.

Demir, İ. (2002). Alt sektörlerde rekabet gücü ölçüm yöntemleri. *Planlama Dergisi, 42*, 229–234.

Doğan, Ö. İ. (2000). *Kalite uygulamalarının işletmelerin rekabet gücü üzerine etkisi*. Dokuz Eylül Üniversitesi.

Dönek, E. (1995). Realızıng Technologıcal change: The new techno Economıc Paradıgm. *Hacettepe Üniversitesi İktisadi ve İdari Bilimler Fakültesi Dergisi, 13*, 101–116.

Dong-sung, C., & Hwy-Chang, M. (2013). *From Adam Smith to Michael Porter: Evolution of competitiveness theory (extended edition)* (Vol. 7). New Jersey: World Scientific.

Drucker, P. F. (1998). The discipline of innovation. *Leader to Leader, 1998*(9), 13–15.

Dunning, J. H. (2013). *Multinationals, technology & competitiveness (RLE international business)*. London: Routledge.

Fagerberg, J. (1988). International competitiveness. *The Economic Journal, 98*(391), 355–374.

Farashahi, M., Hafsi, T., & Molz, R. (2005). Institutionalized norms of conducting research and social realities: A research synthesis of empirical works from 1983 to 2002. *International Journal of Management Reviews, 7*(1), 1–24.

Farinha, L., Gouveia, J. B., & Nunes, S. (2015). Drivers of global competitiveness and economic growth. In *Handbook of research on global competitive advantage through innovation and entrepreneurship* (pp. 13–27). Hershey, PA: IGI Global.

Feurer, R., & Chaharbaghi, K. (1994). Defining competitiveness: A holistic approach. *Management Decision, 32*(2), 49–58.

Fleisher, C. S., & Bensoussan, B. E. (2003). *Strategic and competitive analysis: Methods and techniques for analyzing business competition* (p. 457). Upper Saddle River, NJ: Prentice Hall.

Francis, A. (1989). The concept of competitiveness. In *The competitiveness of european industry* (pp. 3–12). London: Routledge and Kegan.

Francis, A., & Tharakan, P. M. (1989). *The competitiveness of European industry*. London: Routledge Kegan & Paul.

Ganz, C. (2018). *The internet of things, services and people* (In the internet of things) (pp. 189–203). Berlin, Heidelberg: Springer.

Ghose, D., & Kharas, H. (1993). International competitiveness, the demand for exports and real effective exchange rates in developing countries. *Journal of Development Economics, 41*(2), 377–398.

Gilchrist, A. (2016). Introducing industry 4.0. In *Industry 4.0* (pp. 195–215). Berkeley, CA: Apress.

Göker, A. (2000). Prodüktivite, inovasyon yeteneği ve teknoloji. *Rekabet Gücü, Teknoloji ve Verimlilik Toplantısı* (p. 25). Milli Prodüktivite Merkezi, Ankara.

Grandori, A. (Ed.). (1999). *Interfirm networks: Organization and industrial competitiveness* (Vol. 11). London: Routledge.

Gül, E., Ekinci, A., & Konya, S. (2009). *Türkiye'de istihdam politikaları: yapısal bir analiz*. Bursa: Ekin Yayınevi.

Güleş, H. K., & Bülbül, H. (2003). İşletmelerde Proaktif Bir Strateji Olarak Yenilikçilik, 500 Büyük Sanayi İşletmesi Üzerine Bir Uygulama. *Dokuz Eylül Üniversitesi İşletme Fakültesi Dergisi, 4* (1), 40–63.

Güleş, H. K., & Bülbül, H. (2004). *Yenilikçilik*. Ankara: Nobel Yayıncılık.

Hamel, G. (1997). Yarının Avantajlarını Yaratmak. Geleceği Yeniden DüÇünmek, İş Yönetimi, Rekabet, Kontrol, Liderlik, Pazarlar ve Dünya. Drl. Rowan Gibson, Çev. Sinem Gül. İstanbul: Sabah Kitapları, 69–82.

Heckscher, E. F., & Ohlin, B. G. (1991). *Heckscher-Ohlin trade theory*. Cambridge, MA: The MIT Press.

Helms, M. M. (1996). Perspectives on quality and productivity for competitive advantage. *The TQM Magazine, 8*(3), 5–10.

Hermann, M., Pentek, T., & Otto, B. (2016). Design principles for industrie 4.0 scenarios. In *2016 49th Hawaii International Conference on System Sciences (HICSS)* (pp. 3928–3937). New York: IEEE.

Kergroach, S. (2017). Industry 4.0: New challenges and opportunities for the labour market. Форсайт, 11(4 (eng)).

Kim, W. C., & Mauborgne, R. (1999). Strategy, value innovation, and the knowledge economy. *MIT Sloan Management Review, 40*(3), 41.

Krugman, P. (1994). Competitiveness: A dangerous obsession. *Foreign Affairs, 73*, 28.

Kuczmarski, T. D. (1996). *Innovation: Leadership strategies for the competitive edge*. Lincolnwood: NTC Publishing Group.

Lasi, H., Fettke, P., Kemper, H. G., Feld, T., & Hoffmann, M. (2014). Industrie 4.0. *Wirtschaftsinformatik, 56*(4), 261–264.

Markusen, J. R. (1995). The boundaries of multinational enterprises and the theory of international trade. *Journal of Economic Perspectives, 9*(2), 169–189.

Martin, R., & Sunley, P. (2017). Paul Krugman's geographical economics and its implications for regional development theory: A critical assessment. In *Economy* (pp. 25–58). London: Routledge.

Maskell, P., & Malmberg, A. (1999). Localised learning and industrial competitiveness. *Cambridge Journal of Economics, 23*(2), 167–185.

Oks, S. J., Fritzsche, A., & Möslein, K. M. (2017). An application map for industrial cyber-physical systems. In *Industrial internet of things* (pp. 21–46). Cham: Springer.

Oliver, C. (1997). Sustainable competitive advantage: Combining institutional and resource-based views. *Strategic Management Journal, 18*(9), 697–713.

Oral, M. (1986). An industrial competitiveness model. *IIE Transactions, 18*(2), 148–157.

Özdoğan, O. (2017). *Endüstri 4.0: Dördüncü Sanayi Devrimi ve Endüstriyel Dönüşümün Anahtarları*. İstanbul: Pusula.

Porter, M. E. (1985). *Comtipetitive strategy: Techniques for analyzing industries and comlpetitors*. New York: Free Press.

Porter, M. E. (1990). *The competitive advantage of nations* (p. 855). New York: Free Press. isbn:0-333-51804-7.

Porter, M. E. (1993). *Stratejik Grup Kavramı*. New York: Macmillan.

Porter, M. (1994). Ulusların Rekabetçi Üstünlüğü. In M. Özel (Ed.), *Küresel Rekabet*. İstanbul: İz Yayıncılık.

Porter, M. E. (2000). *Rekabet Stratejisi, Sektör ve Rakip Analizi Teknikleri (Çeviri: Gülen Ulubilgen) Sistem Yayıncılık, 1* (p. 16). İstanbul: Basım.

Porter, M. E. (2011). *Competitive advantage of nations: Creating and sustaining superior performance*. New York: Simon and Schuster.

Porter, M. E., & Kramer, M. R. (2002). The competitive advantage of corporate. *Harvard Business Review, 80*, 57–68.

Porter, M. E., & Van der Linde, C. (1995). Toward a new conception of the environment-competitiveness relationship. *Journal of Economic Perspectives, 9*(4), 97–118.

Porter, A. L., Newman, N. C., Roessner, J. D., Johnson, D. M., & Jin, X. Y. (2009). International high tech competitiveness: Does China rank number 1? *Technology Analysis & Strategic Management, 21*(2), 173–193.

Rexhäuser, S., & Rammer, C. (2014). Environmental innovations and firm profitability: Unmasking the Porter hypothesis. *Environmental and Resource Economics, 57*(1), 145–167.

Ricardo, D. (1955). *The works and correspondence of David Ricardo: Volume 10, Biographical miscellany*. Cambridge: Cambridge University Press.

Rodič, B. (2017). Industry 4.0 and the new simulation modelling paradigm. *The Organ, 50*(3), 193–207.

Ruffin, R. (2002). David Ricardo's discovery of comparative advantage. *History of political economy, 34*(4), 727–748.

Rüßmann, M., Lorenz, M., Gerbert, P., Waldner, M., Justus, J., Engel, P., & Harnisch, M. (2015). Industry 4.0: The future of productivity and growth in manufacturing industries. *Boston Consulting Group, 9*(1), 54–89.

Şağbanşua, L., & Bişkek, K. (2006). Strateji, Rekabet ve Rekabet Gücü İlişkileri. Akademik Bakış. *Uluslararası Hakemli Sosyal Bilimler E-Dergisi, 9*, 1–14.

Schumpeter, J. A. (1934). *The theory of economic development*. Cambridge, MA: Harvard University press (originally published in German in 1911; reprinted by Transaction Publishers, New Brunswick, New Jersey in 1997).

Schumpeter, J. A. (2017). *Theory of economic development*. London: Routledge.

Schwab, K. (2017). *The fourth industrial revolution*. Currency.

Schwab, K., & Porter, M. E. (Eds.). (2007). *The global competitiveness report*. Basingstoke: Palgrave Macmillan.

Scott, W. R. (1987). The adolescence of institutional theory. *Administrative Science Quarterly, 32*, 493–511.

Siggel, E. (2006). International competitiveness and comparative advantage: A survey and a proposal for measurement. *Journal of Industry, Competition and Trade, 6*(2), 137–159.

Simpson, D., Love, J., Love, J., & Walker, J. (1987). *The challenge of new technology*. Boulder, CO: Westview Press.

Sirikrai, S. B., & Tang, J. C. (2006). Industrial competitiveness analysis: Using the analytic hierarchy process. *The Journal of High Technology Management Research, 17*(1), 71–83.

Smith, A. (2010). *The theory of moral sentiments*. Harmondsworth: Penguin.

Soylu, A., & Göl, M. Ö. (2010). Yönetim İnovasyonu. *Sosyoekonomi, 11*(1), 113–130.

Summers, L. H. (1988). Tax policy and international competitiveness. In *International aspects of fiscal policies* (pp. 349–386). Chicago: University of Chicago Press.

Teece, D. J. (2010). Business models, business strategy and innovation. *Long Range Planning, 43* (2–3), 172–194.

Thompson, A. A., & Strickland, A. J. (1999). *Strategic management: Cases and concepts*. New York: McGraw Hill.

Tolbert, P. S., & Zucker, L. G. (1999). The institutionalization of institutional theory. In *Studying organization. Theory & method* (pp. 169–184). London, Thousand Oaks, New Delhi: Sage.

Türkkan, E. (2001). *Rekabet teorisi ve endüstri iktisadı*. Ankara: Turhan Kitabevi.

Ulukan, C. (2004). Örgütlerin Kurumsallaşması mı Yoksa Süreçlerin Kurumsallaşması mı. *Yeni bir Perspektif İhtiyacı, 12*, 27–29.

Ungerman, O., Dedkova, J., & Gurinova, K. (2018). The impact of marketing innovation on the competitiveness of enterprises in the context of industry 4.0. *Journal of Competitiveness, 10*(2), 132.

Welford, R., Meaton, J., & Young, W. (2003). Fair trade as a strategy for international competitiveness. *The International Journal of Sustainable Development & World Ecology, 10*(1), 1–13.

White, H. T. (1991). Michael Porter: The competitive advantage of nations. *New Zealand Engineering, 46*(1), 5.

Witkowski, K. (2017). Internet of things, big data, industry 4.0–innovative solutions in logistics and supply chains management. *Procedia Engineering, 182*, 763–769.

Yazıcıoğlu, İ., & Hakan, K. (2009). Aile İşletmelerinin Kurumsallaşma Düzeylerinin Belirlenmesine Yönelik Karşılaştırmalı Bir Araştırma. *Selçuk Üniversitesi Sosyal Bilimler Enstitüsü Dergisi, 21*, 497–507.

Zerenler, M., Türker, N., & Şahin, E. (2007). Küresel Teknoloji, Araştırma-Geliştirme (Ar-Ge) Ve Yenilik İlişkisi. *Selçuk Üniversitesi Sosyal Bilimler Enstitüsü Dergisi, 1*(17), 653–667.

The Spirit of Business Life: Entrepreneurship

Ercan Karakeçe and Murat Çemberci

Abstract This study aims to confirm the importance of entrepreneurship in strategic priorities in competitive environments. In this context, it started with the conceptual structure of the term and proceed conditions the entrepreneur prefers for business success. Furthermore, the fundamental elements that the entrepreneur brings to the market discussed. While explaining these factors, the emphasis placed on the significance of entrepreneurship. Moreover, some crucial determinants are focused on developing entrepreneurship. For this purpose, it is mentioned in both physical and other factors to reach business success in competitive markets.

1 Introduction

The significance of entrepreneurship has increased day by day (Anderson et al. 2019). However, today there is still no obvious definition of entrepreneurial activities. Peter Drucker (2014) refers to this complexity as confusion. We can refer to this confusion as limitlessness of term. We see many clues about entrepreneurial efforts from our daily life even we do not name the works. There are many attempts in both commercial and social areas. Even when we talk about initiatives, we can make distinctions both as private and public. As you see, entrepreneurial spirit has spread all over our lives.

Before going on to the history of the thought of entrepreneurship, it is useful to clarify some issues. It should be noted that when it tells about entrepreneurship, many different points come to mind of people. When we use this term in commercial

E. Karakeçe (✉)
Vocational School of Social Sciences, İstanbul Medipol University, İstanbul, Turkey
e-mail: ekarakece@medipol.edu.tr

M. Çemberci
Department of Business Administration, Faculty of Economics and Administrative Sciences, Yıldız Technical University, Beşiktaş, İstanbul, Turkey
e-mail: cemberci@yildiz.edu.tr

H. Dincer, S. Yüksel (eds.), *Strategic Priorities in Competitive Environments*, Contributions to Management Science, https://doi.org/10.1007/978-3-030-45023-6_7

life, many structures starting from micro SMEs to unicorns can be included in this classification. In the academic section, some disciplines, especially business, economics, sociology, and psychology, have produced studies related to this area. In this sense, entrepreneurship can be considered as a common intersection point.

To make explicit the term, we focus on a short historical story. And also, we step out some relevant stages by pointing out famous personalities and their contributions. And then we make some inquiries about the conceptual background of the term; we effort to describe what an entrepreneur requires, what he gains and dedicates. By defining the above, we detail the importance of entrepreneurial activities. And lastly, after describing the role of it, we follow the visible and invisible factors that encourage entrepreneurs.

2 Entrepreneurial Concept

Our journey begins with Richard Cantillon in 1755. Drawing attention to the uncertainty, he talked about activities to take the risk, evaluate opportunities and profit as a result. Throughout the eighteenth century, it also means to organize, plan, and own products in addition to predecessors. In the 1800s, Jean Baptiste Say mentions that entrepreneurship income and capital income should be separated. So, he demanded that an entrepreneur and an investor should be assumed as different parties. Say also accepting the entrepreneur as the production factor, encouraged the entrepreneur's leadership and managerial role. The entrepreneur is referred to as a coordinator in both production and distribution (Hébert and Link 2009).

In addition to the concepts of risk and uncertainty, Frank Hayneman Knight emphasized the decision-making ability of the entrepreneur. Besides, Joseph Alois Schumpeter added a very different perspective on the system. With its creative destruction concept, it has given entrepreneurship a completely different dimension. With this expression, Schumpeter removed the entrepreneurial activity from the mediocrity. This causes the market to turn a more competitive atmosphere. With the mentioned difference, the entrepreneur changed both his profession or his manner (Schumpeter 2003). On the other hand, Israel Meir Kirzner, unlike Schumpeter, worked to define the entrepreneur's founding role. According to his explanation, the entrepreneur had a role focusing on the market, detecting insufficiencies and completing them (Kirzner 1997).

In addition to those intellectuals, many researchers have contributed to the notion of entrepreneurship. Nicolas Baudeau referred to diminishing costs, enhancing profits and innovation. Johan H. Von Thünen mentioned about unlike the manager, the entrepreneur's taking business risks. Albert Shapero adverted that the entrepreneur guides both commercial and social factors besides the danger of bankruptcy. Gartner emphasized the entrepreneurial process and the value of organizations. Schuler indicated combining innovation with current operations. Robert Hisrich pointed out creating value and satisfaction. Jones and Butler indicated creating opportunities and management with value-added. Shane and Ventakamaran focused on future occasions. Richard Daft underlined the need for success, self-confidence,

Table 1 Keywords in entrepreneurship definitions

Key element	Writer
Innovation	Schumpeter (1947), Cochran (1968), Drucker (1985), and Julien (1989, 1998)
Risk	Cantillon (1755), Knight (1921), Palmer (1971), Reuters (1982), and Rosenberg (1983)
Resource coordination, organization	Ely and Hess (1893), Cole (1942), Aitken (1965), Belshaw (1955), Chandler (1962), Leibstein (1968), Wilken (1979), Pearce (1981), and Casson (1982)
Value added	Say (1815), Bruyat and Julien (2001), and Fayolle (2008)
Project and visionary thought	Longenecker and Schoen (1975) and Filion (1991, 2004)
Action oriented	Baty (1981)
Leadership	Hornaday and Aboud (1971)
Dynamo of the economic system	Weber (1947), Baumol (1968), Storey (1982), and Moffat (1983)
Venture developer	Collins, Moore, and Unwalla (1964), Smith (1967), Brereton (1974), Komives (1974), Mancuso (1979), Schwartz (1982), Carland, Hoy, and Boulton (1984), and Vesper (1990)
Recognizing opportunities	Smith (1967), Meredith, Nelson, and Neck (1982), Kirzner (1983), Stevenson and Gumpert (1985), Timmons (1985), Dana (1995), Shane and Venkatamaran (2000), Bygrave and Zacharakis (2004), and Timmons and Spinelli (2004)
Productive	Zaleznik and Kets de Vries (1976) and Pinchot (1985)
Preoccupation	Lynn (1969) and Kets de Vries (1977, 1985)
Control	Mc Clelland (1961)
Change oriented	Mintzberg (1973) and Shapiro (1975)
Rebellious/guilt	Hagen (1960)

Source: Demirtaş et al. 2017 and Özmen 2016

awareness of opportunities and, tolerance of uncertainty. Tim Burns highlighted development and transformation (Hébert and Link 2009; Godley and Casson 2010; Özmen 2016).

Although some portions of the definitions made were common, some distinctive pieces were highlighted. Notably, subjects on different entrepreneurship definitions discussing this point are confronted. In some articles, investigators utilized some key concepts while describing entrepreneurial activities. All over these studies reveal to us that the descriptions of entrepreneurship have varied as human needs changed. This transformation is already natural. If the entrepreneur is supposed to complement of the human and enriches the life, then the entrepreneurial mindset also modifies as the human desiring shift (Table 1).

To explain the evolution in descriptions, it is valuable to focus on the key statements in the definitions made by the authors. For this reason, the words in the table unveil the determinants that should be included in entrepreneurial motions. Concerning the features of entrepreneurs' and various business circumstances, it is stated that defining a universal entrepreneur definition is difficult. For this purpose, it is beneficial to recall some key terms of entrepreneurship definitions.

First, we have to admit the opinion that the entrepreneur considers uniquely (Baron 1998). He accepts situations as an opportunity where everyone sees as an obstacle. While everyone complains about the problems, he discovers solutions from difficulties, that is, he is the problem solver. We cannot say that he only thinks and imagine. He is also an actioner. He desires to perform as soon as he realizes the solution (Wood and McKelvie 2015). For this purpose, his organizer ability appears. By planning and programming, he also handles the issue of supply coordination. He has to master various details in his plan while exploring opportunities (Schumpeter 2003). With this aspect, it brings the direction of leadership to the fore. In addition to the possibilities he has, he comprehends how to benefit from the resources that he has not. So, he is as collaborative as social (Huda et al. 2019).

In the solutions put forward, he does not only think of the customer who needs satisfaction (Dinçer et al. 2020). He also takes into attention comparable solutions and competitors in the market. If he is not the first in the market, he feels the obligation to differentiate the product or service. For this reason, he knows that he has to make innovation. It is not an easy responsibility to create added value and to satisfy the customer desire (Davis et al. 2016).

He remembers that he should shoulder a computable risk in the competitive market at the same time. Because every change brings resistance to itself. This obstruction can occur both within and outside the company. At its simplest, the target audience may not adopt the solution for various causes. This can lead the entrepreneur from the loss of resources, waste of time and labor to bankruptcy. In other words, the entrepreneur is not a gambler, but he is a good risk-taker (Demirtaş et al. 2017).

He will never feel comfortable himself even if he succeeds. Because being victorious is as vital as remaining strong for the businessperson. The hero recognizes that when he does something accurately, the market trails him. This also means that in most cases he has followers/rivals behind him. Good results will be imitated, that is, competition is part of the nature of entrepreneurship. Sometimes he is forced to price struggle with a lower quality product, sometimes he feels competitive pressure in terms of customer satisfaction with different choices (Özmen 2016).

Even if he is solution-oriented, he realizes that every addition creates a cost-oriented burden for his business. In this respect, the entrepreneur, who should be a good accountant, never gives up the cost-benefit analysis in his actions. Sometimes rational thought may have to limit his productivity. But sometimes, when no one can act, he brings new solutions to life with his imagination. With his rebellious structure, he always creates solutions for his consumers who are waiting for better and newer alternatives (Henrekson and Sanandaji 2020).

Even when the entrepreneur is on the right path, he ponders why not better. Even if he feels he is doing well, the follow-uppers are enough to make him preoccupied. But as a result, he advances and wins with the value-added production. He invests as he earns, and he earns as he invests. So, he is accepted as a dynamo for the economy because he is a consumer as well as a manufacturer. He is the customer of those who produces other solutions for his solutions. For this reason, he satisfies the customers as well as the producers in the market. This means action/work for the market. Investments increase as business turns into earnings. This also leads to employment (Parker et al. 2012). He also shares his earnings with all his stakeholders. Thus, he contributes to consumption and abundance in the economy (Baumol 1996). It is possible to summarize the story of entrepreneurship that key concepts effort to narrate us. Thus, we are able to create a meaningful structure related to the entrepreneurship system through many concepts that stand alone in the first table.

3 Understanding of Entrepreneurship

To better comprehend the term of entrepreneurs, after mentioning the concept, it is necessary to focus on the environment that the entrepreneur prefers. It should be known that regardless of its size and establishment purpose, every attempt efforts to achieve some goals (Mansoori and Lackéus 2019). The first of all is sustainability. By making lots of plans and taking lots of risks, you really desire the establishment you set up to live with you for a very long time. It is your most natural right to anticipate for this wish in return for the effort you endure. However, there are some points you require to achieve this purpose. You should be able to measure inputs and outputs objectively to ensure sustainability. Otherwise, you will not be able to assess. While evaluating, you expect the performance you have shown to be permanent. This leads you to sustainability again (Molina and García-Morales 2019). What you earn should be more than what you spend, so that your business will not be interrupted.

Secondly, you require focusing on another factor after ensuring sustainability. This comes across as profitability. In a nutshell, just as we have expressed sustainability, your organization deals with some activities to achieve its mission. And to perform this action, you have to face some fixed and variable costs. The most important thing is that your product and service meet with the buyer. Thus, you exchange your power (the product and service) with your customer power (money). So, you can assume this stage as a harvest. However, as stated earlier, if your earnings are less than what you spend and if you cannot be changed this situation even in the long run, then you will encounter a more troublesome concept instead of profit; damage. In order not to encounter this nightmare, you have to do your calculations/analysis very well, which will be explained later.

And the entrepreneur will ultimately require to achieve a much more magical object; growth. If you are doing your job well and the client interests your product, this will be augmented your profitability. And if the result will be crowned with sustainability over time, what you lack is growth. We can illustrate this with an example. You are loved in the market; your consumers are satisfied with your commodities and services. Do you believe that this situation will not spread to other users/customers? Your reputation grows longer, and every buyer comes with new ones. You sell and gain. And your production capacity no longer meets solicitations. The golden idea you need is exactly an extension. If you do not grow, you will not be able to respond to your customers' demands. Of course, you may not desire to serve every client. But why do you not satisfy the ones in your target audience? For this purpose, it is not a poor notion to start new investments and allocate some of your profit to extension possibilities (Acs et al. 2008).

With the progression of the three concepts mentioned preceding, strategic management and entrepreneurship have associated. In this way, companies aim to expand and spread to the market with consumer satisfaction. They try to boost earnings by aiming to over-rated profit on the market. They attempt to provide a sustainable competitive advantage by enhancing their research and development expenditures with their incomes. They are able to realize their long-term plans by displaying a stronger position against their rivals.

4 The Significance of Entrepreneurship

While explaining the concept of entrepreneurship, we talked about some tips. However, we should mention the importance of entrepreneurship in more detail. First, we should mention the contribution of the entrepreneur that adds value to human life. According to economic thought, humankind has unlimited needs. When we consider Maslow's basic needs approach, we see that psychological requirements are as vital as physiological ones. Unfortunately, mankind cannot resolve those demands on its own in today's world. At this stage, the entrepreneur comes into action. First of all, he recognizes people and their interests and proposes solutions. It adds value, differentiates and enriches its environment and human life. It regulates production factors, stimulates and preserves them from inertia. In terms of its consequences, it brings many economic and social developments to human life (Mansoori and Lackéus 2019).

Entrepreneur combines many factors (labor, capital, raw material) to execute production. He works as a chef in this aspect. Sometimes he designs and runs the organization. Sometimes he shoulders all works. He efforts to take place in the competitive market by considering consumer pleasure. For this purpose, he attempts to innovate continuously by using creativity. In this sense, innovation and entrepreneurship generate an inseparable couple. Perhaps they feed each other continuously. Every innovation, every advance also activates other entrepreneurs in the system. When we say new designs, new production methods, new market searches, new raw materials, and newer searches never ends (Ibeh et al. 2019). Production and marketing work without stopping which contributes to the growth of employment (Parker 2012). Although the changes brought by Industry 4.0 are discussed, the requirement for qualified employees maintains.

Economic prosperity and social welfare brought on by entrepreneurship progress (Kalkavan and Ersin 2019; Eti et al. 2020). For this purpose, while discussing the essence of entrepreneurship, it should be examined both economically and socially (Hechavarria et al. 2019). With the creation of employment opportunities in the community, the income distribution transferred to individuals is balanced (Acs and Armington 2004; Zhang et al. 2020). Revenue division per household also makes it more accessible to reach other factors. Looking at opportunities such as better living conditions, education, health, and entertainment, all depend on distributed welfare. With this aspect, as long as there is revenue, there will be a revival in the whole market activities. And entrepreneurship has played a highly critical role in generating and distributing assets (Hediger 2000).

When the literature is examined, it will be seen that these statements are not studied just theoretically. Many researchers have produced articles on the effects of entrepreneurship. Although it is part of the business, it has a function that drives the market. For this reason, it acts as a bridge between the micro and the macro dimensions of the economy (Klapper et al. 2006; Kreiser et al. 2019; Shepherd et al. 2019). There are studies related with macroeconomic variables that also emphasizing entrepreneurship. The macroeconomic factors such as development, unemployment, foreign trade figures, current account balance, inflation, crisis etc. are examined with entrepreneurial activities. When some results of the researches are generalized, it is revealed that both the environments chosen by the entrepreneur are under the influence of these factors, and the contribution of the entrepreneurs to these factors (Braunerhjelm et al. 2010; Wennekers and Thurik 1999; Box et al. 2016; Audretsch et al. 2015; Arin et al. 2015; Nițu-Antonie et al. 2017; Henrekson and Sanandaji 2014; Carree et al. 2007; Devece et al. 2016; Khyareh et al. 2019).

5 Fostering of Entrepreneurship

So far, we effort to explain what the entrepreneur is trying to do and the importance of the term. After mentioning so much, the following questions should come to our mind. Since entrepreneurship is so vital; if we decided to become an entrepreneur, what should we consider to be one of them? What can be the factors that trigger entrepreneurship?

Maybe when you first hear this question, a few answers immediately come to your mind. But when we consider deeply, we can decide that the solution is not as simple as it imagines. When we have remembered the definition of entrepreneurship, we have mentioned that there is no definition that everyone has accepted simply. Then let us ask the enigma again! What should be the guidance to reach entrepreneurship that everyone cannot agree on? Our answer is hidden in the question we asked. The entrepreneur is already unique. So, what makes it original is that it is as distinct from others. His similarity with others pushes him to ordinariness (Özmen 2016).

One of the causes of not perceiving a clear answer is hidden in entrepreneurial species. There are almost 20 kinds of entrepreneurship in literature based on various reasons. While the principal determinants in the formation of certain species are quite apparent in some types and not in others. Also, some common points in similar types attract attention. Starting from this point, it is also worth mentioning some familiar points that will ignite the wick of the entrepreneurial environment (Demirtaş et al. 2017; Özmen 2016; Ergen 2014).

The establishment purpose of the enterprises may be different in determining the mentioned criteria. For example, business and social enterprises can sometimes be established for very different reasons. While commercial enterprises make money and do not share what they earn; social enterprises are established for society and distribute their gains with their environment for increasing the effect. Besides, while success is covered with secrets in commercial enterprises, social enterprises agree to share the success of the gain with everyone.

We effort to point out some key points by focusing on business ventures, as they have vital fundamental differences between social and commercial ones. First, if we consider the entrepreneur as a farmer; we must talk about the soil in which he plants the seed (the idea of the entrepreneur). If you have a crop that needs water to grow and have a waterless field, then it would not be a miracle to say that your effort does not worth money (Ergen 2014).

As in the example of waterless field, if there is not enough production environment; the infrastructure is insufficient; the legal infrastructure to promote products is not developed; economic and political stability is not ensured; intellectual property rights are not deemed substantial; there are not enough financial and other resources in the market or cannot accessed; skilled labor force is not supplied; in such an environment, doing business will be troublesome.

If you are ready to pay the price, you can grow products even in the desert. But if you are in a crucial competition; are struggling in a market filled with equivalent products; hardly satisfy your spoiled customers; feel the pressures of your suppliers make your job more difficult; worry that every newcomer will take something out of your market share; then use your resources effectively and efficiently; you also have to act strategically (Porter 2008).

Both the public and private parties must endeavor in order to turn such a hell into an entrepreneurial ecosystem (Motoyama and Knowlton 2017). Structural reforms are mostly accepted on the shoulder of the state. However, it is not significant to attribute the duties to only the state, and if there are no individuals with an entrepreneurial spirit, it is the waste of resources. Taking the fundamental legal, political and economic preoccupation will facilitate the journey of the entrepreneur (farmer) just like in the instance of land.

Something must have caught your attention so far, we always have talked about environmental factors/necessities about ventures. So, are you ready to talk about the actual source? Now it's time to talk about the farmer, let's talk about the entrepreneur, our hero.

6 Entrepreneurial Mindset

Probably one of the biggest differences between natural sciences and social sciences is that natural ones can reach more precise, more repeatable results. However, one of the most important criteria that take this freedom from the social sciences is to work with the human being. Because the human being is ambivalent, varying in nature and so, it is an enigma. No matter how social science tries to fit it to explain it, it always adheres to limitations to ensure the validity of the results. For all these purposes, the variability in all social sciences reflects the origin of this field, as the main actor of entrepreneurship is human.

It is necessary to consider many determinants to apprehend such a strange, unique, changeable existence and its actions. Otherwise, the results obtained are incomplete to reach the truth and to understand the whole. The richness and comprehension that the holistic approach brings will help us reach the accuracy. With the contributions of diverse disciplines, it is more accessible in completing the puzzle of humans (Gartner 2015). For all these reasons, encouragements from many different fields are required to understand entrepreneurship. Many fields such as business, economics, psychology, sociology, history, geography, etc. tell us about the human, its actions, its interactions (Mitchell et al. 2002).

For this reason, we need a statement that covers both the past and the future of man. This should include both his feelings, thoughts, and actions. It should also reflect his physical and mental abilities. It should tell us his social heritage as well as its genetic characteristics. Without just focusing on environmental influences or psychological factors, can any term provide such a panoramic view, other than the entrepreneurial mindset?

How can we explain the same factors producing different results in different individuals without the concept of mindset? Growing in the same family, receiving the same education, working in the same business area, but reaching different results... Our assistant will be the entrepreneurial mindset. One sees only the problem, and the other sees it as a rare opportunity. To explain this situation, here we utilize from the same concept. The entrepreneur differs from others with his mindset (Gartner 1988). Either he does different work or he does his job differently. He is different in his attitude towards risk, in his action, in motivation. Mathisen and Arnulf (2014) talk about the mindset of recognizing and evaluating opportunities.

When the studies managed for the same purpose in the literature are examined, it is seen that the subject is researched with some different key concepts. For example, some sources concentrated on intentionality and personality traits (Rauch and Frese 2007). However, there have been studies criticizing these subjects. Some researchers stated that these efforts evaluating entrepreneurship should be improved (Davis et al. 2016; Baron 1998). The main criticism here was the inability to apprehend the entire system. Bird (1988) directed the intentionality in the study and prioritized the existence of many factors to reach the action stage. When all the determinants are collected until the stage of action, it is seen that the parts in the definition of mindset

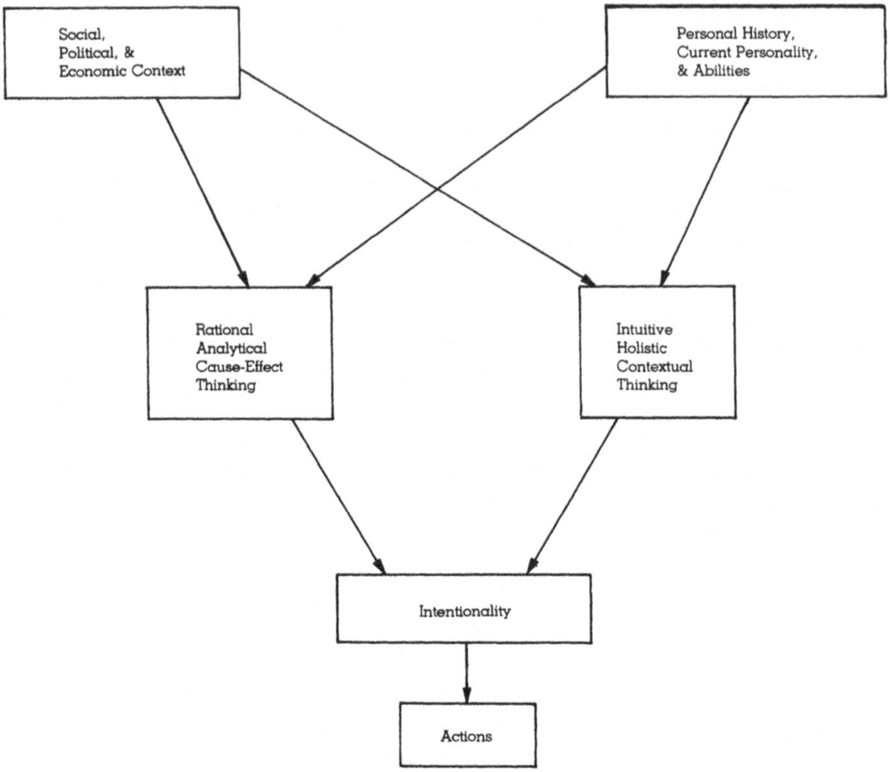

Fig. 1 The context of intentionality (Bird 1988)

appear from that figure. The point should be explained here is whether the intention will be sufficient to take action or not (Fig. 1).

Regarding what to search for the entrepreneurial mindset, we can liken of Bird's shape as a bird. The wing on the left is more rational, more visible factors; that on the right is more individual. A bird can fly with providing both wings must be able to move. In other words, both spiritual and physical effort is required. And for success in entrepreneurship, both lobes of the brain must be activated.

As mentioned in many articles, it should be tried to complete all required physical conditions. On the other hand, the features that will make the entrepreneur powerful should be emphasized. Improvements should be made to the elements that will shape the structure of mindset. Unfortunately, the steps remaining in this section are generally ignored. So, the entrepreneur does not accomplish the desired outcome, despite meeting all visible requirements or imitating a successful model.

Well, if you are asked what is done to reinforce the deficiencies, it is required to start at the beginning, that is, from the family. If we want to raise entrepreneurial individuals, it is essential to raise kids confident, free and equipped. It is crucial to direct children according to their talents and goals. In schools, education and development should be programmed according to requirements (Miller 2002).

Principally, we must allow the individual to discover himself. A person who is aware of his own abilities can prefer the accurate target and reach his target more smoothly. This means the evaluation of intellectual capital. If you pay attention, we do not talk about a goal like everyone should be an entrepreneur. Simply a person should realize that whether he can intentionally be an entrepreneur or not.

It is useful to remind some issues in terms of contributing to this point. Culture has an important contribution to the coding mindset. For this reason, the step to entrepreneurial activities is easy in some societies, but not in others. Since the culture is not very simple to change, the notifications should be more comprehensive. Or one should recognize the social heritage reflected on his behavior and mentality and take precautions accordingly (Miller 2002).

In addition to this matter, we should raise the motivational issue (Zhao et al. 2010). We should also notice the feelings and prejudices that affect the person's motivation and actions. Some studies are examining the relationship of these subjects with entrepreneurship. Some researches prove the effects of prejudices and fears on entrepreneurship (Collins 2007). This declares to us that non-physical concepts are as effective as physical ones on entrepreneurship (Deniz et al. 2011).

As an example, prejudices can affect individuals both positively and sometimes negatively. Due to the negative memories he experienced in the past, individuals may experience pessimism (McKenna 1993). This prevents them from shaking their confidence and making plans. Or vice versa, past successes cause overconfidence, resulting in negligence of potential hazards (Morris et al. 2002). Since the precaution is not taken, the damage becomes very severe when the risk occurs (Lerner and Keltner 2001).

To put it another way, fear has bilateral effects just like biases. When the individual faces fear, he either runs away, freezes or fights. What is important in this circumstance is the perception and management of fear. Even if they have not been experienced in the past, fears learned or inherited can affect the actions of the individual. In positions where fear cannot be deal with, it can cause an individual to lose control. As a result, failure can occur. On the other hand, as a consequence of fear control, the person takes precautions without facing the potential danger, either avoiding the risk or preventing the damage from reaching destructive dimensions. Since there are many different reasons for fear, one should not always consider negative experiences. Sometimes individuals may hesitate to lose what they have (Gerrig et al. 2010). This can also motivate them and cause them to effort more (Cacciotti and Hayton 2015).

7 Conclusion

Entrepreneurship has become an indispensable place for economies in today's world. Every contribution that supports entrepreneurship affects the country's economy. Entrepreneurship will contribute to macro issues such as current balance, terms of trade, economic stability, inflation, and unemployment. For this reason, entrepreneurship may be among the factors that should be emphasized to be prominent in the global competitive market (Acs 2006).

We talked about the factors that will contribute to the development of entrepreneurship. Entrepreneurial activities should be encouraged by structural arrangements (Thurik 2009). Contribution to ecosystems should be provided to support structuring (Isenberg 2010). This contribution should be shared by both the state and the private sector.

Furthermore, individuals should be focused on. Intellectual capital should be used more efficiently and effectively. Entrepreneurial education should be organized (Cheung and Chan 2011). Individuals should be trained to be more creative and courageous (DeTienne and Chandler 2004). This training should give not only in schools but also in houses. We have stated that issues such as culture, personality, perceptions, fears, and prejudices are at least as valuable as other entrepreneurial requirements (George and Zahra 2002).

References

Acs, Z. (2006). How is entrepreneurship good for economic growth? *Innovations: Technology, Governance, Globalization, 1*(1), 97–107.

Acs, Z., & Armington, C. (2004). Employment growth and entrepreneurial activity in cities. *Regional Studies, 38*(8), 911–927.

Acs, Z. J., Desai, S., & Hessels, J. (2008). Entrepreneurship, economic development and institutions. *Small Business Economics, 31*(3), 219–234.

Anderson, B. S., Wennberg, K., & McMullen, J. S. (2019). Enhancing quantitative theory-testing entrepreneurship research. *Journal of Business Venturing, 34*(5), 105928.

Arin, K. P., Huang, V. Z., Minniti, M., Nandialath, A. M., & Reich, O. F. (2015). Revisiting the determinants of entrepreneurship: A Bayesian approach. *Journal of Management, 41*(2), 607–631.

Audretsch, D. B., Belitski, M., & Desai, S. (2015). Entrepreneurship and economic development in cities. *The Annals of Regional Science, 55*(1), 33–60.

Baron, R. A. (1998). Cognitive mechanisms in entrepreneurship: Why and when enterpreneurs think differently than other people. *Journal of Business Venturing, 13*(4), 275–294.

Baumol, W. J. (1996). Entrepreneurship: Productive, unproductive, and destructive. *Journal of Business Venturing, 11*(1), 3–22.

Bird, B. (1988). Implementing entrepreneurial ideas: The case for intention. *Academy of Management Review, 13*(3), 442–453.

Box, M., Lin, X., & Gratzer, K. (2016). Linking entrepreneurship and economic growth in Sweden, 1850–2000. In *Contemporary entrepreneurship* (pp. 31–49). Cham: Springer.

Braunerhjelm, P., Acs, Z. J., Audretsch, D. B., & Carlsson, B. (2010). The missing link: Knowledge diffusion and entrepreneurship in endogenous growth. *Small Business Economics, 34*(2), 105–125.

Cacciotti, G., & Hayton, J. C. (2015). Fear and entrepreneurship: A review and research agenda. *International Journal of Management Reviews, 17*(2), 165–190.

Carree, M., Van Stel, A., Thurik, R., & Wennekers, S. (2007). The relationship between economic development and business ownership revisited. *Entrepreneurship & Regional Development, 19* (3), 281–291.

Cheung, C. K., & Chan, R. Y. C. (2011). The introduction of entrepreneurship education to school leavers in a vocational institute. *International Journal of Scientific Research in Education, 4*(1), 8–16.

Collins, D. D. (2007). *Entrepreneurial success: The effect of fear on human performance*. Doctoral dissertation, Capella University.

Davis, M. H., Hall, J. A., & Mayer, P. S. (2016). Developing a new measure of entrepreneurial mindset: Reliability, validity, and implications for practitioners. *Consulting Psychology Journal: Practice and Research, 68*(1), 21.

Demirtaş, Ö., Mehmet, B., & Mustafa, K. (2017). *Başarılı Girişimciliğin Perde Arkasındaki Güçler*. Konya: Eğitim Yayınevi.

Deniz, N., Boz, İ. T., & Ertosun, Ö. G. (2011). The relationship between entrepreneur's level of perceived business-related fear and business performance. *Procedia-Social and Behavioral Sciences, 24*, 579–600.

DeTienne, D. R., & Chandler, G. N. (2004). Opportunity identification and its role in the entrepreneurial classroom: A pedagogical approach and empirical test. *Academy of Management Learning & Education, 3*(3), 242–257.

Devece, C., Peris-Ortiz, M., & Rueda-Armengot, C. (2016). Entrepreneurship during economic crisis: Success factors and paths to failure. *Journal of Business Research, 69*(11), 5366–5370.

Dinçer, H., Yüksel, S., & Pınarbaşı, F. (2020). Kano-based measurement of customer expectations in retail service industry using IT2 DEMATEL-QUALIFLEX. In *Handbook of research on positive organizational behavior for improved workplace performance* (pp. 349–370). Hershey, PA: IGI Global.

Drucker, P. (2014). *Innovation and entrepreneurship*. New York: Routledge.

Ergen, M. (2014). *Girişimci Kapital, Silikon Vadisi Tarihi ve Startup Ekonomisi*. İstanbul: Koç Üniversitesi Yayınları.

Eti, S., Kalkavan, H., Dinçer, H., & Yüksel, S. (2020). Predicting the role of Islamic banking on sustainable economic development: An analysis for Turkey with ARIMA model. In *Handbook of research on creating sustainable value in the global economy* (pp. 146–164). Hershey, PA: IGI Global.

Gartner, W. B. (1988). "Who is an entrepreneur?" Is the wrong question. *American Journal of Small Business, 12*(4), 11–32.

Gartner, B. (2015). Arts entrepreneurship: Scope, practice and community. *Artivate: A Journal of Entrepreneurship in the Arts, 4*(2), 3–6.

George, G., & Zahra, S. A. (2002). Culture and its consequences for entrepreneurship. *Entrepreneurship Theory and Practice, 26*(4), 5–8.

Gerrig, R. J., Zimbardo, P. G., Zimbardo, P. G., Psychologue, E. U., & Zimbardo, P. G. (2010). *Psychology and life* (Vol. 20). Boston: Pearson.

Godley, A., & Casson, M. (2010). History of entrepreneurship: Britain, 1900–2000. In D. S. Landes, J. Mokyr, & W. J. Baumol (Eds.), *The invention of enterprise: Entrepreneurship from ancient mesopotamia to modern times* (p. 243). Princeton, NJ: Princeton University Press.

Hébert, R. F., & Link, A. N. (2009). *A history of entrepreneurship*. London: Routledge.

Hechavarria, D., Bullough, A., Brush, C., & Edelman, L. (2019). High-growth women's entrepreneurship: Fueling social and economic development.

Hediger, W. (2000). Sustainable development and social welfare. *Ecological Economics, 32*(3), 481–492.

Henrekson, M., & Sanandaji, T. (2014). Small business activity does not measure entrepreneurship. *Proceedings of the National Academy of Sciences, 111*(5), 1760–1765.
Henrekson, M., & Sanandaji, T. (2020). Measuring entrepreneurship: Do established metrics capture high-impact Schumpeterian entrepreneurship? *Entrepreneurship Theory and Practice*, 1042258719844500.
Huda, M., Qodriah, S. L., Rismayadi, B., Hananto, A., Kardiyati, E. N., Ruskam, A., & Nasir, B. M. (2019). Towards cooperative with competitive alliance: Insights into performance value in social entrepreneurship. In *Creating business value and competitive advantage with social entrepreneurship* (pp. 294–317). Hershey, PA: IGI Global.
Ibeh, K., Crick, D., & Etemad, H. (2019). International marketing knowledge and international entrepreneurship in the contemporary multi speed global economy. *International Marketing Review, 36*(1), 2–5.
Isenberg, D. J. (2010). How to start an entrepreneurial revolution. *Harvard Business Review, 88*(6), 40–50.
Kalkavan, H., & Ersin, I. (2019). Determination of factors affecting the South East Asian crisis of 1997 probit-logit panel regression: The South East Asian crisis. In *Handbook of research on global issues in financial communication and investment decision making* (pp. 148–167). Hershey, PA: IGI Global.
Khyareh, M. M., Khair, M., & Torabi, H. (2019). Macroeconomic effects of entrepreneurship: Evidences from factor, efficiency and innovation driven countries. *International Journal of Entrepreneurship, 23*(1), 1–11.
Kirzner, I. M. (1997). Entrepreneurial discovery and the competitive market process: An Austrian approach. *Journal of Economic Literature, 35*(1), 60–85.
Klapper, L., Laeven, L., & Rajan, R. (2006). Entry regulation as a barrier to entrepreneurship. *Journal of Financial Economics, 82*(3), 591–629.
Kreiser, P. M., Kuratko, D. F., Covin, J. G., Ireland, R. D., & Hornsby, J. S. (2019). Corporate entrepreneurship strategy: Extending our knowledge boundaries through configuration theory. *Small Business Economics*, 1–20.
Lerner, J. S., & Keltner, D. (2001). Fear, anger, and risk. *Journal of Personality and Social Psychology, 81*(1), 146.
Mansoori, Y., & Lackéus, M. (2019). Comparing effectuation to discovery-driven planning, prescriptive entrepreneurship, business planning, lean startup, and design thinking. *Small Business Economics*, 1–28.
Mathisen, J. E., & Arnulf, J. K. (2014). Entrepreneurial mindsets: Theoretical foundations and empirical properties of a mindset scale. *International Journal of Management and Business, 5* (1), 84–107.
McKenna, F. P. (1993). It won't happen to me: Unrealistic optimism or illusion of control? *British Journal of Psychology, 84*(1), 39–50.
Miller, P. H. (2002). *Theories of developmental psychology*. New York: Macmillan.
Mitchell, R. K., Busenitz, L., Lant, T., McDougall, P. P., Morse, E. A., & Smith, J. B. (2002). Toward a theory of entrepreneurial cognition: Rethinking the people side of entrepreneurship research. *Entrepreneurship Theory and Practice, 27*(2), 93–104.
Molina, L. M., & García-Morales, V. J. (2019). Combined influence of absorptive capacity and corporate entrepreneurship on performance. *Sustainability, 11*(11), 1–26.
Morris, C. G., Ayvaşık, H. B., & Sayıl, M. (2002). Psikolojiyi anlamak. Türk Psikologlar Derneği.
Motoyama, Y., & Knowlton, K. (2017). Examining the connections within the startup ecosystem: A case study of St. Louis. *Entrepreneurship Research Journal, 7*(1), 1–32.
Nițu-Antonie, R. D., Feder, E. S., & Munteanu, V. P. (2017). Macroeconomic effects of entrepreneurship from an international perspective. *Sustainability, 9*(7), 1159.
Özmen, İ. (2016). Girişimcilik Kavramı ve Girişimciliğin Gelişimi. In K. Çatı (Ed.), *Girişimcilik ve İnovasyon Yönetimi*. Ankara: Nobel Akademik Yayıncılık.
Parker, S. C. (2012). Theories of entrepreneurship, innovation and the business cycle. *Journal of Economic Surveys, 26*(3), 377–394.

Parker, S. C., Congregado, E., & Golpe, A. A. (2012). Is entrepreneurship a leading or lagging indicator of the business cycle? Evidence from UK self-employment data. *International Small Business Journal, 30*(7), 736–753.

Porter, M. E. (2008). The five competitive forces that shape strategy. *Harvard Business Review, 86* (1), 25–40.

Rauch, A., & Frese, M. (2007). Let's put the person back into entrepreneurship research: A meta-analysis on the relationship between business owners' personality traits, business creation, and success. *European Journal of Work and Organizational Psychology, 16*(4), 353–385.

Schumpeter, J. (2003). Theorie der wirtschaftlichen Entwicklung. In *Joseph Alois Schumpeter* (pp. 5–59). Boston, MA: Springer.

Shepherd, D. A., Wennberg, K., Suddaby, R., & Wiklund, J. (2019). What are we explaining? A review and agenda on initiating, engaging, performing, and contextualizing entrepreneurship. *Journal of Management, 45*(1), 159–196.

Thurik, A. R. (2009). Entreprenomics: Entrepreneurship, economic growth and policy. *Entrepreneurship, Growth and Public Policy, 10*(6), 219–249.

Wennekers, S., & Thurik, R. (1999). Linking entrepreneurship and economic growth. *Small Business Economics, 13*(1), 27–56.

Wood, M. S., & McKelvie, A. (2015). Opportunity evaluation as future focused cognition: Identifying conceptual themes and empirical trends. *International Journal of Management Reviews, 17*(2), 256–277.

Zhang, G., Zhou, S., Xia, X., Yüksel, S., Baş, H., & Dincer, H. (2020). Strategic mapping of youth unemployment with interval-valued intuitionistic hesitant fuzzy DEMATEL based on 2-tuple linguistic values. *IEEE Access, 8*, 25706–25721.

Zhao, H., Seibert, S. E., & Lumpkin, G. T. (2010). The relationship of personality to entrepreneurial intentions and performance: A meta-analytic review. *Journal of Management, 36*(2), 381–404.

Transaction Cost Theory

Kudret Celtekligil

Abstract The transaction cost theory focuses on how economic changes are managed the transaction cost theory based on economic operations as the level of analysis is based on limited rationality, opportunism. Transactions are settled within the organizational structure according to their characteristics. These characteristics are stated as uncertainty, frequency, asset characteristics and conformity. As the uncertainty and the need for specific assets increase, the risk of transaction increases. When the dangers of processing are negligible, the least cost-effective management will be preferred as the risk increases, the cost will increase and organizations will develop different methods to reduce costs. At this point, organizations aim to establish management mechanisms that minimize transaction costs, develop specific strategies and develop mechanisms where processes can be structured. This theory deals with the frequency of transactions associated with resources, its appropriateness for the organization, the extent of uncertainty, if any, and the extent to which the resource is specific; These are all factors that increase the transaction costs the use of non-specific assets, vertical integration, long-term contracts, partial ownership agreements and contracts that require parties to invest at the same level are different methods used by organizations to reduce transaction costs.

1 Introduction

The transaction cost theory, which includes the study subject, is the starting point of literature in 1937 by Ronald Coase's transaction Nature of the Firm. By pointing out the effect of Coase's transaction costs on the firm and other institutions, it has linked the market and the company hierarchy, and explained the alternative management models and revealed the costs associated with the operation of the price mechanism (Coase 1937). Transaction cost theory plays a very important role in determining

K. Celtekligil (✉)
Beykent University, Sarıyer, İstanbul, Turkey
e-mail: kcelteklig il@gmail.com

H. Dincer, S. Yüksel (eds.), *Strategic Priorities in Competitive Environments*,
Contributions to Management Science, https://doi.org/10.1007/978-3-030-45023-6_8

how rights are allocated in the economy. In this respect, the processes are not actually the transfer of a property or an object, but a transfer of many complex rights. Therefore, transaction costs are related to the change of rights (Coase 1998). Then, in the Theory of Transaction Costs developed by Oliver Williamson (1975), the study by Coase was elaborated and it was tried to explain that the costs of the internal transactions of the enterprises may be lower than the market purchases due to the factors. Unlike the work of Coase (1937), Williamson (1975) used the concept of Co-hierarchy "instead of" organization (Coase 1998).

They are widely known in the transaction cost theories which are called governance mechanisms. On the other hand, the transaction cost theory is mainly productivity oriented and seeks the answer to whether the efficiency of the transactions will be greater in the business or in the market. Accordingly, it is decided to produce the product or service within the enterprise or to purchase it externally. In theory, this is called as making or buying decision. Transaction cost theory defines the production and transaction costs of using the market, the costs associated with producing a product or providing services to a market, the cost of production, and the exchange between the buyer and the seller as the transaction cost. It is possible to list the transaction costs as costs arising from market research, costs related to the contract process, costs related to performance monitoring, cost of legal procedure, opportunity cost (Williamson 1998).

When entering the international market, businesses must operate at low cost to compete with businesses in the local country. With the transaction costs analysis, it is tried to explain the costs that the transactions entering the international market must endure. However, the costs of the enterprises can be immeasurable due to the costs produced by the agencies in which they co-exist (Hennart 2001). On the other hand, the benefits of co-operation in enterprises in international market activities are more profitable than competing with each other. For example, in the event that the entity has decided to enter the international market by licensing the resource undertaking costs are eliminated, it may be possible for the enterprise it is licensed to exhibit in future competitive activities, and this is taken into account in the calculation of costs in the transaction costs analysis (Hill et al. 1990). In addition, transaction cost theory sets out two assumptions that limit business by identifying business behavior. These are limited rationality and opportunism.

2 Assumptions of Transaction Cost Theory

Transaction cost theory is based on the assumption that people try to maximize their interests and businesses profit. In their efforts to achieve these goals, proxies/ intermediaries have limited rationality and sometimes engage in opportunistic behavior (Williamson 1988).

2.1 Limited Rationality

Although decision-makers aim to make rational decisions, they may be limited to their limited ability to process and communicate and may not be able to evaluate all possible decision alternatives. In this assumption, the individual is equipped with less power in analytical and data processing devices, unlike the economic man definition of the neoclassical economy (Lipman 1991). Limited rationality includes meanings for contract design, which is a formal governance issue (Haltiwanger and Waldman 1989). When the conventions are designed incompletely due to limited rationality, the emergence of any uncertainty may necessitate re-negotiation of contracts, thereby encouraging opportunistic action by re-interpreting the terms of the contract in the interest of one of the parties (Foss 2005). At the same time, while many exchange relations include incomplete, defective or asymmetric information, it is far from being credible to suggest that all relevant cause and effect relationships in contract design can be defined. Asymmetry of information occurs when the parties keep their true intentions before the contract or during the contract process and thus lead to opportunistic behavior in two ways: wrong choice and moral hazard (Akerlof 1970). The wrong choice is caused by confidential information prior to the contract, while the moral hazard is an asymmetric information problem that occurs as a result of the secret actions taken after the contract is signed. Asymmetry of pre-contractual information and the asymmetric information problems, which are labeled as post-contract information asymmetry respectively, provide incentives for pre-contractual opportunism and/or post-contractual opportunism depending on the opportunistic behavior they cause. On the other hand, if one of the parties to the contract encounters submerged costs in investment in specific assets, it is possible that the other party will gain profit from the investment with the threat of withdrawal from the relationship by showing opportunistic behavior and this is called quasi rent (Williamson 1975). In case of high fixed costs of submerged nature, it is difficult for the company to get out of the industry in case of short term damages. In the contracts concerning transaction-specific or relationship-specific investments, one of the parties tries to impose the disadvantaged new provisions on the other side in accordance with their own interests after the contract has been concluded, or does not want to carry out their acts. In transaction cost terminology, processing-specific assets create a collateral problem, which requires the use of mechanisms that hinder opportunistic action or encourage the continuity of the relationship (Zylbersztajn 2018). Other sources of opportunism are relationship-specific factors. A factor that encourages opportunism is the mismatch between the objectives of the buyer and the supplier. Differentiated interests cause one side not to be fully connected to the relationship. Another critical factor is the high gains from opportunistic activities, and such situations create reluctance to act in accordance with written agreements. Also, opportunism can be caused by the lack of commitments to maintain a long-term interaction. The concept of rationality is seen in three steps in the literature. Limited rationality is at medium level. The rationality assumption, in this respect, differentiates transaction cost theory from traditional economic models that assume that other information can be reached from every point of the market (Bahli and Suzanne 2003). The assumption of limited rationality in the transaction cost theory of Simon (1979) suggests that economic actors are rational as intentions but these rationalities are limited in practice. Individuals have limited capabilities in obtaining, storing, retrieving this information, and processing information without error. The limited level of rationality depends on the knowledge and capabilities of the buyer (organization) to determine the conditions, select the appropriate supplier, arrange a firm contract, manage and control the supplier (Fehr and Tyran 2008). The organization cannot predict all future situations during the determination of the conditions.

For these reasons, it is more appropriate to consider the decision-making process as a selection process in which satisfactory results are obtained with limited knowledge, rather than being considered as a realistic selection process that offers the best results. Satisfaction means that the minimum requirements for accepting a result are satisfied. In this respect, instead of the best result in realistic approach, satisfying results are obtained in limited rationality. In his later work, Williamson associated the notion of 'forward-thinking' with limited rationality. They may have limited rationality, but they can determine the limits of their rationality (Rabin 2013). The proxies who have advanced opinions can foresee the unexpected situations that their limited rationalities can create by considering the possibilities of future events and arranging the operations accordingly.

On the other hand, According to the transaction cost theory, high levels of environmental uncertainty increase the adaptation costs of contractual agreements (Rindfleisch 2019). The aim of the organizations is to reduce the costs of the sources of change in the environment and the costs of administrative changes within the organization. According to Williamson (1991), adaptation is the main problem of economic organization. It does not distinguish between Hayek (1945) and Barnard's (1938) adaptation perspectives, and argues that these two types of adaptation point of view are useful for different forms of governance. In responding to price changes, individual participants can demonstrate the right action because the market miracle is based on the principle that, individual participants need little information to get the right position. This type of adaptation is called autonomous adaptation. This is based on neoclassical thinking, in which consumers and producers respond independently to parametric price changes to maximize their benefits and profits. According to Coase (1937), market participants can access incomplete and complete information at any time point as far as they can afford their current costs. Due to the information constraint, companies may not be able to maximize their behavior or optimize their goals. This non-perfect information causes certain degrees of uncertainty in their behavior, achieving their goals and objectives, which the company can not anticipate. There are two ways to eliminate uncertainty in the partner's future behavior. The first may spend resources on obtaining additional information to eliminate transaction uncertainty, and the second, by making a decision based on the available information (Sharland 1993).

2.2 Opportunism

According to the transaction cost theory, any party in the exchange relationship is likely to be opportunistic, and opportunism is defined as the pursuit of self-interest by deceit. The meaning of personal interest has been extended as, reasonable efforts that lead to falsification, manipulation, deceit and deception, misleading, altering, obscuring or other distortions of knowledge. In practice, violations of open or closed commitments such as failure and loss of fulfillment of promises and sanctions are also considered within this scope Information asymmetry, governance problems caused by the characteristics of the process, and relationship-specific factors can be defined as determinants of opportunistic behavior (Jap and Anderson 2003). According to Williamson (1998), opportunism, sometimes subtly, involves bad behaviors such as lying, robbery and deception in the efforts to increase personal interests, but on the basis of being transferred to the missing and wrong at the expense of the other party in economic transactions such as contracts is an act of personal interest. It does not mean that people will profit from opportunism, but this acceptance causes companies to strive to minimize their opportunistic behavior.

There are positive and negative consequences caused by opportunistic behavior: creating a cost and creating sanctions against this situation are the main negative consequences. It is one of the positive results if it provides determination of the features related to the transaction. On the other hand, the transaction cost approach assumes that some actors have an opportunistic approach, rather than assuming that all of the economic actors are constantly opportunistic, but that the distinction of which is not opportunistic is costly. On the other hand, Opportunism includes not transferring information accurately and accurately in economic transactions such as contracts, in a manner that protects the interests of proxies. In the transaction cost approach, the economic actors' preferences for some governance mechanisms are taken as the basis for the assumptions of these opportunistic behaviors. An example of a market governance system rather than a hierarchical governance system, which will reduce this in the face of transactional problems that can create with limited rationality and opportunism. On the other hand, if the established market governance system is not effective in solving the aforementioned transaction problems, it can be decided to switch to a hierarchical governance system with a higher cost than this system. While there arc many buyers and sellers in the market, product performance and quality can be easily controlled, and while the market penetration limits are low in relation, there are few opportunities for companies to act opportunically. However, as market conditions begin to differ from those mentioned above, opportunism increases. Opportunity is "pursuing their own interests" and all economic representatives deceive outside of contractual imperatives whenever they are given or given the opportunity. This acceptance does not always lead to the conclusion that firms will make extra profit from opportunism, but this acceptance causes firms to pursue their partners' opportunity to minimize their opportunistic behavior. So many alternatives and low exchange costs are just two of them (Sharland 1993). These two acceptance firms restrict, guide and guide their activities. Firms take security measures to eliminate the dangers posed by opportunism, while pursuing to reduce limited rationality. The recommended firm can overcome opportunism by improving knowledge, that is, by eliminating limited rationality. For this reason, firms frequently set up infrastructures in their contracts to reduce access to information and opportunism (Sharland 1993).

3 Transaction Costs in Transactions Cost Theory

The assumptions of the transaction cost theory in the previous heading of the study were primarily the constraints of organizational activities related to the transaction cost economy. The process measures and qualities in the transaction cost economy direct this theory. According to Williamson the main dimensions of transaction costs are asset specificity, uncertainty and frequency. These factors are decisive in the formation of transaction costs (Williamson 1988).

3.1 Asset Specificity

According to Williamson (1988), which defines the transaction cost as the most important of the transaction criteria affecting the asset, the authenticity is related to the degree to which a transaction can be offered to alternative users depending on the alternative usage types without losing value during the realization of a transaction. Asset specificity refers to the economic value of the resource (physical or human) other than the relevant transaction. If the machine that produces the products is produced in one brand and one series, this is a sign that the specificity of that machine is very high (Sharland 1993). The height of the specificity in an asset is specific to the transaction and does not have value for another process. If the activity or property does not have a structure that requires technical/specific skills or knowledge, the uniqueness of the asset is in question. Aubert et al. (2004) reported that increased asset specificity led to an increase in transaction costs. The service provider wishes to guarantee the original equipment, personnel, location, time, brand investment, long-term contract guarantee, shipment volume guarantee and certain contractual clauses; It is reported that the transactions in the transactions with high asset specificity have been damaged when such articles in the contract are not fulfilled. In such cases, the beneficiary is faced with contractual penalties and the service provider's investment for this organization is wasted. In order to prevent additional transaction costs such as this, it is seen that the enterprises tend to internalize the transactions with high asset specificity. On the other hand, Any firm needs to highly protect any specific asset it invests in, meaning that the firm loses potential losses and potential opportunities. Asset specificity are assets that are specially prepared for a particular transaction, and their parties are not easy to redistribute or deal outside their relationships. This unique condition of the entity raises security problems, and the competition of the market does not prevent this opportunistic exploitation (Geyskens et al. 2006). The Firm normally guarantees contracts against change if it needs to invest in a specific asset (Sharland 1993). Firms carry out serious infrastructure analysis in the investment of materials with assets. Unfortunately, traditional economic models do not have such requirements with investments. Asset specificity is therefore an important difference between the two economic approaches. Traditional economic models do not consider it necessary to analyze product-specific requirements and attributes, because all outputs are standard. Investing in specific assets is an important part of sustaining the lives of companies both positively and negatively. From a positive perspective, specific assets invested provide high returns, the ability to respond to a wide range of customer demands.

The high asset specificity may cause a lock-in effect to occur in a process. In the economic literature, the lock-in describes how a customer is dependent on the supplier for products and services. The addiction is so advanced that the customer cannot turn to any other supplier without having to undergo high transit costs (switching cost). As the authenticity of the asset increases, the degree of substitution of the asset and therefore of the transaction decreases, which in turn increases the two-way dependence and contractual hazards between the parties. The approach suggests that transactions with low asset specificity will be appropriate to be managed under the market structure and transactions with high asset specificity should be managed by hierarchical structuring. In order to prevent the threats of opportunistic behavior, which are increased by highly original assets, it may be necessary to try to turn the articles into favorable articles or to make the transactions within the organization. It is also possible to increase the costs associated with the transaction in the market with the increase in specificity in the asset due to the fact that the establishment of contracts that contain sound collateral for the protection of the original assets affects the costs of ensuring compliance, monitoring and compliance with the contract conditions (Williamson 1991).

The authenticity of the entity is, in particular, those prepared for a particular transaction. Asset uniqueness refers to the economic value of the resource outside the relevant process. The authenticity of the asset shows significant investments that are rarely seen or not present for any other process except for the process in which they are original (Anderson and Gerbing 1988). If the activity or property does not have a structure that requires technical/specific skills or knowledge, the uniqueness of the asset is low. As the authenticity of the asset increases, the transaction cost of the organization increases; the number of trade partners and the bargaining power of the organization are reduced (Bunduchi 2005). It is a structure whose asset specificity can be measured with four variables. The first is product complexity. Simple parts are often sold successfully by market suppliers. However, complex components, modules, and finished products require intensive coaching, thoughtful supplier development, and time-consuming transfer of information. Second, product and supplier strategic importance is measured as the reason for transaction costs. If a product or supplier is important to a buyer, the buyer tries to strengthen the buyer-supplier relationship. Strategic importance may be related to single-source situations, the supplier with special technical competence, the finished product due to delivery conditions, or intermediate special requirements due to sub-production processes. Third, special assets for the production provided by the buyer determine transaction costs. The buyer invests in supplier-specific machines, auxiliary parts and tools and further increases processing costs. Fourth, its expertise in international trade affects the effective management of the global supply chain. This variable is related to the size of the company and the existence of markets where accepted local purchases are made. Long distances initiated by small and medium-sized buyers can create big additional efforts in the global supply chain.

According to Williamson, there are 6 different originalities. These; place specificity, physical specificity, specificity of human resources, brand names, dedicated assets and temporal originality.

Place Specificity: The place where the assets are located is special. In other words, if the elements that make up the production and/or service process require to be arranged in stages following each other, the originality of the place in the transaction is concerned.

Physical Specificity: It is the special nature of the physical structure of assets. When a supplier of products and/or services needs to invest in special equipment to meet the specific requirements of customers, physical authenticity is in question.

Branded assets: The positive image/reputation that makes an asset attractive.

Dedicated assets: Valuable investments that cannot be made outside of a specific transaction. To fulfill a commitment to serve a large customer. Specific materials, working procedures or systems are sources such as software.

Temporal Specificity: The fact that assets are related to time. Temporal originality, a process that requires completion in a very short time, the completion of the parties to be completed for a variety of reasons cannot be completed.

3.2 Uncertainty

It is called the difficulty situation in predicting the possible occurrences of a process. Uncertainty according to Coase (1937); individuals cannot have the ability to foresee the future. Businesses can internalize transactions within the control of uncertainty or try to minimize the uncertainties in contracts by careful study. It is desirable that the costs and benefits of outsourcing contracts are explained in a logical manner. In cases of high uncertainty, the process in the realization of the contract is likely to be very costly, as it may contain substances with very complicated conditions. Instead of dealing with such costs that can be created by the process of making the contract, businesses can choose to carry out their transactions within themselves. Williamson (1991) mentions two types of uncertainty. The primary type defines uncertainty as masking and deflecting information, including unforeseen behavioral changes between partners and associated with utilitarianism.

If the business partner can observe this type of uncertainty is low, if the business partner's behavior cannot predict for future situations, the primary type of uncertainty is high. The second type of uncertainty, rather than environmental factors, which are accidentally caused by the lack of strategic importance, such as inflation, demand uncertainty includes situations. In cases where uncertainty increases in transaction cost theory, it is assumed that transactions will be more likely to be provided with internal resources, in other words, no outsourcing will be used or less will be applied. Uncertainty includes four different variables. Regulatory uncertainty is the first of these. It is about rapid changes in the global supply chain. Constantly changing value added tax refunds are examples of regulatory uncertainties in China. Local dependencies make it easy and accurate to access information. The second is price variables. The most important ones are labor and raw materials. The third is foreign currency risks. In particular, currency fluctuations increase due to crises. Supplier unpredictability is the fourth factor affecting transaction costs in terms of uncertainty. In developing markets, especially in fast growing companies, business relations can be canceled due to strategic arrangements. It can be integrated into the model in cultural uncertainty. However, it was not effective in research (Bremen et al. 2010).

3.3 Frequency

The frequency of how often the transactions are performed is related to the economies of scale. The frequency of procedures has many effects. Increasing the frequency of transactions provides opportunities for evaluating the product/service that an enterprise puts in, creating the behaviors it wants on the suppliers and reducing the operational risks. Another effect relates to the size and form of the organization. At this point, the theory predicts: the increase in the amount of products/services to be procured reduces the low productivity and cost-effectiveness of in-house production. In case the requirements reach high levels compared to market size, the economies of scale should be taken into consideration. As a result, the integration of elements by large enterprises is more likely than that of small enterprises. In this direction; In the transaction cost approach, it is assumed that in cases where the frequency increases, transactions will be more likely to be provided with internal resources, in other words, the use of outsourcing will not be used or less will be applied. On the other hand, Management does not establish schemes that include special installation and maintenance costs for operations where seldom occurring opportunity and potential losses are high. Frequency also brings uncertainty. When high performance is expected in the future, it brings about opportunistic behavior in uncertainty. As a result, organizations should establish their contracts not only on institutional knowledge, but also on situations that arise from opportunism and deviations from expectations (Sharland 1993).

4 Integrating Transaction Cost Theory with Other Outstanding Theoretical Perspectives

4.1 Transaction Cost Theory and Strategic Alliances

The focus of the transaction costs approach is the way in which economic changes are managed. The transaction cost approach based on economic transaction cost theory focuses on difficult complex situations, including non-material capital, fixed assets and even capital structure. The cost variable provides a tremendous benefit in the routine and non-routine decisions of a business. The main advantage of this is that it creates a realistic basis for the cost variable and shows exactly where the costs are entered. As internalization effectively controls transaction costs, this is preferred when the transaction cost of a trade is high. On the other hand, market changes tend to process costs but avoid production costs, so that when transaction costs are low and production costs are high. Strategic alliances have combined the characteristics of internal change and market changes because they have partially internalized a change. As a result, researchers suggest that alliances will be preferred when a currency-related transaction costs is not high enough to justify medium and vertical integration. Given that alliances reflect semi-internalization, internalization has a slightly different understanding that internal alliances can be justified when more cost-effective, but different types of constraints prohibit full internalization (Das and Teng 2000). Transaction costs represent a cost incurred in carrying out inter-organizational transactions, such as contract costs, but also include costs such as stocking, coordinating and learning, including raw materials required for production (Das and Teng 2000). Organizations fall into an alliance to reduce these costs. In the economy of transaction costs, alliances are seen as intermediate forms that unite the market and hierarchy, and organizations make alliances to bring economic and production costs together. Costs arising from procurement, production processes, limiting the use of the market and trading based on relations can be considered among the reasons leading alliances.

4.2 Transaction Cost Theory and Resource Dependence Theory

Transaction cost theory focuses on how economic changes are managed. The transaction cost theory based on economic operations as the level of analysis is based on limited rationality opportunism (March and Simon 1958). Transactions are settled within the organizational structure according to their characteristics. These characteristics are stated as uncertainty, frequency, asset characteristics and conformity. As the uncertainty and the need for specific assets increase, the risk of transaction increases. When the dangers of processing are negligible, the least cost-effective management will be preferred, the cost will increase as the danger increases, and the organizations will be able to develop different methods to reduce costs. At this point, organizations aim to establish management mechanisms to minimize transaction costs, and develop specific strategies and mechanisms in which processes can be structured (Donaldson 1990). This theory deals with the frequency of transactions associated with resources, its appropriateness for the organization, the extent of uncertainty, if any, and the extent to which the resource is specific. These are all factors that increase the transaction costs (Kogut 1988). The use of non-specific assets, vertical integration, long-term contracts, partial ownership agreements and contracts that require parties to invest at the same level are different methods used by organizations to reduce transaction costs.

4.3 Transaction Cost Theory and Agency Theory

It can be said that the foundations of Agency theory are based on Max Weber. The theory of power of Agency, in essence, deals with the problems experienced and the costs arising from the violations of rights and obligations of the parties based on the principal proxy relationships between the principal and the proxy, and aims to reduce the problems by trying to understand this mechanism. According to Shavell (1979), the noble-proxy agreement can be defined as a contract which briefly refers to a person or institution (noble) making a service on behalf of another person (proxy) and receiving a fee in return. The relationship between the noble-surrogate problem and the transaction cost approach within the framework of the theory of proxy can be briefly stated as follows. The noble-surrogate problem is a problem that can arise between the professional managers of the companies and the owners. Transaction costs are the costs that may arise during the management of professional managers and constitute an area where noble-surrogate problems can occur. Transaction costs include all the cost elements that make it difficult to perform transactions such as the number of parties involved in an economic activity, not being conciliatory, the information is not open to all parties and resistance to change. There are many transaction cost sources that affect the level of activity of a firm. For example, it may lead to uncertainty and asymmetric data processing costs incurred by the manager during the control phase of the workforce. According to Grossman and Hart (1983), the principal-surrogate problem may arise due to the transaction costs and moral hazard that may arise in cases such as the owner or owners of the company or the professional company manager to manage the company and the wage is paid on a fixed amount or on the basis of profit. In such cases, company profits are determined as the criteria for evaluating the activity results of the proxy. In this case, the principal who is the owner of the company cannot follow the actions and actions of the manager, i.e. the proxy, but it is assumed that he can observe the results of these acts and transactions. Company profits may also depend on the company manager's actions and transactions, as well as random external variables outside the manager's transaction and control. In this case, the owner of the company does not know exactly whether the profit of the company is due to the good work of the manager or the fortune of the manager and that he should be given the chance to determine the optimal wage to be paid to the managers. This chance factor can lead to the emergence of a noble surrogate problem (Grossman and Hart 1983). In some cases, transaction costs may coincide with noble-surrogate problems. There are also opinions that examine the transaction cost and the noble-surrogate problem within the scope of corruptions and bribery payments as well as unnecessary corporate spending. Company executives shall bear certain transaction costs in order to obtain tenders.

5 Conclusion

The transaction cost theory is based on the idea that a company does not create the cost of the time it does not buy in the market. These costs are called transaction costs. Trading Firms and individuals aim to save on transaction costs (not in production costs). The use of markets is expensive because of the costs of coordination, such as the presence of remote suppliers, monitoring of communications, insurance purchase and information about the product (Williamson 1988). The Theory of Transaction Costs has become the dominant theoretical framework in explaining decisions that define organizational boundaries. As with all other theories, most of the studies have not developed their perspective, but are based on reformulation, explanation and proof. The Transaction Cost Theory assumes that managers and firms do not always have access to excellent information. This assumption distinguishes the Theory of Transaction Costs from traditional economic models that assume that other information can be accessed from any point of the market. Market participants can access incomplete and complete information at any time point as far as they can afford their current costs. Due to the information constraint, companies may not be able to maximize their behavior or optimize their goals. The importance of information constraint in the Cost of Transaction Theory emerges at the point of examining the flow of information from the supplier. This non-perfect information causes certain degrees of uncertainty in achieving the goals and objectives of the firm's actions that the company is not able to predict. Traditionally, companies have attempted to further reduce transaction costs: they recruit more employees, integrate vertically, purchase their own suppliers and distributors, move to new markets, develop horizontally, take over small companies, and even develop monopolies. The transaction cost theory focuses on how economic changes are managed (Williamson 1975). The transaction cost approach based on economic transactions at the level of analysis is based on limited rationality and opportunism. Transactions are settled within the organizational structure according to their characteristics. These characteristics are specified as uncertainty, frequency, asset characteristics and conformity.

References

Akerlof, G. A. (1970). The market for lemons: Quality uncertainty and the market mechanism. *Quarterly Journal of Economics, 84*, 488–500.

Anderson, J. C., & Gerbing, D. W. (1988). Structural equation modeling in practice: A review and recommended two-step approach. *Psychological Bulletin, 103*(3), 411–433.

Aubert, B. A., Rivard, S., & Patry, M. (2004). A transaction cost model of IT outsourcing. *Information & Management, 41*(7), 921–932.

Bahli, B., & Suzanne, R. (2003). The information technology outsourcing risk: A transaction cost and agency theory-based perspective. *Journal of Information Technology, 18*(8), 211–221.

Barnard, C. I. (1938). *The functions of the executive*. Cambridge, MA: Harvard University.

Bremen, P., Oehmen, J., Alard, R., & Schönsleben, P. (2010). Transaction costs in global supply chains of manufacturing companies. *Journal of Systemics, Cybernetics & Informatics, 8*, 19–25.

Bunduchi, R. (2005). Business relationships in internet-based electronic markets: The role of goodwill trust and transaction costs. *Information Systems Journal, 15*(4), 321–341.

Coase, R. H. (1937). *The nature of the firm*. Retrieved October 20, 2017, from http://purao.ist.psu.edu/532/Readings/Coase1937.pdf

Coase, R. H. (1998). *The firm, the market and the law*. Chicago: The University of Chicago Press.

Das, T. K., & Teng, B. S. (2000). A resource-based theory of strategic alliances. *Journal of Management, 26*(1), 31–61.

Donaldson, L. (1990). The ethereal hand: Organizational economics and management theory. *Academy of Management Review, 15*(3), 369–381.

Fehr, E., & Tyran, J. R. (2008). Limited rationality and strategic interaction: The impact of the strategic environment on nominal inertia. *Econometrica, 76*(2), 353–394.

Foss, N. J. (2005). Transaction cost economics in Scandinavian business administration. *Scandinavian Journal of Management, 21*, 5–17.

Geyskens, I., Steenkamp, E. J.-B., & Kumar, N. (2006). Make, buy, or ally: A transaction cost theory meta-analysis. *Academy of Management Journal, 49*(3), 519–543.

Grossman, S. J., & Hart, O. D. (1983). An analysis of the principal-agent problem. *Econometrica, 51*(1), 7–46.

Haltiwanger, J., & Waldman, M. (1989). Limited rationality and strategic complements: The implications for macroeconomics. *The Quarterly Journal of Economics, 104*(3), 463–483.

Hayek, F. A. (1945). The use of knowledge in society. *The American Economic Review, 35*(4), 519–530.

Hennart, J. F. (2001). Theories of the multinational enterprise. In A. M. Rugman & A. Verbeke (Eds.), *The Oxford handbook of international business*. New York: Oxford University Press.

Hill, C. W. L., Hwang, P., & Kim, W. C. (1990). An eclectic theory of the choice of international entry mode. *Strategic Management Journal, 11*(2), 117–128.

Jap, S. D., & Anderson, E. (2003). Safeguarding interorganizational performance and continuity under ex post opportunism. *Management Science, 49*(12), 1684–1701.

Kogut, B. (1988). Joint ventures: Theoretical and empirical perspectives. *Strategic Management Journal, 9*, 319–322.

Lipman, B. L. (1991). How to decide how to decide how to...: Modeling limited rationality. *Econometrica: Journal of the Econometric Society, 59*, 1105–1125.

March, J. G., & Simon, H. A. (1958). *Organizations*. New York: Wiley.

Rabin, M. (2013). Incorporating limited rationality into economics. *Journal of Economic Literature, 51*(2), 528–543.

Rindfleisch, A. (2019). Transaction cost theory: Past, present and future. *AMS Review*, 1–13.

Sharland, A. P. (1993). *Internal outsourcing an empirical study of the role of transactions cost and Competitive advantage in the international buyer supplier relationship*. The Florida State University College of Business.

Shavell, S. (1979). Risk sharing and incentives in the principal and agent relationship. *The Bell Journal of Economics, 10*, 55–73.

Simon, H. A. (1979). Rational decision making in business organizations. *The American Economic Review, 69*(4), 493–513.
Williamson, O. E. (1975). *Markets and hierarchies: Analysis and antitrust implications*. New York: Free Press.
Williamson, O. E. (1988). Technology and transaction cost economics: A reply. *Journal of Economic Behavior & Organization, 10*(3), 355–363.
Williamson, O. E. (1991). Comparative economic organization: The analysis of discrete structural alternatives. *Administrative Science Quarterly, 36*, 269–296.
Williamson, O. E. (1998). Transaction cost economics: How it works; where it is headed. *The Economist, 146*, 23–58.
Zylbersztajn, D. (2018). Measurement costs and governance: Bridging perspectives of transaction cost economics. *Caderno de Administração, 26*(1), 1–19.

Strategies for the Robust Banking System and the Determinants of the Commercial and Participation Banks Performance in Turkey Evidence from a Panel Data Analysis

Zafer Adalı and Mustafa Uysal

Abstract The primary purpose of this study is to investigate the internal determinants of commercial and participation banks operated profitability in Turkey over the time from 2010Q1 to 2018Q4 and recommend strategies for the robust banking system regarding The Turkish bank system. Within this context, quarterly data of 20 commercial and three participation banks were analyzed by using the fixed panel regression model. The bank performance is measured by using return on asset (ROA) and return on equity (ROE). As a result, it was found that size has a negative and significant impact on participation banks ROE and commercial banks both ROE and ROA. It was also concluded that credit risk (CR) has an adverse and significant effect on participation banks. However, non-interest income to the total asset (OFFBS) has a positive and significant impact on all bank profitability. The results also showed that the coefficient of capital adequacy for participation bank ROA is positive and significant. At the same time, its effect is negative and significant for commercial bank ROE and participation bank ROE. Finally, liquidity management is positively related to participation bank ROE. Concerning the results of the model, the commercial and participation bank profitability are associated with the bank-specific determinants. Because of this situation, bank managements and policymakers should initially focus on improving bank management, the lending policy and banking activities so the bank performance will continue in a crisis period.

Z. Adalı · M. Uysal (✉)
The Department of Applied Disciplines, Artvin Çoruh University, Artvin, Turkey
e-mail: zaferadali@artvin.edu.tr; muysal@artvin.edu.tr

H. Dincer, S. Yüksel (eds.), *Strategic Priorities in Competitive Environments*, Contributions to Management Science, https://doi.org/10.1007/978-3-030-45023-6_9

1 Introduction

Every economic system contains the units which have financing needs and have excessive financing surpluses. Matching these units and eliminating the obstacles in the financial relation need some mechanism called as financial intermediaries. Many researchers pointed out the role of financial intermediaries. For example, Diamond (1984) suggested that financial intermediaries play a vital role in the delegated monitor, which leads to a decrease in monitoring cost and free-rider problem resulting from markets. Furthermore, Hubbard (1994) also emphasized that financial intermediaries have an essential function which solves principal-agent issues (Kalkavan and Ersin 2019). All of the financial intermediaries, banks are prime and dominant ones. Banks are the financial intermediaries which are collecting deposits from the units having external funds and providing these funds to deficit units that need funds (Peek and Rosengren 1995; Casu et al. 2006).

An efficient and robust working financial system plays a crucial role in economic development. The finance industry has encountered many developments since the last 20 years. The regulation, globalization, technological innovations, financial product diversification, and the areas of operation are some significant developments and challenges (Zhang et al. 2020). The banking industry has been redesigned and operated through these developments. At the same time, regulation, deregulation and product diversification and globalization are main factors changing banking structure; hence, policymakers and supervisory authorities have not noticed the weakness of the banking industry, causing many crises. The 2008 global financial crisis is an essential example in terms of the importance of monitoring the banking industry. The recent global financial crisis arose from the weak capital structure, incoherent financial product diversification and unsustainable operations resulting in huge profits. The effects of the collapse of the global financial system resulting from the 2008 financial crisis were the European sovereign-debt crisis, a decline in whole economic activity causing The Great Recession of 2008–2012, declining housing prices, the collapse of the vital industry and prolonged unemployment. As a result, the monitoring and evaluating of the banking industry have been the leading and essential topic on the policymakers, markets players and other authorities' agenda. Considering this purpose, examining the relationship between bank-specific determinants and profitability can generate beneficial information since the resistance and sustainability of a banking system is strongly linked to its profitability.

The banking system is the dominant financial intermediaries for developed, especially for emerging countries. As for Turkey, the banking system is unquestionably the most critical element of the finance industry, and the performance of the banking system seems to be a significant indicator to evaluate the Turkish economy in every way. In spite of the increasing role of other financial intermediaries such as the capital markets, the banking industry continues to be leading financial intermediaries in Turkey (Topak and Talu 2016). The 2018 Annual Report of BRSA emphasized that the banking sector assets account for 83% of the total assets of the financial sectors. In the history of the Turkish economy, November 2000 and

February 2001 were the most devastating banking crisis. In order to prevent potential crisis and mitigate its effects, the Turkish banking industry has been built on a robust construction through "Banking Sector Restructuring Program". All banks operating in Turkey are to adopt this program by improving the screening and monitoring activities (Ozgur and Gorus 2016). With the help of the program, the global financial crisis did not lead to the collapse of the Turkish banking system. However, many global financial institutions either collapsed or shrunk profitability (Artar 2012). The effects of the 2008 global crisis can be classified as expectation, trade and financial channel, which lead to a sharp declining in export, worsened credit condition arose from sharply stop in financial flow. As a result, the Turkish economy encountered one of the worst economic down. Still, there was no collapse of the financial markets with the help of the main structural change in the financial market (Adalı and Bari 2017).

Turkish banking system consists of commercial and participation banks though commercial banks are the dominant actors (Eti et al. 2020). The number of commercial banks operating in the Turkish banking system is 34 as of April 2019, but the number of participation banks is only 6. The main feature of the participation banks is that they are associated with Islamic rules in their banking operation, such as lending and deposit activities. On the contrary to the commercial bank, the participation banks do not operate through promising a fixed interest payment to their savers. The funds collected from the savers should be used or utilized in trade and industry, and the saver units share the obtaining profit or loss as a result of using funds. In spite of a few participation banks in Turkey, the participation banking system has drawn massive attention because they have been robust and resistance against the devastating effect of the 2008 global financial crisis. The main reasons for the participation banks resistance against the 2008 financial crisis are that the participation bank engages in real economic activities containing production, service, and investment (Dinçer et al. 2020). In spite of increasing global attention, the share of the participation bank in the Turkish banking system is quite low, so the topic of the determinants of participation banks performance is naturally not enough. In the literature, Macit (2012) made a study to the determinants of the participation banks profitability. As a result, in this study, commercial bank, as well as participation banks, will be separately analyzed by using panel regression to investigate the Turkish banking system in every aspect. ROA and ROE, which have been the preferable profitability indicators in the literature, are employed as the dependent variables for both commercial and participation banks. For this purpose, monthly data of 22 commercials and five participation bank for the period between 2007:01 and 2019:03 was evaluated. According to the results of the analysis, it will be possible to give some recommendation to policymakers, supervisory authorities, investors and banking industry regarding this concept.

This paper is organized as follows: Sect. 2 provides the existing literature relating to the determinants of banks profitability. Sect. 3 presents the strategies for a robust banking system regarding Turkish experiences, while Sect. 4 presents data and methodology. Then, the empirical results will be presented in Sect. 5, and finally, conclusions and policy recommendation are provided in the final section.

2 Literature Review

The topics of banking profitability's determinants have attracted many researchers, and some of them are provided in Table 1.

There is plenty of literature related to investigating the determinants of bank profitability. However, there is no strong consensus because studies linked to mentioned literature used different scope, methods and a wide variety of external and internal determinants. In terms of the literature, studies conducted by Short (1979) and Bourke (1989) are pioneers research examining the determinants of bank profitability. According to Short (1979), government ownership banks are negatively related to profitability. Bourke (1989) tried to understand the factors affecting bank profitability in Europe, North America and Japan. It was proven that there is a result supporting the Edward-Heggestad-Mingo Hypothesis in which higher-level concentration leads lower staff expense inducing higher profitability; however, the expense preference expenditure theories are not confirmed.

There are various studies focusing on EU bank performance. For example, Molyneux and Thornton (1992) made a prime study to evaluate the determinants of European bank profitability for the period 1986–1989 by using standardized accounting data. They employed the model built by Bourke (1989) and focused on 18 European countries. As a result of the model's output, it was defined that liquidity harms the banks' profitability while the profitability is positively related to efficiency. Besides, Staikouras and Wood (2003) tried to investigate the determinants of banks profitability in the EU with the help of the regression model. They used a data set covering the period 1994–1998. According to their findings, it was identified that the external macroeconomic environment seems to have more powerful effects than banks-specific determinants in terms of banks' profitability. Moreover, Abreu and Mendes (2002) conducted a study to investigate the effects of bank-specific determinants along with other variables on 4 EU countries' commercial banks from 1986 to 1999. It was emphasized that low bankruptcy costs and higher interest rate margins on assets are associated with well-capitalized banks. They also found that operating expenses stimulate the net interest margin, and the loan-to-asset ratio positively influences profitability and interest margins. Furthermore, Goddard et al. (2004) focused on the performance of six European countries' bank. They suggested that there is a weak relationship between size and profitability. However, their results also posed that off-balance business has a significant and positive impact on the profitability only in the UK.

There is also a large number of studies focusing on the determinants of US banks' performance. Initially, Rhoades (1985) tried to investigate the factors affecting the banks' profitability and analysis used in the model is based on a sample 6492 bank and control for market concentration, scale economies, and explicit product differentiation are used as the determinants influencing the banks' performance. It was underlined that market share per se is an essential source for profitability, and there is a significant relationship between risk and profitability. Berger (1995) conducted a study to investigate the relationship between the return on equity and capital asset

Table 1 Major studies related to the determinants of bank profitability

Author	Scope	Methods	Results
Acaravci and Çalim (2013)	Turkey	Johansen and Johansen-Juselius Cointegration analysis	It was determined that banking specific determinants seem to be more effective factors affecting the profitability of banks than the macroeconomic determinants.
Ongore and Kusa (2013)	Kenya	Panel regression	It was concluded that board and management decisions play a vital role in the financial performance of commercial banks, whereas macroeconomic variables have no significant contribution.
Javaid et al. (2011)	Pakistan	Panel regression	It was emphasized that there is a strong relationship between internal factors and return on asset (ROA).
Ramadan et al. (2011)	Jordan	Panel regression	It was identified that internal factors is important determinants of the profitability.
Wasiuzzaman and Tarmizi (2010)	Malaysia	Regression	It was found that capital and asset quality lead to lower profitability, whereas liquidity and operational efficiency lead to higher profitability.
Obamuyi (2013)	Nigeria	Regression	The results posed that efficient expenses management and favorable economic condition contribute to profitability.
Mohamad et al. (2019)	Malaysia	Regression	It was defined that all variables used in the model have a fundamental impact on Islamic banks' profitability.
Athanasoglou et al. (2008)	Greece	GMM	It was concluded that all internal factors, apart from size, play a pivotal role in the profitability of Greek banks in the excepted way.
Sufian and Habibullah (2010)	Malaysia	Regression	It was found that economic freedom, business in doing business and corruption has a great impact on the profitability.
Uhomoibhi	Nigeria	Regression	Their finding showed that corruption has an effect on profitability.
Alkassim (2005)	GCC countries	Regression	It was defined that interest free lending has a negative effect on Islamic banks and total expenses leads to lower conventional bank profitability.
Masood et al. (2009)	Saudi Arabia	Johansen's Cointegration and Granger causality analysis	It was suggested that there is a cointegrated relationship between the ROA and the ROE.
Amor-Tapia et al. (2006)	OECD countries	Regression	Higher leverage ratio and lower overheads ratio improve profitability.

(continued)

Table 1 (continued)

Author	Scope	Methods	Results
Ramlall (2009)	Taiwan	Regression	It was found that credit risk harm profits, whereas capital stimulates Taiwan's banking profits.
Anbar and Alper (2011)	Turkey	Regression	Asset size, non-interest income, size of the credit portfolio, loan under follow-up, and real interest rate are important determinants of bank's profitability.
Berger (1995)	US	Regression	It was underlined that there is a positive relationship between the return on equity and the capital asset ratio.
Angbazo (1997)	US	Regression	It was identified that default risk, management efficiency and leverage seem to have a positive impact on bank interest margin.
Masood and Ashraf (2012)	12 Countries	Regression	It was defined that larger asset size and efficient management have a positive effect on the return on assets.
Ahmad and Ahmad (2004)	Malaysia	Regression	It was identified that bank-specific determinants seem to have a meaningful impact on Islamic banks credit risks.
Hassan and Bashir (2003)	21 Countries	GLS method	Islamic banks' profitability is positively associated with loans activities and capital adequacy.
Tan and Floros (2012)	China	GMM method	It was confirmed that higher banks profitability arises from cost efficiency, banking sector development and inflation. In contrast, a higher volume of non-traditional activities and higher taxation.
Molyneux and Thornton (1992)	EU	Regression	It was posed that liquidity harms the banks' profitability.
Staikouras and Wood (2003)	EU	Regression	The results were proven that external macroeconomic determinants have more powerful effects than banks-specific determinants in terms of banks' profitability.
Goddard et al. (2004)	6 EU countries	VAR model	There is no powerful relationship between the size and profitability.
Smirlock (1985)	US	Regression	It was reported that there is an adverse relationship between size and bank profitability.
Rhoades (1985)	US	Regression	There is an important and adverse effect of risk on bank profitability.

(continued)

Table 1 (continued)

Author	Scope	Methods	Results
Berger (1995)	US	Granger causality analysis	It was defined that there is positive causality relationship from capitalization to profitability.
Mirzaei et al. (2013)	Advanced and emerging countries	Regression	It was posed that lower competitive condition has a positive impact on profitability for advanced countries, whereas this situation is not a case for emerging countries.
Lee et al. (2014)	22 Asian countries	GMM method	It was found that non-interest activities have no powerful effect on bank profitability.
Dietrich and Wanzenried (2014)	118 Countries	GMM method	It was identified that bank profitability is associated with the level of a country's income.
Bourke (1989)	Europe, North America and Japan	Regression	There is a result supporting the Edward-Heggestad-Mingo hypothesis; however, the expense preference expenditure theories are not confirmed.
Short (1979)	Canada, Western Europe, and Japan	Regression	It was concluded that government owned banks are negatively related to profitability.
Erdoğan and Aksoy (2016)	Turkey	Regression	It was defined that internal factors have a substantial impact on banks' profit.
Isik (2017)	Turkey	Regression	It was proven that banks' performance is totally related to all bank-specific factors.
Ozgur and Gorus (2016)	Turkey	Regression	It was indicated that the impact of the 2008 global financial crisis on bank profitability is significantly adverse.
Akbaş (2012)	Turkey	Regression	Loans loss provision, total cost over total income and inflation lead to lower bank performance.
İskenderoğlu et al. (2012)	Turkey	GMM method	It was showed that size, growth and capital structure increase the banks' profitability.
Demirhan (2013)	Turkey	GMM method	It was found that deposits banks' performance is just positively associated with non-interest income over total assets.
Ata (2009)	Turkey	GMM method	It was proven that banks performance is related to banks specific determinants.
Kaya (2002)	Turkey	Regression	It was underlined that banks performance is linked to internal and external determinants.

ratio in the US for the 1983–1992-time period. According to regression's results, it was underlined that there is a positive relationship between the return on equity and capital asset ratio. Within the same scope, Angbazo (1997) tried to investigate the effects of factors on net interest rate margin. It was emphasized that leverage, default risk, management efficiency, the opportunity cost of interest-bearing reserves play a pivotal role in the net interest rate margin positively. Furthermore, Berger (1995) focused on the causality relationship between the determinants and the banks' profitability. As a result of the finding, there is a positive causality relationship from capitalization to profitability.

Ongore and Kusa (2013) investigated the determinants of commercial banks' performance in Kenya. With the help of linear multiple regression and Generalized Least Square model, they concluded that bank-specific factors related to the control of managers are the most critical essential determinants of commercial banks' performance in Kenya. Javaid et al. (2011) conducted a study to investigate the relationship between the internal factors related to banking sectors and ROA in Pakistan by using regression. As a result of the analysis, they found that internal factors have a significant impact on profitability. Among the internal factors, equity and deposits seem to be more effective determinants of profitability. Ramadan et al. (2011) conducted a study to investigate the effects of internal and external factors on the profitability of banks in Jordan. They suggest that the banks' characteristics determinants play a pivotal role in the profitability of banks. According to their results, the profitability of banks is positively associated with low credit risk, well-capitalized banks, high lending activities, and the efficiency of cost management.

Wasiuzzaman and Tarmizi (2010) tried to analyze the determinants of Islamic banks' profitability. For this purpose, the bank characteristics and macroeconomic variables are used to investigate the effects of the variables on Islamic banks by using regression. They posed that inflation and growth have a positive impact on profitability, and bank characteristics such as liquidity and operational efficiency also have a positive effect on profitability. However, capital and asset quality harm profitability. Obamuyi (2013) tried to examine the effects of internal and external factors on the banks' performance in Nigeria. According to the results, it was underlined that improved bank capital, interest income, efficient expenses management, and higher economic performance are important factors to increase profitability. Mohamad et al. (2019) analyse the profitability of Malaysian's Islamic banking system. The study uses annually data of 17 top Malaysian Islamic banks over the period 1994–2015. According to the results of regression model, it was found that all determinants employed in the model are important determinants of banks' profitability, but their effects are not uniform.

Athanasoglou et al. (2008) tried to investigate the determinant of bank profitability in Greek. To account for the profitability, the effects of bank-specific, industry-specific factors and determinants related to the macroeconomic condition on profitability was investigated by using Generalized Methods Moments (GMM). The results posed that all internal factors, apart from size, have an impact on bank profitability in the excepted way. Besides, favorable macroeconomic conditions stimulate bank profitability, but there is an asymmetric relationship between the macroeconomic determinants and bank profitability. Sufian and Habibullah (2010) conducted a study to investigate the determinants of the banking sector's performance in Malaysia. They focus on the effects of bank specification, economic freedom, and macroeconomic variables using panel data from 1999 to 2007. Their result showed that low economic freedom and business in doing business are essential determinants to reduce banks' performance. It was also determined that corruption has an intense impact on the Malaysian banking sector's performance. Uhomoibhi also investigate the effects of determinants on the bank's performance in Nigeria, similar to Sufian and Habibullah (2010). The researchers emphasized that the bank's performance is positively linked to corruption because the development of corrupt practices induce banks in Nigeria to increase their proliferate activities.

Amor-Tapia et al. (2006) tried to investigate the commercial banks' performance of OECD countries. They reached a conclusion that higher profitability arises from a higher leverage ratio, and lower overhead ratio leads to reducing the type of costs that improve profitability. Masood et al. (2009) have done an empirical study to examine whether there is a long-run relationship between the ROA and the ROE in the kingdom of Saudi Arabia with the help of cointegration and causality analysis. It was identified that there is a cointegrated relationship between the ROE and the ROA. Tan and Floros (2012) focused on the determinants of Chinese commercial banks' profitability by using GMM method. The empirical result exhibited that cost efficiency, banking sector development and inflation are essential factors that positively influenced the banks' profitability. At the same time, the volume of non-traditional activities and taxation seem to have a detrimental effect on the banks' profitability. Another comparative study conducted by Alkassim (2005) on the performance of conventional and Islamic banks in GCC countries throughout 1997–2004. According to the results obtained from regression methods, it was found that conventional banks are more stable than Islamic banks in terms of asset quality. The study also suggests that interest-free lending has an impact on the profitability of the Islamic Bank, and total expenses have a detrimental effect on the conventional bank.

Ramlall (2009) reviews the determinants of the Taiwan banking system's performance. A quarterly panel data, including banking industry and macroeconomic factors through March 2002 to December 2007. It was found that credit risk influences profit adversely, while capital influences profits positively. Masood and Ashraf (2012) aimed to inspect the effects of banks-specific and macroeconomic determinants on Islamic banks' profitability in the selected countries from different regions. They concluded that larger asset size and efficient management lead to a higher return on asset. A study conducted by Ahmad and Ahmad (2004) focused on the determinants of Islamic banks credit risks in Malaysia for the 1996–2002-time period. The study's result posed that Islamic banks credit risk is associated with asset size, risky asset ratio, and banks management efficiency.

Hassan and Bashir (2003) conducted a study that covered 21 countries' Islamic banks' performance by using GLS method. They found that Islamic banks' profitability is positively associated with loans activities and capital adequacy. Mirzaei et al. (2013) focused on a sample of banks from emerging countries as well as advanced countries by using the regression model. They suggested that banks in developed countries benefit from the lower competitive environment; however, it is not a case for banks operating in emerging countries. Lee et al. (2014) conducted a study focusing on the banks' performance in 22 Asian countries by using GMM method. They found that non-interest activities do not affect banks' profitability.

2.1 Studies for Turkey

The determinants of bank profitability have been received considerable attention. Studies related to this topic reached a different conclusion because of data set, empirical methods, and defining determinants. Mainly, the panel regression model and GMM methods are applied to investigate the determinants of banks profitability in Turkey, and banks data were employed without distinction. In this part, some of the studies focusing on Turkish banks profitability are listed. Anbar and Alper (2011) aimed to examine the determinants of banks' profitability in Turkey for the 2002–2010 period time. The profitability of the banks seems to have decreased along with increasing size of credit portfolio and loans under follow-up. It is also concluded that asset size and non-interest income stimulate the banks' profitability. In addition to the banks-specific factors, the real interest rate has a significantly and positively impact on the banks' profitability.

Acaravci and Çalim (2013) made a study related to the effects of the bank and macroeconomic determinants on the commercial banks' profitability. For this purpose, annual data for the period between 1998 and 2011 is investigated by using Johansen (1988) and Johansen–Juselius Cointegration (1990) Analysis. Their test results proved that bank-specific determinants have more effects on banks' profitability than macroeconomic determinants. They also emphasized that the 2001 economic crisis has a detrimental impact on banking sectors. Erdoğan and Aksoy (2016) conducted a study focusing on 36 Turkish banks for the period 1995–2007 by analyzing Prais-Winsten regression method. The empirical results showed that capital, size, liquidity, loans, off-balance sheet transactions have a positive impact on performance; however, quality of loans and concentration have a detrimental effect on banks' performance.

Isik (2017) tried to analyze the internal determinants of state, private, and foreign-owned commercial banks' performance. The estimation method is based on fixed and random effects panel data covering for the period 2009Q1–2016Q3. According to empirical test results, it was indicated that income diversification, deposit level, bank stability and bank scale are determinants positively impacting banks' profitability. However, credit risk, lending level and capital adequacy and operating expenses seem to be determinants negatively influencing banks' performance. All in all, all internal determinants affect banks' profitability, but their intense and effects depend on the bank ownership structure. Ozgur and Gorus (2016) made a study to investigate the determinants of deposit banks performance by using OLS methodology. Their data is based on monthly covering the period over 2006:1–2016:2.

Their empirical test result suggested that net interest revenues, non-performing loans, central bank policy interest rate, equity over total assets have a substantial effect on return on assets. However, there is no relationship between factors including non-interest income, market share, exchange rate, operational expenses and banks' performance. In addition to these findings, it is also indicated that the 2008 global financial crisis harmed banking industry profitability. The Similar empirical method is also employed by Akbaş (2012). Furthermore, some Turkish studies in the literature employed GMM method to examine the determinants of banks profitability (Demirhan 2013; Ata 2009). According to Demirhan (2013), banks performance in both pre and post-global financial crisis are positively associated with non-interest income over total assets. Iskerderoglu (2012) also suggested that growth in assets and size are determinants inducing higher profitability.

3 Strategies for the Robust Banking Industry

The repercussion of the 2008 Global Financial Crisis all over the world economy is that sharp decline in private consumption, stagnant investment figures, sudden decrease in commodity price, and rapid contraction credit volume can be classified. The global development arising from reduced global demand made the 2008 Global Crisis to be named as the great recession. The devastating effects of the crisis were felt quietly in the last quarter of 2008, and the Turkish economy is also one of the countries affected by the crisis because of limited external financing, highly unprecedented unemployment figure, the sharp decrease in export. As for the public sector, narrowed current account deficit, increase in the budget deficit, and an increase in the public sector borrowing requirement are some the recent crisis' output which swamps the policymakers and government. By contrast with the real sector, the banking sector in Turkey was not influenced by the crisis such as American and European counterpart. Examining the structure of the Turkish banking sector and applying policies against the 2008 Global Crisis may lead to essential strategies which could be used to mitigate and pretend the potential financial and real economic crisis.

It is vital to understand and examine the history of the Turkish banking system for investigating the strategies applied by the Turkish banking authorities and policymakers to mitigate the repercussion of the 2008 Global Financial Crisis. The Turkish banking system has encountered many challenges and experienced various financial and economic events which changed the structure and mindings of the banking sectors. The first significant event in the history of the Turkish banking industry was financial liberalization during early 1980. This experience has increased the competition among the banks and other financial institutions. However, the liberalization step was imposed by global institutions such as the IMF, so the authorities did not properly manage this process. This unplanned experienced step negatively systemized the structure of the banking industry to both internal and external events. Then, the 1990s seemed to be a crucial period for the banking system because an unstable macroeconomic environment including high inflation, dollarization, capital flights and high exchange rate risk lead to a weak banking system. As a result, these volatile economic conditions ended in bankruptcy for three banks in 1994.

The Turkish economy has experienced many economic bottlenecks, and highly devastating crisis like mentioned before but the disaster that occurred in 2000 and 2001 are considered as the milestone in the Turkish economy. Then, the policymakers and authorities have taken the brave step not to let it happen again. The characteristic features of these crises were the vulnerability of commercial banks. First, the intervention of the political figures and the domination of state in the banking industry are one of the leading culprits resulting in the vulnerable banking industry in Turkey before the 2001s. For example, the assets of the banking industry were mainly utilized to finance public deficit which deteriorates banks' balance sheet. Additionally, the relationship based on mutual interest between bank conglomerates and political leads to inadequate supervision, regulation and moral hazard which augment risk. Second, the banking industry was highly dependent on the international capital market. In this context, the funds borrowed from the global market in foreign currency were invested in public sector securities to finance current account and budget deficit in spite of investing private sector. Shortly, the reasons for the weakness of the Turkish banking industry beginning with the liberalization attempt in the 1980s are the banking industry based on foreign funds financing to higher current account deficit, increasing public debt, inadequate regulation, supervision, uncertainties resulting from political, global and economic factors (Ari and Cergibozan 2016).

After the crises experienced by the Turkish economy, the root reasons for the crisis have been tried to eliminate to achieve a stronger and sustainable economy. Firstly, the stabilization program in charge of the IMF was announced and assiduously implemented by the government. The stabilization program was based on tight fiscal policies and the inflation-targeting regime, which recovered budget deficit, inflation and dollarization problem. All of the recoveries helped the Turkish economy to achieve high and steady growth rates. Other remarkable achievements resulting from the stabilization program are that the central bank became independent, activating the floating exchange rate regime and focus only on price stability by controlling the short-term interest rate (Erdem 2010). Remarkable improvements in the macroeconomic fundamentals such as inflation, budget deficit, and economic growth lead to the more sustainable economic environment which minimizes the externalities encountered by the financial market (Ari and Cergibozan 2016). With the help of these improvements, the banking industry has not concentrated on government debt instruments and the previous critical weakness causing vulnerability banking system could be annihilated (Özatay and Sak 2002).

In addition to the macroeconomic recovery arising from Transition to the Strong Economy, former institutions framework causing the fragile banking system were changed from top to toe. New institutions frameworks related to the banking system, is named The Banking Sector Restructuring Program, which aims to control and supervises the banking industry for avoiding any fragilities like older ones. Briefly, four major blocks shaped the program. The first block suggested that public banks restructured financially and operationally, which decreased short-term liabilities and cleared the functional loss receivables. It also focused on the frameworks leading to the effective management of loan portfolio. The second block was that The SDIF prompted the resolution of the troubled banks by funding. Furthermore, the third one emphasized that BRSA generated new regulatory frameworks to supervise the banks. For example, the capital adequacy norms were employed, principles regarding the supervision were imposed on the banking system under the legal sanctions. Besides, BRSA regulated the laws and procedures based on the independent audit. Finally, the fourth block was associated with assessing banking sector soundness. For example, penalties and judicial crimes related to the banking sectors were regulated and re-arranged. The Turkish banking system, based on the mentioned four blocks, showed management success during the 2008 global financial crisis. The central banks and The BRSA gave confidence to the market and solved the liquidity problems which guaranteed the banking system robust against the crisis and generated no financial burdens. To understand the success of banking management, the capital adequacy ratio (CAR), return on assets (ROA), return on equity (ROE), FX exposure, asset quality and liquidity risks are outstanding views. Indeed, it is emphasized that the health banking sectors are strongly linked to these factors. For example, FX exposure was shallow at year-end 2008 and represented 29% of total lending, whereas the overall average of FX figures in European countries was over 50%. In terms of asset quality, the non-performing loans (NPL) ratio is essential figures, and NPL decreased from 17 to 5.3% between 2003 and 2009. This figures showed that asset quality seemed to be healthy and have little deterioration in credit quality. Among these factors, the capital adequacy ratio (CAR) is one of the leading trust-building factors guaranteeing the banking system to remain healthy against any crisis (Morrison and White 2005). According to BASEL II criteria, the target ratio should be at least 12% but the Turkish banking system improved to 20 from 9.3% in 2000 which strengthened the banks' prudent and risk-averse perception (Pomerleano 2009). Furthermore, ROA as 3% and ROE as 25.1% during the crisis showed that the Turkish banks not only remain robust against the crisis but also they worked with high profits.

As for countries affected by the 2008 financial crisis, their banks had extremely high toxic loans, deregulation, implement new instruments equipped with highly financial engineering and risk-taking which lead them to a weak structure in the face of the global crisis. Taking into Turkish experiences consideration, it is worth to note that regulation, supervision, risk-averse or prudent new financial instrument dissembling risk are one of leading and essential strategies which contribute to critical tools addressing any crisis in a stronger position.

4 Data and Methodology

This study is aimed to investigate the determinants of commercial and participation banks in Turkey by using a panel regression model. The study sample is a balanced panel dataset of 22 commercial and three participation banks observed over the period 2010q1–2018q4. The reason for the selected banks is that all banks used in this study operated continuously mentioned period, and whose financial data can be accessed without interruption. Their financial data can be The bank-specific variables are obtained from income statements and balance sheets of both banks via www.finnet.com. There are seven variables used in the model, and two of them are the dependent variables and the others associated with bank-specific variables are employed as explanatory variables. Within this purpose, the determinants of banks profitability and performance are measured through a model improved by Demirgüç-Kunt and Huizinga (1999, 2000). The model is presented as follow:

$$BPi, t = \beta 0 + \beta 1\ BVi, t + uit$$

i and t represent banks and years, respectively. BP is the dependent variable and also represents bank profitability and performance. However, β refers to intercept term and BV also refers to bank-specific variables. Finally, u represents standard error.

Regarding the literature, banks profitability has been measured by using different factors but return on asset (ROA) and return on equity (ROE) are the preferable variables to analyze banks profitability. ROA states net profit divided by total assets and is expressed in percent. ROE is verbalized as net profit divided by shareholders' equity and is also expressed in percent.

Bank specific determinants are based on the bank's management decision and policy objectives including liquidity management, capital adequacy, size, credit risk and off-balance income. The five bank-specific determinants used in this study are detailed as follows:

Capital adequacy is measured as the ratio of equity to total assets and accepted as one of the leading indicators for capital strength. When a bank has higher capital adequacy, it seems to need lower external funds and can mitigate losses and handle risk exposure with the shareholder. The effects of CAR on bank profitability is ambiguous. Still, most of the authors emphasized that higher capitalization stimulates the profitability because of lower funding cost, engaging in prudent lending, the importance for creditworthiness (Molyneux 1993; Bourke 1989; Haron and Azmi 2004; Bashir 2001). However, it is also expected a negative relationship between CAR and bank profitability since a lower capital ratio reflects a relatively risky position (Berger 1995).

Banks size is related to potential economies and diseconomies of scale in the banking sector. The size ratio is associated with controlling factors for cost differences, product and risk diversification. There is a controversial debate related to the effects of size on bank performance. According to Akhavein et al. (1997) and Goddard et al. (2004), large scale economies and scope lead to reducing cost, which maintains and increase returns while decreasing risk. On the other hand, larger size beyond certain point results in bureaucratic issues which raise the burden of management banks increasing the cost of bank management (Eichengreen and Gibson 2001).

Another controversial ratio is liquidity management (LIQ) measured by total loans and liabilities to total asset. When a bank has a larger share of loans to total asset, there is a positive relationship between liquidity and profitability because of gaining more interest revenue. On the other hand, larger LIQ ratio implies that a bank can encounter credit risk because of shrinking liquidity. Additionally, credit risk measured by non-performing loans to total loans is another ratio reflecting the balance sheet of the bank and the quality of loans. Higher credit risk means that there are high-risk loans which raising the accumulation of unpaid loans and hence decrease in the profitability (Miller and Noulas 1997).

Finally, non-interest income to the total asset (OFFBS) implies that the bank can obtain more income by diversifying their income resources consisting of trades in derivatives or currencies and credit card provisions and reducing the dependence of usual banking activities (Jiang et al. 2003). However, OFFBS also emphasized that the bank can be easily affected by the macroeconomic environment (Gischer and Jüttner 2001).

5 Empirical Results from Panel Data Analysis

In this study, the bank-specific determinants of commercial and participation banks profitability were tried to determine by using panel data analysis. The Models for each bank have been formed with ROA and ROE as dependent variables.

There are some necessary steps in order to build an appropriate panel regression model. First, the existence of individual and/or time effects for each model should be detected by using the various test. The results of the LR test employed to identify whether the model is related to individual and/or time effects, or not. According to the results of the LR test, it was found that the impact of bank-specific determinants on both ROA and ROE in the commercial should be tested through individual effects. On the other hand, as for the participation banks, the time effects for each equation is the most appropriate. Hausman test is to be employed to determine whether the individual or time effects are fixed or random in the second step. Table 2 posed that fixed model has to be used for all models with ROA and ROE.

Moreover, the third part is related to the prior condition for modelling panel regression. The panel data model is associated with some assumptions. The homoscedasticity, no autocorrelation and cross-sectional dependence generating the presumption should be investigated. The modified Wald test is employed to examine the homoscedasticity. The null hypothesis in the analysis stated that there is no heteroscedasticity. As a result of the modified Wald test, the null hypothesis is rejected for each model; in other words, there are heteroscedasticity problems for each model. Panel Durbin Watson test (Bhargava et al. 1982) and Local Best

Table 2 The results of panel regression model

	The commercial bank		The participation bank	
	ROA	ROE	ROA	ROE
LIQ	0.0069 (0.0044)	−0.0073 (0.0210)	0.0004 (0.0009)	0.1265** (0.0524)
CR	0.0208 (0.0341)	−0.1283 (0.00061)	−0.0965*** (0.0106)	−1.5933*** (0.2448)
OFFBS	1.20267** (0.5613)	4.5699*** (1.1310)	0.2315*** (0.0390)	5.2181*** (1.6040)
CAR	−0.0096 (0.0196)	−0.1597*** (0.0393)	0.0302*** (0.0040)	−1.8724*** (0.4498)
ln_size	−0.0061** (0.0028)	−0.0158*** (0.0047)	−0.0566 (0.0316)	−1.0609*** (0.3222)
Cons	0.1024 (0.0437)	0.3488*** (0.0674)	1.3797*** (0.4556)	28.8806*** (8.0925)
Observations	720	720	108	108
Number of id	20	20	3	3
R-squared	0.5958	0.1614	0.4930	0.5576
Prob > F	0.0000	0.0000	0.0000	0.0000
LR test vs. linear model	0.0000 (individual)	0.0000 (individual)	0.0011 (time)	0.0000 (time)
Chow	0.0000	0.0000	0.0048	0.0000
Hausman	0.0000	0.0000	0.0002	0.0000
Modified Wald test	0.0000	0.0000	0.0000	0.0000
Baltagi-Wu LBI	1.5577	1.1171	2.487228	2.7048746
Durbin-Watsons	1.4250	0.8134	1.7308419	2.057312
Breusch-pagan LM (N < T)	0.0000	0.0000	0.0000	0.0000

Robust standard errors in parentheses (Drisc/Kraay)
$^{***}p < 0.01$, $^{**}p < 0.05$

Invariant Test (Baltagi and Wu 1999) are used to investigating whether there is autocorrelation or not. The results of the tests indicated that there is autocorrelation problem for the third model, except that the panel model is associated with the effects of internal factors on ROE in the participation banks. Additionally, the Breusch-Pagan LM (N < T) Test is used to determine the Cross-Sectional Dependence. The findings of the test suggested that there is a cross-sectional correlation for all models. Finally, Driscoll and Kraay standard errors were employed to robust the model.

Initially, the interpretation of the model for commercial banks will be detailed. According to the result of the model, it was underlined that the coefficient of OFFBS poses a significantly positive sign in ROA and ROE. It means that the commercial banks most engage in non-traditional activities or market activities. This result in line with (Jiang et al. 2003; Erdoğan and Aksoy 2016). Moreover, there is also a significant relationship between size and bank profitability. As understood from Table 2, banks size has a detrimental effect on commercial banks. It is understood from the result that commercial banks in Turkey are beyond a certain point which harms the management efficiency and increase the cost of bank management. This conclusion is also suggested by Eichengreen and Gibson (2001).

Moreover, the coefficient of CAR is found as unfavorable for commercial banks ROE. This finding indicated that commercial banks are risk-averse and unperturbably acting in lending activities. The relationship between CAR and bank profitability was also found by Isik (2017).

Additionally, it was understood that the participation banks are highly associated with the bank-specific determinants on the contrary to the commercial banks in Turkey. For example, LIQ, CR, OFFBS, CAR, and SIZE play a vital role in the participation banks' performance. Similar to the commercial banks, the effect of size is adverse for ROE. Besides, credit risk is an essential factor affecting the participation of bank profitability. The coefficient of CR is significantly harmful. It means that high-risk loans are increasing the accumulation of unpaid loans in Turkish participation banks. In other words, the balance sheet of the bank and the quality of loans in the participation banks are unhealthy.

Furthermore, the coefficient of OFFBS is significantly positive, like commercial banks results. On contrast to commercial banks, liquidity management is substantial determinants impacting ROE in the participation banks. The effects of LIQ is significantly positive. This result implies that participation banks have a larger share of loans to total assets which raise interest revenue. This result is also achieved by Wasiuzzaman and Tarmizi (2010). Besides, the effects of CAR on both ROA and ROE are controversial because the coefficient of CAR on ROA is significantly positive. Still, there is the exact opposite situation for ROE.

6 Conclusion

Profitability is leading factors to measure the performance banks; especially, the banking system is dominant financial intermediaries which their lending activities and performance have a direct impact on the real economy, like Turkey. Parallel to this concept, this study aims to investigate the banks-specific determinants of both commercial and participation operated in Turkey. Therefore, quarterly data of 20 commercial banks and three participation banks for the period between 2010Q1 and 2018Q4 was focused. Furthermore, the panel fixed regression model was employed, and Driscoll and Kraay standard errors were used to robust model as a result of diagnostic tests.

The effects of the fixed panel regression model identified that the impact of OFFBS on both commercial and participation banks is significantly positive. However, it is also emphasized that banks size increases in the costs of banking management which shrinks banks profitability. Regarding the quality of the participation banks' balance sheet is unhealthy. In other words, the participation banks engage in riskier lending activities, and it will be recommended that the participation banks should abandon give the credit to risk business and households who may not afford to repay loans. Parallel with credit risk ratio, and there is a positive relationship between liquidity and bank profitability while the participation banks may encounter potential bad loans. Another important bank-specific determinant is capital adequacy which reflects one of the most leading indicators for capital strength. Capital adequacy is served as a safeguarding system, and its effects on banks profitability are ambiguous. As a result of the panel regression model, there is a negative relationship between CAR and ROE, but there is a positive relationship between CAR and ROA.

With this study, it was aimed to investigate the determinants of bank profitability and recommend some policies for the robust banking system by examining the Turkish banking crisis experience and then structural transformation. Thus, it will be recommended that the Turkish banking system should change their management system because the size indicator is negative for all banks. However, there is a credit risk situation in the participation banks, and their lending activities should depend on the rational view to preventing the crisis because all crises in the history is associated with lousy lending activities such as the 2008 Global Financial Crisis.

References

Abreu, M., & Mendes, V. (2002). *Commercial bank interest margins and profitability: Evidence from*.

Acaravci, S. K., & Çalim, A. E. (2013). Turkish banking sector's profitability factors. *International Journal of Economics and Financial Issues, 3*(1), 27–41.

Adalı, Z., & Bari, B. (2017). Monetary policy and bank lending channel in Turkey. *International Journal of Finance & Banking Studies (2147-4486), 6*(2), 22–36.

Ahmad, N. H., & Ahmad, S. N. (2004). Key factors influencing credit risk of Islamic bank: A Malaysian case. *The Journal of Muamalat and Islamic Finance Research, 1*(1), 65–80.

Akbaş, H. E. (2012). Determinants of bank profitability: An investigation on Turkish banking sector. *Öneri Dergisi, 10*(37), 103–110.

Akhavein, J. D., Berger, A. N., & Humphrey, D. B. (1997). The effects of megamergers on efficiency and prices: Evidence from a bank profit function. *Review of Industrial Organization, 12*(1), 95–139.

Alkassim, F. A. (2005). The profitability of Islamic and conventional banking in the GCC countries: A comparative study. *Journal of Review of Islamic Economics, 13*(1), 5–30.

Amor-Tapia, B., Tascón, M. T., & Fanjul, J. L. (2006). *Determinants of commercial banks' residual profitability: An industry approach*. https://doi.org/10.2139/ssrn.894440.

Anbar, A., & Alper, D. (2011). Bank specific and macroeconomic determinants of commercial bank profitability: Empirical evidence from Turkey. *Business and Economics Research Journal, 2*(2), 139–152.

Angbazo, L. (1997). Commercial bank net interest margins, default risk, interest-rate risk, and off-balance sheet banking. *Journal of Banking & Finance, 21*(1), 55–87.

Ari, A., & Cergibozan, R. (2016). The twin crises: Determinants of banking and currency crises in the Turkish economy. *Emerging Markets Finance and Trade, 52*(1), 123–135.

Artar, O. K. (2012). Küresel finansal krizin Türkiye'de bankacılık sektörü mali yapısına etkileri.

Ata, H. A. (2009). Kriz Sonrası Türkiye'de mevduat bankalara karlılığına etki eden faktörler. *Dokuz Eylül Üniversitesi İşletme Fakültesi Dergisi, 10*(2), 137–151.

Athanasoglou, P. P., Brissimis, S. N., & Delis, M. D. (2008). Bank-specific, industry-specific and macroeconomic determinants of bank profitability. *Journal of International Financial Markets, Institutions and Money, 18*(2), 121–136.

Baltagi, B. H., & Wu, P. X. (1999). Unequally spaced panel data regressions with AR (1) disturbances. *Econometric Theory, 15*(6), 814–823.

Bashir, A. H. M. (2001). Assessing the performance of Islamic banks: Some evidence from the Middle East. *Topics in Middle Eastern and North African Economies, 3*, 1–11.

Berger, A. N. (1995). The relationship between capital and earnings in banking. *Journal of Money, Credit and Banking, 27*(2), 432–456.

Bhargava, A., Franzini, L., & Narendranathan, W. (1982). Serial correlation and the fixed effects model. *The Review of Economic Studies, 49*(4), 533–549.

Bourke, P. (1989). Concentration and other determinants of bank profitability in Europe, North America and Australia. *Journal of Banking & Finance, 13*(1), 65–79.

Casu, B., Girardone, C., & Molyneux, P. (2006). *Introduction to banking* (Vol. 10). Harlow: Pearson Education.

Demirgüç-Kunt, A., & Huizinga, H. (1999). Determinants of commercial bank interest margins and profitability: Some international evidence. *The World Bank Economic Review, 13*(2), 379–408.

Demirgüç-Kunt, A., & Huizinga, H. (2000). *Financial structure and bank profitability*. World Bank Policy Research Working Paper (2430).

Demirhan, D. (2013). Effects of the recent financial crisis on the determinants of bank profitability: Case of Turkish banking industry. *Journal of Yaşar University, 8*(31), 5203–5228.

Diamond, D. W. (1984). Financial intermediation and delegated monitoring. *The Review of Economic Studies, 51*(3), 393–414.

Dietrich, A., & Wanzenried, G. (2014). The determinants of commercial banking profitability in low-, middle-, and high-income countries. *The Quarterly Review of Economics and Finance, 54* (3), 337–354.

Dinçer, H., Yüksel, S., & Pınarbaşı, F. (2020). Kano-based measurement of customer expectations in retail service industry using IT2 DEMATEL-QUALIFLEX. In *Handbook of research on positive organizational behavior for improved workplace performance* (pp. 349–370). Hershey, PA: IGI Global.

Eichengreen, B., & Gibson, H. D. (2001). *Greek banking at the dawn of the new millennium*. CFR Discussion Paper 2791, London.

Erdem, M. S. (2010). Turkish banking system in the face of the global crisis. *International Journal of Islamic and Middle Eastern Finance and Management, 3*(4), 351–362.

Erdoğan, M., & Aksoy, E. E. (2016). Banking regulation and determinants of banks' profits: Empirical evidence from Turkey. *Eurasian Journal of Business and Economics, 9*(17), 109–124.

Eti, S., Kalkavan, H., Dinçer, H., & Yüksel, S. (2020). Predicting the role of Islamic banking on sustainable economic development: An analysis for Turkey with ARIMA model. In *Handbook of research on creating sustainable value in the global economy* (pp. 146–164). Hershey, PA: IGI Global.

Gischer, H., & Jüttner, D. J. (2001). *Profitability and competition in banking markets: An aggregative cross country approach*. Otto-von-Guericke-Univ. Magdeburg, Faculty of Economics and Management.

Goddard, J., Molyneux, P., & Wilson, J. O. (2004). Dynamics of growth and profitability in banking. *Journal of Money, Credit and Banking, 36*(6), 1069–1090.

Haron, S., & Azmi, W. N. W. (2004, December). Profitability determinants of Islamic banks: A Cointegration approach. In *Electronic Version), Islamic Banking Conference, Union Arab Bank, Beirut, Lebanon* (pp. 5–7).

Hassan, M. K., & Bashir, A. H. M. (2003, December). Determinants of Islamic banking profitability. In *10th ERF annual conference, Morocco* (Vol. 7, pp. 2–31).

Hubbard, R. G. (1994). *Is there a credit channel' for monetary policy?* (No. w4977). National Bureau of Economic Research.

Isik, O. (2017). Internal determinants of profitability of state, private and foreign owned commercial banks operating in Turkey. *Journal of Economics Finance and Accounting, 4*(3), 342–353.

İskenderoğlu, Ö., Karadeniz, E., & Atioğlu, E. (2012). Türk bankacılık sektöründe büyüme, büyüklük ve sermaye yapısı kararlarının karlılığa etkisinin analizi. *Eskişehir Osmangazi Üniversitesi İktisadi ve İdari Bilimler Dergisi, 7*(1), 291–311.

Javaid, S., Anwar, J., Zaman, K., & Ghafoor, A. (2011). Determinants of bank profitability in Pakistan: Internal factor analysis. *Journal of Yasar University, 23*(6), 3794–3804.

Jiang, G., Tang, N., Law, E., & Sze, A. (2003). The profitability of the banking sector in Hong Kong. *Hong Kong Monetary Authority Quarterly Bulletin, 3*(36), 5–14.

Johansen, S. (1988). Statistical analysis of cointegration vectors. *Journal of Economic Dynamics and Control, 12*(2-3), 231–254.

Johansen, S., & Juselius, K. (1990). Maximum likelihood estimation and inference on cointegration—With applications to the demand for money. *Oxford Bulletin of Economics and Statistics, 52*(2), 169–210.

Kalkavan, H., & Ersin, I. (2019). Determination of factors affecting the South East Asian crisis of 1997 probit-logit panel regression: The South East Asian crisis. In *Handbook of research on global issues in financial communication and investment decision making* (pp. 148–167). Hershey, PA: IGI Global.

Kaya, Y. T. (2002). Türk bankacılık sektöründe karlılığın belirleyicileri. *MSPD Çalışma Raporları, BDDK Yayınları*, 1–21.

Lee, C. C., Yang, S. J., & Chang, C. H. (2014). Non-interest income, profitability, and risk in banking industry: A cross-country analysis. *The North American Journal of Economics and Finance, 27*, 48–67.

Macit, F. (2012). Bank specific and macroeconomic determinants of profitability: Evidence from participation banks in Turkey. *Economics Bulletin, 32*(1), 586–595.

Masood, O., & Ashraf, M. (2012). Bank-specific and macroeconomic profitability determinants of Islamic banks. *Qualitative Research in Financial Markets, 4*(2/3), 255–268.

Masood, O., Aktan, B., & Chaudhary, S. (2009). An empirical study on banks profitability in the KSA: A co-integration approach. *African Journal of Business Management, 3*(8), 374.

Miller, S. M., & Noulas, A. G. (1997). Portfolio mix and large-bank profitability in the USA. *Applied Economics, 29*(4), 505–512.

Mirzaei, A., Moore, T., & Liu, G. (2013). Does market structure matter on banks' profitability and stability? Emerging vs. advanced economies. *Journal of Banking & Finance, 37*(8), 2920–2937.

Mohamad, M. T., Sulaiman, A. A., Hamimah, K., & Muslim, N. (2019). The determinants of bank profitability: How Malaysian Islamic banks response to the financing risk. *Advances in Social Sciences Research Journal, 6*(12), 1–15.

Molyneux, P. (1993). *Structure and performance in European banking*. Doctoral dissertation, Prifysgol Bangor University.

Molyneux, P., & Thornton, J. (1992). Determinants of European bank profitability: A note. *Journal of Banking & Finance, 16*(6), 1173–1178.

Morrison, A. D., & White, L. (2005). Crises and capital requirements in banking. *American Economic Review, 95*(5), 1548–1572.

Obamuyi, T. M. (2013). Determinants of banks' profitability in developing economy: Evidence from Nigeria. *Organizations and Markets in Emerging Economies, 4*(08), 97–111.

Ongore, V. O., & Kusa, G. B. (2013). Determinants of financial performance of commercial banks in Kenya. *International Journal of Economics and Financial Issues, 3*(1), 237–252.

Özatay, F., & Sak, G. (2002, April). The 2000–2001 financial crisis in Turkey. In *Brookings trade forum* (pp. 121–160). Washington, DC: Brookings Institution Press.

Ozgur, O., & Gorus, M. S. (2016). Determinants of deposit bank profitability: Evidence from Turkey. *Journal of Applied Economics and Business Research, 6*(3), 218–231.

Peek, J., & Rosengren, E. (1995). The capital crunch: Neither a borrower nor a lender be. *Journal of Money, Credit and Banking, 27*(3), 625–638.

Pomerleano, M. (2009). *What is the impact of the global financial crisis on the banking system in East Asia?* (No. 146). ADBI Working Paper.

Ramadan, I. Z., Kilani, Q. A., & Kaddumi, T. A. (2011). Determinants of bank profitability: Evidence from Jordan. *International Journal of Academic Research, 3*(4), 180–191.

Ramlall, I. (2009). Bank-specific, industry-specific and macroeconomic determinants of profitability in Taiwanese banking system: Under panel data estimation. *International Research Journal of Finance and Economics, 34*(2), 1450–2887.

Rhoades, S. A. (1985). Market share as a source of market power: Implications and some evidence. *Journal of Economics and Business, 37*(4), 343–363.

Short, B. K. (1979). The relation between commercial bank profit rates and banking concentration in Canada, Western Europe, and Japan. *Journal of Banking & Finance, 3*(3), 209–219.

Smirlock, M. (1985). Evidence on the (non) relationship between concentration and profitability in banking. *Journal of Money, Credit and Banking, 17*(1), 69–83.

Staikouras, C., & Wood, G. (2003, June). The determinants of bank profitability in Europe. In *European Applied Business Research Conference, Venice* (Vol. 913).

Sufian, F., & Habibullah, M. S. (2010). Does economic freedom fosters banks' performance? Panel evidence from Malaysia. *Journal of Contemporary Accounting & Economics, 6*(2), 77–91.

Tan, Y., & Floros, C. (2012). Bank profitability and inflation: The case of China. *Journal of Economic Studies, 39*(6), 675–696.

Topak, M. S., & Talu, N. H. (2016). Internal determinants of bank profitability: Evidience from Turkish banking sector. *International Journal of Economic Perspectives, 10*(1), 37–49.

Wasiuzzaman, S., & Tarmizi, H. A. B. A. (2010). Profitability of Islamic banks in Malaysia: An empirical analysis. *Journal of Islamic Economics, Banking and Finance, 6*(4), 53–68.

Zhang, G., Zhou, S., Xia, X., Yüksel, S., Baş, H., & Dincer, H. (2020). Strategic mapping of youth unemployment with interval-valued intuitionistic hesitant fuzzy DEMATEL based on 2-tuple linguistic values. *IEEE Access, 8*, 25706–25721.

Classification Performance Comparison of Artificial Neural Networks and Support Vector Machines Methods: An Empirical Study on Predicting Stock Market Index Movement Direction

Şenol Emir

Abstract In this study, Artificial Neural Networks and Support Vector Machines which are widely used machine learning methods were examined. Usability of these methods for the prediction of the Istanbul Stock Exchange (ISE) National 100 Index (currently named BIST—100) movement direction was investigated. In the analysis, performances of these methods on the 2005–2011 period data sets containing technical indicators, other stock market indices and common macroeconomic indicators were compared. The results showed that technical variables give better performances than other variables. Later, a data set that predicts the stock index movement direction most accurately with a minimum number of variables was formed by feature selection on the aggregation of the mentioned data sets. Artificial Neural Networks gave better results than Support Vector Machines for all analyzes.

1 Introduction

The stock markets are complex systems that a huge number of transactions are made every day. Prediction in a dynamic, non-linear and highly complex systems is not an easy task. There exists no single method that exactly predicts the price behavior in the markets. Therefore, studies in the field have been very active for a long time.

Classical statistical methods have been partially successful in this area. In recent years, the usage of machine learning methods that have the ability to learn from examples, generalization, and have fewer assumptions than statistical methods increased dramatically. Artificial Neural Networks (ANN) and Support Vector

This study is a summary of Ph.D. thesis written by Şenol Emir in the Department of Quantitative Methods (Institute of Social Sciences, Istanbul University, 2013).

Ş. Emir (✉)
Faculty of Economics, Econometrics Department, Istanbul University, İstanbul, Turkey
e-mail: senol.emir@istanbul.edu.tr

H. Dincer, S. Yüksel (eds.), *Strategic Priorities in Competitive Environments*, Contributions to Management Science, https://doi.org/10.1007/978-3-030-45023-6_10

Machines (SVM) methods are examples of two of the most commonly used machine learning methods.

ANN are mathematical models that were inspired by the learning process in biological neural networks. In ANN, calculations are handled by simple computation units that are connected to each other. The processing of information is carried out by using connections between these units. ANN are flexible models that can detect the patterns in the noisy, nonlinear data. These properties of the method enable the usage of it in dynamic systems such as the stock market. It is theoretically proved that, through learning, an ANN with an adequate number of nonlinear units can explore complex relationships in the data with high accuracy. There are many studies in which the successful results are obtained by applying ANN to problem types such as classification, regression, and clustering.

SVM is a machine learning method that is backed by Statistical Learning Theory and can be applied in classification, regression problems. SVM has become a commonly preferred method for stock market prediction problems due to its ability to configure the model complexity, generalization, and to employ of kernel functions. In a binary classification case, if data is linearly separable then the method chooses the decision boundary that gives the least generalization error among infinitely many linear decision boundaries. The optimization problem that is constructed to find optimal decision boundaries can be solved by standard quadratic programming techniques. In a non-separable case, by configuring optimization problem it is possible to reach a solution. By using kernel functions inputs are mapped to a higher dimensional space and the classification problem is solved in this higher-dimensional space.

In this study, classification performances of ANN and SVM which are commonly used techniques for stock market predictions were compared to predict the movement direction of the Istanbul Stock Market (ISE) 100 Index. In addition, it is intended to reveal which type of variables have the most effect on the stock market movement direction.

This paper is organized as follows: In theoretical parts of the study, conceptual and mathematical discussions of Artificial Neural Networks and Support Vector Machines were included. In the application part, the datasets which contain technical indicators, percentages of change of other stock market indices, and common macroeconomic indicators were used to predict movement direction of ISE-100. On each data set, ANN and SVM methods were applied and their prediction performances were reported. At the end of the application, a summary is given as a conclusion.

2 Literature Review

A literature review of some of the studies using technical indicators in stock market index prediction is presented below.

Kim and Han used Stochastic %K, Stochastic %D, Stochastic slow %D, Momentum, ROC, William's %R, A/D, Disparity 5-day, Disparity 10-day, OSCP, CCI, RSI technical indicators to estimate the Korea Stock Exchange (KOSPI) index (Kim and Han 2000). Kara and others used 10 technical indicators to estimate the direction of the ISE-100 index. These technical indicators are simple 10-day moving average, weighted 10-day moving average, Momentum, Stochastic K%, Stochastic D%, RSI, MACD, William's R%, A/D Oscillator and CCI (Kara et al. 2011).

Diler used simple moving average, weighted moving average, Momentum, Stochastic, RSI and MACD technical indicators in his model to estimate the daily direction of the ISE-100 index (Diler 2003). Dunis and others employed MACD and RSI technical indicators to predict the weekly change of direction of the Madrid stock exchange (Dunis et al. 2012).

Several studies investigating the degree of interdependence between ISE and other stock exchanges summarized.

Vuran studied the long-term relationship between the ISE-100 Index and the stock market indices of some developed and developing countries. The results of the study concluded that the ISE-100 index for the period indicated was related to the FTSE-100, DAX, Bovespa, MERVAL and IPC indices over the long term (Vuran 2010). In the study by Ozun, the impact of developed country stock exchanges on developing countries stock exchanges such as Brazil and Turkey was examined. The daily closing values of Bovespa, ISE-100, NIKKEI-225, FTSE-100, DAX, CAC-40, S&P-500 and NASDAQ stock exchanges were analyzed. As a result, it was stated that the ISE index was affected in a weak positive direction by the developed stock markets (Ozun 2007). According to results in the study conducted by Korkmaz and others, the S&P-500 index affects the ISE-100 Index (Korkmaz et al. 2011).

The studies in which the relations between macroeconomic indicators and the ISE index are examined are listed below. Türsoy and others measured the effects of 13 macroeconomic variables on returns of shares. These variables include fundamental economic indicators: money supply (M2), industrial production, crude oil prices, consumer price index, import, export, gold prices, exchange rates, interest rates, National Domestic Product (GDP), foreign reserves, unemployment rate, market pressure (Türsoy et al. 2008). Erdem and others examined the impact of macroeconomic variables on the ISE index. According to the study, among the macroeconomic variables examined, only inflation, interest rate, and exchange rate affect the return on the ISE (Erdem et al. 2005). Zügül and Sahin investigated whether or not there is a relationship between consumer-price index and macroeconomic variables using monthly data of January 2004–December 2008 period and ISE-100 index, dollar exchange rate, M1 money supply, interest rate as variables. The results showed that there was a negative correlation between the M1 money supply, exchange rate, and interest rate and the stock return index, whereas there was a positive correlation between the inflation rate and the ISE-100 index (Zügül and Şahin 2009). Gençtürk tried to determine the relationship between stock prices and macroeconomic factors in the period of crises and the period of non-crises by using multiple linear regression analysis. As a result of the research, macroeconomic variables affecting the ISE index in times of crisis emerged as the money supply and the consumer price index. In the period when there were no crises, the index of industrial production, consumer price index, gold, dollar, money supply, and treasury bond interest rate were significantly correlated with the index. In this period, there was a positive correlation between gold, consumer price index and money supply and index, additionally a negative correlation between industrial production index, dollar and treasury bond interest rates and the index (Gençtürk 2009). Dogan and Yalçın investigated the effect of exchange rate changes on the ISE-100 index. (Dogan and Yalcin 2007). In the study conducted by Eryiğit ISE index values were examined and the effect of oil prices on the change of the stock market index based on dollars was tried to be found. In the analysis, the Turkish lira-denominated oil price, dollar-denominated oil prices, and TL-US dollar exchange rate were used as input variables (Eryiğit 2009).

ANN studies in Turkey have generally been used to predict financial failures and bankruptcies. Although there are studies on stock market index forecasting abroad, there is a lack of such studies in Turkey.

Çinko and Avcı used ANN and linear regression to estimate the ISE-100 Index and compared the results. They used delayed values and moving averages of the index and transaction volume as variables of the model. In the study, ANN showed generally better results than regression models (Çinko and Avcı 2007). Akcan and Kartal tried to estimate the stock prices of the seven companies that make up the ISE insurance sector index with ANN. In the model, the daily closing value of the ISE-100 index, consumer price index, dollar effective sales rate, daily gold price were used (Akcan and Kartal 2011). Kutlu and Badur used ANN to estimate the ISE index direction. The variables used in the study are previous day's index value, previous day's US dollar value, previous day's overnight interest value, five dummy variables indicating the days of the week, previous day's index values of France, Germany, UK, Brazil, Japan, NASDAQ, DOW JONES and S&P-500 stock markets (Kutlu and Badur 2009). In the study conducted by Yıldız and others, ANN was used to estimate the direction of the ISE-100 index using the highest, lowest, closing values of ISE and the US Dollar rate as model inputs (Yıldız et al. 2008). Boyacioğlu and Avci used the ANFIS (Adaptive Neuro-Fuzzy Inference System) method to accurately predict the ISE index. Six macroeconomic variables (gold price, U.S. dollar rate, interest rates, consumer price index, industrial production index, treasury interest rates) and three stock market indices (DOW JONES, DAX and BOVESPA) were used as inputs (Boyacioglu and Avci 2010).

The applications in which the SVM method is applied to ISE data are very limited. Below are the applications of stock market movement prediction achieved by using SVM in the worldwide and Turkey.

The study by Kim used SVM and ANN methods to estimate the direction of the Korea Stock Exchange (KOSPI) index with daily data. Twelve technical indicators were used in the analysis. These indicators were %K, %D, Slow %D, Momentum, ROC, William's %R, A/D Oscillator, Disparity 5-day, Disparity 10-day, OSCP, CCI, RSI technical indicators. 2347 observations were used for training (80%) and 581 observations were used for testing (20%). The test performance results of the methods were SVM (57.83%) and ANN (54.73%) (Kim 2003). Huang and others used the SVM method to estimate the weekly change direction of the NIKKEI-225 index. The S&P-500 index and the Japanese Yen-US Dollar rate were used as inputs to predict the direction change of the NIKKEI Stock Exchange (Huang et al. 2005). Özdemir and others applied the SVM method on the monthly data to predict the index movement of ISE-100. A total of 11 variables were used in the analysis, 8 of which were macroeconomic indicators and 3 of which were indices of other stock markets (Özdemir et al. 2011). Kara and others used the SVM method to estimate the direction of the ISE-100 index with data from the period 1997–2007 (Kara et al. 2011).

3 Artificial Neural Networks

For classification, regression, clustering problems many statistical methods have been developed. Some of these methods yield successful results if their assumptions about data are provided. But they are not flexible enough to perform well for observations outside of the training set in which they are built. Artificial neural networks (ANN) are used as an alternative approach to classical methods (Jain et al. 1996). They are most commonly used in pattern recognition (classification) applications. In particular, the steady increase in computing power of computers has made them be used more widely and effectively for complex data sets. The most important feature of ANN is the way it provides information processing. It is possible to perceive the artificial neural networks as "a whole consisting of a large number of computing units working together harmoniously in order to solve a particular problem."

3.1 Biological Motivation

ANN originated from the idea of mimicking the inner working principles of the brain on computers. The findings of studies on the brain show that each neuron receives some information from neighboring neurons and that this information is converted into output according to biological neuron dynamics (Efe and Kaynak 2000). ANN consists of a large number of simple information processing (computing) units connected by weighted connections. If an analogy is to be made, its units can be likened to neurons. Each unit receives inputs from many other units and generates an output. The output is distributed as input to other units in the network (Reed and Marks 1999).

It wouldn't be random for these units to come together. In general, these units run parallel and are distributed in the input, hidden, and output layers of the network. The information that is sent from one neuron to another in the brain is very tiny. This suggests that critical information in the brain is not carried directly, it is held and distributed in interconnections between neurons. Another name of ANN, "the connectionist model" comes from this feature (Mehrotra et al. 1997).

3.2 *Advantages of ANN*

The main advantages of ANN can be listed as follows.

3.2.1 Learning

ANNs have a strong learning ability. They can adapt to the environment in which they work by changing network parameters. What makes these abilities possible is their powerful learning algorithms. Learning is the most prominent feature of artificial neural networks. Given input samples and their expected output, there are different learning algorithms that change weights to generate the correct output for each training input. Among these algorithms, backpropagation is the most widely used (Reed and Marks 1999).

3.2.2 Generalization

As a result of efficient training, an ANN model not only learns training observations but also learns the relationship between input and output to generate the correct output when observations that are not included in the training set presented to the network. In short, a well-trained ANN can show a good generalization (Du and Swamy 2006).

3.2.3 Nonlinearity

A typical property of ANN is its ability to model nonlinear relationships effectively and easily. ANN aims to solve problems by using "universal approximation" capability. Thus, need to have very detailed information about the problem or to analyze the structure of the problem deeply is eliminated (Warren 1994).

3.2.4 Self-Organizing

Some types of artificial neural networks (e.g. self-organizing maps and competitive learning-based networks) have the ability to change their internal structure and function in response to external changes. The training of these networks is achieved using unsupervised learning algorithms (Zurada 1992).

3.2.5 Parallelism

Its parallel structure allows ANN to implement software and hardware applications that run in a high degree of parallelism. Another benefit is that it allows for very fast computation. The output of a unit at time t depends only on inputs at time $t - 1$. Since the units on the same layer are independent of each other, these units can be processed at the same time (Mehrotra et al. 1997). An L-Layer forward-oriented network can respond to the change in the input after the L step since the layers are connected in series.

3.2.6 Robustness and Fault Tolerance

ANN has the characteristics of robustness and fault tolerance. An ANN model can process fuzzy, incomplete, noisy and probability-based data. It is a distributed information processing system due to the fact that information is distributed throughout the network structure. Since many inputs are used to generate the output of each unit the system is not very sensitive to small distortions. In a case that a few units are out of use, due to the distributed structure, it does not result in a complete crash (Munakata 2008). In any deterioration, the network can immediately improve performance by recalibrating the weights. Thus, it repairs itself and gains the ability to tolerate errors.

3.3 Basic Elements of Artificial Neural Networks

The basic elements involved in artificial neural networks are described below.

3.3.1 Layers

Most networks consist of three layers as input, hidden, and output layers. There may be more hidden layers, but only one hidden layer is enough for many applications. Each connection between the two units has a weight denoted by w.

The input layer retrieves input values from the dataset and passes these values to the hidden layer without holding any processing. The number of input units depends on the types and number of features in the dataset. This layer has no errors because there are no calculations on these units. Therefore, it does not have a detailed unit structure like the hidden and output layers.

The units in the hidden layer are the source of the nonlinearity of the network, due to their nonlinear behavior. As a greater number of hidden layer units are considered to increase the network's ability and flexibility to identify complex patterns, it may be tempting to use too many units in this layer. On the other hand, an overgrowth hidden layer leads to a reduction of generalization ability by memorizing the training set, i.e. overfitting. In this case, the number of units in the hidden layer can be reduced or vice versa if the training results are not at the desired level, the number of units in the hidden layer can be increased (Mehrotra et al. 1997). Each time a new hidden layer is added to the network, local minimum points where the error function can be stuck during the training process are added. Therefore, a single hidden layered network is created first. However, if this network is insufficient then a new hidden layer can be added. Applications attempt to use the least number of hidden layers to meet the requirement (Kriesel 2007). An analytic method has not been developed that gives the optimal number of units in the hidden layer(s). Therefore, the only way to overcome this ambiguity is trial and error (Munakata 2008). There is no need to use hidden layers for "linearly separable" problems. Because multi-layer models have no superiority over single-layer models in such problems (Kecman 2001).

The output layer is responsible for generating outputs corresponding to the observations presented from the input layer by processing information flowing from the hidden layer. In the output layer, for the binary classification problems, it is common to use a single unit where a "threshold" value is assigned a priori to separate classes. A single output unit can also be used in problems where there is more than one class. In the same way, the threshold values for each class must be determined to distinguish these classes from each other. Assessment by field experts is required to determine the threshold values correctly. In many networks, computing units generate output in the following manner.

$$y = f\left(\sum_i w_i x_i\right)$$

x_i represents the output of other units (input values from outside), w_i denotes connection weights, and f( ) denotes a nonlinear function. In other words, each unit calculates the weighted sum of the inputs coming to it and sends it to a nonlinear function for the purpose of generating a scalar output. Generally, f is a bounded, non-decreasing, nonlinear function (Reed and Marks 1999).

3.3.2 Weights

In ANN models, the information is represented by weights. Weights indicate the importance of information coming to a unit in the calculation to be made by the unit. The fact that the weight is zero indicates that the incoming information has no effect. Weights can be positive or negative.

3.3.3 Combining Function

For each unit, the combining function produces a value called "net input" from the linear combination of the input values and weights of the corresponding unit. The most commonly used combining function is the weighted sum. The net input for any *j*th node (unit) using the weighted sum is found as:

$$\text{net input}_j = \sum_i w_{ij}x_{ij} = w_{0j}x_{0j} + w_{1j}x_{1j} + \cdots + w_{lj}x_{lj}$$

x_{ij}, is the *i*th input that comes to unit *j* and w_{ij} indicates the weight between *j*th unit that has a total of l + 1 incoming inputs and *i*th input. $x_1, x_2, \ldots, x_l$ represent total inputs flowing to the unit. $x_{0j} = 1$ meaning that it always takes the constant value 1. Therefore, each hidden or output layer unit has an extra input with a value of 1 (Rumelhart et al. 1986).

3.3.4 Activation Function

One of the important factors determining the behavior of units in ANN is the activation functions used. In biological neurons, if the sum of the weighted inputs of a neuron exceeds a certain threshold value, it is known that this neuron sends electrical signals to other neurons. In addition, in biological neurons, the output changes nonlinearly with respect to changes in the inputs. Thus, nonlinear activity functions are used to achieve a behavior similar to this in artificial neurons. The most commonly used activity function is the sigmoid function as shown:

$$f(x) = \frac{1}{1 + e^{(-ax)}}$$

Inputs of the sigmoid functions are net input values. The output of each unit (values between 0 and 1) in the hidden layer is calculated by activation function according to net input flowing to these units. Calculated output values are sent to the output layer (Zurada 1992). *a* denotes the slope parameter in the function definition. By changing this parameter, sigmoid functions with different slopes can be obtained. On the origin slope is a/4. When the slope approaches infinity, the sigmoid function transforms into the threshold function. The sigmoid function can combine linear, curvilinear and near-constant behaviors based on the input (Larose 2005). In the places close to the center, it shows a straight line. As it starts to move away from the center, it shows curvilinear and almost constant behavior when it approaches the extreme values. Therefore, small increases in the input value depending on the location it is in creates different increases in the value of the function. While small increases in the points close to the center create small increases in the function, increasing the input value at the endpoints creates very small increases in the value of the function.

3.3.5 Loss Function

Although the choice of loss functions is application dependent, most applications use standard loss functions. The advantages of standard loss functions are that they are easily differentiable, errors are not affected by the trends and magnitudes of previous errors, and that the costs of equal errors are equal regardless of input. This makes the models easier to analyze. Sum of Squared Errors (SSE) is used in many ANN models as a loss function. SSE is the sum of squares of prediction errors in all output units of all observations in the training set (Zurada 1992).

$$\text{SSE} = \sum_{\text{inputs}} \sum_{\text{outputs}} \left(\begin{matrix} \text{actual} \\ \text{output} \end{matrix} - \begin{matrix} \text{predicted} \\ \text{output} \end{matrix} \right)^2$$

There are several common loss functions in applications in addition to the SSE. Mean Sum of Squared Errors (MSSE) normalizes the SSE. When the network output is asked to give a probability estimate, the "cross-entropy" loss function is used (Mitchell 1997).

3.4 Backpropagation Learning Algorithm

Theoretically, learning in artificial neural networks can be managed by creating (new connections, new units) or removing (existing connections, existing units) or changing (connection weights, threshold values of units, activity function). The most common way of learning is through changing weights (Kriesel 2007).

The backpropagation algorithm is used to learn weights in multilayer feedforward networks. İt is computationally effective as its computational complexity varies linearly with respect to the number of weights in the network. With the development of this algorithm, feed-forward multilayer networks have become the most widely used architecture (Yegnanarayana 2005).

The gradient descent method is employed in the backpropagation algorithm. Multi-layer networks can have many local minimums. Gradient descent only guarantees convergence to a local minimum point. It does not guarantee convergence to the point that will give global minimum error value. Despite this obstacle, it is seen that in many real applications the backpropagation algorithm yields superior results (Rumelhart et al. 1986).

The backpropagation algorithm creates a network based on the number of hidden units that are determined beforehand. All weights are randomly assigned small values. Once the network structure is fixed, all training observations are presented to the network respectively.

In learning processes, a coefficient called "learning rate" is often used, which takes a value between (0, 1). The size of the update in the weights depends on this learning rate η. If this value is too large, the impact of recent observations will be greater. When this coefficient is small, a greater number of update steps are required for convergence (Alpaydın 2011). In the backpropagation algorithm, each weight is updated in proportion to the learning coefficient (η), the input (x_{ji}) to which the weight is applied, and the error δ_j that occurs in the output of the unit (Mitchell 1997).

4 Support Vector Machines

In this section, the Support Vector Machines (SVM) method and the basic concepts of Statistical Learning Theory are examined from a mathematical perspective. SVM, proposed by Vladimir Vapnik, is a powerful method for solving many common problems such as classification, regression, clustering, anomaly detection, and density estimation.

Support Vector Machines (SVM) is a method that brings together different mathematical concepts such as margin, duality, and kernel representation. Although these concepts have been used in different applications, they have been known for a long time. However, because they lacked the solid foundations provided by the Statistical Learning Theory, they were unable to be used to create viable learning algorithms (Cherkassky and Mulier 2007: 408). For example, the idea of using kernels was introduced in the 1960s. The concept of margin was developed again in the 1960s in order to classify linearly separable data. However, applying kernels in the SVM method and the classification of linearly inseparable occurred after approximately 30 years later (Boser et al. 1992; Cortes and Vapnik 1995). After that, the SVM method was adapted to other types of learning problems and successfully applied in many different applications.

According to Cover's Theorem (Cover 1965), an input space consisting of linearly non-separable observations can be transformed into a higher-dimensional feature space where observations can be linearly separated with high probability when the required conditions are met (Haykin 1999). In applications, it is also common to map entries to a new set of variables called features according to a priori assumption about the learning problem. The learning algorithm uses these features instead of the original entries. It is therefore important that observations are mapped to higher-dimensional space (feature space), where they can be easily separated by a linear decision boundary. Linear decision functions generated in the feature space correspond to nonlinear decision functions in the input space (Cristianini and Schölkopf 2002). For this, the mapping must be non-linear and the size of the feature space must be large enough. In the SVM method, the input space is mapped to the higher-dimensional feature space by a nonlinear transformation. The feature space can be very large or even infinite because there is no restriction on the number of features in SVM (Pontil and Verri 1998). The SVM method uses linear functions to distinguish high-dimensional observations since the complexity of linear models can be accurately determined and optimization methods are available that give the global minimum for empirical risk (Moguerza and Muñoz 2006).

The SVM method is based on Statistical Learning Theory. It was originally used only for the theoretical analysis of the function approximation problem that fits a given set of data. Later, it was found that it could be used in the design of new learning algorithms as well as theoretical analyses (Vapnik 1999).

4.1 Statistical Learning Theory

Statistical Learning theory which is also known as the "Vapnik-Chervonenkis (VC) Theory" attempts to build a mathematical infrastructure of machine learning. It is considered one of the best approaches for making flexible predictions using a limited number of observations. It contains mathematical proofs that have important consequences for learning. All the concepts necessary to construct a general framework of the learning problem are defined in this theory.

The basic questions that the theory tries to answer can be sorted as follows (Von Luxburg and Schölkopf 2008):

1. Which learning tasks can be performed by computers in general?
2. Which assumptions must be made for machine learning to be successful?
3. Which basic characteristics does a learning algorithm need to be successful?
4. Which performance guarantees can be given on the results of a learning algorithm?

VC theory was first developed to theoretically study the "Empirical Risk minimization (ERM)" induction principle. The conditions for good generalization have been determined and these conditions have been shown to be closely related to uniform convergence. The results found provided quantitative expression of the compromise (tradeoff) between model complexity and knowledge at hand (training set consisting of a limited number of observations).

VC theory consists mainly of four parts (Vapnik 1998).

1. Determination of consistency conditions of Empirical Risk Minimization principle
2. Finding the generalization limits of the learning machine under consistency conditions.
3. Finding the necessary principles for making inductive inference from finite observations depending on the limits of generalization.
4. Creating algorithms that apply induction principles developed.

One of the main characteristics that any induction principle must provide is asymptotic consistency. This property refers to the asymptotically (as the number of training observations increases) convergence of the value of the function minimizing empirical risk to the value that would be achieved if the actual risk could be directly minimized (Schölkopf and Smola 2001).

The best generalization performance can be achieved if the correct tradeoff between empirical error on the training set and the capacity of the learning machine which demonstrates the learning ability of the model on any training set can be achieved. A person says "it is not a tree" when a tree is shown to him because the number of leaves of the new tree is different from the number of leaves of the trees he has seen before. This is an example of a learning machine with a very high capacity, on the other hand, a learning machine with low capacity is like someone who accepts every object as a tree when a green object is shown. In either case, the generalization that is the main purpose cannot be achieved. How to establish this tradeoff is theoretically explained very successfully in the VC theory (Burges 1998).

4.1.1 VC Dimension

VC (Vapnik–Chervonenkis) dimension is a measure of the capacity (complexity) of classifiers. For example, it measures how well a binary classifier can model the decision boundary between classes. When the VC size is large, the classifier's capacity is higher and it is better able to distinguish training observations by their class. In general, as a classifier's capacity increases, it can separate observations in training set more successfully (Hamel 2009).

4.1.2 Generalization Bounds

It is always possible to find a function from all possible classes of functions to reduce the empirical risk to zero. Clearly, the empirical risk has no benefit in finding the optimal model because it is too optimistic. So, Vapnik developed the concept of "VC confidence " based on the VC dimension to determine the generalization error of a model.

Generalization bound is shown as $R(\omega) \leq R_{amp}(\omega) + \psi(n, h, \delta)$ denoting expected risk and empirical risk as $R(\omega)$ and $R_{amp}(\omega)$ respectively. This bound is valid with a probability at least $1-\delta$ for all loss functions that are bounded and nonnegative. The term $\psi(n, h, \delta)$ shows the VC Confidence and n, h corresponds to the size of the training set and VC dimension respectively. Sum of empirical risk and VC Confidence give an upper bound for the expected risk of a model. When the set of different learning machines namely $f(x, \omega)$ functions are given and for the fixed, small enough δ value, the machine that gives the smallest upper limit on the real risk is chosen. This shows a principal way of choosing a learning machine for a particular task (Burges 1998).

More explicitly, VC Confidence can be written as (Clarke et al. 2009):

$$\psi(n, h, \delta) = \sqrt{\frac{h\left(\log\left(\frac{2n}{h}\right) + 1\right) - \log\left(\frac{\delta}{4}\right)}{n}}$$

Looking at $\psi(n, h, \delta)$ it can be seen that VC confidence is directly proportional to the VC dimension (h). A high VC dimension increases the complexity of the model, resulting in a high generalization error. Over-complicated models tend to overfit training data and therefore cannot generalize well. The sum of empirical risk and VC confidence represent an envelope formed by these two curves. This envelope shows the generalization limit. The optimal model is reached at the point where this limit is minimal (Hamel 2009). Additionally, VC confidence is inversely proportional to the size (n) of the training set. Therefore, as the training set grows, a lower generalization error occurs because more information about the input space will be known.

4.1.3 Structural Risk Minimization

Structural Risk Minimization (SRM) induction principle is a mechanism developed for the purpose of selecting optimal model complexity for limited observations. Since the sets of functions are infinitely large, it is not a practical approach to examine all the elements of these sets of functions one by one in order to find the optimal function without any additional information. Therefore, Vapnik proposed to use VC dimensions of function classes as a guide to finding the optimal model to match capacity and training data and capture the best generalization performance (Evgeniou et al. 2002).

There are two SRM strategies that can be used to minimize the generalization bound: Keeping model complexity (VC dimension) constant and minimizing empirical risk or alternatively keeping the empirical risk constant (small) and minimizing the VC dimension. Many statistical methods and artificial neural networks implement the first strategy, while support vector machines implement the second alternative (Wang and Zhong 2003).

To solve the learning problem with a limited number of observations, the SRM principle uses a priori structure definition on the set of approximating functions. For this purpose, a structure such as $S_1 \subset S_2 \subset \ldots S_k \subset \ldots$ is created. Sets of loss functions are subsets of each other and of each subset (S_k) VC dimension is finite and denoted by h_k. By definition, the constructed structure allows subsets to be ordered according to their capacity (VC size) such that $h_1 \leq h_2 \leq \cdots \leq h_k \leq \cdots$. After this structure is determined, the optimal model selection includes selecting the elements of the structure with optimal capacity and then estimating the model from this element steps. To be able to implement the SRM principle VC size of each subset S_k in the structure is calculated and empirical risk is minimized for each subset (Cherkassky and Mulier 2007). SRM principle doesn't specify a certain class of approximating function. Such a choice is outside of Statistical Learning Theory and is determined by a priori knowledge (Evgeniou et al. 2000).

The SRM principle has also shaped the idea of "maximum margin classifier", which is at the base of the support vector machines method. In such classifiers, it is intended to find models with the largest margin for good generalization (Cox and Adhami 2002). In this case, the relationship between the concept of margin and the concept of capacity (VC dimension) becomes important.

4.1.4 Margin and Complexity Relation

In the SVM method, complexity control is managed using margin-based loss functions. Empirical results show that margin-based methods are more robust than classical methods when the number of observations is limited. Vapnik analytically proved that for the VC dimension of γ-margin hyperplanes

$$h \leq \min\left(\frac{r^2}{\gamma^2}, d\right) + 1$$

bound is valid (Belousov et al. 2002). r is the radius of the smallest hypersphere containing all training observations. Accordingly, it is possible to directly control the complexity (VC dimension) of the hyperplane independently of the dimension (d). Also as an important result, it can be observed that the separating hyperplane with the minimum complexity, hence the highest generalization ability, is the hyperplane with the widest margin.

4.2 Maximum Margin Classifiers

The main goal in classification models based on maximum margin is to find a decision surface that is equidistant to the class boundaries at the position where the two classes are closest to each other. If a hyperplane is parallel to the linear decision surface and all observations of the class are below or above the hyperplane, it is called "support hyperplane" (Bennett and Campbell 2000). The support hyperplane can be considered as a copy of the decision surface moved to the point where it touches the boundary of the class concerned. In binary classification problems, there are typically two support hyperplanes. One of them was moved in the direction of the class labeled as positive, the other was moved in the direction of the class that was labeled as negative. In addition, the distance between class boundaries (margin) is attempted to be maximized. Models using this approach are called "maximum margin classifiers" (Steinwart and Christmann 2008: 14). When the decision surface is placed in a position equal to the class boundaries, the probability of correct classification of observations not included in the training set increases. Maximizing the distance from the decision surface to class boundaries further increases this probability (Ramon and Christodoulou 2006).

Considering the concepts of support hyperplane and margins, the "optimal separating hyperplane" criteria can be expressed as follows: The hyperplane found for the binary classification problem is the optimal separating hyperplane if it is equidistant to the two support hyperplanes and maximizes the margin value (Abe 2010). The optimal separating hyperplane is unique because it is the separating hyperplane with the largest margin.

4.2.1 Maximum Margin Classifiers Optimization Problem

Finding optimal separating hyperplane is an optimization problem where the appropriate (feasible) solutions are different supporting hyperplanes. The objective function calculates the margin of each appropriate solution. Since the maximum margin is desired, the objective is $m^* = \max \phi(w, b)$. The function $\phi(w, b)$ calculates the margin of the separating hyperplane $w \cdot x = b$. The maximum margin (m^*) shows the margin of the optimal separating hyperplane $w^* \cdot x = b^*$. But for computational purposes, this maximization objective is transformed to a minimization objective. Constraints are the positions of support hyperplanes that are not allowed to cross their class boundaries. By using geometry and linear algebra it can be found that maximum margin is $m^* = \text{maks } \frac{2}{\|w\|}$. Since any maximization problem can also be expressed as a minimization problem, the same objective function can also be written as $m^* = \min \frac{\|w\|}{2}$. Since the squaring operation is monotonically increasing, minimizing value and minimizing the square of this value means the same. The optimization result is also independent of multiplication by a constant value (Boyd and Vandenberghe 2004). If the objective function is rearranged based on this information it finally becomes

$$\min \frac{\|w\|}{2} = \min \frac{\|w\|^2}{2} = \frac{1}{2} w \cdot w = \min \frac{1}{2} w \cdot w$$

The term b is not included in objective function but it has an effect on the constraints. During optimization, support hyperplanes are not allowed to exceed the class bounds to which they belong. In other words, they must remain as support hyperplanes during optimization. In this case constraints

$$w^* \cdot x_i \geq 1 + k, \quad \forall y_i \in \{\text{Class} + 1\}$$
$$w^* \cdot (-x_i) \leq 1 - k, \quad \forall y_i \in \{\text{Class} - 1\}$$

must be satisfied. These constraints can be written more compactly as:

$$w \cdot (y_i x_i) \geq 1 + y_i b$$

In this notation, it is seen that all observations are involved in constraints. Constraints define only appropriate solutions (Mavroforakis and Theodoridis 2006). In summary; given a binary classification problem with a linearly separable training set optimal separating hyperplane can be reached by solving the optimization problem that has an objective function

$$\min \phi(w, b) = \min \frac{1}{2} w \cdot w$$

and constraint

$$w \cdot (y_i x_i) \geq 1 + y_i b$$

The maximum margin objective function is not overly sensitive to small changes in *w* parameters. In the case of small parameter changes, the probability of misclassification is minimized for maximum margin (Boser et al. 1992). The convexity of the objective function suggests that the global minimum can be found. In another word, a method such as quadratic programming, to ensure that the objective function gets its optimal (the smallest) value given the appropriate set of solutions. This is a significant superiority of maximum margin classifiers over algorithms such as artificial neural networks whose solution depends on initial states or parameters that are difficult to control.

4.2.2 Margin-Based Loss Function

Margin-based loss functions divide observations into two regions, zero-loss observations and greater-than-zero-loss observations. Considering the binary classification problem, the decision boundary ($f(x, w) = 0$) divides the input space into positive ($f(x, w) > 0$) and negative ($f(x, w) < 0$) regions. Observations that are correctly classified by the model and located at a certain distance from the decision limit are assigned zero losses; observations that are misclassified or close to the decision boundary are assigned positive losses.

A decision function needs to achieve the optimal balance between goals of:

1. Minimizing the total empirical loss of observations within the margin.
2. Maximizing margin.

Apparently, these two goals contradict each other. Because greater margin size leads to greater empirical loss. Therefore, it is crucial to find the optimal margin size for good generalization. For classification problems, SVM uses a loss function parameterized with the margin size (γ) called Hinge Loss. This function is defined as:

$$L_\gamma(y, f(x, \omega)) = \max \ (\gamma - yf(x, \omega), 0)$$

4.3 SVM Classification

SVM's conceptual approach to the classification problem can be more easily understood by starting from an idealized starting point and making generalizations. The starting point is the special case where the data set is assumed to be linearly separable.

4.3.1 Hard Margin Linear Classifier

For classification problems, the separating hyperplane is a linear function that can separate the training set without error. Thus, a training set denoted as $(x_1, y_1), \ldots.$ $(x_n, y_n),\ x \in R^d,\ y \in \{-1, +1\}$, by appropriate *w*, *b* parameters can be separated by the linear decision function $D(x) = (w \cdot x) + b$.

To find the optimal separating hyperplane it is necessary to determine *w*, *b* values that minimize the objective function

$$\frac{1}{2}\,(w \cdot w)$$

under

$$y_i[(w \cdot x_i) + b] \geq 1$$

constraint.

The solution of the primal problem shown contains d + 1 parameters. For medium-sized dimensions (d), this problem can be solved by quadratic programming. It is not applicable in very high dimensional spaces. The primal problem is therefore converted to the dual problem, whose complexity depends not on dimension but on the number of observations. Even for very high dimensional spaces, the dual problem can be easily solved with standard quadratic optimization techniques. The optimal solution can be reached in polynomial time (Alpaydın 2009).

It is possible to switch from primal form to dual form in two steps. In the first step, the unconstrained optimization problem is created using Lagrange multipliers shown as

$$L(w, b, \alpha) = \frac{1}{2}(w \cdot w) - \sum_{i=1}^{n} \alpha_i(\ y_i[(w \cdot x_i) + b] - 1.)$$

A large portion of the Lagrange multipliers (α_i), has a value of a zero ($\alpha_i = 0$). These observations provide the constraint $y_i[(w \cdot x_i) + b] > 1$ meaning that they represent observations that are sufficiently far from the separating hyperplane and have no effect on the position of the separating hyperplane. Since they do not carry any information to determine the decision boundary, even if they are removed, the same solution is obtained.

The second step is to use the Karush-Kuhn-Tucker (KKT) conditions to show the parameters w and b in $L(w, b, \alpha)$ only in terms of α_i. After this, the primal problem becomes the dual problem, which requires the only maximization with respect to the Lagrange multipliers (Abe 2010). Optimal parameters (w^*, b^*, α^*) according to KKT conditions must satisfy equations below:

$$\frac{\partial L(w^*, b^*, \alpha^*)}{\partial b} = 0$$

$$\frac{\partial L(w^*, b^*, \alpha^*)}{\partial w} = 0$$

The following properties of optimal hyperplane are found as a result of solving partial derivative equations.

- α_i^* coefficients must satify constraint $\sum_{i=1}^{n} \alpha_i^* y_i = 0, \quad \alpha_i^* \geq 0$
- w^* (optimal separating hyperplane) is a linear combination of observations in the training set. Namely, $w^* = \sum_{i=1}^{n} \alpha_i^* y_i x_i, \quad \alpha_i^* \geq 0.$

According to complementary slackness condition, it is necessary to satisfy $\alpha_i^* [y_i(w^* \cdot x_i + b^*) - 1] = 0$ equality. By using the obtained results decision function can be written in terms of $\alpha_1^*, \ldots, \alpha_n^*$ and b^* as:

$$D(x) = \sum_{i=1}^{n} \alpha_i^* y_i (x \cdot x_i) + b^*$$

Parameter b^* is found using a special property of support vectors. For any support vector (x_s, y_s), the condition $y_s[(w^* \cdot x_s) + b^*] = 1$ is provided because the support vectors are exactly on the margin boundary. If this condition is substituted in the decision function, equality for b^* is obtained as:

$$b^* = y_s - \sum_{i=1}^{n} \alpha_i^* y_i (x_i \cdot x_s)$$

The third term in the equation has a value of 0 due to the condition $\left(\sum_{i=1}^{n} \alpha_i^* y_i = 0\right)$. Again by substituting the result $(w^* = \sum_{i=1}^{n} \alpha_i^* y_i x_i, \ \alpha_i^* \geq 0)$ in the Lagrangian, dual objective function $L(\alpha)$ is constructed as:

$$L(\alpha) = -\frac{1}{2} \sum_{i,j=1}^{n} \alpha_i \alpha_j y_i y_j (x_i \cdot x_j) + \sum_{i=1}^{n} \alpha_i$$

This function needs to be maximized with respect to parameters $\alpha_1, \ldots, \alpha_n$.

Summarizing, the dual optimizing problem is to find α_i parameters to maximize the objective function

$$L(\alpha) = \sum_{i=1}^{n} \alpha_i - \frac{1}{2} \sum_{i,j=1}^{n} \alpha_i \alpha_j y_i y_j (x_i \cdot x_j)$$

under constraints

$$\sum_{i=1}^{n} y_i \alpha_i = 0 \qquad \alpha_i \geq 0$$

Observations with corresponding α_i^* values that are greater than zero in the dual solution are support vectors. Since the support vectors are the observations closest to the decision surface, they are the observations that are most difficult to classify and determine the position of the optimal separating hyperplane (Cherkassky and Mulier 2007). Support vectors carry all the information about the classification problem. Even if all observations except the support vectors are removed, the same solution is obtained. This property is known as "sparsity of solution" and has important consequences both in practice and in the analysis of the algorithm (Cristianini and Schölkopf 2002).

4.3.2 Linear Soft Margin Classifiers

Maximum margin classifiers are allowed to make mistakes on the training set using the concept of slack variable. It may seem pointless to allow a classifier to make a mistake. But it should be taken into account that many of the data in the actual applications contain noise. Noise can cause the boundary between classes to be too complex in a classification problem. A classifier that is not allowed to make mistakes also creates very complex decision surfaces (Mammone et al. 2009). It is possible to create much simpler decision functions by acknowledging that the observations that force decision surfaces to be too complex are noise and ignoring these points. Maximum margin classifiers where misclassification is allowed are called "soft margin" classifiers. Classifiers that are not allowed to make classification errors are known as "hard margin" classifiers (Steinwart and Christmann 2008). In the soft margin approach, observations that remain within the margin are ignored to be on the wrong side of the separating hyperplane. So the constraints on hard margin classifiers are relaxed.

The sum of errors is tried to be minimized instead of the number of errors due to the easiness of reaching the solution. The empirical risk is found by using "slack variables" defined as $\xi_i = \max(1 - y_i f(x_i, \omega), 0)$ (Cherkassky and Mulier 2007). The sum of these variables gives the total deviation from the margin. Not only observations that are misclassified, but observations that are correctly classified but within the margin are also punished for better generalization. Soft margin optimal separating hyperplane is found by minimizing the objective function

$$\frac{1}{2}(w \cdot w) + \frac{C}{n}\sum_{i=1}^{n}\xi_i$$

under the constraint

$$y_i[(w \cdot x_i) + b] \geq 1 - \xi_i$$

The C parameter in the objective function controls the tradeoff between complexity and empirical risk and is determined by the model designer (Cortes and Vapnik 1995).

Dual of the problem can be shown as:

Objective function

$$\text{maks } L(\alpha) = \sum_{i=1}^{n}\alpha_i - \frac{1}{2}\sum_{i,j=1}^{n}\alpha_i\alpha_j y_i y_j (x_i \cdot x_j)$$

Constraints

$$\sum_{i=1}^{n} y_i\alpha_i = 0$$

$$0 \leq \alpha_i \leq C/n$$

The only difference with the linearly separable case is that the upper limit of C/n is added to the Lagrange multipliers (Mavroforakis and Theodoridis 2006). The soft margin problem becomes the hard margin problem when all the values of ξ_i are 0.

Possible results for the dual of soft margin (Abe 2010).

1. $\alpha_i = 0,\ \xi_i = 0$, observation x_i is classified correctly.
2. İf $0 < \alpha_i < C$, then according to the complementary slackness $y_i[w^T x_i + b] - 1 + \xi_i = 0$ and $\xi_i = 0$ conditions must be satisfied. Thus, $y_i[w^T x_i + b] = 1$ and x_i is a support vector. Support vectors that satisfy $0 \leq \alpha_i \leq C$ inequality are called "free support vectors".
3. If $\alpha_i = C$, $y_i[w^T x_i + b] - 1 + \xi_i = 0$, $\xi_i \geq 0$ then x_i is a support vector. Support vectors that satisfy $\alpha_i = C$ condition are called "bounded support vectors". They are on the wrong side of the margin. If $0 \leq \xi_i < 1$ then x_i is correctly classified, if $\xi_i >= 1$ then x_i is misclassified.

Decision function is the same as the linearly separable case and is given as:

$$D(x) = \sum_{i=1}^{n}\alpha_i^* y_i (x \cdot x_i) + b^*$$

4.3.3 Nonlinear SVM Classifiers

In the soft margin approach, constraints are relaxed, allowing a certain degree of misclassification. But if the problem is largely not linearly separable misclassification error will be too high then the soft margin will not work. In most real applications it is necessary to create nonlinear decision functions. It becomes possible to classify linearly non-separable training sets if nonlinear decision functions can be constructed (Huang et al. 2006).

To transform a linearly non-separable problem into a linearly separable problem, inputs are mapped to the higher-dimensional feature space using "mapping functions" (Wu et al. 2010).

The basic idea is that a nonlinear separating hyperplane in an n-dimensional input space can be mapped to a linear hyperplane in a higher N-dimensional feature space. Unfortunately, there is no analytical method that gives the optimal mapping function. Therefore, mapping functions are tried to be found by trial and error.

Each input in the training set is mapped to a point in higher dimensional (N) space using φ mapping function as $x = (x_1, x_2, \ldots, x_n) \xrightarrow{\varphi} \varphi(x) = (\varphi_1(x), \varphi_2(x), \ldots, \varphi_N(x))$. As a result of the mapping, the set $\{ (\varphi(x_1), y_1), (\varphi(x_2), y_2), \ldots, (\varphi(x_n), y_n) \}$ is obtained which contains the images in the feature space.

Here are two main points to consider when mapping an input space to a higher dimensional feature space.

1. The chosen $\varphi(x)$ mapping function should be able to create a wide class of hyperplanes.
2. It can become very difficult to make computations when the number of features (the size of the feature space) is too large.

If the decision function for hard-margin and soft-margin classifiers is rewritten for the feature space

$$D(\varphi(x)) = \sum_{i=1}^{N} \alpha_i^* y_i (\varphi(x) \cdot \varphi(x_i)) + b^*$$

is obtained. It is seen that in the decision function the only operation requiring observations is the dot product $\varphi(x) \cdot \varphi(x_i)$. This is the fundamental property that allows the decision function to be transformed into a nonlinear form (Cristianini and Schölkopf 2002).

4.4 *Kernel Functions*

The painless generalization of linear classifiers to nonlinear classifiers has extended the application areas of the SVM method extensively. At the center of this generalization are "kernel functions". A kernel function is the criterion of application-specific similarity between observations and shapes the feature space according to its definition of similarity (Alpaydın 2009). It is very difficult to calculate dot products in very high dimensional spaces thus kernel functions are used for this purpose. A kernel is a function providing

$$K(x_i, x_j) = \varphi^T(x_i) \cdot \varphi(x_j)$$

property. It can be seen that kernel functions operate in the input space. The main advantage of using the kernel function is that it does not require $\varphi(x)$ mapping. The dot product $\varphi^T(x_i) \cdot \varphi(x_j)$ which must be done in the feature space, is done directly on the training observations in the input space using the kernel. So, using a kernel it is possible to create a model that will process in an infinite-dimensional feature space. The "kernel trick" is that there is no obligation to know what the $\varphi(x)$ mapping is. All that is needed is the calculation of the K_{ij} kernel, which can be generated from any mapping (Abe 2010). Under proper circumstances, a dot product in the feature space has an equivalent kernel in the input space. Decision function for nonlinear SVM classifiers is $D(x) = \sum_{i=1}^{n} \alpha_i^* y_i K(x_i, x) + b$

4.4.1 Kernel Types

Kernel functions can map different types of observations, such as text documents, images, or DNA chains, into space where the learning algorithm can be run. This is one of the important innovations of the kernel approach (Cristianini and Schölkopf 2002). The maximum margin method is independent of the kernel used. Kernel selection is made according to field knowledge or other techniques after the maximum margin is determined. Field experts know the effective similarity criteria between observations. Therefore, many kernels specific to problem areas are being developed.

Common types of kernels are as follows (Ivanciuc 2007):

4.4.1.1 Linear Kernel

The dot product of *x* and *y* values defines the linear kernel as:

$$K(x_i, x_j) = x_i \cdot x_j$$

It is used to test the linear separability of the training set and to track the increase in classification performance as a result of the use of nonlinear kernels.

4.4.1.2 Polynomial Kernel

The polynomial kernel provides a simple and efficient way to model nonlinear relations defined as

$$K(x_i, x_j) = (1 + x_i \cdot x_j)^d$$

the *d* parameter shows the degree of the kernel. As degrees increase, the risk of overfitting increases.

4.4.1.3 Radial Kernel

The radial-based kernel is defined as:

$$K(x_i, x_j) = \exp\left(-\frac{\|x - y\|^2}{2\sigma^2}\right)$$

Parameter σ controls the shape of the hyperplane.

4.4.1.4 Sigmoidal Kernel

Kernel corresponding to the hyperbolic tangent (tanh) function, which is one the most commonly used activity function in artificial neural networks is defined as:

$$K(x_i, x_j) = \tanh(ax_i \cdot x_j + b)$$

5 Stock Index Movement Prediction

In this section, Artificial Neural Networks (ANN) and Support Vector Machines (SVM) methods were used in the prediction of index movement direction for the ISE-100 index. For this purpose, five separate data sets were created, including technical indicators, index change percentages of other stock markets, macroeconomic indicators, an aggregated form of the first three data sets mentioned, and the data obtained after feature selection was performed on this data set. It has been attempted to determine which of these datasets is more useful in ISE-100 index direction prediction. In addition, how ANN and SVM methods perform in this classification problem has been studied.

After giving basic information about data sets, model details and the performances of ANN and SVM methods will be presented on each data set.

5.1 Technical Indicators Used in Analysis

The first dataset which will be used for the direction movement estimation of the ISE-100 index consists of 11 technical indicators with variable names such as MASS, ATR, Mo (Momentum), CCI, MACD, TRIX, MOV (moving average), MFI, RSI, Stochastic, WILLR (William's %R). Table 1 has basic statistical information about these technical indicators.

There are no missing observations in the technical indicators. They all have 1747 values, the number of days the stock market was open during the period under review. The technical indicators with the largest standard deviation are MOV, MACD, ATR, and CCI, respectively. The calculations of the technical indicators used in the analysis are given briefly (Perşembe 2010; Erdinç 2004).

5.1.1 Moving Averages

Simple Moving Average is calculated as follow:

$$SMA_t = P_t + P_{t-1} + P_{t-2} + \cdots + P_{t-n}/n$$

SMA_t Simple Moving Average
P Price
t Current date
n Time period moving average calculated

The exponential moving average takes into account all available data points, as opposed to the simple moving average, in addition to highlighting the last days. The calculation is done as follows:

Table 1 Basic statistics about technical indicators

Technical indicator	Number of observations	Average	Minimum	Maximum	Standard deviation
MASS	1747	25.01	22.19	29.04	1.14
ATR	1747	1055.30	421.15	2232.72	327.58
MO	1747	100.75	70.77	119.70	6.53
CCI	1747	15.51	−309.54	333.47	110.60
MACD	1747	114.91	−2893.93	2014.85	890.32
TRIX	1747	0.05	−1.43	0.91	0.35
MOV	1747	44,499.06	23,800.36	69,595.72	12,583.81
MFI	1747	56.54	6.53	99.61	16.30
RSI	1747	53.45	13.21	88.37	12.93
STOCH	1747	56.83	3.04	99.72	26.77
WILLR	1747	−41.45	−100.00	0.00	30.51

$$\mathrm{EMA_t} = \mathrm{EMA_{t-1}} + (\mathrm{CF} * (\mathrm{P_t} - \mathrm{EMA_{t-1}}))$$

EMA_t Exponential Moving Average
CF Correction factor (2/(n + 1))

5.1.2 Moving Average Convergence Divergence (MACD)

It is used to detect harmony or mismatch between two moving averages. Prices have one long-term (26-day) and one short-term (12-day) exponential moving average. Once these are found, the long-term moving average is subtracted from the short-term moving average. Then, the signal curve utilized in the detection of rotation movements and mismatch is calculated by taking the 9-day exponential moving average of the MACD value.

$$\mathrm{MACD} = \mathrm{EMA}(12) - \mathrm{EMA}(26)$$

$$\mathrm{Signal} = \mathrm{EMA}(\mathrm{MACD}, 9)$$

5.1.3 Commodity Channel Index (CCI)

CCI is a trend-following indicator and the calculation steps are as follows.

$$\text{Typical Price (TP)} = (\text{Highest Price} + \text{Lowest Price} + \text{Closing Price})/3$$

1. 20-period Simple Moving Average (SMA) of Typical Price (TP) is calculated.
2. Mean Deviation (MD) = TP − SMA
3. The total of the mean deviations (TMD) of the last 20 periods is found.

$$\mathrm{CCI} = (\mathrm{TMD} * 0.015)/(\mathrm{SMA} - \mathrm{TP})$$

5.1.4 Relative Strength Index (RSI)

It is one of the most widely used indicators among overbought/oversold indicators. This simple yet simple as well as a reliable indicator can be used in a wide variety of ways. In this context, AU(n) is the average of closing prices higher than the current price value over the previous n days where AD(n) is the average of closing prices lower than the current price value over the previous n days. The details are given below.

$$\mathrm{RSI} = 100 - (100/1 + \mathrm{RS}) \text{ and } \mathrm{RS} = \mathrm{AU}_{(n)}/\mathrm{AD}_{(n)}$$

5.1.5 Stochastic

Stochastic is an overbought/oversold indicator. It is built on the assumption that closures in an upward trend will be concentrated on the upper sides of the daily trading range and in a downward trend on the lower sides. The stochastic formula calculates the value called %K.

$$\%K_t = ((\text{Closing Price}_t - \text{Lowest Price}_n)/(\text{Highest Price}_n - \text{Lowest Price}_n)) * 100$$

5.1.6 William's %R

%R is from the same family of indicators such as RSI and Stochastic (an overbought/oversold indicator). It is actually a variation of the stochastic indicator. %R is short for Range, which means the range of operations (the distance between the highest and lowest of the selected period, for example, one day). As with the assumption behind the stochastic indicator, the closing price is close to the highest of the trading range of the selected period, a picture of the market buying and starting to swell. If the closing price is at the bottom of the selected trading range, the market is assumed to be oversold. The formula %R built on these assumptions is:

$$\%R_t = ((\text{Highest Price}_n - \text{Closing Price}_t)/(\text{Highest Price}_n - \text{Lowest Price}_n)) * 100$$

5.1.7 Momentum

The most important feature of the Momentum indicator is that it is used in both trending and horizontal markets. Momentum is calculated by a very simple formula:

$$\text{Momentum} = P_S - P_{s-n}$$

P_s The last period closing price
P_{s-n} n period previous price

5.1.8 Money Flow Index (MFI)

MFI is a trading volume indicator. It is calculated based on the typical price of the day.

$$\text{Typical Price (TP)} = (\text{Highest Price} + \text{Lowest Price} + \text{Closing Price})/3$$

This value is multiplied by the volume of the transaction and the raw flow of money is found.

$$\text{Raw Money Flow} = \text{Typical Price} * \text{Volume}$$

If the average price of the most recent period is higher than the average price of the previous period, there has been money inflows and money outflows if it is lower. Money entry is the sum of money inflows in the selected period (for example, the last 14 days), and money out is the sum of money outflows. The money flow ratio using two values is

$$\text{Money Flow Ratio} = \frac{\text{14 Period Money Inflows}}{\text{14 Period Money Outflows}}$$

Finally, MFI is computed as

$$\text{Money Flow Index} = 100 - (100/(1 + \text{Money Flow Ratio}))$$

5.1.9 Average True Range (ATR)

ATR measures the extent of the volatility in prices. An increasing value indicates that the change in its prices (volatility) is increasing; otherwise, the fluctuation in its prices is decreasing. So this indicator increases when prices suddenly start to fall or suddenly start to rise. If prices fluctuate around a given value they fall. The calculations are done as follows:

$$\text{HCP : Highest Closing Price, LCP : lowest Closing Price, CP : Closing Price}$$

$$\text{TR}_t : \text{Time Range at period t}$$

$$\text{TR}_t = \text{Max}(|\text{HCP}_t - \text{LCP}_t|, |\text{HCP}_t - \text{CP}_{t-1}|, |\text{LCP}_t - \text{CP}_{t-1}|)$$

$$\text{ATR}_0 = \text{TR}_0$$

$$\text{ATR}_t = \frac{(n-1)\text{ATR}_{t-1} + \text{TR}_t}{n}$$

5.1.10 TRIX

TRIX is a momentum indicator and is calculated by averaging three consecutive exponential movements of closing prices for specified periods to eliminate small ups and downs in prices. In this way, the trend of prices can be seen and interpreted much more clearly when charted. The following is the TRIX formula.

$$\mathrm{TRIX} = \frac{\mathrm{EMA3_t} - \mathrm{EMA3_{t-1}}}{\mathrm{EMA3_{t-1}}}$$

5.1.11 Mass Index

It is an indicator that aims to inform trend changes. When calculating this index, the distance between the lowest and highest prices increases and decreases. If the distance between the highest and lowest prices widens, the mass index increases, if it shrinks, it decreases. The calculation is as follows:

$$\mathrm{Mass\ \ Index} = \sum_{1}^{27} \left[\frac{9 - \mathrm{period\ EMA(HCP - LCP)}}{9\ \mathrm{period\ EMA(9\ period\ EMA(HCP - LCP))}} \right]$$

5.2 Stock Market Index Data

The second dataset used to predict the index movement direction includes stock market index values. Information about stock exchanges and indices are given in Table 2.

In the analysis, a total of 18% change ratios, with 1 and 2 days delay of 9 stock exchanges closing prices, were used. Percentage change rates were calculated using

Table 2 Indices used in analysis

Abbreviation	Index	Country
ISE-100	ISE-100 Index	Turkey
BOVESPA	São Paulo Stock Exchange	Brazil
DAX	Deutscher Aktien IndeX	Germany
DJIA	Dow Jones Industrial Average	USA
FTSE-100	Financial Times Stock Exchange 100 Index	England
NIKKEI-225	Nihon Keizai Shimbun Index 225 Index	Japan
NYSE	New York Stock Exchange	USA
SP-500	Standart and Poors 500 Index	USA
HSI	Hang Seng Index	Hong Kong

$((Closing_t - Closing_{t-1})/Closing_{t-1}) * 100$ formula for the days stock exchange was open. In the analysis, since the direction of the ISE-100 index is tried to be predicted, only the days that the ISE was open was considered. If any stock market used as an independent variable was not open on a day when ISE was open, it was accepted that the percentage change ratio of this stock exchange index is the same as the change rate of the previous open day.

5.3 Macroeconomic Indicators

In the literature, it is seen that very different macroeconomic variables are used in the prediction of capital markets. Since most of these variables are published in weekly, monthly or quarterly periods, they were not included in the analysis. There are macroeconomic variables in the third data set. These variables are 1-day delayed values of Euro, Pound, USA Dollar, Yen exchange rates and 1-day delayed value of gold per ounce.

5.4 Data Collection and Preparation

The ISE closing price data was taken from the http://www.imkb.gov.tr web page. The closing price data of other stock exchanges are obtained from the Yahoo Finance (http://finance.yahoo.com) page. For the macroeconomic data ("http://evds.tcmb.gov.tr"), the Central Bank's Electronic Data Distribution System was used. MetaStock software was used to obtain technical analysis indicators. The daily direction change was labeled as "−1" and "1". If the ISE-100 index closed at a higher value than the $t - 1$ day on day t, it was "1"; if it closed at a lower value, it was shown as "−1".

The data used in the analysis belongs to the period of 03.01.2005–30.12.2011. The total number of observations consisted of 1747 trading days. In this period, while the number of days the ISE-100 index increasing was 921, there were 826 days when the index was in a decreasing direction. In this case, increasing days constitute 52.8% of all trading days and the remaining 47.2% constitute decreasing days (Table 3). Since these values are close to each other, it can be said that the upward and downward movement classes are balanced.

The number of days when the stock market was open by years is close to each other. The number of days traded varies between 247 and 251. Considering the increase and decrease in percentages by years, it is seen that these rates are also close to each other. The percentage of up days ranges from 41.8% (in 2008) to 58.8% (in 2009). The percentages of upward direction were higher than the percentages downwards, except for 2008.

In the analysis, the period 2005–2009 (5 years) was used as a training set and the period 2010–2011 (2 years) was used as a test set. The increase and decrease data for

Table 3 Number of days in which ISE-100 index increased and decreased by years

	Years							
	2005	2006	2007	2008	2009	2010	2011	Total
Upward	145	131	126	104	147	140	128	921
%	57.8	52.4	50.6	41.8	58.8	56.7	51	52.8
Downward	106	119	123	145	103	107	123	826
%	42.2	47.6	49.4	58.2	41.2	43.3	49	47.2
Total	251	250	249	249	250	247	251	1747

Table 4 Upward and downward percentages of training and testing sets

	Period	
	2005–2009 (Training)	2010–2011 (Testing)
Upward	653	268
%	52.2	53.9
Downward	596	230
%	47.8	46.1
Total	1249	498

these periods is also given in Table 4. Accordingly, the training set consists of 1249 observations and the test set consists of 498 observations. When the percentages of upwards are examined, it is seen that the rates in the training and test sets (52.2% and 53.9% respectively) are close together. According to this, class distributions in training and testing sets can be said to be similar to each other.

Ninety percent of the training data set was used for training and the remaining 10% for validation. The number of hidden units in ANN models was searched in a range of min = 4, max = 14. Sum of Square (SSE) and cross-entropy functions were used as loss functions. While creating ANN classifiers, it was asked to software to report the performance results of 4 of the 20 networks trained on each dataset, which yielded the best results in the training and validation set. Identity, Logistic, Tanh, Exponential, and Sine functions were used as activation functions for the hidden and output layers. In order to prevent the network from being too complex, the weight decay method with default range values (min = 0.0001, max = 0.001) in the input and output layers was utilized. As a result of the training, the parameters of the networks that gave the best results on the validation set were recorded in a file. Then, this file was loaded on the test set so that the same networks could run. While creating SVM models Linear, Polynomial, RBF (radial based function) and Sigmoid kernels were tested in order. 10-fold cross-validation was performed to prevent overfitting. In order to find the optimal C parameter, the C parameter was searched in the range 1–10.

5.5 *Index Direction Prediction with Technical Indicators*

SVM classifiers using Linear, Polynomial, RBF, and Sigmoid kernels have been constructed on the first dataset containing technical indicators. The classification accuracy rates of these classifiers on the test set are given in Table 5.

The SVM classifier, which showed the best performance on the technical indicators dataset, used the RBF kernel with an accurate classification rate of 73.7%. The Linear kernel shows performance in training (71.2%) close to the RBF kernel, but test performance (69.3%) is lower.

The classification summary on the test set of the RBF kernel is given in Table 6. Accordingly, the days of an increase in the index can be predicted correctly at a good rate of 78.7%. The correct estimate of the days of the decrease in the index was 67.9%.

During constructing ANN models on the first dataset, the number of hidden units was searched between 4 and 14. The results of the four networks with the best results are also summarized in Table 7.

Of the networks created, the network that had an 11-11-2 architecture, gave the highest training (86%) and validation (83%) performance. The loss functions and activity functions of all networks were the same. The test performances found by running these networks on the test set are shown in Table 8.

According to results, the network that showed the highest performance (80%) over the test set was the 11-12-2 network. ANN models seem to better predict the direction of increase, as do SVM models. For example, the 11-4-2 network was able

Table 5 Training and test performances of SVM classifiers (technical indicators)

Kernel type	Training performance (%)	Testing performance (%)
Linear	71.2	69.3
Polynomial	67.7	64.4
RBF	73	73.7
Sigmoid	62.3	63.6

Table 6 Classification summary of the RBF kernel on the test set

Direction	Total	True	False	True (%)	False (%)
Downward	230	156	74	67.9	32.1
Upward	268	211	57	78.7	21.3

Table 7 Best ANN models on training and validation sets (technical indicators)

Network no.	Network architecture	Training performance	Validation performance	Loss function	Hidden layer activation function	Output layer activation function
1	11-4-2	79.8	77.4	Entropy	Tanh	Softmax
2	11-9-2	79.8	79	Entropy	Tanh	Softmax
3	11-12-2	84	80.6	Entropy	Tanh	Softmax
4	11-11-2	86	83	Entropy	Tanh	Softmax

Table 8 Test performances of ANN models (technical indicators)

Architecture	Result	Downward	Upward	Total
11-4-2	True (%)	70.9	87	79.5
	False (%)	29.1	13	20.5
11-9-2	True (%)	67.4	79.1	73.7
	False (%)	32.6	20.9	26.3
11-12-2	True (%)	75.7	83.6	80
	False (%)	24.3	16.4	20
11-11-2	True (%)	70.9	86.1	79.1
	False (%)	29.1	13.9	20.9

Table 9 SVM results (stock market index values)

Kernel type	Training performance (%)	Test performance (%)
Linear	62.1	55.8
Polynomial	52.3	53.8
RBF	60.4	56.8
Sigmoid	59.5	56.8

to accurately predict the direction of increase at a very good rate of 87%. Other networks could also predict the direction of increase at satisfactory rates. The network that best predicted the downward direction with a 75.7% success rate was also the 11-12-2 network that showed the best performance on average.

Given these results, it is possible to predict the direction of the ISE-100 Index more accurately by ANN classifiers with an 80% true classification rate compared to the SVM classifiers with 73.7% performance.

5.6 *Index Direction Prediction with Stock Market Index Data*

The second dataset contains stock market index values. The results of the SVM models on the test set are presented in Table 9. SVM classifiers that showed the highest test performance (56.8%) were classifiers using RBF and Sigmoid kernels. Although the Linear kernel showed the highest (62.1%) performance in the training set, the test performance remained in second place.

On the second dataset, although the performances of the best four ANN models selected were close to each other, both training (62%) and validation performance (59.8%) were the highest in the network of 18-11-2 architecture. This network used Entropy as loss function and Tanh activation function for both the hidden and output layer.

The results obtained by running four selected models on the test set are shown in Table 10. The best performance (57.2%) on the test set was yielded by the 18-11-2 model. All models were able to predict the direction of the increase better. The model with an 18-9-2 architecture was able to predict the direction of increase by 73.1%

Table 10 ANN test results (stock market index values)

Architecture	Result	Downward	Upward	Total
18-17-2	True (%)	41.3	68.7	56
	False (%)	58.7	31.3	44
18-9-2	True (%)	34.8	73.1	55.4
	False (%)	65.2	26.9	44.6
18-5-2	True (%)	39.6	70.9	56.4
	False (%)	60.4	29.1	43.6
18-11-2	True (%)	41.3	70.9	57.2
	False (%)	58.7	29.1	42.8

Table 11 SVM results (macroeconomic variables)

Kernel type	Training performance (%)	Test performance (%)
Linear	55.2	48.4
Polynomial	52.3	53.8
RBF	55.4	53.8
Sigmoid	54.8	46.2

while showing a very low performance (34.8%) in estimating the downward movement.

According to these results, SVM and ANN classifiers provide close results (56.8% and 57.2%, respectively) if percentage change values of other stock markets were used to predict ISE-100 direction. Considering these low testing performances, it is seen that changes in other stock markets are not very effective in predicting the ISE-100 index.

5.7 Index Direction Prediction with Macroeconomic Indicators

The third dataset contains macroeconomic variables. The performance of SVM classifiers on this dataset is summarized in Table 11. Accordingly, the highest training (55.4%) and test performance (53.8%) again showed by the RBF-based kernel. The test performance of Linear and Sigmoid kernels remained below 50%.

The best ANN model that gave the best validation performance (58.9%) was a 5-9-2 network. This network used Entropy loss function and Exponential activation function for the hidden layer and Softmax for the output layer.

The test performances of the obtained networks are included in Table 12. Accordingly, the best performance achieved on macroeconomic data was a 5-4-2 network with a 54.4% score. While the classification accuracy for the upward direction of this network was 70.5%, it was able to predict the direction with very low accuracy (35.7%).

Table 12 ANN test results (macroeconomic indicators)

Architecture	Result	Downward	Upward	Total
5-3-2	True (%)	46.1	57.8	52.4
	False (%)	53.9	42.2	47.6
5-7-2	True (%)	3	97	53.6
	False (%)	97	3	46.4
5-9-2	True (%)	32.6	64.8	49.6
	False (%)	67.4	35.8	50.4
5-4-2	True (%)	35.7	70.5	54.4
	False (%)	64.3	29.5	45.6

Table 13 SVM results (combined data set)

Kernel type	Training performance (%)	Test performance (%)
Linear	71.5	71.7
Polynomial	64	65
RBF	73.4	71.9
Sigmoid	70	70.5

Table 14 RBF kernel test results (combined data set)

Direction	Total	True	False	True (%)	False (%)
Downward	230	149	81	64.8	35.2
Upward	268	209	59	78	22

When the results were examined, the SVM and ANN models yielded very close results (53.8% and 54.4%, respectively) with a data set of macroeconomic variables. Both methods predicted upward direction movement more successfully. When the SVM classifiers were examined, it was determined that the RBF-based kernel performed better than the others. As a summary, the lagged stock market index percentage changes and macroeconomic indicators showed significantly worse results in the ISE-100 index's direction prediction than in the technical indicators.

5.8 *Index Direction Prediction with Combined Data*

The fourth dataset combines all 34 independent variables, including 11 technical indicators, 18 stock market index values and 5 macroeconomic indicators. The results given by the SVM classifiers on this combined dataset are given in Table 13. Classifiers using Linear, RBF, and Sigmoid kernels have yielded close test results. The SVM classifier using an RBF-based kernel showed the best test performance with 71.9%.

The classification summary of the SVM classifier using the RBF-based kernel on the test set is presented in Table 14. Examining results shows that 78% of the days of the upward movement in the index can be estimated successfully. The true prediction rate of the days of the downward movement in the index was 64.8%.

Table 15 Best ANN models on training and validation sets (combined dataset)

Network no	Network architecture	Training performance	Validation performance	Loss function	Hidden layer activation function	Output layer activation function
1	34-24-2	84	82.3	SSE	Tanh	Tanh
2	34-8-2	89.7	87.1	SSE	Tanh	Tanh
3	34-8-2	91	84.7	SSE	Logistic	Identity
4	34-18-2	88.7	86.3	Entropy	Tanh	Softmax

Table 16 ANN test results (combined dataset)

Architecture	Result	Downward	Upward	Total
34-24-2	True (%)	81.3	58.6	69.1
	False (%)	18.7	41.4	30.9
34-8-2	True (%)	95.2	49.6	70.7
	False (%)	4.8	50.4	29.3
34-8-2	True (%)	88.3	61.2	73.7
	False (%)	11.7	38.8	26.3
34-18-2	True (%)	90	49.3	68.1
	False (%)	10	50.7	31.9

Table 15 provides the results of the networks that show the best performance on the training and validation data sets. Accordingly, the training performances of the networks are markedly higher than the training performances of the SVM classifiers. The 34-8-2 network showed the best training performance with 91%.

Detailed classification results on the test set of these networks are presented in Table 16. Accordingly, the highest test performance was 73.7% with a 34-8-2 network. All ANN models seem to predict the downward direction better than the upward direction.

If the results obtained so far are summarized, the highest test performance on the first 3 datasets was achieved on the dataset of technical indicators both by the SVM and by the ANN. A true classification rate of SVM classifiers with 73.7% on technical indicators has dropped to 71.9% on the fourth (combined) dataset. True classification rate, which was 80% of ANN classifiers, decreased to 73.7% on this dataset. It can be concluded that the higher dimensionality problem (the curse of dimensionality) affects the ANN classifiers more than the SVM classifiers on this specific application.

5.9 *Index Direction Prediction by Feature Selection*

A feature selection procedure was performed on the fourth data set (combined set with 34 variables). For this purpose, Chi-Square results were used. Independent variables that had a p-value less than 0.01 were selected. As a result of the feature

Table 17 Chi-Square and *p* values used in feature selection

Variable	Chi-Square	*p*-value
CCI	149.2221	0.000000
WILLR	292.4849	0.000000
RSI	105.2608	0.000000
STOCH	101.7980	0.000000
MO	45.9494	0.000001
MFI	40.4241	0.000006
DJIA1 CHANGE	24.1802	0.001059
DOLLAR EXC RATE	21.7172	0.005468

Table 18 SVM results (reduced dataset)

Kernel type	Training performance (%)	Test performance (%)
Linear	64.3	64.5
Polynomial	66.5	65
RBF	69	68.5
Sigmoid	63.3	66.3

Table 19 Model details of RBF kernel (feature selected dataset)

Property	Values
Kernel type	Radial based
# of support vectors	878 (854 bounded)
C (capacity)	8

selection, the number of variables, which was 34, was reduced to 8. Details are given in Table 17.

As expected, most of the variables were selected from technical indicators that give the best results from. Of the 11 technical indicators, 6 were selected (CCI, WILLR, RSI, STOCH, MO, MFI). Of the 18 lagged stock market index variables, only 1 lagged stock market change percentage (DJIA1_CHANGE) of the DOW JONES index and 5 macroeconomic variables, only the US Dollar rate (DOLLAR_EXC_RATE) were selected. With these results, it is clear that technical indicators are more effective in predicting the direction of the ISE-100 index than other stock market indices and macroeconomic indicators.

The performance results of SVM classifiers on the dataset that was created after the feature selection procedure are also shown in Table 18. According to this, the highest true classification was performed by the SVM classifier using the RBF-based kernel. The true classification rate of this classifier was 68.5%. The training and test performances of SVM classifiers appear to be very close together. This is an indication that SVM classifiers have a high ability to generalize.

Model details of RBF Kernel is given in Table 19.

The classification performance summary of the SVM classifier using the RBF-based kernel on the test set is given in Table 20. Accordingly, the days of the upward movement of the index can be estimated successfully at 77.2%. True prediction of the days of the downward movement in the index was 58.3%.

Table 20 Classification summary of RBF kernel on test set

Direction	Total	True	False	True (%)	False (%)
Downward	230	134	96	58.3	41.7
Upward	268	207	61	77.2	22.8

Table 21 ANN models on feature selected dataset

Network no.	Network architecture	Training performance	Validation performance	Loss function	Hidden layer activation function	Output layer activation function
1	8-11-2	80.2	75.8	Entropy	Tanh	Softmax
2	8-9-2	75.5	75	Entropy	Exponential	Softmax
3	8-9-2	81.1	75	Entropy	Tanh	Softmax
4	8-9-2	80.4	75	Entropy	Exponential	Softmax

Table 22 Test performance of ANN models on feature selected dataset

Architecture	Result	Downward	Upward	Total
8-11-2	True (%)	64.3	81.3	73.5
	False (%)	35.6	18.7	26.5
8-9-2	True (%)	57.4	82.8	71.1
	False (%)	42.6	17.2	28.9
8-9-2	True (%)	68.7	77.2	73.3
	False (%)	31.3	22.8	26.7
8-9-2	True (%)	64.8	79.5	72.7
	False (%)	35.2	20.5	27.3

The four best networks obtained on the fifth dataset are ranked in Table 21. Accordingly, the highest training performance was 81.1%.

The performance of these networks on the test set is also included in Table 22. It is seen that the networks give very close results. The 8-11-2 network achieved the highest classification success with a ratio of 73.5%.

The performance of SVM classifiers (68.5%) on the reduced size dataset decreased slightly compared to the performance (71.9%) in the dataset in which all variables were used. In the ANN classifiers, the performance (73.7%) in the data set where all variables are used is very close to the performance (73.5%) in the reduced data set. Based on this, it is seen that with fewer (8) variables obtained as a result of feature selection, very close performance can be achieved by using all (34) variables.

6 Conclusion

In this study, a literature review on approaches and variables used to predict stock markets are presented. With these results in mind, different data sets have been created to use in the analysis. Explanations related to variables in each data set and various statistical information related to these data sets were provided. The performance comparisons of the classifiers that are employed in the analyses are given in tables. It was investigated which data set more effective in predicting movement direction, which of the methods of Artificial Neural Networks and Support Vector Machines yielded more successful results.

For this purpose, five different data sets (1—technical indicators, 2—stock exchange indices, 3—macroeconomic indicators, 4—aggregated version of the first three data sets, 5—the reduced version of data set four constructed by using feature selection) were created to determine which data set can best predict the direction of the stock index. The daily data for the period 2005–2009 was used for training, and the period of 2010–2011 was used for testing purposes. After the training using ANN and SVM methods on each training set, the resulting classifiers were run on the corresponding test sets and their performances were compared.

According to the results found, technical indicators calculated based on the historical values of the index were much more beneficial in determining the index direction than other stock market indices and macroeconomic variables. The best test performance achieved using the first data set with 11 technical indicators was 80%, compared to 57.2% on the second with 18 stock market indices. On the third data set with five macroeconomic indicators, the test performance was 54.4%. The highest test performance achieved on the fourth dataset with 34 variables (constructed by combining the first three data sets) was 73.7%, By applying a feature selection procedure on this dataset, we tried to create a dataset that could predict the index direction movement at the maximum performance using the least number of variables. Therefore, the total number of variables, which was 34, was reduced to 8. This new data set contains six technical indicators, one foreign stock market index, one macroeconomic indicator. The best result of this reduced sized data set was 73.5%.

ANN has always shown the highest performance on all data sets compared to SVM. Accordingly, although it is seen that these methods are useful tools for predicting the index direction in a developing stock market such as Borsa Istanbul (BIST), it is concluded that the ANN method generates lower prediction errors on test sets than SVM method.

For future studies, to further develop the results found, hybrid methods in which fuzzy logic and ANN or SVM methods are used together can be used. Using genetic algorithms to searching optimal parameters is another option. The performance of classifiers can be improved in several ways. One option is tuning the model parameters more precisely by searching over wider ranges. The second way is to add other variables that may be related to the subject and are not in the data set now.

References

Abe, S. (2010). *Support vector machines for pattern classification*. London: Springer.

Akcan, A., & Kartal, C. (2011). İMKB Sigorta Endeksini Oluşturan Şirketlerin Hisse Senedi Fiyatlarının Yapay Sinir Ağları İle Tahmini. *Muhasebe ve Finansman Dergisi*, 27–40.

Alpaydın, E. (2009). *Introduction to machine learning*. Cambridge: MIT.

Alpaydın, E. (2011). *Yapay Öğrenme*. İstanbul: Boğaziçi Üniversitesi Yayınevi.
Belousov, A. I., Verzakov, S. A., & von Frese, J. (2002). A flexible classification approach with optimal generalisation performance: Support vector machines. *Chemometrics and Intelligent Laboratory Systems, 64*(1), 15–25.
Bennett, K. P., & Campbell, C. (2000). Support vector machines: Hype or hallelujah? *ACM SIGKDD Explorations Newsletter, 2*(2), 1–13.
Boser, B. E., Guyon, I. M., & Vapnik, V. N. (1992). A training algorithm for optimal margin classifiers. In *Proceedings of the Fifth Annual Workshop on Computational Learning Theory* (pp. 144–152).
Boyacioglu, M. A., & Avci, D. (2010). An adaptive network-based fuzzy inference system (ANFIS) for the prediction of stock market return: The case of the Istanbul stock exchange. *Expert Systems with Applications, 37*(12), 7908–7912.
Boyd, S., & Vandenberghe, L. (2004). *Convex optimization*. London: Cambridge University Press.
Burges, C. J. C. (1998). A tutorial on support vector machines for pattern recognition. *Data Mining and Knowledge Discovery, 2*(2), 121–167.
Cherkassky, V., & Mulier, F. (2007). *Learning from data: Concepts, theory, and methods*. New York: Wiley-IEEE Press.
Çinko, M., & Avcı, E. (2007). A comparison of neural network and linear regression forecasts of the ISE-100 index. *Öneri, 7*(28), 301–307.
Clarke, B., Fokoue, E., & Hao, Z. (2009). *Principles and theory for data mining and machine learning*. New York: Springer.
Cortes, C., & Vapnik, V. (1995). Support-vector networks. *Machine Learning, 20*(3), 273–297.
Cover, T. M. (1965). Geometrical and statistical properties of systems of linear inequalities with applications in pattern recognition. *IEEE Transactions on Electronic Computers, 14*, 326–334.
Cox, P. G., & Adhami, R. (2002). Multi-class support vector machine classifier applied to hyper-spectral data. In *Proceedings of the Thirty-Fourth Southeastern Symposium on System Theory* (271–274).
Cristianini, N., & Schölkopf, B. (2002). Support vector machines and kernel methods: The new generation of learning machines. *AI Magazine, 23*(3), 31–41.
Diler, A. İ. (2003). İMKB Ulusal 100 Endeksinin Yönünün Yapay Sinir Ağları Hata Geriye Yayma Yöntemi ile Tahmin Edilmesi. *İMKB Dergisi, 7*(25), 65–81.
Dogan, N., & Yalcin, Y. (2007). The effects of the exchange rate movements on the Istanbul stock exchange. *Applied Financial Economics Letters, 3*(1), 39–46.
Du, K. L., & Swamy, M. N. S. (2006). *Neural networks in a Softcomputing framework*. New York: Springer.
Dunis, C. L., Rosillo, R., & de la Fuente, D. (2012). Forecasting IBEX-35 moves using support vector machines. *Neural Computing and Applications, 23*(1), 229–236.
Efe, M. Ö., & Kaynak, O. (2000). *Yapay Sinir Ağları Ve Uygulamaları*. İstanbul: Boğaziçi Üniversitesi Yayınları.
Erdem, C., Arslan, C. K., & Erdem, M. S. (2005). Effects of macroeconomic variables on Istanbul stock exchange indexes. *Applied Financial Economics, 15*(14), 987–994.
Erdinç, Y. (2004). *Yatırımcı ve Teknik Analiz Sorgulanıyor*. Ankara: Siyasal Kitabevi.
Eryiğit, M. (2009). Effects of oil price changes on the sector indices of Istanbul stock exchange. *International Research Journal of Finance and Economics, 25*, 209–216.
Evgeniou, T., Pontil, M., & Poggio, T. (2000). Statistical learning theory: A primer. *International Journal of Computer Vision, 38*(1), 9–13.
Evgeniou, T., Poggio, T., Pontil, M., & Verri, A. (2002). Regularization and statistical learning theory for data analysis. *Computational Statistics & Data Analysis, 38*(4), 421–432.
Gençtürk, M. (2009). Finansal Kriz Dönemlerinde Makroekonomik Faktörlerin Hisse Senedi Fiyatlarına Etkisi. *Süleyman Demirel Üniversitesi İktisadi ve İdari Bilimler Fakültesi Dergisi, 14*(1), 127–136.
Hamel, L. H. (2009). *Knowledge discovery with support vector machines*. Hoboken, NJ: Wiley-Interscience.

Haykin, S. (1999). *Neural networks: A comprehensive foundation*. Upper Saddle River: Prentice Hall.

Huang, W., Nakamori, Y., & Wang, S. Y. (2005). Forecasting stock market movement direction with support vector machine. *Computers & Operations Research, 32*(10), 2513–2522.

Huang, T. M., Kecman, V., & Kopriva, I. (2006). *Kernel based algorithms for mining huge data sets: Supervised, semi-supervised, and unsupervised learning*. New York: Springer.

Ivanciuc, O. (2007). Applications of support vector machines in chemistry. *Reviews in Computational Chemistry, 26*, 291–400.

Jain, A. K., Mao, J., & Mohiuddin, K. M. (1996). Artificial neural networks: A tutorial. *Computer, 29*(3), 31–44.

Kara, Y., Boyacioglu, M. A., & Baykan, Ö. K. (2011). Predicting direction of stock price index movement using artificial neural networks and support vector machines: The sample of the Istanbul stock exchange. *Expert Systems with Applications, 28*(5), 5311–5319.

Kecman, V. (2001). *Learning and soft computing: Support vector machines, neural networks and fuzzy logic models*. Cambridge: A Bradford Book.

Kim, K. J. (2003). Financial time series forecasting using support vector machines. *Neurocomputing, 55*(1), 307–319.

Kim, K. J., & Han, I. (2000). Genetic algorithms approach to feature discretization in artificial neural networks for the prediction of stock price index. *Expert Systems with Applications, 19*(2), 125–132.

Korkmaz, T., Çevik, E. I., Birkan, E., & Özataç, N. (2011). Causality in mean and variance between ISE 100 and S&P 500: Turkcell case. *African Journal of Business Management, 5*(5), 1673–1683.

Kriesel, D. (2007). *A brief introduction to neural networks*. Retrieved from http://www.dkriesel.com

Kutlu, B., & Badur, B. (2009). Yapay Sinir Ağları Ile Borsa Endeksi Tahmini. *Yönetim, 20*(63), 25–40.

Larose, D. T. (2005). *Discovering knowledge in data: An introduction to data mining*. Hoboken, NJ: Wiley-Interscience.

Mammone, A., Turchi, M., & Cristianini, N. (2009). Support vector machines. *Wiley Interdisciplinary Reviews: Computational Statistics, 1*(3), 283–289.

Mavroforakis, M. E., & Theodoridis, S. (2006). A geometric approach to support vector machine (SVM) classification. *IEEE Transactions on Neural Networks, 17*(3), 671–682.

Mehrotra, K., Mohan, C. K., & Ranka, S. (1997). *Elements of artificial neural networks. Complex adaptive systems series*. Cambridge: MIT.

Mitchell, T. (1997). *Machine learning*. New York: McGraw-Hill.

Moguerza, J. M., & Muñoz, A. (2006). Support vector machines with applications. *Statistical Science, 21*(3), 322–336.

Munakata, T. (2008). *Fundamentals of the new artificial intelligence: Neural, evolutionary, fuzzy and more*. London: Springer.

Özdemir, A. K., Tolun, S., & Demirci, E. (2011). Endeks Getirisi Yönünün İkili Sınıflandırma Yöntemiyle Tahmin Edilmesi: IMKB-100 Endeks Örneği. *Niğde Üniversitesi İİBF Dergisi, 4* (2), 45–59.

Ozun, A. (2007). Are the reactions of emerging equity markets to the volatility in advanced markets similar? Comparative evidence from Brazil and Turkey. *International Research Journal of Finance and Economics, 9*, 220–230.

Perşembe, A. (2010). *Teknik Analiz mi Dedin? Hadi Canım Sen De! Üçüncü Kitap*. İstanbul: Scala Yayıncılık.

Pontil, M., & Verri, A. (1998). Properties of support vector machines. *Neural Computation, 10*(4), 955–974.

Ramon, M. M., & Christodoulou, C. (2006). *Support vector machines for antenna array processing and electromagnetics*. San Rafael, CA: Morgan & Claypool.

Reed, R. D., & Marks, R. J. (1999). *Neural smithing: Supervised learning*. Cambridge: MIT.

Rumelhart, D. E., Hinton, G. E., & Williams, R. J. (1986). Learning representations by back-propagating errors. *Nature, 323*, 533–536.

Schölkopf, B., & Smola, A. J. (2001). *Learning with kernels: Support vector machines, regularization, optimization, and beyond*. Cambridge, MA: MIT.

Steinwart, I., & Christmann, A. (2008). *Support vector machines*. New York: Springer.

Türsoy, T., Nil, G., & Rjoub, H. (2008). Macroeconomic factors, the APT and the Istanbul stock market. *International Research Journal of Finance and Economics, 22*, 49–57.

Vapnik, V. N. (1998). *Statistical learning theory*. New York: Wiley-Interscience.

Vapnik, V. N. (1999). An overview of statistical learning theory. *IEEE Transactions on Neural Networks, 10*(5), 988–999.

Von Luxburg, U., & Schölkopf, B. (2008). Statistical learning theory: Models, concepts, and results. *arXiv Preprint* arXiv:0810.4752.

Vuran, B. (2010). The determination of long-run relationship between ISE 100 and international equity indices using cointegration analysis. *Istanbul University Journal of the School of Business Administration, 39*(1), 154–168.

Wang, X., & Zhong, Y. (2003). Statistical learning theory and state of the art in SVM. In *Proceedings of the Second IEEE International Conference on Cognitive Informatics* (pp. 55–59).

Warren, W. S. (1994). Neural networks and statistical models. In *Proceedings of the Nineteenth Annual SAS Users Group International Conference*. Dallas, TX: SAS.

Wu, C. H., Ken, Y., & Huang, T. (2010). Patent classification system using a new hybrid genetic algorithm support vector machine. *Applied Soft Computing, 10*(4), 1164–1177.

Yegnanarayana, B. (2005). *Artificial neural networks*. New Delhi: Prentice-Hall of India.

Yıldız, B., Yalama, A., & Coşkun, M. (2008). Forecasting the Istanbul stock exchange national 100 index using an artificial neural network. *World Academy of Science, Engineering and Technology, 46*, 36–39.

Zügül, M., & Şahin, C. (2009). İMKB 100 Endeksi ile Bazı Makroekonomik Değişkenler Arasındaki İlişkiyi İncelemeye Yönelik Bir Uygulama. *Akademik Bakış, 16*, 1–16.

Zurada, J. M. (1992). *Introduction to artificial neural systems*. St. Paul: West Group.

Increase in Expected Returns on the Investment

Selin Sarılı

Abstract Although the main purpose of the enterprises is to increase their profitability, they actually want to increase the service and service quality they provide in order to reach their profit targets. For this purpose, companies aim to grow and increase their potential customer base through a horizontal and vertical merger strategy. The perception in the market, especially for public companies, is that the mergers and acquisitions will increase the stock price. Is there a significant difference between stock returns in real terms before and after purchase, or is it merely a market perception? Or are investors able to generate higher returns in the market after news of mergers and acquisitions? When the effective markets hypothesis mentions information efficiency, it means that it is not possible to obtain a return above the market since all information in the market will be reflected on the stock price. In order to find the answer to these questions, it has been analyzed whether the stock returns of the bank shares, which are selected from Turkey, developed and developing countries' have abnormal return and cumulative abnormal return before and after the merger and acquisition.

1 Introduction

The globalization in the financial markets and the facilitation of money transfer has caused the increase of countries' demand for global capital. The increase of commercial activity volume made it necessary to bring a larger amount of capital together, which led to the establishment of multi-partner enterprises (Micklethwait and Wooldridge 2003). This increase of capital demand has accelerated the competition of the countries to attract both direct and indirect foreign capital investments. As the developing countries need capital to increase their level of development, different strategies are taken against foreign capital.

S. Sarılı (✉)
Banking and Insurance, İstanbul Sisli Vocational School, Istanbul, Turkey
e-mail: selin.sarili@sisli.edu.tr

H. Dincer, S. Yüksel (eds.), *Strategic Priorities in Competitive Environments*, Contributions to Management Science, https://doi.org/10.1007/978-3-030-45023-6_11

Damodaran (2002) says in his corporate finance theory that the main purpose of companies is to maximize the share values of the company owners, in other words the shareholders. The companies need more capital, investment and qualified workforce than before in order to cope with international competition in the current economic structure and to reach lucrative areas outside their regional markets, which makes it difficult for companies to exist solely. The developments in the global economy force all enterprises to change. Companies that do not improve their activities and adapt to the change lose their competitive advantage over time or are sold to other companies or are completely vanquished from the market. Using the international competitive advantage in the last 10 years in the best way, China has become one of the fastest growing economies in the world that creates difference in this sense.

The basic underlying reason for global capital movements is the willingness of companies to internationalize for different reasons. Although there are different motivations for company mergers and acquisitions, the factors such as increasing service quality, the need for technology and capital are important for developing countries while factors such as increasing market share and having an international customer portfolio can be mentioned more important in developed countries. Therefore, countries and companies develop different strategies to benefit from the existing global capital.

2 Literature Review

Mergers and acquisitions have a wide range in the literature. The studies include analysis on the balance sheet, as well as analysis on stock value after merger or acquisition. Looking at the history of mergers and acquisitions, it is seen that there are different waves that carry different features from time to time. However, the basic goal of all of them is to increase the company values. Since especially for public companies, the change in stock prices is more important, stock price changes before and after the merger have found wide coverage in the literature. Generally, studies have investigated whether stocks have abnormal returns after merger compared to before merger.

DeLong (2003), in his study examining the effects of mergers in United States and non-U.S. countries on stock returns found out that combined partners earn 1.3% profit over stocks of non-US merging banks. When a bank was bought in US, 2.1% depreciation occurred in stocks, while there had been no depreciation in non-US.

In studies conducted in Turkey, Mandacı (2004) tested if mergers and acquisitions decisions of the companies traded on the ISE between 1998 and 2003 brought abnormal returns to shareholders. As a result of the study, it was determined that the abnormal return with statistical significance was obtained on the first and second days before the merger announcement and the first day after.

Seghal et al. (2012) examined whether announcements after merger and acquisition affected stock returns. In the study conducted between 2005 and 2009 in Brazil,

Russia, India, China, South Korea and South Africa, it was concluded that five out of these six countries had pre-announcement abnormal returns. In India, South Korea and China, significant negative returns were generated after the announcement, while abnormal returns were observed in South Africa.

Çıtak and Yıldız (2007) calculated the holding abnormal returns and cumulative abnormal returns after the acquisition in line with the public information of 40 companies that were traded in BIST (the name of the ISE at the time of operation) and performed purchases. It was concluded that the abnormal returns of the companies after the acquisition were not statistically significant.

Cybo-Ottone and Murgia (2000) conducted from 1988 to 1997 stock exchange valuation of the largest mergers and acquisitions between banks and financial institutions in 14 European countries. As a result of their study, they found that there was a positive and significant increase in the average value of the stock at the time of the agreement's announcement, and they found a cumulative excessive return of 2.19% for buyers and 15.3% for target company partners.

Moeller and Zhu (2016) examined from 2012 to early 2016 the short-term effects of mergers and acquisitions of companies, which are publicly traded in China with companies in the UK. In the windows consisting of four different time periods, the case study analysis was used. It was concluded that the Chinese companies, which are the transferee of the merge obtained significant positive abnormal returns on the first day following the announcement date of the merger and acquisition agreements, but these positive returns disappeared over time.

Yeh and Hoshino (2002) investigated 86 merger activities in the Tokyo Stock Exchange between 1970 and 1994 and concluded that the mergers of the Japanese companies did not increase the efficiency of the company, and even caused a deterioration in the companies' operational performance.

Campa and Hernando (2006) examined the return on mergers and acquisitions in the European Union financial sector between 1998 and 2002. The merger announcements brought positive excessive returns to the shareholders of the target company since the announcement date and provided a slight positive excess return in the 3-month period prior to the announcement.

3 Methodology

It is widely used in the studies to analyze whether there is a change in stock returns before and after the merger in order to analyze the effects of acquisitions and mergers on company's performance. There are many areas in the literature where event study is used. The advantage of the event study method for companies is that the magnitude of the extraordinary performance that occurs when an event occurs is measuring the impact on the assets of shareholders. In this study, whether significant mergers or acquisitions in developed and developing countries create values for the purchasing company and the target company shareholders are examined by applying the event study method.

In the short-term analysis applying the event study method, the short-term stock price performances covering the period before and after the announcement is measured for the buyer, target firm and the merging firm. It is stated that this method is a very reliable method for effective markets. As it is known, stock prices in effective markets are immediately corrected by the introduction of new information or by any changes in the market at any point (Bouwman et al. 2003).

Expected returns are calculated by using the Market Model. According to the model, the expected return of a financial asset is directly proportional to the systematic risk of that asset, defined as the scale of that asset to act together with the market or its sensitivity to the market (Weston et al. 1990).

The study covers a total of five banks mergers or acquisitions in nine countries. The selection was made based on the countries and the event windows were determined only according to the selected merger or purchase announcement date in that country. In the study, the daily data of bank stocks were examined, and the data was obtained from banks' websites.

In this process, first of the entire event window is determined and then the actual returns or realized yields are calculated for each day of the specified period on a company basis. Equation (1) is used to calculate the actual returns of the stocks.

$$R_{it} = \frac{P_{it} - P_{it-1}}{P_{it-1}} \tag{1}$$

t −10, …, +10 days.
P_{it} Price of common stock outstanding for firm i at the day t end.
P_{it-1} Price of common stock outstanding for firm i at the day t − 1 end.

Expected return for each firm is as follow:

$$E(R)_i = \alpha_i + \beta_i(R_{mit}) \tag{2}$$

The systematic risk coefficient β_i in the model is calculated as follows:

$$\beta_i = \frac{COV(R_m, R_i)}{VAR(R_m)} \tag{3}$$

$COV(R_m, R_i)$ Covariance between market return and return on assets.
$VAR(R_m)$ Variance of market return.

After calculating the expected and actual returns of stocks, abnormal returns were calculated. Abnormal returns are unpredictable stock value changes that occur outside of systematic effects across the market. In other words, abnormal returns are independent of market movements. In the event studies, it is the unpredictable change in the stock value resulting from the event.

Abnormal return (AR) occurs when the expected returns (ER) of the stocks are above or below their actual returns:

$$AR_{it} = R_{it} - E(R_{it}) \tag{4}$$

R_{it} Actual return of the stocks
$E(R_{it})$ Expected return of the stocks

Cumulative Abnormal Return (CAR) method is used to determine if there is a difference between stock returns in the time-period of the pre- and post-merger announcements in bank mergers and acquisitions experience in US, European Union and Turkey. CAR is the cumulative total of the differences between the real value and expected value of the stock in the market.

In CAR measurement, the event study method divides the event window into two, before the news and the news period. In the study, the event window covers the period (21 days) up to the 10th day before and after the event. CAR is used to measure short-term returns. The sum of the abnormal returns in the 21-day event window constitutes the cumulative abnormal return.

$$CAR_{i\tau} = \sum\nolimits_{\tau=1}^{T} AR_{i\tau} \tag{5}$$

The study examines whether it is possible at mergers for both purchasing and target companies to obtain abnormal returns. Within this framework, two separate hypothesis groups have been created for purchasing companies and target companies.

1st Group (From the Perspective of Purchasing Companies)

$H_{1,\,0}$ The abnormal return of the purchasing companies is 0 on the announcement date of the merger and the 10-day period around it.
$H_{1,\,1}$ The abnormal returns of the shareholders of the purchasing companies are different than 0 on the announcement date of the merger and the 10-day period around it.

2nd Group (From the Perspective of Target Companies)

$H_{1,\,0}$ The abnormal return of the target companies is 0 on the announcement date of the merger and the 10-day period around it.
$H_{2,\,1}$ The abnormal returns of the target companies are different than 0 on the announcement date of the merger and the 10-day period around it.

Abnormal returns and cumulative abnormal returns on the announcement date of the merger and the days around them are subjected to the t-test in order to test these hypotheses. The t statistic of CAR has been calculated with the equation numbered 6.

$$t_{CAR} = \frac{CAR(t_1, t_2)}{S_t \sqrt[2]{T}} \tag{6}$$

$CAR(t_1, t_2)$ Cumulative abnormal return between periods t_1 and t_2.
S_t Standard deviation.
T The number of days in the event window.

After the abnormal returns are calculated, the sum of the abnormal returns obtained is divided by the number of companies in the sample and the Average Abnormal Return (AAR) is calculated (Brown and Warner 1985):

$$AAR_{it} = \frac{1}{N}\sum_{i=1}^{N} AR_{it} \tag{7}$$

AR_{it} Abnormal return on day t for share i,
AAR_{it} The average abnormal return on day t for i share.
N Number of shares in the sample on t date

$$t(AAR_t) = \frac{1}{\sqrt{N}}\sum_{i=1}^{n} \frac{AR_{it}}{\sigma_i} \tag{8}$$

Cumulative Average Abnormal Returns are obtained by adding the calculated average abnormal returns (Dodd and Warner 1983):

$$CAAR_{it} = \sum_{i=1}^{N} AAR_{it} \tag{9}$$

AAR_{it} Average abnormal return on day t for share i
$CAAR_{it}$ The sum of the average abnormal returns on day t for the i share.

In the last stage of the event study method, for the event day and other days in the event window, the t statistic is calculated by the following formula (Brown and Warner 1985):

$$t(CAAR_t) = \frac{AAR}{S(AAR_t)} \tag{10}$$

t t statistics
AAR Average abnormal return
$S(AAR_t)$ Standard deviation of abnormal return on day t

4 Analysis and Findings

Examples from developed and developing countries were selected to measure how banks' stock returns are affected in mergers and acquisitions. It is seen in the literature that generally the effects of different mergers on the same country are examined. Thereby, it is thought that different country examples and national and international bank mergers, which are less common in the literature, will contribute to the literature.

Another bank merger from developed countries is the acquisition between BNP Paribas and BGL. Although BNP Paribas is a bank that had been purchased many times in its history, it had changed its name for the first time as BGL BNP Paribas after the purchase by BGL. Therefore, it was deemed appropriate to be included it in the analysis.

The first example from developing countries is the bank purchase between Turkey and the United Arab Emirates (UAE). Since its foundation in Turkey, Denizbank had had many different owners. It was announced in 2018 that Denizbank, owned by Russia-based Sberbank, was going to be acquired by UAE-based Emirates NBD. The interest of Arab capital in Turkish market especially in recent years has been effective in this study to examine the impact of the merger.

As example of another developing country, China, where national bank merger took place, was chosen. In addition to its desire to enter international markets in recent years, ICBC Bank has preferred to grow in the national market. Therefore: the bank wanted to buy some of the shares of Hang Seng, the third largest bank of China.

The last merger example used in the study is a private banking acquisition made by the Swiss-based UBS, one of the largest banks in the world. Interested in Finland-based Nordea Bank, Switzerland has been used as an example of an international bank merger in developed countries.

Firstly, the systematic risk coefficients (Beta) of he selected banks are calculated and presented in Table 1.

Looking at the systematic risk coefficients of banks listed in Table 1; It is seen that Sun Trust, Denizbank, ICBC and UBS banks are bigger than 1. This proves us that the said bank stocks are riskier compared to the market. Denizbank and Sun Trust Bank had negative coefficients; this might mean there is a reverse movement between the markets. BNP Paribas has the lowest systematic risk coefficient among selected banks.

Table 1 Beta coefficient of banks

Banks	Beta
SunTrust Bank	−1.44772
BBT	0.33312
BNP Paribas	0.00756
Denizbank	−1.32142
NBD	−0.32904
ICBC	1.26837
Hang Seng	0.25501
UBS	1.48731
Nordea	0.54334

4.1 United States

Before BB&T Corp Bank purchased the SunTrust Banks, it was a bank offering retail and commercial banking, securities, asset management, mortgage and insurance products and services, with 2049 branches in 15 states and Washington DC. According to its assets, it was among the largest banks in the United States. As of December 31, 2018, SunTrust Bank was a bank with an asset size of $216 billion, whose main activities were deposits, lending, credit cards, and trust and investment services.

In December 2019, BB&T Corp. in Winston-Salem, North Carolina merged with SunTrust Banks, Inc. in Atlanta, Georgia and took the name of Truist Financial Corp. The first announcement of the merger negotiations was made on February 7, 2019. The merger of the two banks constituted the sixth largest bank in the USA, and it was stated that the bank would manage $442 billion of assets, $301 billion of loans and $324 billion of deposits and will serve more than ten million households in the US alone. Within the scope of the merger agreement, a SunTrust share would be traded in return for 1.295 shares of BB&T, and the shareholders' profit share would increase 5.0% after the transaction was completed. Moreover, this bank merger has been the largest bank merger in the USA after the 2007–2008 crisis. Stocks of both banks are traded on the New York Stock Exchange. Thus, NYSE Composite Index was used as market return in the analysis.

Excess returns of Sun Trust and BBT stock are shown in Fig. 1.

As it can be seen in Fig. 1, there was a significant increase in Sun Trust stock returns on the day of announcement. This acquisition might have enabled increase in stock return on the day of the announcement for Sun Trust, which was purchased by BB&T Corp Bank but this trend did not continue in the following days. Looking at the returns graph of the BBT, which bought the Sun Trust, it is seen that it followed a different course. Comparing the BBT Corp. Bank and Sun Trust graphs, the two series show different responses to the purchase announcement. On the day of the merger announcement, the Sun Trust stock reached its highest level among 21-day returns, while BBT's share returns continued to fall. In a sense, investors reacted to the BBT purchase with a delay, and the return started to increase in the days after the announcement.

The abnormal returns of the Sun Trust are included in column 2 of Table 2. Considering the statistical significance of returns, it was concluded that only the return on July 7, when the purchase announcement was made, was significant. No significant abnormal return was found for other event days. Based on the event days, the lowest abnormal return was seen on the 5th day. It is seen that the cumulative returns in the +10/−10 day event window reached the highest level again at the announcement date.

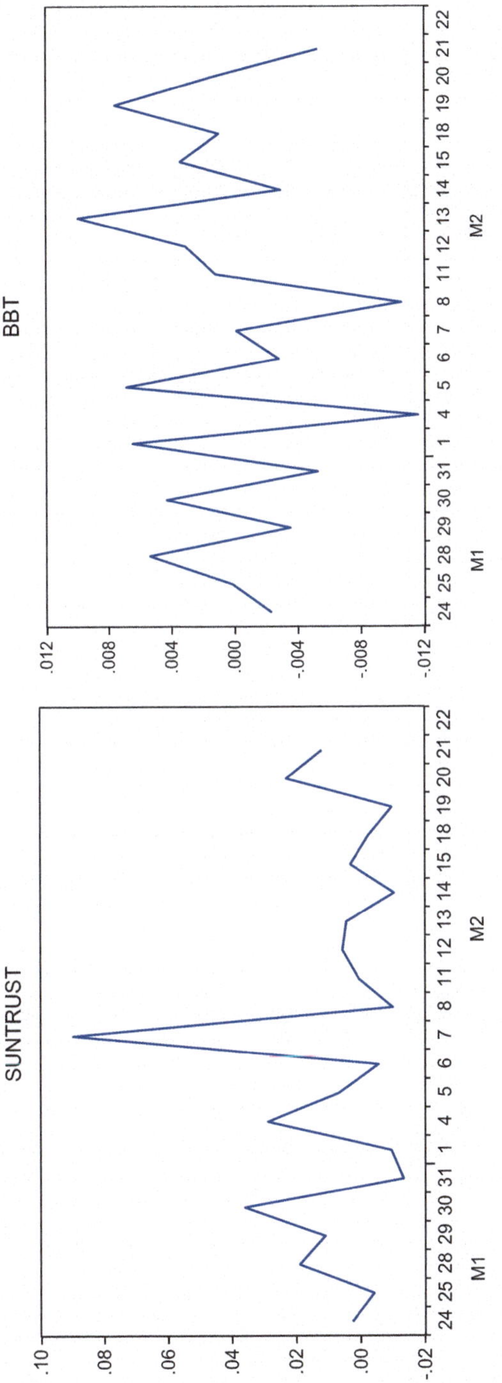

Fig. 1 Sun trust and BBT return graphs

Table 2 SunTrust and BBT AR and CAR values

Date	Suntrust	T stats.	CAR	% CAR	BBT	T stats.	CAR	% CAR
22.02.2019	0.0025	0.2593	0.1755	0.0144	−0.00234	0.47379	0.00651	−0.35863
21.02.2019	−0.0043	0.5620	0.730	−0.0244	0.00014	0.03022	0.00885	0.02171
20.02.2019	0.0189	−0.4672	0.1772	0.1075	0.00539	−0.90995	0.00871	0.82786
19.02.2019	0.0110	−0.1180	0.1584	0.0627	−0.00353	0.68777	0.00332	−0.54212
15.02.2019	0.0360	−1.2283	0.1474	0.2051	0.00432	−0.71801	0.00685	0.66329
14.02.2019	−0.0135	0.9730	0.1114	−0.0771	−0.00526	0.99691	0.00253	−0.80719
13.02.2019	−0.0097	0.8021	0.1249	−0.0552	0.00649	−1.10645	0.00778	0.99635
12.02.2019	0.0288	−0.9085	0.1346	0.1641	−0.01163	2.13727*	0.00129	−1.78501
11.02.2019	0.0068	0.0690	0.1058	0.0388	0.00690	−1.17964	0.01292	1.05911
08.02.2019	−0.0058	0.6275	0.0990	−0.0328	−0.00281	0.55808	0.00602	−0.43091
07.02.2019	0.0898	−3.6188*	0.1048	0.5116	−0.00011	0.07558	0.00883	−0.01719
06.02.2019	−0.0103	0.8273	0.0150	−0.0585	−0.01058	1.95049*	0.00894	−1.62485
05.02.2019	0.0004	0.3515	0.0252	0.0026	0.00118	−0.15601	0.01952	0.18139
04.02.2019	0.0056	0.1224	0.0248	0.0319	0.00310	−0.49947	0.01834	0.47589
01.02.2019	0.0044	0.1770	0.0192	0.0249	0.00995	−1.72596	0.01524	1.52757
31.01.2019	−0.0107	0.8458	0.0148	−0.0608	−0.00293	0.57944	0.00529	−0.44923
30.01.2019	0.0031	0.2335	0.0255	0.0177	0.00344	−0.56103	0.00822	0.52868
29.01.2019	−0.0025	0.4828	0.0224	−0.0143	0.00098	−0.11968	0.00478	0.15024
28.01.2019	−0.0100	0.8153	0.0249	−0.0569	0.00758	−1.30141	0.00380	1.16353
25.01.2019	0.0229	−0.6465	0.0349	0.1305	0.00150	−0.21308	−0.00378	0.23033
24.01.2019	0.0120	−0.1612	0.0120	0.0683	−0.00528	1.00114	−0.00528	−0.81082

*Significant at 0.05 level

Looking at the t statistics of BBT stock excess returns, it is seen that the returns on the −1st day and on the 3rd day are statistically significant. The increase in excessive return 1 day before the announcement is remarkable. Looking at CAR figures, the highest CAR in 21 days is on day −2 while CAR percentage took place on the day −4.

4.2 *Luxembourg-France*

BGL is a Luxembourg bank founded on 29 September 1919, which is the fifth-largest bank in the Grand Duchy of Luxembourg and is the country's second-largest employer. BNP Paribas Group was founded in 2000 and had become a strong European leader following its integration with many rich banks. Cac40, the main index of France, was used as the market return.

On May 13, 2009, the BNP Paribas group became the majority shareholder of the banks with a share of 65.96%, while the Luxembourg State continued to be an important shareholder with a share of 34%. On September 21, 2009, the bank was renamed BGL BNP Paribas. In 2009, BNP Paribas took control of Fortis Bank and BGL (Banque Générale du Luxembourg), thereby becoming the European leader in the retail market with four domestic markets. In Luxembourg, the shares of BGL Bank are not traded. Therefore, only BNP Paribas analysis of the purchase shall be presented. The return series of BNP Paribas is given in Fig. 2.

Looking at Fig. 3, it is seen that stock returns entered an upward trend 2 days before the announcement date. On the day of the announcement, the increase trend continued with a lower slope than the previous increase. During the event window

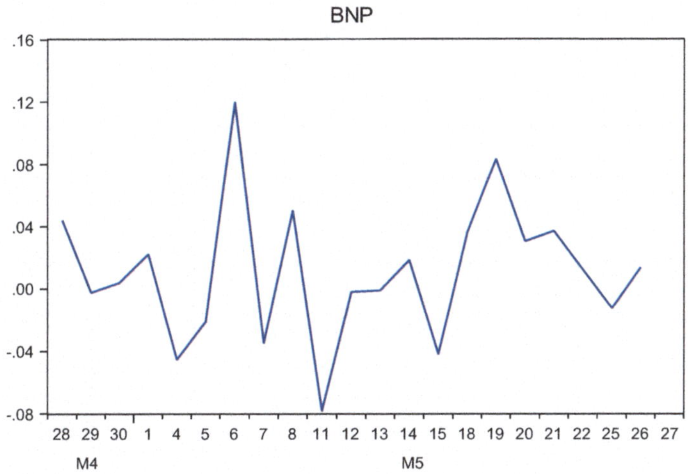

Fig. 2 BGL BNP Paribas return graphs

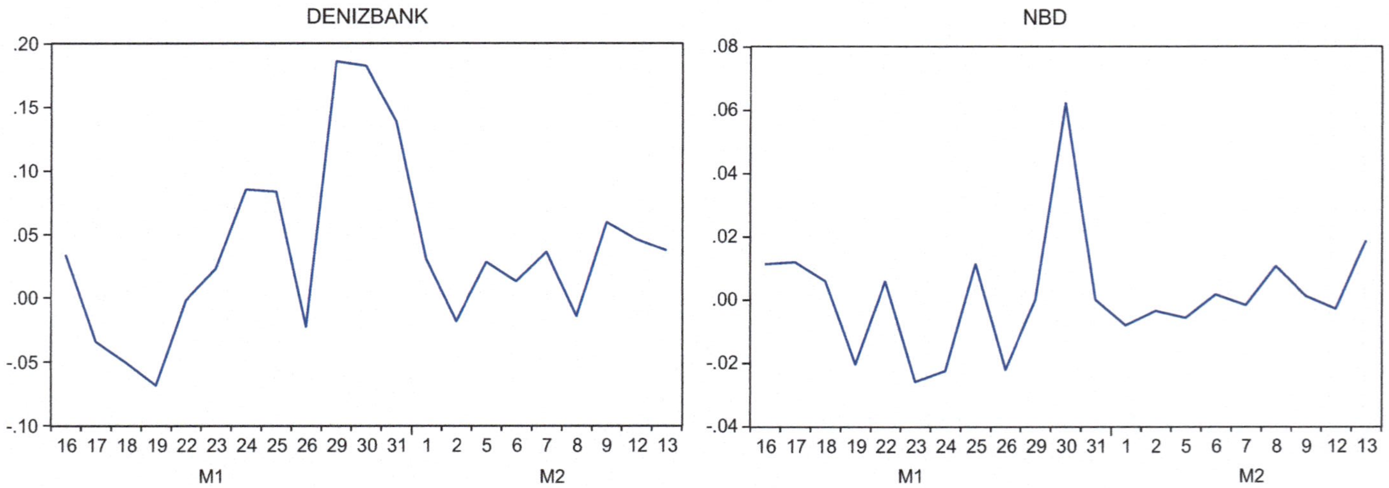

Fig. 3 Denizbank and NBD return graphs

Table 3 BGL BNP Paribas AR and CAR values

Date	BNP	T stats.	CAR	% CAR
27.05.2009	0.04410	−0.75567	0.23621	0.18670
26.05.2009	−0.00213	0.30770	0.19211	−0.00901
25.05.2009	0.00415	0.16338	0.19424	0.01755
22.05.2009	0.02240	−0.25643	0.19010	0.09481
21.05.2009	−0.04520	1.29844	0.16770	−0.19135
20.05.2009	−0.02087	0.73884	0.21290	−0.08836
19.05.2009	0.11989	−2.49911∗	0.23377	0.50757
18.05.2009	−0.03466	1.05595	0.11388	−0.14672
15.05.2009	0.05041	−0.90072	0.14854	0.21339
14.05.2009	−0.07801	2.05306∗	0.09813	−0.33024
13.05.2009	−0.00182	0.30062	0.17614	−0.00771
12.05.2009	−0.00085	0.27839	0.17796	−0.00362
11.05.2009	0.01858	−0.16861	0.17881	0.07865
08.05.2009	−0.04164	1.21651	0.16023	−0.17627
07.05.2009	0.03640	−0.57862	0.20187	0.15411
06.05.2009	0.08345	−1.66072∗	0.16547	0.35327
05.05.2009	0.03064	−0.44601	0.08202	0.12971
04.05.2009	0.03725	−0.59818	0.05138	0.15771
30.04.2009	0.01266	−0.03251	0.01413	0.05360
29.04.2009	−0.01228	0.54129	0.00147	−0.05200
28.04.2009	0.01375	−0.05761	0.01375	0.05822

∗Significant at 0.05

period, stock returns could not catch the peak that occurred in the days before the announcement.

According to Table 3, excessive return values of BNP were found statistically significant at three points of the event window. In the event window, returns in the days −5, +1, +4 were found above market returns and it was concluded that they were statistically significant. Contrary to the results obtained in other bank analyzes, excessive return was found significant on the day after the announcement day, not on the day of the announcement. It can be said that there was a delayed reaction.

4.3 *Turkey-United Arab Emirates*

Emirates National Bank of Dubai (Emirates NBD) which is one of the leading banks in the United Arab Emirates, offers both corporate and retail banking and financial products. By purchasing the Dexia, one of the leading financial groups in Europe, in October 2006, Denizbank became the subject of the largest investments made at a time by Russia in Turkey and as of September 28, 2012 started to provide service under Sberbank, one of Europe's biggest banks. Borsa Istanbul 100 index was used to calculate market returns.

Emirates NBD announced on January 30, 2018 that they started to negotiate with Sberbank for the sale of Denizbank. Emirates NBD and Sberbank announced that they signed a final agreement on the sale of 99.85% of Denizbank shares to Emirates NBD. Upon the completion of the transaction, Sberbank's shareholding in Denizbank ended. Denizbank stocks are traded on Borsa Istanbul. DFM General Index was used for market return. The return graphs of the series are given in Fig. 3.

When the income graphs of the banks presented in Fig. 3 are analyzed, it is noteworthy that before the merger announcement, both banks started to increase their stock returns. The stock returns of both banks started to decline from the day after the announcement. As of January 26, the negative course in the stock returns of both banks is seen to have turned to positive. The situation will be better evaluated with the t statistical values calculated in Table 3.

If the excessive return values of Denizbank are interpreted according to Table 3; the increase on the first day and the day after the event was found statistically significant. Although there had been an increase in returns before the announcement day, no statistically significant value was found before the event day. The excess returns of Emirates NBD, which purchased Denizbank, were also found significant on the day of announcement. Therefore, this merger provided significant returns both for bank investors in Turkey and United Arab Emirates.

4.4 China

Seng Heng Bank (SHB) is the third largest bank in terms of total assets and is the largest independent bank in Macau with local capital. In 29 August 2007, Industrial and Commercial Bank of China Limited (ICBC) announced that it has entered into an agreement to acquire a 79.9333% interest in Seng Heng Bank Limited.

As a result of the merger between Seng Heng Bank Limited and ICBC Macau Branch, it was renamed Industrial and Commercial Bank of China (ICBC Macau) after the purchase was completed. ICBC Macau Branch and Seng Heng Bank merge to become ICBC Macau. Shanghai index is used for market returns in both banks' excess return calculations. Figure 4 contains the return graphs of the two banks' stocks.

When the graphs in Fig. 4 are analyzed, it is seen that the return series for both banks stocks move in parallel on the day of the merger announcement. Both banks followed a downward trend until the announcement of the purchase while they started to follow a positive trend on the day of the announcement. Therefore, it can be said that the news of merger had a positive effect on the market. In Table 4, excessive returns, t values and CAR and CAR percentages of two banks are given.

Considering the excessive returns of ICBC Bank listed in Table 5; it is seen that the values on the 1st and 4th days after the event are statistically significant. The purchase announcement led to a significant increase in these days in the returns of

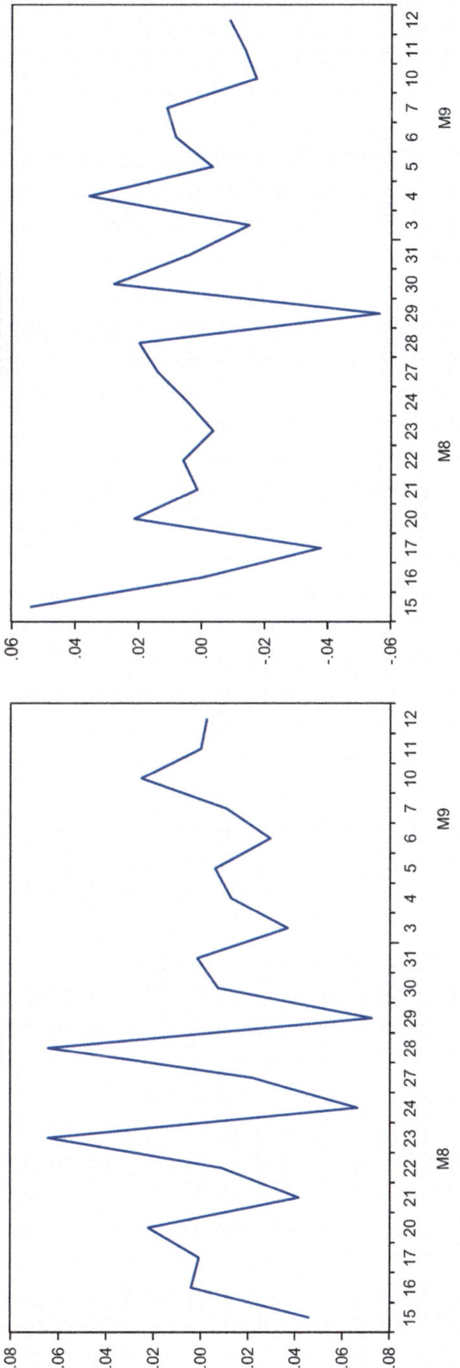

Fig. 4 ICBS and Hang Seng return graphs

Table 4 Denizbank and NBD AR and CAR values

Date	Denizbank	T stats.	CAR	% CAR	NBD	T stats.	CAR	% CAR
13.02.2018	0.03379	0.04394	0.77155	0.04379	0.01127	−0.54668	0.02763	0.40794
12.02.2018	−0.03462	1.06232	0.73776	−0.04487	0.01184	−0.57764	0.01636	0.42834
9.02.2018	−0.05082	1.30348	0.77238	−0.06587	0.00589	−0.25124	0.00452	0.21321
8.02.2018	−0.06884	1.57167	0.82320	−0.08922	−0.02051	1.19811	−0.00137	−0.74206
7.02.2018	−0.00229	0.58098	0.89204	−0.00296	0.00591	−0.25212	0.01914	0.21379
6.02.2018	0.02264	0.20993	0.89433	0.02934	−0.02595	1.49688	0.01323	−0.93898
5.02.2018	0.08528	−0.72260	0.87169	0.11053	−0.02249	1.30716	0.03918	−0.81393
2.02.2018	0.08362	−0.69790	0.78641	0.10838	0.01131	−0.54896	0.06167	0.40944
1.02.2018	−0.02292	0.88814	0.70278	−0.02971	−0.02213	1.28717	0.05035	−0.80076
31.01.2018	0.18620	−2.22494*	0.72571	0.24133	0.00000	0.07225	0.07248	0.00000
30.01.2018	0.18272	−2.17316*	0.53950	0.23683	0.06214	−3.33973*	0.07248	2.24885
29.01.2018	0.13869	−1.51770	0.35678	0.17976	0.00007	0.06832	0.01034	0.00259
26.01.2018	0.03051	0.09280	0.21809	0.03954	−0.00814	0.51901	0.01027	−0.29446
25.01.2018	−0.01862	0.82416	0.18758	−0.02414	−0.00352	0.26541	0.01840	−0.12732
24.01.2018	0.02832	0.12540	0.20621	0.03670	−0.00572	0.38645	0.02192	−0.20709
23.01.2018	0.01313	0.35146	0.17789	0.01702	0.00167	−0.01970	0.02765	0.06060
22.01.2018	0.03610	0.00957	0.16476	0.04679	−0.00165	0.16274	0.02597	−0.05964
19.01.2018	−0.01445	0.76201	0.12866	−0.01873	0.01054	−0.50663	0.02762	0.38154
18.01.2018	0.05969	−0.34168	0.14311	0.07737	0.00123	0.00485	0.01708	0.04442
17.01.2018	0.04616	−0.14023	0.08341	0.05983	−0.00284	0.22799	0.01585	−0.10265
16.01.2018	0.03725	−0.00763	0.03725	0.04828	0.01868	−0.95365	0.01868	0.67617

*Significant at 0.05 level

Table 5 ICBC and Hang Seng AR and CAR values

Date	ICBC	T stats.	CAR	% CAR	HangSeng	T stats.	CAR	% CAR
12.09.2007	−0.04622	1.09982	−0.17997	−0.25684	0.05420	−2.20020*	0.05171	1.04807
11.09.2007	0.00412	−0.37057	−0.13375	0.02287	−0.00004	0.10645	−0.00249	−0.00079
10.09.2007	0.00082	−0.27426	−0.13787	0.00455	−0.03791	171.681	−0.00245	−0.73303
7.09.2007	0.02237	−0.90373	−0.13868	0.12430	0.02145	−0.80733	0.03546	0.41472
6.09.2007	−0.04159	0.96442	−0.16105	−0.23108	0.00134	0.04777	0.01402	0.02590
5.09.2007	−0.00882	0.00744	−0.11947	−0.04903	0.00587	−0.14482	0.01268	0.11347
4.09.2007	0.06451	−2.13456*	−0.11064	0.35844	−0.00369	0.26151	0.00681	−0.07129
3.09.2007	−0.06635	1.68783	−0.17515	−0.36869	0.00467	−0.09403	0.01050	0.09038
31.08.2007	−0.02189	0.38911	−0.10880	−0.12164	0.01398	−0.48976	0.00582	0.27032
30.08.2007	0.06450	−2.13431*	−0.08690	0.35839	0.01983	−0.73869	−0.00816	0.38351
29.08.2007	−0.07245	1.86584*	−0.15140	−0.40255	−0.05642	2.50409*	−0.02799	−1.09102
28.08.2007	−0.00733	−0.03627	−0.07896	−0.04072	0.02790	−1.08165	0.02843	0.53946
27.08.2007	0.00147	−0.29317	−0.07163	0.00815	0.00381	−0.05728	0.00053	0.07367
24.08.2007	−0.03683	0.82548	−0.07309	−0.20465	−0.01505	0.74463	−0.00328	−0.29097
23.08.2007	−0.01280	0.12344	−0.03626	−0.07110	0.03565	−1.41148	0.01177	0.68943
22.08.2007	−0.00605	−0.07371	−0.02347	−0.03360	−0.00334	0.24685	−0.02388	−0.06463
21.08.2007	−0.02946	0.61025	−0.01742	−0.16371	0.00829	−0.24764	−0.02054	0.16023
20.08.2007	−0.01072	0.06278	0.01204	−0.05956	0.01108	−0.36666	−0.02882	0.21434
17.08.2007	0.02529	−0.98907	0.02276	0.14053	−0.01738	0.84390	−0.03991	−0.33611
16.08.2007	0.00001	−0.25062	−0.00253	0.00006	−0.01371	0.68782	−0.02253	−0.26514
15.08.2007	−0.00254	−0.17615	−0.00254	−0.01411	−0.00882	0.47970	−0.00882	−0.17050

*Significant at 0.05 level

the bank shareholders. Excess return values of Hang Seng are significant on the day of the announcement like ICBC Bank's return values, but the values were found statistically significant on the 10th day after the event. The calculations in the table show that the merger of these two banks in the Chinese stock market was positively interpreted in the market. Moreover, the fact that the values of excessive returns in the days before the announcement day are not statistically significant means that there had been no insiders.

4.5 Switzerland-Finland

UBS provides financial consultancy and solutions to wealthy corporate customers worldwide and private customers in Switzerland. Nordea Bank AB is a Nordic Financial Services group operating in Northern Europe. The bank was established with the merger of Merita Bank, Unibank, Kreditkassen and Nordbanken, Finnish, Danish, Norwegian and Swedish, which took place between 1997 and 2000. OMX Helsinki index was used for the excessive market return calculation of Nordea Bank.

UBS and Nordea announced on January 25, 2018 that they signed an agreement and UBS would take over a part of the Luxembourg-based private banking business of Nordea. While the acquisition envisages the integration of UBS into the consultation platform, it aims to access customers' global offerings and local expertise. The acquisition aims to concentrate Nordea's private banking activities to Scandinavians, expand UBS's presence in Europe, and further develop its position as a key Asset Manager for Scandinavian customers. As market return, SMI, the main stock index of the UBS Bank is used. Figure 5 includes the return graphs of the banks.

Bank graphs in Fig. 5 show an increase especially in Nordea Bank stock returns, at the date of the announcement. However, in order to talk about the excessive return significance of the two banks, it would be more accurate to examine the excess returns according to the stock market indexes where the banks are traded.

In Table 6 where excessive returns are listed, the values of UBS were found statistically significant one day before the announcement day and on the 5th day of the event day. The fact that UBS had excessive returns one day before the day of the announcement brings to mind the idea that there might have been insiders. When the excess returns of Nordea are analyzed, it is seen that the excess return obtained on the day of the announcement is statistically significant. In other event days, no statistically significant degree was found.

In the next stage, the average abnormal returns and the cumulative average abnormal returns of the purchasing bank and the target bank are calculated, and the results are given in Table 7. Table 7 shows the average abnormal returns (AAR), cumulative average abnormal returns (CAAR) and the t statistical results of these returns calculated for 10 days before and after of companies whose announcements of purchase or merger are accepted as the event date.

While the cumulative average abnormal return shows the total effect of the announcements made by the companies; average abnormal return is used to

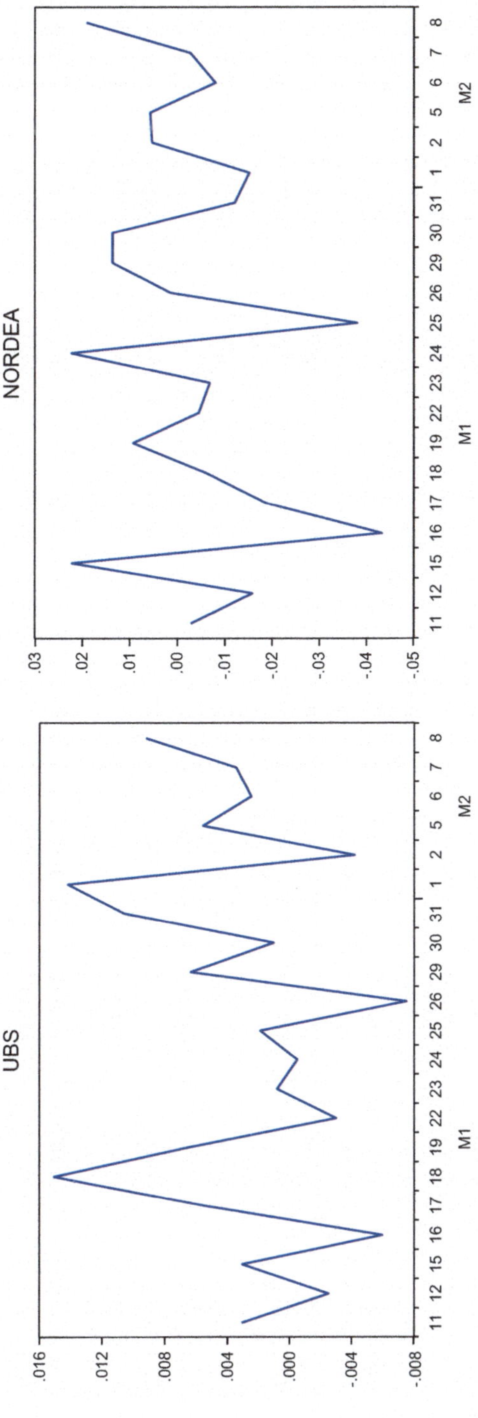

Fig. 5 UBS and Nordea return graphs

Table 6 UBS and Nordea AR and CAR values

Date	UBS	T stats.	CAR	% CAR	Nordea	T stats.	CAR	% CAR
08.02.2018	0.0031	0.0037	0.0649	0.0473	−0.0028	−0.0054	−0.0615	0.0461
07.02.2018	−0.0025	0.9469	0.0619	−0.0388	−0.0159	0.7535	−0.0587	0.2579
06.02.2018	0.0031	0.0051	0.0644	0.0472	0.0223	−1.4671	−0.0428	−0.3617
05.02.2018	−0.0060	1.5327	0.0613	−0.0922	−0.0433	2.3526*	−0.0651	0.7040
02.02.2018	0.0054	−0.3953	0.0673	0.0837	−0.0187	0.9210	−0.0218	0.3046
01.02.2018	0.0151	−2.0287*	0.0619	0.2327	−0.0061	0.1856	−0.0030	0.0994
31.01.2018	0.0065	−0.5818	0.0468	0.1007	0.0093	−0.7127	0.0031	−0.1512
30.01.2018	−0.0030	1.0280	0.0402	−0.0462	−0.0045	0.0894	−0.0062	0.0726
29.01.2018	0.0008	0.3867	0.0432	0.0123	−0.0068	0.2247	−0.0017	0.1103
26.01.2018	−0.0005	0.6074	0.0424	−0.0078	0.0223	−1.4716	0.0050	−0.3630
25.01.2018	0.0019	0.2026	0.0429	0.0291	−0.0381	2.0485*	−0.0173	0.6192
24.01.2018	−0.0075	1.7959*	0.0410	−0.1162	0.0014	−0.2540	0.0208	−0.0233
23.01.2018	0.0064	−0.5519	0.0486	0.0980	0.0136	−0.9632	0.0194	−0.2211
22.01.2018	0.0010	0.3510	0.0422	0.0156	0.0136	−0.9639	0.0058	−0.2213
19.01.2018	0.0106	−1.2604	0.0412	0.1626	−0.0121	0.5351	−0.0078	0.1969
18.01.2018	0.0142	−1.8749*	0.0306	0.2186	−0.0152	0.7137	0.0043	0.2467
17.01.2018	−0.0042	1.2324	0.0164	−0.0648	0.0053	−0.4803	0.0194	−0.0864
16.01.2018	0.0056	−0.4180	0.0207	0.0858	0.0057	−0.5043	0.0141	−0.0931
15.01.1900	0.0025	0.1065	0.0151	0.0379	−0.0080	0.2951	0.0084	0.1300
12.01.2018	0.0034	−0.0572	0.0126	0.0528	−0.0027	−0.0142	0.0164	0.0436
11.01.2018	0.0092	−1.0308	0.0092	0.1417	0.0191	−1.2825	0.0191	−0.3102

*Significant at 0.05 level

Table 7 AAR and CAAR of banks

	Purchasing bank				Target Bank			
Days	AAR	t AAR	CAAR	t CAAR	AAR	t AAR	CAAR	t CAAR
10	0.0020	0.1714	0.0311	0.1697	0.0219	2.0609*	0.2343	1.1648
9	0.0023	0.1438	0.0291	0.1966	−0.0137	−1.0149	0.2124	−0.7283
8	0.0039	0.8610	0.0268	0.3315	−0.0119	0.3892	0.2261	−0.6325
7	0.0029	−0.7156	0.0229	0.2531	−0.0199	0.1503	0.2380	−1.0588
6	−0.0142	−0.1070	0.0200	−1.2212	0.0041	2.9593*	0.2579	0.2166
5	−0.0092	−0.2474	0.0342	−0.7862	0.0022	−0.8798	0.2538	0.1176
4	0.0350	2.5370*	0.0434	3.0035*	0.0203	0.1479	0.2516	1.0789
3	−0.0209	−2.1027*	0.0084	−1.7911	0.0282	3.6031*	0.2313	1.4964
2	0.0028	0.3021	0.0292	0.2419	−0.0022	0.6301	0.2032	−0.1186
1	−0.0034	−0.2228	0.0264	−0.2888	0.0557	2.4963*	0.2054	2.9575*
0	−0.0021	0.6946	0.0298	−0.1777	0.0445	8.0342*	0.1497	2.3648*
−1	−0.0052	−1.5199	0.0319	−0.4505	0.0394	1.4634	0.1052	2.0960*
−2	0.0039	0.5853	0.0371	0.3339	0.0121	0.6943	0.0658	0.6426
−3	−0.0156	−0.6712	0.0332	−1.3370	−0.0036	0.0731	0.0537	−0.1920
−4	0.0077	1.6606	0.0488	0.6591	0.0141	1.5190	0.0573	0.7470
−5	0.0181	1.6582	0.0411	1.5511	−0.0040	−1.1181	0.0433	−0.2134
−6	−0.0002	−0.1521	0.0230	−0.0212	0.0132	0.9981	0.0473	0.7015
−7	0.0087	1.0008	0.0233	0.7490	0.0000	−0.0027	0.0341	−0.0019
−8	0.0098	1.2834	0.0146	0.8450	0.0061	−0.8015	0.0341	0.3232
−9	−0.0020	0.1833	0.0047	−0.1748	0.0132	2.1657*	0.0280	0.6997
−10	0.0068	0.8387	0.0068	0.5805	0.0149	1.5379	0.0149	0.7906

*Significant at %5 level

determine the impact of these announcements on the average market value for each day (Nagm and Kautz 2008).

When Table 7 is analyzed, it is seen that the AAR value of the purchasing banks is statistically significant on the 3rd and 4th days after the announcement date. Average abnormal returns before the announcement date are not statistically significant. CAAR values of the purchasing banks are found to be statistically significant on the 3rd and 4th days after the announcement, in parallel with AAR.

Looking at the companies purchased in Table 7, t statistics of both AAR and CAAR values were found significant on the day of the announcement and on the 1st day following the announcement. If it is necessary to make a comparison between the purchased and purchasing companies; the increase in the stock returns of the banks, the shares of which were bought by a large capital bank, is seen on the day of the announcement. However, on a cumulative basis, the cumulative average return of the purchasing bank stock is higher than the bank purchased.

Therefore, it can be stated that the merger and acquisition announcements of the companies have an impact on the stock returns of the companies in question, which is an indication that the market is not active in a semi-strong form.

In the next stage, the statistical significance of the cumulative average abnormal returns of the purchaser and target bank stocks in developed and developing countries was tested and the values are given in Table 8.

Looking at the values given in Table 8, it is seen that the CAAR values of the purchasing bank are higher in developed countries. It is determined that the target bank's CAAR values in developing countries are higher than both developed and developing countries. Considering the statistical significance of CAAR values in both country groups, it is seen that it is significant in both developed and developing countries on the day when the merger is announced. In developing countries, the values one day after the announcement are significant, whereas in developed countries, CAAR values are found significant 5 days before and 4 days after the merger.

Cumulative abnormal returns are examined in five different windows, including pre-event and post-event periods. Test statistics for cumulative returns for −10/+10, −7/+7, −5/+5, −3/+3 and −1/+1 days were calculated as the event window and the results are given in Table 9.

When the t statistics of banks' CAR values in Table 9 are analyzed, it is seen that the calculations of four banks are statistically significant. The banks in question, two of which are purchasing, two of which are target banks are Sun Trust, Denizbank, NBD and UBS. Cumulative returns for Sun Trust purchased by BBT were found to be significant at days +1, −1, and +3, −3. It is possible to say that the said purchase provided extra returns to the bank shareholders in this period. Cumulative returns were found statistically significant in all window ranges for Denizbank purchased by NBD.

The cumulative returns of NBD, one of the purchasing banks were found to be statistically significant on window range +1, −1. Cumulative returns for UBS, one of the other purchasing banks, were found to be significant at window intervals +5, −5, +7, −7, +10, −10. Therefore, the +10, −10 period in the selected event window can be said to be statistically significant.

Table 8 Developing and developed country comparison

Developing countries				Developed countries			
Purchasing bank		Target bank		Purchasing bank		Target bank	
CAAR	t CAAR	CAAR	t CAAR	CAAR	t CAAR	CAAR	t CAAR
−0.0762	−1.1962	0.4116	1.2724	0.1026	0.9411	0.0570	−0.0144
−0.0587	0.5460	0.3676	−0.5012	0.0876	−0.0945	0.0571	−0.9283
−0.0667	0.2297	0.3850	−1.2831	0.0891	0.2645	0.0672	1.8943*
−0.0700	0.0638	0.4293	−0.6853	0.0849	0.2703	0.0466	−1.4881
−0.0710	−1.2212	0.4530	−0.0137	0.0806	−0.7440	0.0628	0.7948
−0.0531	−1.1901	0.4535	0.4122	0.0924	−0.2314	0.0542	−0.9053
−0.0357	1.4380	0.4392	1.1799	0.0961	2.7900*	0.0640	−0.0177
−0.0567	−1.8838	0.3985	1.2768	0.0518	−1.0344	0.0642	1.1209
−0.0292	−1.5066	0.3543	−0.1293	0.0682	1.2196	0.0520	0.0007
−0.0072	2.2075*	0.3588	2.9794*	0.0489	−1.7069	0.0520	0.7633
−0.0395	−0.3527	0.2558	1.8265*	0.0760	−0.0009	0.0437	2.3809*
−0.0343	−0.2484	0.1926	2.4090*	0.0760	−0.3984	0.0179	−0.4067
−0.0307	−0.2283	0.1093	0.4962	0.0823	0.5483	0.0223	0.6474
−0.0273	−1.3810	0.0922	−0.4869	0.0736	−0.7877	0.0153	0.8853
−0.0072	−0.6338	0.1090	0.9251	0.0861	1.1945	0.0057	−0.3567
0.0021	−0.1496	0.0770	0.1416	0.0671	1.9881*	0.0095	−1.1910
0.0043	−1.0648	0.0721	0.6418	0.0356	0.6271	0.0225	0.3878
0.0198	−0.0060	0.0499	−0.0486	0.0256	0.9193	0.0183	0.1483
0.0199	0.9076	0.0516	0.6119	0.0110	0.4765	0.0167	−0.8284
0.0067	−0.0967	0.0304	0.4693	0.0034	−0.1543	0.0256	0.9313
0.0081	0.6930	0.0142	0.4112	0.0059	0.3709	0.0155	1.4312

*Significant at 0.05 level

5 Conclusion

In this study, the effect of mergers and acquisitions, which is one of the growth ways of companies, on public company stock returns was investigated. The banking sector was chosen as the sector and an event study was carried out with examples from developed and developing countries. As a review interval, 10-day periods before and after the announcement were selected and a total of 21-day period was included in the analysis for each bank. Abnormal and cumulative abnormal returns were calculated in order to measure the reaction of the companies towards the investment announcements in the days around the investment announcement dates. Sharpe model, also called market model, was used in calculating abnormal returns. Then, the average abnormal returns and the average cumulative excess returns of the purchasing and target companies were calculated.

Firstly, beta coefficients of banks were calculated for the analysis. Beta coefficients of UBS and ICBC, which are among the purchasing banks, are higher than 1, they have a high systematic risk coefficient, and this means that their returns will also be high. Sun Trust Bank and Denizbank, which are among the target banks, are

Table 9 Cumulative abnormal return t statistics

windows	ICBC	Hang Seng	SunTrust	BBT	BNP	Denizbank	NBD	UBS	Nordea
+1, −1	−0.2576	−0.2134	1.8927*	−1.3958	−1.0715	4.3628*	1.9722*	−0.6004	−0.4820
+3, −3	−1.5333	−0.0205	1.9387*	−0.9440	−0.7650	3.2645*	0.8248	−0.0626	0.0360
+5, −5	−0.8987	0.4259	1.1509	−0.3073	0.9077	3.2746*	−0.2109	2.3120*	−0.3947
+7, −7	−1.2176	0.8276	1.5318	−0.0223	1.0451	2.6141*	−0.2615	2.0151*	−1.1053
+10, −10	−1.1471	0.4799	1.7020	0.2545	1.1857	2.5064*	0.3311	2.3922*	−0.7821

*Significant at 0.05 level

also among the banks with high Beta coefficient. The CAR values calculated for these four banks were also found to be statistically significant.

Abnormal returns of bank stock returns were calculated, and excessive returns were found to be statistically significant on the day of announcement, except for two banks. Considering BBT Corp. Bank's excess returns, it is noteworthy that the value on the day before the announcement was statistically significant. This situation brings to mind that there might have been an insider. Another bank belongs to BNP Paribas and the excessive return value one day after the merger was found statistically significant. The investors' reaction to this purchase was one day delayed in the market.

After calculating excess returns, cumulative excess returns are calculated. As with AR, the CAR values of the BBT Corp. Bank are high in the days before the announcement day. There are two main sources of significant cumulative abnormal returns that occur before the disclosures. The first is that information that will be disclosed to the public on a subject is often spread to the market before the date of the announcement. For this reason, the announcement loses its quality of new information and the investor's reaction to the disclosure can be reflected in the prices without any explanation. The second reason is the possibility of learning the information in advance. When the data on the calculated abnormal returns, t statistics and cumulative abnormal returns are analyzed, the positive returns of the relevant shares before the event date indicate that the investment news were used before being announced to the public. The same situation is not observed in the target company Sun Trust, in the purchase made by BBT. Looking at merger news in the market, CAR values of bank stocks; it is seen that CAR values increase with the announcement for Sun Trust, BNP Paribas, NBD Emirates, Denizbank, ICBC and UBS banks.

The effects of merger announcements on average abnormal returns and average abnormal cumulative returns for purchasers and target banks were investigated. When the CAAR values are analyzed, it is seen that the value of the target banks is higher than that of the purchasing bank. Therefore, it turns out that smaller-scale banks purchased by higher capital banks provide more returns to their investors in their announcements for acquisitions and mergers.

Another analysis is the comparison of CAAR values of purchasing and target banks in developed and developing country groups. The highest CAAR value obtained in all groups belongs to target banks in developing countries. It is determined from the CAAR values in developed countries that the purchasing bank returns are higher than the target bank. According to the results, it is concluded that in developing countries, investors obtain higher average abnormal cumulative returns from purchased bank shares. The result of the analysis reveals that in developing countries, investments in target bank stocks are more effective.

The significance of the cumulative abnormal returns of banks was analyzed by creating five event windows. −10/+10, −7/+7, −5/+5, −3/+3 and −1/+1 days were determined as the event window. While ICBC and NBD Emirates had the highest CAR rate in −1/+1 days, Nordea had the highest CAR rate in the −3/+3 range. In other banks, the highest CAR rates were achieved in the longer maturity range. As a result, banks that provide more excessive cumulative in the short term are ICBC, NBD and Nordea.

In line with the findings obtained from the banks subject to the study, it was determined that the investment announcements of the companies had an impact on the stock returns, and this also gave information about the efficiency of the market. In the findings obtained in the study, the cumulative average abnormal returns and excess returns are greater than zero, and it was concluded that the investment announcements of the bankers had an impact on the stock returns, as abnormal returns were obtained at the time of the investment announcement. This contradicts with the market distinction in semi-strong form of the effective market hypothesis. According to the effective market hypothesis, it is not possible for investors to earn excessive profits from stock announcements; it is revealed in this study that excessive returns can be obtained.

This study is important for those who plan to invest in the banking sector stocks in terms of showing how the shares are affected by the investment decisions of the banks. The fact that the abnormal returns of the stocks occur on the announcement day or one day after except BBT, which is one of the banks operating in the USA, is another finding that may be effective in investment decisions.

References

Bouwman, C., Fuller, K., & Nain, A. (2003). The performance of stock-price driven acquisitions (Published as 'Market valuation and acquisition quality: Empirical evidence'). *Review of Financial Studies, 22*(2), 635–679.

Brown, S. J., & Warner, J. B. (1985). Using daily stock returns: The case of event studies. *Journal of Financial Economics, 14*, 3–31.

Campa, J., & Hernando, I. (2006). M&As performance in the European financial industry. *Journal of Banking and Finance, 30*(12), 3367–3392.

Çıtak, L., & Yıldız, F. K. (2007). Devralmanın Devralan İşletmelerin Hisse Senedi Getirileri Üzerindekı Etkisi: Sermaye Piyasası Kurulu İzni İle Gerçekleşen Devralmaların Devralan İşletmelerin Hisse Senedi Getiri Oranları Üzerindeki Etkisinin İncelenmesi. *Dokuz Eylül Üniversitesi İktisadi ve İdari Bilimler Fakültesi Dergisi, 22*(2), 273–295.

Cybo-Ottone, A., & Murgia, M. (2000). Mergers and shareholder wealth in European banking. *Journal of Banking and Finance, 24*(6), 831–859.

Damodaran, A. (2002). *Investment valuation*. New York: Wiley.

DeLong, G. L. (2003). Does long-term performance of mergers match market expectations? Evidence from the US banking industry. *Financial Management, 32*(2), 5–26.

Dodd, P., & Warner, J. B. (1983). On corporate governance a study of proxy contestes. *Journal of Financial Economics, 11*, 401–438.

Mandacı, P. E. (2004). Şirketlerin Birleşme ve Satın Alma Duyurularının Hisse Senedi Fiyatları Üzerine Etkileri. *İktisat İşletme ve Finans, 19*(225), 118–124.

Micklethwait, J., & Wooldridge, A. (2003). *The company: A short history of a revolutionary idea* (Paperback Edition). New York: Modern Library.

Moeller, S., & Zhu, L. (2016). An analysis of short-term performance of UK cross border mergers and acquisitions by Chinese listed companies. *City Research Online*.

Nagm, F., & Kautz, K. (2008). The market value impact of IT investment announcements – An event study. *Journal of Information Technology Theory and Application (JITTA), 9*(3), 61–79.

Seghal, S., Banerjee, S., & Deisting, F. (2012). The impact of M&A announcement and financing strategy on stock returns: Evidence from BRICKS markets. *International Journal of Economics and Finance, 4*(11), 76–90.

Weston, F., Chung, K. S., & Hoag, S. E. (1990). *Mergers, restructuring and corporate control.* Englewood Cliffs, NJ: Prentice Hall.

Yeh, T., & Hoshino, Y. (2002). Productivity and operating performance of Japanese merging firms: Keiretsu-related and independent mergers. *Japan and the World Economy, 14*(3), 347–366.

Increasing Customer Satisfaction in Strategic Communication Studies: Excellence Awards in the Transportation Sector

Ihsan Eken and Başak Gezmen

Abstract As a partner of the European Foundation for Quality Management (EFQM), KalDer (Quality Foundation) annually gives Excellence Awards to companies and non-governmental organizations operating in various sectors as a result of certain criteria and studies in line with EFQM criteria. The awards given since 2013 include companies and NGOs from different sector groups. IETT (Istanbul Electricity, Tramway, and Tunnel) General Directorate, which is one of these companies, has the largest share in Istanbul's public transportation after service transportation (Excluding Private Public Bus and Bus). IETT, which transports thousands or even millions of individuals from a certain point to a certain point every day, carries out studies to increase the existing customer satisfaction with its efforts. Within the scope of the research, it is aimed to analyze the satisfaction of individuals about IETT by conducting a face-to-face survey with individuals in transfer stations located in different regions of Istanbul (Beylikduzu, Avcılar, Cevizlibag, Zincirlikuyu, Uzuncayır, and Sogutlucesme). The transfer stations were selected from the main line stops on the IETT website. The research population consists of approximately 2 million people. Since it is not possible to reach all of these people, it is planned to conduct a survey with 829 people (351 females to 478 males) representing the population. The survey study will be randomly selected from the individuals at the transfer station. The research will be conducted between December 27, 2019 and January 4, 2020 at selected transfer stops. Three scales will be used for the study. In the research, questions in Chinomona (2013)'s "*The Influence Of Brand Experience On Brand Satisfaction, Trust And Attachment In South Africa*" scale, Bobâlcă et al. (2012)'s "*Developing a scale to measure customer loyalty*" scale and Imam (2014)'s "*Measuring Public Transport Satisfaction from User Surveys*" scale will be used.

I. Eken (✉) · B. Gezmen
The School of Communication, İstanbul Medipol University, Istanbul, Turkey
e-mail: ieken@medipol.edu.tr; bgezmen@medipol.edu.trh

H. Dincer, S. Yüksel (eds.), *Strategic Priorities in Competitive Environments*, Contributions to Management Science, https://doi.org/10.1007/978-3-030-45023-6_12

1 Introduction

Today, the global competitive environment has created an environment where companies or organizations constantly develop and renew themselves. All developments and transformations affect the achievement of companies or organizations. Among these factors, customer satisfaction can be considered as one of the most important. While the companies or organizations that have succeeded in ensuring customer satisfaction get shares from the market, the companies or organizations that cannot ensure or keep up with customer satisfaction are observed to get smaller or even vanish within the intensive competitive environment (Dinçer et al. 2020). Another important factor that increases the success of companies or organizations is to increase the existing satisfaction level. Companies or organizations perform constant studies on this issue.

Companies or organizations try to make their goods and services perfect by improving them consistently. Companies and organizations may develop many models in this process. Accordingly, EEA-The European Excellence Award which is rewarded upon this viewpoint within certain criteria and inspections since 1992 brings so many criteria to the companies and organizations. These criteria make their product or services perfect. According to Kalder, there are three remarkable excellence awards among others. The "Deming Award" in Japan since 1951, the "Malcolm Baldrige National Excellence Award (MBNQA)" in the United States since 1988, and the "EFQM European Excellence Award (EEA-The European Excellence Award)" in Europe since 1992 (Kalder & TUSIAD 2017).

Having started in 1992, the EFQM European Excellence Award reached its current state by improving and growing in time. EFQM has started to be applied in many organizations today. In our country, the implementation of the EFQM started with the joint efforts of TUSIAD and Turkish Quality Association for National Quality Award in 1992, which is known today as the Turkey Excellence Award. The evaluations of the Turkey Excellence Award applications are carried out with reference to the EFQM Excellence Model for all categories. Excellence Awards organizations have started to symbolize perfection within the business world due to the fact that, instead of assessing institutions only by single-dimensional parameters such as turnover, efficiency, and loss indicators, they reviewed them with all processes, goals and positions in the competitive environment besides measuring their holistic management systems (Kalder & TUSIAD 2017).

EFQM was established with the aim of appreciating and promoting success as well as providing guidance to the organizations that are willing to achieve sustainable success. This goal is accomplished by three elements, which are integrated with each other and embody the EFQM Excellence Model (Kalder 2014):

- *Basic Concepts of Excellence: Principles underpinning the process of achieving sustainable excellence by any organization*
- *EFQM Excellence Model: Basic Concepts of Organizations and the framework that would assist the RADAR application*

- *RADAR: A dynamic assessment framework and a powerful management tool that can be used to support an organization, which aims to achieve sustainable success, in overcoming the difficulties within this process.*

The use of these three integrated elements enable various institutions of all dimensions and sectors to compare the characteristics and qualifications of institutions that have already achieved sustainable success as well as the results obtained by them. Organizations can use these elements to create a corporate culture of excellence, to ensure consistency in the understanding of management, to learn about good practices, to drive innovation and to improve the obtained results. If used appropriately, together with RADAR and Basic Concepts, the EFQM Excellence Model ensures that all management tools used by an organization create a system that is continuously improved, realizes the intended strategy and works in harmony (Kalder 2016).

In the study, the Metrobus transportation system, which is an organization of IETT, was selected. Metrobus is one of the most important fleet transportation systems in the world. Metrobus, which was established in 2007, has brought many awards to IETT at the national and international level. The reason for analyzing Metrobus in this study is its pioneering role in the path towards quality by starting to implement EFQM standards as well as the Turkey Perfection Award it won in the public category.

Metrobus is one of the most important parts of land transportation in Istanbul, with its 45 stops and 8 different routes in 52 kilometers. Metrobuses, which can be integrated to different transportation lines, connect different means of transportation such as land transportation, rail systems and even sea transportation to each other. Metrobus, making up 13.4% of Istanbul's total transportation activity, can quickly carry the individuals from the start point to the end point in around 100 min (Istanbul Büyüksehir Belediyesi 2018).

The survey method, one of the quantitative research methods, has been used in the study. A face-to-face survey has been conducted with the participants at the metrobus stops. The most important advantage of conducting a survey at the metrobus stops with the participants is that this technique is a fast and convenient data collection method. The face to face surveys have been digitally recorded thanks to the surveymonkey program. In the study, the scales in Chinomona (2013)'s "The Influence Of Brand Experience On Brand Satisfaction, Trust And Attachment In South Africa", Bobâlcă et al. (2012)'s "Developing a scale to measure customer loyalty" and Imam (2014)'s Measuring Public Transport Satisfaction have been used and a factor analysis has been performed for each scale. In this study, the age, gender, type of Istanbulcard usage of Metrobus using individuals and the average number of stops visited by them, as well as their satisfaction have been studied. The aim of the study is to determine the relation between the current satisfaction of the individuals regarding the metrobus usage and the enhancement of this current satisfaction level and related solution offers.

2 Customer Satisfaction and Improving the Current Satisfaction

The main purpose of public relations activities is to influence the feelings and thoughts of the target audience about the institution based on the policies and strategies of the institutions in addition to striving to become a trustworthy and prestigious institution. At this point, it is aimed to bring the economic and social interests of the organization to the highest level. In general, it is aimed to create a positive image and make it sustainable for organizations (Onal 2000).

No matter whether they are referred to as public relations, corporate communication or reputation management, all public relations applications have the duty to ensure the relationship between the institution and the target audience, contribute to the professional targets and establish a common base (Balta Peltekoğlu 2016).

Satisfaction, which is an emotional reaction, can be defined as the extent of meeting the needs and expectations; and it reveals the quality of the public relations activities as a part of the strategic tools of the competitive environment. By increasing the common values and targets, a positive ascension would be achieved in attitudes and the quality of satisfaction would increase gradually. According to the evaluations of Celebi, Hon and Grunig on the satisfaction relationship, it was stated that when one of the parties took a step towards the other party for maintaining positive relations, this resulted in a satisfactory relationship. Satisfaction is an effective tool to understand the quality within the communication process of the target audience and the organization (Celebi 2019). Increasing satisfaction requires serious work for every organization as well as requiring time and spending of resources.

Customer satisfaction, which is an indispensable element for all financial organizations, has been increasingly emphasized in recent years. The most valuable assets of organizations are satisfied customers, who would enable future cash flow. Customer satisfaction increases with better quality and service, and each organization is now performing strategic activities for increasing customer satisfaction to the peak level and increase its profit margins. Creating an image, which is a long-term work, also has a great impact on satisfaction. The development of this whole process will be supported by making the product quality, service and public relations activities productive.

Customer satisfaction measurements, which have gained importance in recent years, are directly related to the income to be obtained both for the organizations and for shareholders, government agencies and buyers. The useful information obtained is used in studies on how the existing customer base could be sustained and preserved. Within the increasing competition environment where the customer satisfaction gradually improves, competition methods that decrease price flexibility for buyers should be considered with respect to the increasing price pressure. In addition to maintaining the existing customer base, gaining new customers from the market requires longer term studies and efforts. Many organizations use a combination of Aggressive and Defensive Strategies and develop strategies to maintain their existing customer base as well as gaining new customers (Schukies 1998).

Satisfaction, which is an emotional reaction, can be defined as the extent of meeting the needs and expectations; and it reveals the quality of the public relations activities as a part of the strategic tools of the competitive environment. By increasing the common values and targets, a positive ascension would be achieved in attitudes and the quality of satisfaction would increase gradually. According to the evaluations of Celebi, Hon and Grunig on the satisfaction relationship, it was stated that when one of the parties took a step towards the other party for maintaining positive relations, this resulted in a satisfactory relationship. Satisfaction is an effective tool to understand the quality within the communication process of the target audience and the organization (Celebi 2019). Increasing satisfaction requires serious work for every organization as well as requiring time and spending of resources.

Organizations should adopt the ultimate goal of gaining customers of other businesses or increasing the loyalty of existing customers and perform activities to achieve this goal. Every institution, including the best, may experience service breaks or failures from time to time. Customers, whose problems are solved, remain as loyal customers. At this point, training of personnel facing the customer is also very important. Within the technological developments and global competition environment, it is difficult to gain new customers and it is important to ensure loyalty in changing customers (Aktepe 2018).

Managing the public relations activity surrounding the results of strategic alliances has become an important financial option for organizations (Oliver 2010, s. 45). Today, businesses face complex stormy markets that are constantly changing and developing. Now, every consumer evaluates the products and services they purchase in the most detailed way with modern technology and digitalization. Customers are demanding more service by paying less. Within this competition environment, institutions have to develop new strategies for new methods. With the tendency towards quality, activities that focus on customer satisfaction have accelerated. For customers, the concept of value is prominent. The common point where all concepts meet is the *you should focus on your customers* expression.

The meaning of creating value for the customer lies in the response to the questions, "what does the customer want?" and, "what does the customer get after purchasing and using the product?" That is, it is the state of gaining more than what is expected in return of the price paid by the customer (Odabaşı 2015).

Brand loyalty is a type of relationship that is integrated with all components of marketing. Quality, product performance, distribution network, promotional activities, the balance of price and value are among the elements increasing brand loyalty. With respect to relational marketing, brand loyalty could be defined as the state of making the type of relationship between the consumer and the brand sustainable by the consumer. Within this communication network, the relationship based on interest between the brand and the consumer is interesting. At this point, the companies have to address the common interest between the brand and the consumer. The concepts of establishing trust, ensuring successful and effective communication, customer satisfaction activities, empathy, cooperation, addiction and reciprocality could be listed among the factors that affect brand loyalty (Islamoğlu and Fırat 2016).

3 Background

The metrobus, which appeared in September 2007 in order to facilitate the transportation in the city, emerged as a design model that is completely unique to Istanbul. In 2007, when it first emerged, metrobus started its rounds between Avcılar and Topkapı; after 1 year, by connecting two sides of Istanbul, it was extended from Avcılar to Söğütlüçeşme. In 2012, the Avcılar-Beylikdüzü destination was introduced. Metrobus became the only means of transport that connects two continents and won many awards for IETT at the national and international level. As of 2017, with its 2756 (1669 single, 1087 hooded) vehicles, Metrobus is one of the most important fleet transport systems of the world (Istanbul Büyüksehir Belediyesi 2018).

Metrobus serves with comfortable vehicles that have high passenger capacity on the Metrobus line of 52 kilometers. There are 45 stations on the Metrobus line, which is integrated with the other means of mass transport. From Beylikdüzü (first/last stop) to Söğütlüçeşme (first/last stop), it takes about 100 min. In other words, it takes 100 min from one end of Istanbul to the other. Operational information regarding the Metrobus is as follows (Istanbul Büyüksehir Belediyesi 2018).

According to data dated 2017, the maximum passenger, excluding those of private automobiles, is 10,095,485. 37.5% of the passengers transported using the land routes is with buses and metrobuses, which makes 3,785,791 persons, 25.4% of them are transported via services, which makes 2,560,270, 20.5% of them are transported with minibuses, which makes 2,073,600 and 16.6% of them are transported with taxis, which makes 1,675,824. 1400 IETT busses and metrobuses, there is Internet service and 1100 of them have USB chargers. 520 vehicles have the black box system and this system is planned to be installed to all the vehicles (Istanbul Büyüksehir Belediyesi 2018).

IETT has five different card systems within the Istanbulcard system, which is used as an electronic cash system. Anonymous Istanbulcard (is an individualized card system that anyone can use). Mavikart (subscription) is a card system which has certain terms and conditions of use, and can be obtained in return of a certain monthly fee. Discount Istanbulcard (is the discount subscription system for students, teachers and people over the age of 60). Free Istanbulcard is a free transportation system for people who meet certain criteria or work in certain businesses. 65 Plus, city police card, disabled card, veteran card, veteran family card, Police Force Systems (EHS) card, yellow press card, martyr spouse and family card, Turkish Statistical Institute (TUIK) card, national athlete card and PTT card are the cards that are used for free transport. Limited-use cards (a type of card, which can be purchased by all citizens, gives a certain amount of right to use and is available at various locations in Istanbul) (Belbim 2016).

According to the Istanbul Public Transportation vehicles report dated in 2019, the daily share of IETT Bus/Metrobus vehicles in the highway category is 13.4%. In other words, the daily number of passengers of the transportation vehicles is 2,059,151. The other two transportation vehicles ranking before IETT Bus/Metrobus in Istanbul transportation are school busses (18.9%—2,867,502) and minibuses (19.2%—2,911,163) (IETT 2020a, b).

4 Research

4.1 Method

In this study, the survey method, which is one of the quantitative research methods, was used. Face-to-face surveys were conducted with the participants at the metrobus stops. The most important advantage of conducting surveys at the metrobus stops with the participants is that this technique is a quick and convenient data collection method. Face to face surveys were digitally recorded through the SurveyMonkey program. The survey method is the method of obtaining data from respondents, who answer questions that have been previously determined for an academic, commercial or official purpose. 61 questions of different scales were prepared for the implementation of the survey. Before the final survey form was prepared for the research and data was collected, ten people traveling with metrobus were contacted and their opinions about the questions and statements in the survey were taken. After the opinions of the individuals in the preliminary study were taken, some statements were modified. Ten people, who participated in the preliminary study, were not included in the main study group.

First of all, some questions were asked to the participants to reveal their demographic information. These questions included age, gender and working status of the participants as well as their use of cards according to the type of Istanbulcard and the number of stops they traveled daily on average.

4.2 Objective and Importance

Transportation is one of the most important problems for Istanbul, which is attributed as one of the most important cities in the world by various experts and research sites. There are three types of transportation in Istanbul, being the railway, land and sea freight. Even though the importance of rail systems increases day by day, the main transportation vehicle of the city is not the railway system. The share of rail systems in transportation system of Istanbul is 18.6% (2,822,291). The share of sea transport vehicles is 4.3% (644,851). The most important means of transportation in

Istanbul is land transportation. The rate of land transportation is 77.1% (11,682,191). One of the most important transportation vehicles that is used in land transportation is IETT buses/Metrobus. The share of metrobus in Istanbul transportation is 13.4%. Due to such reasons as speed, safety and punctuality, the importance of metrobuses in transportation is increasing day by day. Customer satisfaction is one of the most vital issues in using metrobus, which transfers more than 2 million people from one place to another. In order to increase customer satisfaction, Metrobus, which is in constant competition with different means of transportation, offers its customers various innovations both on digital media and on busses. In this study, satisfaction states of individuals, who use Metrobus, were researched together with their ages, genders, Istanbulcard usage methods and the average number of stops they used on daily basis. The aim of the study is to determine the relation between the current satisfaction levels of the individuals regarding the utilization of the metrobus and the enhancement of this current satisfaction level as well as the proposals for solution.

4.3 Limitations

There are 45 stations on the Metrobus line with a total length of 52 km. Six of these stations are defined as the main station and the stations with direct services. Within the scope of the study, only these six (Söğütlüçeşme, Uzunçayır, Beylikdüzü, Avcılar, Cevizlibağ and Zincirlikuyu) metrobus stops were included. The remaining 39 metrobus stops and individuals using these metrobus stops were not included in the study.

4.4 Universe and Sampling

The sampling of the study is either judicial or purposeful. The researcher makes use of his/her own judgement and judgements of other experts to determine who will be included in the sampling. At this point, subjectivity and ease are taken into consideration; as a result, some members of the mainstream have less chance to be selected than the others (Burns and Bush 2014).

The universe of the study is Söğütlüçeşme and Uzunçayır in the Anatolian Part of Istanbul and Beylikdüzü, Avcılar, Cevizlibağ and Zincirlikuyu in the European Part of Istanbul, which are described as the main stops of the Metrobus line and are announced during the Metrobus rounds (34 Avcılar—Zincirlikuyu; 34A Söğütlüçeşme—Cevizlibağ; 34AS Avcılar—Söğütlüçeşme; 34BZ Beylikdüzü—Zincirlikuyu; 34C Beylikdüzü—Cevizlibağ; 34G Beylikdüzü—Söğütlüçeşme; 34U Uzunçayır—Zincirlikuyu; 34Z Zincirlikuyu—Söğütlüçeşme). In six metrobus stations, a total of 829 individuals were surveyed face to face (IETT 2020a, b).

4.5 Data Collection Tools

Following the demographic questions, the scale of brand satisfaction that Chinomona (2013) designed in the study called "The Influence Of Brand Experience On Brand Satisfaction, Trust And Attachment In South Africa" was used in the study. In these questions, the 5-point Likert-type scale was used. After these questions, the scale related to customer loyalty used by Bobâlcă et al. (2012) in their study called "Developing a scale to measure customer loyalty" was used. In these questions, the 5-point Likert-type scale was used. In the study, the satisfaction scale on public transportation from the 'Measuring Public Transport Satisfaction from User Surveys' study by Imam (2014) was used as the third and last scale. In these questions, the 1–9 scoring system was used for satisfaction and importance separately.

Factor analysis was applied to the responses given by individuals using metrobus. Factor analysis is a good way to identify hidden or underlying factors from a range of important variables. Factor analysis, more generally, is a technique that analyzes correlations between variables and collects them under fewer factors (explaining most of the original data) by economically reducing their number (Malhotra 2002). Data obtained after factor analysis in the study were applied the KMO (Kaiser-Meyer-Olkin) sampling competence. In the study of Chinomona (2013), while KMO value was divided into subtitles (.69, .78, .87, and .91), in this study, the KMO value of the Chinomona scale in this studywas .82. While the KMO value of satisfaction title was .87 in the study by Chinomona, the KMO value in this study was .83. Therefore, the study can be deemed to have high reliability. KMO value of all criteria used in the scale of Bobâlcă et al. (2012) was over .67. A similar result was obtained with the scale of Bobâlcă et al. (2012) used in the study. KMO value of all criteria used in the study was over .73.

4.6 Finding

When the ages of the individuals using the metrobus were examined, it was seen that 224 individuals were between the ages of 31–40. Percentage of individuals in this age group was 27%. In other words, one out of every four people participating in the study belonged in the 31–40 age group. It was determined that 175 individuals were between the ages of 41–50. The percentage of individuals in this age group was 21.1%. 171 individuals were found to be between the ages of 19–24. The percentage of individuals in this age group was 20.6%. The number of individuals in the 25–30 age group was 119. The percentage of individuals in the 25–30 age group was 14.4%. It was determined that 93 individuals were in the 51 and plus age group. The percentage of individuals in this age group was 11.2%. Finally, the number of individuals at the age of 18 and below was 47. The percentage of individuals in this group was 5.7%. The total number of passengers participating in the study was

829. 351 of these passengers were female and 478 were male. The percentage of female passengers was 44.8%, while the percentage of the male was 55.2%.

When the working status of the participating individuals using the metrobus was examined, the number of individuals working in a full time (or full day) job was wound to be 505. The percentage of individuals working full-time was 60.9%. In other words, more than half of the individuals participating in the study worked full time. It was seen that 200 individuals participating in the study were students. The percentage of students was 24.1%. 69 individuals were found to be unemployed. The percentage of the unemployed was 8.3%. The number of individuals working in a part-time job was 32. The percentage of individuals working in this category was 3.9%. The number of individuals in the "retired" category was 23. The percentage of individuals in the "retired" category was 2.8%.

When the participants of the study were analyzed according to the types of Istanbulcard they used, it was determined that 441 participants had student cards. The percentage of individuals with student cards is 53.2. In other words, more than half of the participants participating in the study used a student card. The number of metrobus users with blue cards was 265. The percentage of users using blue cards was 32%. 51 individuals had free cards. The percentage of individuals using free cards was 6.2%. 43 individuals used anonymous cards. The percentage of individuals using anonymous cards was 5.2. 29 users used cards listed in the other category. In the other category, the number of users using teacher Istanbulcard was 29, and their percentage was 3.5.

When the average number of stops used daily by the individuals using the metrobus was examined, it was seen that individuals using 21 stops and over were 342 in number. The percentage of individuals traveling 21 stops and over was 41.3. It was determined that 176 individuals travelled between 16 and 20 stops per day. The percentage of individuals traveling in this category was 21.2. The number of individuals traveling between 11 and 15 stops was 146. The percentage of individuals traveling between 11 and 15 stops was 17.6. 125 individuals travelled between 6 and 10 stops. The percentage of individuals traveling in this category was 15.1. The number of individuals using 5 and less stops was 40. The percentage of individuals using 5 and less stops was 4.8.

Within the scope of the study, data obtained from the hypothesis tests were analyzed and explanations were made according to the findings. The Chi-Square (X^2) test was used for the hypothesis tests. The Chi-Square test was generally used to test whether the observed values or frequencies were in accordance with the claimed theoretical frequencies and whether the distribution of the sampling was consistent with a recognized distribution (Gürbüz and Şahin 2016).

Participants of the study were tested to identify whether there was a significant difference in their transportation card (akbil) usage status and the amount of distance they travelled by the metrobus (number of stops) at 0.05 significance rate. In the study, a survey with 5-point Likert-type scale was administered to 829 students who participated in the study based on certain criteria and their opinions were collected. For this activity, 1H0 and 1H1 hypotheses were formed as follows.

1H0: There is no relationship between the transportation card (akbil) usage status of the participants and their metrobus travel distance (number of stops) per day
1H1: There is a relationship between the transportation card (akbil) usage status of the participants and their metrobus travel distance (number of stops) per day

The results of the Chi-Square test, which was performed with the aim of determining whether there was a relationship between the transportation card (akbil) usage status of the participants and their metrobus travel distances (number of stops). There is a statistically significant relationship between the transportation card (akbil) usage status of the participants and their metrobus travel distances (number of stops) (X2 (16) = 68,429; P < 0.05). The observed and expected frequency values were found to be very close or equal to each other. As a result, the 1H0 hypothesis has been rejected; the 1H1 hypothesis has been accepted. In other words, the transportation card (akbil) usage status (akbil) of the participants differed significantly according to their metrobus travel distances (number of stops).

It was tested whether there was a significant difference between "the transportation card usage status (akbil) of the participants and their working status" at 0.05 significance rate. In the study, a survey with 5-point Likert-type scale was administered to 829 students who participated in the study based on certain criteria and their opinions were collected. For this activity, $2H^0$ and $2H^1$ hypotheses were formed as follows.

$2H^0$: There is no relationship between the transportation card (akbil) usage status of the participants and their working status
$2H^1$: There is a relationship between individuals' transportation card (akbil) usage status and their working status

The results of the Chi-Square test, which was performed with the aim of testing whether there was a relationship between the transportation card (akbil) usage status of the participants and their working status. There is a statistically significant relationship between the transportation card (akbil) usage status of the participants and their working status (X^2 (16) = 1117.160; $P < 0.05$). The observed and expected frequency values were found to be very close or equal to each other. As a result, the $2H^0$ hypothesis has been rejected; the $2H^1$ hypothesis has been accepted. In other words, there is a significant difference between the transportation card (akbil) usage status of the participants and their working status.

It was tested whether there was a significant difference between the daily metrobus travel distances (number of stops) of the participants and their state of being somehow dependent on the metrobus, at the 0.05 significance rate. In the study, a survey with 5-point Likert-type scale was administered to 829 students who participated in the study based on certain criteria and their opinions were collected. For this activity, $3H^0$ and $3H^1$ hypotheses were formed as follows.

$3H^0$: There is no relationship between the daily metrobus travel distances (number of stops) of the participants and their state of being somehow dependent on the metrobus

3H[1]: There is a relationship between the daily metrobus travel distances (number of stops) of the participants and their state of being somehow dependent on the metrobus.

The results of the Chi-Square test, which was performed to identify whether there was a relationship between the daily metrobus travel distances (number of stops) of the participants and their state of being somehow dependent on the metrobus. There was no statistically significant relationship between the daily metrobus travel distances (number of stops) of the participants and their state of being somehow dependent on the metrobus ($X2\ (16) = 23{,}378;\ P > 0.05$). The observed and expected frequency values were found to be distant or different from each other. As a result, the 3H1 hypothesis has been rejected; the 3H0 hypothesis has been accepted. In other words, the daily metrobus travel distances (number of stops) of the participants does not differ significantly according to their state of being somehow dependent on the metrobus.

It was tested whether there was a significant difference between the daily metrobus travel distances (number of stops) of the participants and their state of being very satisfied with the metrobus, at the 0.05 significance rate. In the study, a survey with 5-point Likert-type scale was administered to 829 students who participated in the study based on certain criteria and their opinions were collected. For this activity, 4HO and 4H1 hypotheses were formed as follows.

4H0: There is no relationship between the daily metrobus travel distances of the individuals (number of stops) and their states of being very satisfied with the metrobus

4H1: There is a relationship between the daily metrobus travel distances of the individuals (number of stops) and their states of being very satisfied with the metrobus

The results of the Chi-Square test, which was performed with the aim of testing whether there was a relationship between the daily metrobus travel distances of the individuals (number of stops) and their states of being very satisfied with the metrobus. There was a statistically significant relationship between the daily metrobus travel distances of the individuals (number of stops) and their states of being very satisfied with the metrobus ($X2\ (16) = 22{,}134;\ P < 0.05$). The observed and expected frequency values were found to be very close or equal to each other. As a result, the 4H0 hypothesis has been rejected; the 4H1 hypothesis has been accepted. In other words, the daily metrobus travel distances of the individuals (number of stops) differed significantly according to their states of being very satisfied with the metrobus.

It was tested whether there was a significant difference between the working status of the participants and their state of being very satisfied with the metrobus, at the 0.05 significance rate. In the study, a survey with 5-point Likert-type scale was administered to 829 students who participated in the study based on certain criteria and their opinions were collected. For this activity, 5H0 and 5H1 hypotheses were formed as follows.

5H0: There is no relationship between the working status of the participants and their states of being very satisfied with the metrobus
5H1: There is a relationship between the working status of the participants and their states of being very satisfied with the metrobus

The results of the Chi-Square test, which was performed with the aim of testing whether there was a relationship between the working status of the participants and their states of being very satisfied with the metrobus. There was a statistically significant relationship between the working status of the participants and their states of being very satisfied with the metrobus ($X2\ (16) = 26{,}970$; $P < 0.05$). The observed and expected frequency values were found to be very close or equal to each other. As a result, the 5H0 hypothesis has been rejected; the 5H1 hypothesis has been accepted. In other words, the working status of the participants differed significantly according to their states of being very satisfied with the metrobus.

It has been tested whether there was a significant difference between "the transportation card usage of the participants and their state of being very satisfied with the metrobus" at 0.05 significance rate. In the study, a survey with 5-point Likert-type scale was administered to 829 students who participated in the study based on certain criteria and their opinions were collected. For this activity, 6H0 and 6H1 hypotheses were formed as follows.

6H0: There is no relationship between the transportation card (akbil) usage status of the participants and their state of being very satisfied with metrobus
6H1: There is a relationship between the transportation card (akbil) usage status of the participants and their state of being very satisfied with metrobus

The results of the Chi-Square test, which was performed with the aim of testing whether there was a relationship between the transportation card (akbil) usage status of the participants and their state of being very satisfied with metrobus. There is no statistically significant difference between the transportation card (akbil) usage status of the individuals and their state of being very satisfied with metrobus ($X2\ (16) = 21{,}162$; $P > 0.05$). The observed and expected frequency values were found to be distant or different from each other. As a result, the 6H1 hypothesis has been rejected; the 6H0 hypothesis has been accepted. In other words, the transportation card usage of the individuals did not differ significantly according to their status of being very satisfied with the metrobus.

The Anova test, which is known as the variance analysis or f-test, is used to analyze group averages and the relevant operations. One or more factors may be involved in models where the Anova test is applied. The purpose of this analysis is to test whether there was a difference at a certain significance rate in a single factor by comparing the averages of more than two groups (Gürbüz and Sahin 2016).

Whether the opinions of individuals about the usage of metrobus displayed a significant difference according to their satisfaction status was investigated through data obtained from 829 people. Some statistics related to the sampling are shown in Table 1 together with the single factor variance analysis results and multiple

Table 1 One way Anova results of Imam's Scale

	P-value		P-value
Stops (protection against weather conditions, lightning, etc.)	.001	Ease of getting on/off the vehicle	0.93
Hygiene of the vehicle	.000	Ease of payment	.002
Availability of the air conditioner	.002	Coverage in Istanbul (number of routes)	.013
Privacy	.585	Travel cost	.361
Seat comfort	.000	Attitudes of employees	.023
Noise	.000	Travel time	.000
Crowd	.037	Waiting time	0.29
Availability of the services	.000	On-board safety	.009
Availability of the wheelchair area	.000	Personal security	.001

Table 2 Metrobus satisfaction and importance scale

Rank	Most satisfied	Least satisfied	Most important	Least important
1	Travel cost	Crowd	Travel time	Availability of the wheelchair area
2	Ease of payment	Stops (protection against weather conditions, lightning, etc.)	Waiting time	Seat comfort
3	Hygiene of the vehicle	Attitudes of employees	Travel cost	Privacy
4	Availability of the services	Waiting time	Availability of the air conditioner	
5	Availability of the air conditioner	Ease of getting on/off the vehicle	Stops (protection against weather conditions, lightning, etc.)	

comparison results. According to the results in Table 1, the significance rate in some items is less than .05 and in some items it was observed to be greater than .05.

In Table 2, looking at the criteria that the individuals using metrobus were most satisfied with, it was seen that the most satisfied criterion was the travel cost. Other criteria that followed the travel price were the ease of payment, hygiene of the vehicle, availability of the services and availability of air conditioning. When the criteria for the least satisfaction of individuals using Metrobus were examined, the most dissatisfactory criterion of individuals was that the metrobus was very crowded. Other criteria that followed the dissatisfaction of the individuals due to the crowd were the stops (protection against weather conditions, lightning, etc.), attitudes of the employees, waiting time and ease of getting on/off the vehicle.

For individuals using metrobus, the most important criterion in the metrobus was the journey time. Other criteria that followed the journey time were the waiting time, travel cost, availability of air conditioning and Stops (protection against weather conditions, lightning, etc.). When the most insignificant criteria for individuals using metrobus were examined, the most insignificant criterion for individuals was the availability of the wheelchair area in the metrobus. Other criteria following the availability of the wheelchair area were the seat comfort and privacy.

5 Conclusion

Customer relationship management, which includes many elements in its structure, covers a strategic working process. At this point, the strategy stands for the all methods that should be applied in order to differ from the competitors in line with the competitor analysis made based on the market conditions. The differentiations that have emerged with the technological developments have facilitated the analysis. In the development period, it is important to know the customer and implement individual production and marketing for them.

Successful customer relationship management also creates customer satisfaction. Satisfied customers can also be defined as the loyal customers. Therefore, ensuring this loyalty and managing to maintain it is very important. High customer satisfaction is seen as one of the most important aspects of loyalty. Customer satisfaction is essential in terms of finance. In the study, the Metrobus transportation system, which is one of the most important parts of Istanbul transportation, is discussed, the satisfaction status of individuals regarding this issue is evaluated and assessments and solution offers regarding the issue aiming to increase the satisfaction level are presented.

Individuals in different age groups have participated in the study. The percentage of individuals under the age of 30 is about 40%, while the percentage of participants over the age of 30 is about 60%. Although a homogeneous study was aimed in the proportion of male and female individuals, this was not fully realized in the study. The percentage of women is about 45%, while the percentage of men is about 55%. When the working status of the individuals participating in the study was examined, it was found out that approximately 61% of the individuals participating in the study were working full-time. In addition to the individuals working full-time, it was also observed that the students also used the metrobus as the means of transport intensively. One of the important results of the study is that although there are 200 people who identify themselves as students, 441 individuals use the transportation card for the students. In other words, due to the fact that the student discount card is lower than the blue card as of price in the monthly Istanbulcard subscription, it was discovered that although some of the individuals were not students, they had received a discount student card by registering in systems such as open education faculties of the universities. When the average number of stops that individuals travel per day with metrobus is examined, it is seen that approximately 41% of individuals travel 21 or more stops. It has been observed that approximately 5% of the individuals using the Metrobus travel 5 or less than 5 stops. In other words, it has been concluded that individuals using the metrobus generally use the metrobus for their long-distance travels and other transportation vehicles for short distances.

When the statistical relationship between the transportation card (akbil) usage status of the individuals and the metrobus traveling distance per 1 day (number of stops) was examined, it was discovered that there was a significant relationship between these two variables. When the statistical relationship between the transportation card (akbil) usage status of the individuals and their working status was examined, it was discovered that there is a significant relationship between these two variables. In other words, there is a significant difference between usage of transportation card by individuals (akbil) and their working status. When the statistical relationship between individuals' travel distance with metrobus per 1 day (number of stops) and their dependence on metrobus in a sense was examined, it was seen that there was no significant relationship between these two variables. In other words, it does not differ significantly between the two variables. When the statistical relationship between individuals' metrobus traveling distance per 1 day (number of stops) and their status of being highly satisfied with the metrobus was examined, it was seen that there was a significant relationship between these two variables. In other words, the traveling distance of individuals per 1 day varies significantly according to their status of being highly satisfied with the metrobus. When the statistical relationship between the working status of the individuals and the traveling distance with metrobus per 1 day (number of stops) was examined, it was seen that there is a significant relationship between these two variables. When the statistical relationship between individuals' transportation card (akbil) usage status and being highly satisfied with metrobus is examined, it was seen that there is no significant relationship between these two variables. In other words, the transportation card usage status of the individuals does not vary significantly according to their status of being highly satisfied with the metrobus.

When the results of the one way Anova test are examined, it is observed that the significance rate of some items is in some items less than .05 and in some items greater than .05. Items less than 0.05; Stops (protection against weather conditions, lightning, etc.), cleanness of the vehicle, existence of the air conditioning, seat comfort, noise, crowd, existence of services, existing of the wheelchair area, easiness of payment, employee attitude, journey time, waiting time, vehicle safety and personal security. Items greater than .05 are privacy, the easiness of getting on/off the vehicle, travel price and waiting time.

When the subjects that the participants are most satisfied with the metrobus are examined, the individuals are mostly satisfied with the travel price, easiness of payment, travel time, existence of services and existence of air-conditioning. When the subjects that exist in IETT's strategic report regarding the subjects which individuals are most satisfied, the similar results are observed. For example, the same data was discovered both in IETT's strategic report's "verbal notifications and on board screen (LCD) indications to the individuals" and "total traveling time" items and the results from the study in items "existence of services" and "traveling time". Unlike the IETT strategic report, the subjects that indicate the highest satisfaction with the metrobus are the benefits of Metrobuses in reducing environmental pollution and the notifications made in emergency cases.

When the subjects where the participants are least satisfied with the metrobus are examined, they are: crowd, stops (protection against weather conditions, lightning, etc.), attitude of the employees, waiting time and easiness of getting on/off the vehicle. When the subjects the individuals are least satisfied of, which exist in IETT's strategic report were examined, the similar results were observed. For example, the same data was discovered both in IETT's strategic report's "the passenger traffic in stations and on board" and "the convenience of stations to bad weather conditions" items and the results from the study in items "crowd" and "stops (protection against bad weather conditions, lightning etc.)". Unlike the IETT strategic report, the subjects that indicated the least satisfaction from the metrobus were the accessibility of the elevators and ramps at the station, the waiting time of the nostalgic tram, the sufficiency of the information on the website, the distance of the nostalgic tram stops to the transfer points and the security systems.

The most important issues that individuals participating in the study expect from the metrobus transportation system are traveling time, waiting time, travel cost, availability of air conditioning and stops (protection against weather conditions, lightning, etc.). The least important issues that the individuals participating in the study expect from the metrobus transportation system are the availability of the wheelchair area, seat comfort and privacy.

This study tries to present solutions about discovering the relationship between the current satisfaction status of the individuals about metrobus and increasing the satisfaction level and related solution offers. The aim here is to provide troubleshooting and solutions to the authorities in order to make the metrobus transportation system closer to perfect by eliminating the deficiencies in the, system.

References

Aktepe, C. (2018). Müşteri Ilişkileri Yönetiminde Müsteri Hizmetleri. In C. Aktepe, M. Baş, & M. Tolon (Eds.), *Müşteri İilşkileri Yönetimi* (pp. 59–96). Ankara: Detay Yayıncılık.

Balta Peltekoğlu, F. (2016). *Halkla Iliskiler Nedir?* Istanbul: Beta Yayınları.

Belbim. (2016). *Istanbulcard.* Retrieved from Kartlarımız https://www.Istanbulcard.istanbul/kartlarimiz-45

Bobâlcă, C., Gătej, C., & Ciobanu, O. (2012). Developing a scale to measure customer loyalty. *Emerging Markets Queries in Finance and Business, 3*, 623–628.

Burns, A., & Bush, R. (2014). *Marketing research.* London: Pearson Education.

Celebi, E. (2019). *Halkla İlişkiler Uygulamaları Nasıl Olmalı? Özel Sektör Kuruluşlarında Kamu Kuruluşlarında Sivil Toplum Kuruluşlarında Dijital Ortamlarda Kültürler Arası Ortamlarda.* Ankara: Nobel Yayınları.

Chinomona, R. (2013). The influence of brand experience on brand satisfaction, trust and attachment in South Africa. *International Business & Economics Research Journal, 12*, 1303–1316.

Dinçer, H., Yüksel, S., & Pınarbaşı, F. (2020). Kano-based measurement of customer expectations in retail service industry using IT2 DEMATEL-QUALIFLEX. In *Handbook of research on positive organizational behavior for improved workplace performance* (pp. 349–370). Hershey, PA: IGI Global.

Gürbüz, S., & Sahin, F. (2016). *Sosyal Bilimlerde Araştırma Yöntemleri*. Ankara: Seçkin Yayıncılık.

IETT. (2020a). *Toplu Ulasım*. Retrieved from İstanbul'da Toplu Ulaşım Tablosu 2019 https://www.iett.istanbul/tr/main/pages/istanbulda-toplu-ulasim/95

IETT. (2020b). *Toplu Ulaşım*. Retrieved from Metrobüs Hatları https://www.iett.istanbul/tr/main/pages/metrobus-hatlari/90

Imam, R. (2014). Measuring public transport satisfaction from user surveys. *International Journal of Business and Management, 9*, 106–114.

Islamoğlu, A., & Fırat, D. (2016). *Startejik Marka Yönetimi*. Istanbul: Beta Yayınları.

Istanbul Büyüksehir Belediyesi. (2018). *IETT 2018-2022 Yıl Stratejik Planı*. Istanbul: Istanbul Büyüksehir Belediyesi.

Kalder. (2014). *2014 Türkiye Mükemmellik Ödülü*. Istanbul: Türkiye Mükemmellik Ödülü Yürütme Kurulu.

Kalder. (2016). *2016 Türkiye Mükemmellik Ödülleri*. Istanbul: Türkiye Mükemmellik Ödülleri Yürütme Kurulu.

Kalder & TUSIAD. (2017). *2017 Türkiye Mükemmellik Ödülleri*. Istanbul: Türkiye Mükemmellik Ödülleri Yürütme Kurulu.

Malhotra, N. (2002). *Marketing research - An applied orientation*. New Delhi: Pearson.

Odabaşı, Y. (2015). *Satış ve Pazarlamada Müşteri İlşkileri Yönetimi (CRM)*. Istanbul: Aura Kitapları.

Oliver, S. (2010). *Public relations strategy*. London: Kogan Page; CIPR.

Onal, G. (2000). *Halkla İlişkiler*. İstanbul: Türkmen Kitabevi.

Schukies, G. (1998). *Halkla İlişkilerde Müşteri Memnuniyetine Dönük Kalite Örgütsel İletişimde Yeni Yönelimler* (p. 10). İstanbul: Rota Yayınları; IPRA-Uluslararası Halkla İlişkiler Derneği Altın Kitap Sayı.

Significance of Non-Monetary Forms of Capital: Importance of Social Capital

Arif Orçun Söylemez

Abstract There exists non-monetary forms of capital, which are utterly important for better economic performance. However, the non-monetary forms of capital are usually either neglected by or unknown to managers. In sum, their significance is almost always overlooked. This article scrutinized one such important non-monetary capital, the social capital. Social capital is a vague term which is broadly used by economists to refer to the social associations and relations between individuals, groups and institutions in an economy. According to a popular classification, it is possible to classify social capital into three classes. These three classes namely are the bonding, bridging and linking social capital classes. While bonding and bridging capital refer to horizontal social relations between constituents with no hierarchical positioning against each other, linking capital reflects a vertical structure and mostly refers to the relations of individuals and social groups with formal institutions. Empirical studies have shown that high levels of social capital stock is usually beneficial in the economic sense. However, too much bonding capital might have adverse economic impact as well. Bonding capital includes our relations with and associations to the others in our closest circle. It includes the social relations and networks established between the closest friends, kins etc. That is why so strong bonding feelings may lead us to making favors to others in our bonding circle even when such favors reflected worse than optimal choices from the pure economic rationale. Nepotism or favoritism, as two examples, may result in job offers to people with whom we are bonded but not so talented in fact. That said, social capital, especially the bridging and linking types, have the capacity to make positive economic contributions to the society through enabling efficient buildup of teams, facilitating idea sharing, reducing contract costs, boosting productivity, mitigating informational asymmetry issues and supporting entrepreneurial activities.

A. O. Söylemez (✉)
Economics Department, Marmara University, Kadıköy/İstanbul, Turkey
e-mail: orcun.soylemez@marmara.edu.tr

H. Dincer, S. Yüksel (eds.), *Strategic Priorities in Competitive Environments*,
Contributions to Management Science, https://doi.org/10.1007/978-3-030-45023-6_13

1 Introduction

Return on capital employed (ROCE) remains as one of the most significant measures of profitability for managers, if not the most significant one. The term "capital employed" conventionally includes all the fixed and working capital that have been put to use by the firm. The following chart presents the average ROCE figures during the 1996–2006 period for a number of industries in Europe. The interesting one in this chart is undoubtedly the software industry for the fact that its decade-long ROCE average is more than double of the runner-up Pharmaceuticals industry. As the chart indicates, software industry is a ROCE outlier with no other industry in the list even getting somewhere close to it as shown in Fig. 1.

What could be the reason behind this observed anomaly? As well known, the monetary value of the capital that is used by any firm in any industry is estimated from the balance sheet figures. Since capital employed is equal to the sum of the fixed capital and working capital, we only need to dive into the balance sheet figures to read the sum of the long-term assets and current assets in excess of the current liabilities. But there obviously is a catch here. It is only impossible to translate all the capital in use into monetary figures and make a recording on the financial documents. Financial documents, such as the balance sheet, would therefore fall short of recognizing the stock value of the non-monetary capitals of the firms such as the human capital and the social capital.

If we go back to the above chart, software industry is a human-capital abundant industry. Or put it differently, the most valuable asset in this industry is not the hardware or the software that the programmers use but the programmers themselves and the harmony between them which enables the build-up of effective teams on various projects. Unfortunately, we know no reliable way of estimating the value of the programmers or the value of intangible things such as the friendship and harmony between them for the accounting purposes. Nonetheless, we could devise a back-of-the-envelope method for roughly estimating a ballpark figure for the value of non-monetary, human-related stocks like those.

Let us take the average of the ROCEs of all the industries in the chart except the software industry. It would be 9.7%. Let us now assume that the ROCE figure of the software industry had to be in the vicinity of that number if we could somehow estimate the monetary value of the non-monetary stock in this industry. Hence, we can write the following equalities.

$$ROCE_1 = \frac{NOPAT}{Value\ of\ Monetary\ Capital\ Employed} = 49.7\%$$

$$ROCE_2 = \frac{NOPAT}{Value\ of\ Monetary\ and\ Nonmonetary\ Capital\ Employed} = 9.7\%$$

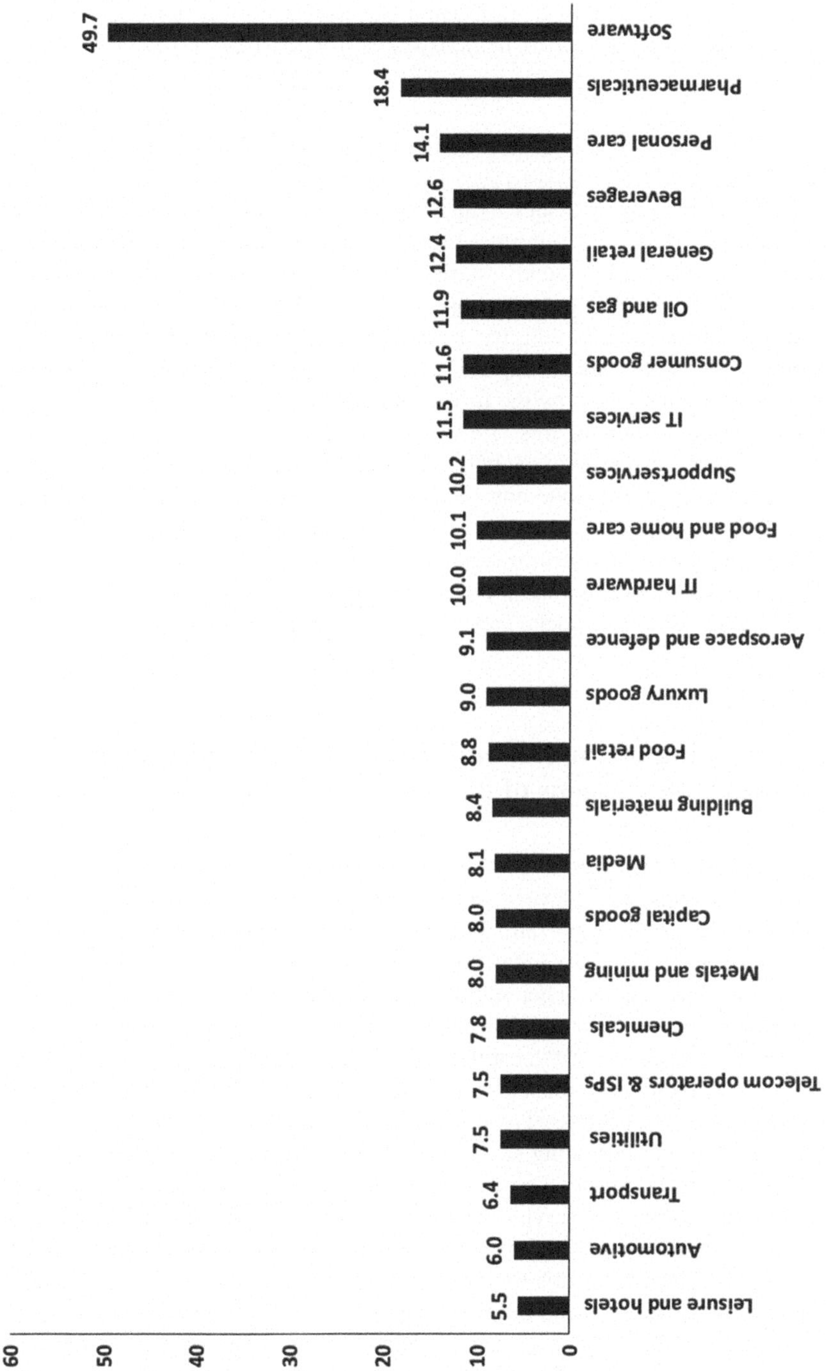

Fig. 1 Average ROCEs for 23 European Industries from 1996–2006 (Source: Vernimmen P., Le Fur Y., Dallochio M., Salvi A. and P. Quiry 2017)

Note that *NOPAT*, i.e. net operating profit after tax figure, is the same in both equations. Let us use the abbreviations *MCE* and *nMCE* for the *Value of Monetary Capital Employed* and *Value of Nonmonetary Capital Employed* terms, respectively. Then, we could write the following.

$$0.497MCE = 0.097MCE + 0.097nMCE \implies nMCE \cong 4MCE$$

This rough estimation indicates us that the intrinsic value of the non-monetary capital stock might be almost four times higher than the value of the monetary capital in the software business. In conclusion, the non-monetary capital of firms, which is usually overlooked, is likely to be an important stock that needs more attention as a matter of fact. This article will try to underline the importance of one such non-monetary stock, i.e. social capital, which is a form of capital that is either unknown or totally neglected by the firm managers.

The remaining sections of this article are organized as follows. Section 2 is a discussion about the meaning of capital with regard to whether capital is a monetary phenomenon, or it could include non-monetary assets as well. Section 3 introduces social capital as an important non-monetary form of capital with reference to the historical accounts on the usefulness social bonds and traditions etc. Section 4 is spared for more recent discussions about social capital. Section 5 argues the potential economic benefits of strong social capital stock. Section 6 concludes.

2 The Meaning of Capital and the Need for Recognizing Non-Monetary Forms of it

Social capital roughly refers to the social associations both within and between different social groups, social layers, people, institutions that take part in society. In a simpler way, one could argue any kind of bond or relation between the social elements make up the social capital. Since capital is an economic term, probably the first step one has to take, in her attempt to understand the already vague meaning of social capital, should be questioning the fit of this term to the definition.

From a Marxian point of view, capital is a term with strict meaning. According to Marx, himself, capital was a monetary phenomenon and could only exist within the economic reproduction process. The economic reproduction according to Marx is a cycle that involves the following steps. Initially the physical production and distribution of goods and services take place. Secondly, trading activity occurs allowing the exchange of goods and services. Goods and services are then used either for further production purposes as intermediate goods and services or consumed out by their final users. In the end, this reproduction scheme becomes the cause of many voluntary and involuntary social relations in the form of competition or cooperation of social classes. Put in this way, there seems to be nothing novel in this Marxist conceptualization of capitalism that is in fact different than the dynamics of any other type of social and economic organization. After all, production and exchange take place almost in every economic and social arrangement. However, the novelty in the capitalist setting is the dependence of this reproduction process on capital. Capital, as aforesaid, is a monetary phenomenon and neither production nor exchange would take place without the promise of growing capital according to the Marxist view. In a capitalist setting, no economic entity would bother with producing and exchanging unless there were economic rewards in the end. As one might notice, capital is definitely and only a monetary issue for Marxists. It is the reward for which the capitalist functions and it is also what makes production and formation of a functioning market economy possible. Defined in this way, according to Marxists, capital would have a narrow meaning excluding all the non-monetary and human forms of capital.

Classicals, however, has a broader definition for capital. As an example, Adam Smith accepts any stock that affords a person a revenue as a capital of that person. Therefore, capital could be anything ranging from the stock value of machines that a master uses to the intangible tacit knowledge of a doctor which allows her medical practice. Additionally, there might be times even a dramatic face acts as a capital—for an actress for instance.

In our view, the discussion that has been made in the introduction part above is a proof of the fact that the classical approach to defining capital in a broader fashion makes more sense. Software industry might be posting ROCE figures that are unprecedentedly high but if we look at the profits of that industry in Dollar terms, what we see there is its sales profit margins' not being that dramatically over the margins of other highly profitable industries. Its margins are even lower than the margins we observe in the pharmaceuticals or banking industries as shown in Fig. 2.

A situation like this could arise if some of the expenditures of software firms were recorded as current expenses but not counted as investment expenditures. This would align the margin measures while causing an overestimation of ROCE since the invested capital would be artificially depressed. That is why, from an empirical point of view, such radical differences between the ROCE figures of the software industry and the rest are not reasonable because given the software industry's more modest margin-based profits in contrast to its wild ROCE figures, we believe something should be missing in the capital assessment of that industry. In our view again, that might be an outcome of the fact that margin-based metrics account for all expenses, but ROCE adjusts the return with respect to the capital employed. If an expense is not recognized as capital investment, ROCE could just go sky high levels as in the case of software industry. As a result, we believe the capital should be assessed in a broader sense and all the forms of stock that afford a revenue for its holder should be accepted as capital.

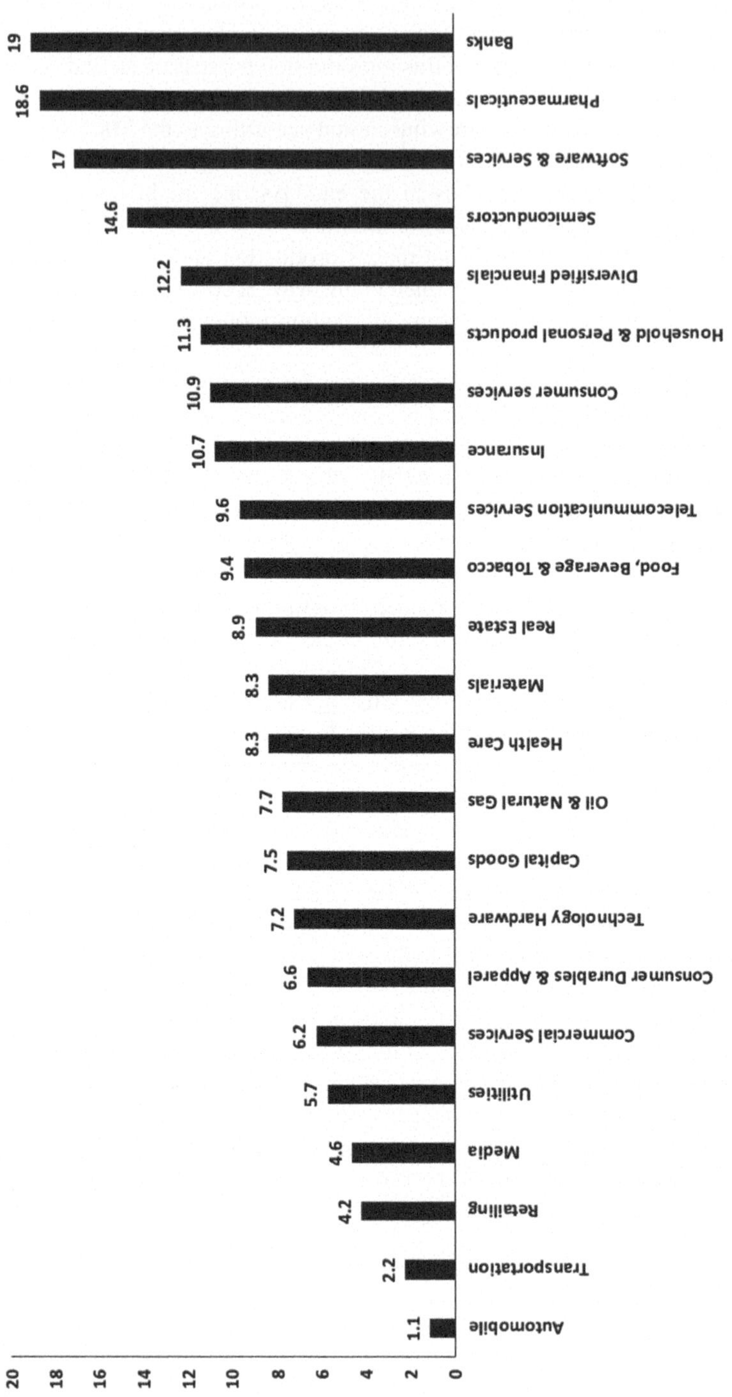

Fig. 2 Sales Profit Margins of US Industries (Source: Derzko 2007)

3 Social Capital: An Important Non-Monetary Form of Capital in Retrospect

Social capital is an important non-monetary sort of capital that is usually overlooked. In fact, it has so much capacity to generate wealth. Social capital came into popularity in economics especially during the 1990s following the seminal contributions of Robert Putnam, a Harvard University professor of public policy. The interest paid by the international organizations such as the World Bank and the OECD also supported the rise of its popularity among economists.

Although, we have aforementioned social capital in this text and said how it refers to the associations between different social elements such as the institutions, classes, layers and individuals, in fact there is no clear and unquestionable definition of it for substantive and ideological reasons (Dolfsma and Dannreuther 2003; Foley and Edwards 1997). Socialcapitalresearch.com, a world wide web page dedicated to social capital research and training provides excellent information regarding this ambiguity around the concept. That said, social capital is not a concept that is just in the interest of economists. Along with economists, social scientists from various backgrounds such as political sciences, sociology and international relations do have active research interests in social capital matters. Given all these differing frameworks for analyzing social capital, there exists substantial disagreement and disputation in the definitions of the concept (Adler and Kwon 2002). As it is written on the socialcapitalresearch.com with reference to Adam and Roncevic (2003), due to the difficulties in describing social capital, scholars usually tend to discuss the intellec tual origins of the concept along with the diverse ways of its applications and some of its unresolved issues before adopting a school of thought and adding their own definition. We are not going to make an attempt to add our own definition, still we find it useful as well to discuss the intellectual origins of social capital before discussing the diverse ways of its applications in and usefulness for the corporations.

Although the social capital concept gained outstanding fame in economics only in the last three decades, as Söylemez (2019) shows, the intellectual discussions somehow related with the concept has a significant past. From the historical perspective, early nineteenth century thinkers such as Alexis de Tocqueville and James Madison were among the first ones to discuss the concept. However, they never used the term social capital. Therefore, we need to trace the concept in their thoughts. Take the ideas of Alexis de Tocqueville for example. He ardently believed that effectiveness of democracy in the US society was directly related with the American society's traditions. Americans had a tendency to discuss all matters on a broad range of subjects from economics to politics in a collective manner. Alexis de Tocqueville seems to have noticed that this decentralized form of solution seeking to communal issues was not only a simple tradition but it was indeed a social capacity helping Americans build a democratic nation. Alexis de Tocqueville noted this capacity as a useful cause of social effectiveness but never called it explicitly as a form of capital.

Söylemez (2019) details the various resembling views in the discussions of John Bates Clark, Edward Bellamy, Henry Sidgwick, and Karl Marx among numerous other nineteenth century thinkers. Among all these names, Karl Marx was the first one to use the term social capital explicitly, in German, his native tongue, as 'gesellschaftliche kapital' in 1867. In the English-speaking world, John Bates Clark is known to have used the term social capital first in 1885. It is no surprise that Clark employed a Marxist term at the time because in his younger period, as an economist schooled in Switzerland and Germany between 1872 and 1875, he was heavily influenced from German socialists. Clark would become an advocate of capitalism gradually over the years. But in this early stage of his career, he was refusing the classical political economic view of the time. Along with Clark, Marx and Sidgwick were also upset with the classical political economic view of their age, according to which capitalists had the entrepreneurial prudence and abstinence from daily consumption and their prudence and abstinence were enabling their funds and power to profit. Workers were the labor they hired with their own funds, which were resulting from the capitalists' prior abstinences. However, Sidgwick, Clark, and Marx were refusing the thought that payments to laborers were made from the capitalist's own pocket. According to them, production was not related with only the past activities of the capitalist but it was more of a potential result of the society's all funds. According to Sidgwick, the sum of all the tools, inventions, infrastructural elements like roads and bridges and even the intangibles such as the organizational structure of the country and the goodwill among the constituents were the parts of a social capital. Sidgwick, Clark and Marx all believed in the existence of such a social aggregation of many things in the society providing an expanding fund for more production. Thus, social capital was a productive and prospective aggregation of many things in the society. It was a part of every produce.

As these examples indicate us that the earlier discussions related to a form of social capacity, a capital of social aggregations, were made from a very macro standpoint. An excellent discussion regarding the early views about the social capital from a macro perspective could be found in Farr (2014). Quite interestingly, the social capital in economics literature today took a more micro turn. In today's literature, social capital is not a social aggregate but it is more a bilateral form of relations between individuals and/or institutions. Let us now focus on the contemporary definitions of social capital.

4 Classification of Social Capital

Contemporary definitions of social capital could be grouped under four approaches. Following table presents the stylized facts of these four different approaches to social capital with reference works in each one of them (Table 1).

Among these approaches, we choose to focus on the network approach in the following discussion for its usefulness for economic analyses. The modern economic classification of social capital tends to count three distinct classes of social capital

Table 1 Four contemporary theories on social capital

Approach	Stylized facts	References
Institutional approach	• Social networks and associations are strongly shaped by the legal, political and institutional environment. • This approach is especially useful for understanding the social associations from a top-down perspective. • However, it is weak in providing a micro-level explanation of social relations	• Knack and Keefer (1995, 1997) • Collier and Gunning (1999) • Collier (1998, 2002) • Rodrik (1998, 1999) • Easterly (2000)
Communitarian approach	• Social capital is a produce of local organizations like clubs, associations, civic groups etc. • Communitarians correlate the level of social capital with the number and density of local organizations. • More local organizations translate into more social capital and more social capital, according to this approach, is beneficial for the social welfare. • Social welfare is a vague term, which surely means more than economic prosperity. If we nonetheless focus on prosperity as a narrow definition of welfare, empirical literature finds that high levels of social solidarity or density of informal groups does not always yield more prosperity.	• Putnam (1993, 1995) • Fukuyama (1995, 1997)
Synergy approach	• Synergy approach attempts to reconcile the institutional and network approaches • Synergy approach theorists attempt to provide the policy makers and researchers with useful insights on the interaction between the institutions and the communal relations. • The proponents of that approach place special emphasis on improving the social associations between horizontally and vertically different groups, individuals and institutions within the society. • According to synergy approach, improvements in cooperation, interpersonal trust and institutional efficiency could suppress sectarianism, isolationism and corruption.	• Fox (1992) • Evans (1992, 1995, 1996) • Rose (1998) • Woolcock (1998) • Narayan and Pritchett (1999) • Fox and Brown (1998)
Network approach	• Network approach is probably the most fitting approach to social capital analysis from the economic angle since it takes into account the economic benefits and disadvantages of social capital more thoroughly than the others. • It analyzes both the vertical and the horizontal relations between constituents and institutions including a wide range of entities from the legal system to public offices and to private sector firms. • Focuses mainly on the two types of social capital that are named the bonding and bridging social capital in the recent literature.	• Granovetter (1973) • Burt (1992, 1997, 1998) • Lin (1999, 2001) • Portes (1998) • Portes and Sensenbrenner (1993)

that overlap with the network approach. These classes namely are the (i) bonding, (ii) bridging and (iii) linking classes of social capital.

Among these, the social networks that occur between similar social units form the bonding capital. Those networks occurring between relatively more distinct social units form the bridging capital. Both bonding and bridging capital refer to the social networks on a horizontal basis, which means the social units that are networking in a bonding or bridging way do not associate with each other in a hierarchical structure. Linking capital, however, refers to vertical relations. It is the relations between the different social layers in a hierarchical way. Linking social capital may even refer to the relations between the constituents and the formal institutions. Let us now explain all these classes in further detail.

4.1 Bonding Social Capital

Robert Putnam describes the bonding type of social capital as the social associations between the individuals that are close to each other through commonalities like friendship, kinship etc. Bonding capital therefore refers to the relations between the individuals who share a common identity and form a homogenous group together.

The associations of members in such close-knit groups are naturally strong. Social capital, on the other hand, is whatever that facilitates collective action within such groups. For example, by tradition, young women must be obliged to serve their elderly relatives in a certain ethnic group. However, traditional values might not be enough to facilitate collective actions. Younger generation might be feeling discomfort in the presence of the elderly people owing to the strict behavioral code between the generations. In such case, although tradition brings the young and elderly together and oblige the young to servicing the elderly, it is not going to be enough for establishing a true bond between them. However, trust, respect and similar feelings, plus everything that creates such feelings, would be counted as social capital.

When we look at the economic benefits of bonding relations, we usually observe that close horizontal ties tend to reduce business costs, boost productivity, improve coordination and cooperation within the group. In the US, 70% of the new positions are filled up quite rapidly based on personal recommendations so that these positions are even not posted (Söylemez 2019). According to some estimates, the percentage of such unposted vacancies could be as high as 80% of all the open positions. That indicates us how well the information flows in the labor market thanks to private connections among individuals. This situation is also helpful for resolving the potential matching problems between the job-seekers and worker-seekers. Finally, the possible labor force loss from the open position until the recruitment is minimized. Of course, such benefits would be reaped only if the position is filled with a capable person. However, Portes and Landolt (2000) provides a persuading discussion on how bonding capital could produce social bad instead of social good. That negative outcome would occur if people showed favor to their group members although the group members were not fitting very well to the open positions. As they argued, bonding type of social relations could result in economic losses if they caused nepotism, group favoritism which could lead to choosing the lesser candidates from a pool or prejudice against others which could lead to eliminating the better candidates.

4.2 Bridging Social Capital

Bridging type social capital also refers to horizontal relations. However, different from the bonding relations, bridging relations occur between distant (heterogenous) members of the society. From an economic perspective, network management is a way of building bridging social capital in business life. Ford and McDowell (1999) draw attention to business fairs and company visits. Both fair and company visits enable interaction between sellers and prospective and/or current buyers. Such interaction helps either to establishing new business relations or to strengthening the existing ones and making them permanent. In business management literature, since mid-1990s, an increasing number of articles reported findings on the significance of human relations in professional life (see Kanter 1994; Contractor and Lorange 2002; Dyer and Singh1998; Inkpen and Tsang 2005).

4.3 Linking Social Capital

Although the bonding and bridging types of social relations come into being on a horizontal basis, linking type relations happen in a vertical structure since linking relations occur between distant people, groups or institutions in a hierarchical order. As Söylemez (2019) claims, in a narrower sense linking social relations with the interference of formal institutions have the capacity to set social norms. The abstract entities such as the legal system and the political regime are therefore a part of social capital.

The legal system and the political structure could enhance the formation social capital stock in a linking sense or adversely could destroy it. As The World Bank claims, in order to create the economically rewarding social relations, we need "enabling social and political environments". Democracy in that respect provides an efficient backdrop for the buildup of promising linking structures since the democratic environment fosters accountability, responsibility and transparency of institutions and officials.

5 A Concise Discussion on the Possible Economic Benefits of Higher Social Capital

We have already sketchily touched on the economic benefits of bonding, bridging and linking types of social capital above. Let us now categorize these and additional benefits from high stock of social capital. The empirical literature usually use the level of interpersonal trust as a proxy for the social capital level. Interpersonal trust, which could be estimated from survey studies, is indeed a good proxy variable especially for the density and strength of bridging and linking types of social relations.

5.1 Mitigation of Adverse Selection Problems

Informational asymmetry problems are known to cause severe 'market failure' issues. Market failure, as well known, is an economic term. It simply refers to the situations that could prevent a freely functioning economic system from finding the socially optimum market equilibrium. In this respect, the existence of market failures would deter an economy from achieving allocative efficiency. Adverse selection and moral hazard problems, together, are known as the informational asymmetry problems and are among the severe causes of market failures. Of these two, adverse selection problems could be mitigated significantly by higher stocks of bridging and linking social capital.

To provide better insight, adverse selection happens whenever one of the economic agents has more information to her advantage in an economic transaction than the other agent. Take for instance the loan making transaction. Assume that a bank has 100 loan applications waiting for assessment. Also assume that the highly reliable historical data tells the overall ratio of crooked applicants should be 10%, which would mean 10 out of the 100 loan applicants on the wait-list should be crooked from a purely statistical standpoint. However only applicant themselves know whether they are crooked or honest in their loan application. The crooked ones are those who has no intention to pay back. They will get the money and flee away. Honest ones are those regular customers who ask for a loan with decent intention of paying it back. If we use interpersonal trust as a proxy variable and claim that it would be low whenever social capital level is low, we could then argue that the loan officers in a society with low social capital (therefore low trust) would be more inclined to exaggerating the ratio of crooked applicants. As the result, their expected losses from the loan wait-list would be unrealistically high, causing them to ask for very high average interest rates for their loans. This would lead some applicants to withdrawing their loan applications. Knowing that only the honest ones must have withdrawn, the expected loss would now be even higher, triggering higher average interest rates to compensate for the higher expected losses. That would of course result in a vicious cycle of more application withdrawals, higher interest rates and so on and so forth. In the end, a much needed loan market could remain unestablished.

As this example indicates, trust issues in the society due to low social capital levels could aggravate adverse selection problems.

5.2 Productivity Enhancement

High stock of bridging social capital could facilitate effective team formation. Considering the importance of idea sharing and partnering in modern economic settings, we could claim bridging social capital would therefore be a valuable latent variable for the success of modern organizations.

Linking social capital, on the other hand, has the potential to augment entrepreneurial activities. Especially a legal environment, which effectively punishes the wrongdoers in a cooperative arrangement (like those people who dishonor their duties from an agreement) would improve the entrepreneurship in the society.

In the end, effective teams, idea sharing environment and supportive legal setting would be positive contributors to total factor productivity as the literature on endogenous growth has empirically indicated many times.

5.3 Cost Cutting

Contract making is a costly endeavor. It consumes time and money. In a society with low interpersonal trust, contract making would be even harder. Plus, high legal costs would accompany all the other costs in such societies. High contract costs would of course reduce the expected returns from projects, reduce the net present value and internal rate of return estimations and as a result a lesser number of projects would be undertaken in such economies. Strong linking social relations would be effectively helpful in reducing the contract costs and stimulating the economic activity.

6 Conclusions

As this article attempted to explain, there exists non-monetary forms of capital, which are utterly important for economic activity in the overall and for firm's performances in specific. However, the non-monetary forms of capital are usually either neglected by or unknown to managers. In sum, their significance is almost always overlooked. This article scrutinized one of them, namely, the social capital.

Social capital is a vague term which is broadly used by economists to refer to the social associations and relations between individuals, groups and institutions in an economy. Current literature on this vague concept seems to have forked into four approaches. Among these four, in this article we put special emphasis on to analyzing the social capital concept from the perspective of the network approach, which is in our consideration the most meaningful approach for economic analysis.

Social capital could be assessed in three classes from the angle of the network approach. These three classes namely are the bonding, bridging and linking social capital classes. While bonding and bridging capital refer to horizontal social relations between constituents with no hierarchical positioning against each other, linking capital has a vertical structure and mostly refers to the relations of individuals and groups with formal institutions.

Empirical studies have shown that high levels of social capital stock is mostly beneficial in the economic sense. However, too much bonding capital might have adverse economic impact as well. Bonding capital includes our relations with and associations to the most others in our closest circle. It is established between the closest friends, kins etc. Therefore, so strong bonding feelings may lead us to making favors to others in our bonding circle in economically meaningless ways. Nepotism or favoritism, as two examples, may result in job offers to people with whom we are bonded but not so talented and fitting for the job otherwise.

That said, social capital, especially the bridging and linking types, have the capacity to make positive economic contributions to the society through enabling efficient buildup of teams, facilitating idea sharing, reducing contract costs, boosting productivity, mitigating informational asymmetry issues and supporting entrepreneurial activities.

References

Adam, F., & Roncevic, B. (2003). Social capital: Recent debates and research trends. *Social Science Information, 42*, 155–183.

Adler, P. S., & Kwon, S. (2002). Social capital: Prospects for a new concept. *The Academy of Management Review., 27*, 17–40.

Burt, R. (1992). *Structural holes: The social structure of competition*. Cambridge: Harvard University Press.

Burt, R. (1997). The contingent value of social capital. *Administrative Science Quarterly, 42*, 339–365.

Burt, R. (1998). The gender of social capital. *Rationality and Society, 10*, 5–46.

Claridge, T. (2004). *Social capital and natural resource management: An important role for social capital?* Unpublished thesis, University of Queensland, Brisbane, Australia. Retrieved October 1, 2020, from http://www.socialcapitalresearch.com

Clark, J. B. (1885). *The philosophy of wealth*. Boston: Ginn and Company.

Collier, P. (1998). *Social capital and poverty*. Washington, DC: World Bank.

Collier, P. (2002). Social capital and poverty: A microeconomic perspective. In T. Van Bastelaer (Ed.), *The role of social capital in development* (pp. 19–41). Melbourne: Cambridge University Press.

Collier, P., & Gunning, J. W. (1999). Explaining African economic performance. *Journal of Economic Literature, 37*, 64–111.

Contractor, F. J., & Lorange, P. (2002). The growth of alliances in the knowledge-based economy. *International Business Review, 11*, 485–502.

Derzko, W. (2007). What industries to avoid? Lessons from Canadian billionaire Seymour Schulich. Retrieved January 24, 2020, from https://smarteconomy.typepad.com/entrepreneurship_and_inno/2007/09/the-industries-.html

Dolfsma, W., & Dannreuther, C. (2003). Subjects and boundaries: Contesting social capital-based policies. *Journal of Economic Issues., 37*, 405–413.

Dyer, J. H., & Singh, H. (1998). The relational view: Cooperative strategy and sources of interorganizational competitive advantage. *The Academy of Management Review, 23*(4), 660–679.

Easterly, W. (2000). *Happy societies: The middle class consensus and economic development.* Washington, DC: World Bank, Development Research Group.

Evans, P. (1992). The state as problem and solution: Predation, embedded autonomy, and structural change. In R. Kaufman (Ed.), *The politics of economic adjustment: International constraints, disruptive conflicts and the state*. Princeton, NJ: Princeton University Press.

Evans, P. (1995). *Embedded autonomy: States and industrial transformation*. Princeton, NJ: Princeton University Press.

Evans, P. (1996). Government action, social capital and development: Reviewing the evidence on synergy. *World Development, 24*, 1119–1132.

Farr, J. (2014). The history of social capital. In A. Christoforou & J. B. Davis (Eds.), *Social capital and economics: Social values, power, and social identity*. London: Routledge.

Foley, M. W., & Edwards, B. (1997). Escape from politics? Social theory and the social capital debate. *American Behavioral Scientist, 40*, 550.

Ford, D., & McDowell, R. (1999). Managing business relationships by analyzing the effects and value of different actors. *Industrial Marketing Management, 28*(5), 429–442.

Fox, J. (1992). Democratic rural development: Leadership accountability in rural peasant organisations. *Development Change, 23*, 1–36.

Fox, J., & Brown, L. D. (1998). *The struggle for accountability: The World Bank, NGOs and the grassroots movement*. Cambridge: MIT Press.

Fukuyama, F. (1995). *Trust: The social virtues and the creation of prosperity*. London: Hamish Hamilton.

Fukuyama, F. (1997). Social capital and the modern capitalist economy: Creating a high trust workplace. *Stern Business Magazine, 4*, 1–16.

Granovetter, M. (1973). The strength of weak ties. *American Journal of Sociology, 78*, 1350–1380.

Inkpen, A. C., & Tsang, E. W. K. (2005). Social capital, networks, and knowledge transfer. *The Academy of Management Review, 30*(1), 146–165.

Kanter, R. M. (1994, July–August). Collaborative advantage: The art of alliances. *Harvard Business Review, 4*, 96–108.

Knack, S., & Keefer, P. (1995). Institutions and economic performance: Cross-country tests using alternative institutional measures. *Economics and Politics, 7*(3), 207–227.

Knack, S., & Keefer, P. (1997). Does social capital have an economic payoff? A cross-country investigation. *Quarterly Journal of Economics, 112*(4), 1251–1288.

Lin, N. (1999). Social networks and status attainment. *Annual Review of Sociology, 25*, 467–487.

Lin, N. (2001). Building a network theory of social capital. In R. Burt (Ed.), *Social capital: Theory and research* (pp. 3–30). New York: Aldine de Gruyter.

Marx, K. (1867). *Capital: A critique of political economy. Volume I. book one: The process of production of capital.* Moscow: Progress publishers. Retrieved October 12, 2019, from www.marxists.org/archive/marx/works/download/pdf/Capital-volume-I.pdf

Narayan, D., & Pritchett, L. (1999). Social capital: Evidence and implications. In I. Serageldin (Ed.), *Social capital: A multifaceted perspective* (pp. 269–296). Washington, DC: World Bank.

Portes, A. (1998). Social capital: Its origins and applications in modern sociology. *Annual Review of Sociology, 24*, 1–25.

Portes, A., & Landolt, P. (2000). Social capital: Promise and pitfalls of its role in development. *Journal of Latin American Studies, 32*(2), 529–547.

Portes, A., & Sensenbrenner, J. (1993). Embeddedness and immigration: Notes on the social determinants of economic action. *American Journal of Sociology, 98*, 1320–1350.
Putnam, R. D. (1993). The prosperous community: Social capital and public life. *The American Prospect, 4*, 35–42.
Putnam, R. D. (1995). Bowling alone: America's declining social capital. *Journal of Democracy, 6* (1), 65–78.
Rodrik, D. (1998). *Where did all the growth go? External shocks, social conflict and growth collapses*. Cambridge: National Bureau of Economic Research.
Rodrik, D. (1999). *Making openness work*. Baltimore: John Hopkins University Press.
Rose, R. (1998). *Getting things done in an anti-modern society: Social capital networks in Russia*. Washington, DC: World Bank, Social Development Department.
Söylemez, A. O. (2019). Past discussions and current evidence on the importance of social capital. *SETSCI Conference Proceedings, 4*(8), 267–270.
Vernimmen, P., Le Fur, Y., Dallochio, M., Salvi, A., & Quiry, P. (2017). *Corporate finance: Theory and practice* (5th ed.). Boca Raton, FL: Wiley.
Woolcock, M. (1998). Social capital and economic development: Towards a theoretical synthesis and policy framework. *Theory and Society, 27*, 151–208.

The Role of R&D Investments on Labor Force: The Case of Selected Developed Countries

Halim Baş and İsmail Canöz

Abstract Whether the change in R&D spending creates technological unemployment, in particular, is a controversial issue. Acceptance of this hypothesis might not be possible under all circumstances. At this point, especially if country-based research is conducted, it might be the right choice to consider the countries with the highest R&D expenditure. This study empirically analyses the role of R&D spending on unemployment by using annual data from 1996 to 2017 of 15 developed countries. In empirical results, it was first determined that there is no co-integration between the ratio of R&D expenditures to GDP and the unemployment rate. Therefore, an attempt was made to determine the existence of a hidden co-integration among the shocks of these variables. The direction of asymmetric causality among them was investigated as a result of the detection of findings that is evidence of hidden co-integration. Although there is an otherwise observation, asymmetric causality analysis results predominantly show that there is causality from R&D expenditures to unemployment.

1 Introduction

There are different perspectives on the role of R&D spending on unemployment. The first perspective defends that process innovation will bring technological unemployment. Another perspective recognizes that unemployment will decrease with product innovation (Gerçeker et al. 2019; Zhang et al. 2020). Product innovation means improving existing goods or launching new goods. Product innovation is considered to increase consumer demand. Increasing demand also creates a suitable ground for the establishment of new companies, the creation of new sectors, and

H. Baş (✉)
Vocational School of Social Sciences, Istanbul Medipol University, Kadıköy/İstanbul, Turkey
e-mail: hbas@medipol.edu.tr

İ. Canöz
Faculty of Political Sciences, Istanbul Medeniyet University, Kadıköy/İstanbul, Turkey
e-mail: ismail.canoz@medeniyet.edu.tr

H. Dincer, S. Yüksel (eds.), *Strategic Priorities in Competitive Environments*, Contributions to Management Science, https://doi.org/10.1007/978-3-030-45023-6_14

therefore the creation of new businesses (Oberdabernig 2016). From this point of view, the increase in R&D spending has an increasing effect on employment and thus unemployment decreases. An opposite view argues that automation systems reducing the need for labor will increase unemployment. Especially, the increase in the R&D expenditures of the companies might provide technologies reducing the need for labor. As a result, unemployment will increase in such a situation.

When the studies conducted at the firm level are analyzed, the firms generally focus on innovation are handled and the employment effect at these firms' level is measured. In studies examining R&D expenditures and unemployment based on innovation firms, unemployment of neither competitors in the same sector nor competitors in the other sector might be measured. Moreover, they might not be observed on a general economic basis as a whole (Eti et al. 2020). Researches approaching the event from a macro-economic perspective might reveal a phenomenon that covers the entire economy (Feldmann 2013). Unlike some previous studies on the role of R&D spending on the labor market, this research focuses on the macroeconomic field, which allows considering its impact on the economy as a whole.

The theoretical and conceptual background is discussed in the following two sections. The fourth section summarizes empirical and conceptual research in the literature and presents their results. The fifth section describes the measure of R&D expenditure and unemployment used in co-integration and causality analysis. The sixth section explains the estimation method as a summary. In the seventh section, the tests accepted as the prerequisite of the seventh section are carried out and in the eighth section, findings related to empirical research are presented. The last part is the section where the results of the research are discussed, and the study is concluded.

2 Technological Unemployment and Artificial Intelligence

Employment and unemployment are among the main determinants of economic welfare for each country (Ersin and Ergeç 2018). They are among the major issues in economic researches. Current unemployment in an economy produces social effects if it emerges due to technological reasons. With this regard, technological unemployment is described as a complex concept (Gregory 1930). Besides, there are norm differences generally defined by the possible effects of technological change on existing or potential labor (Dankert 1959). The conceptualization efforts of technological unemployment also include Keynes' views, starting with Ricardo's views. Furthermore, it has a long history until the effects of robots and automation on different sectors and professions recently (Calvino and Virgillito 2018). The classic view describes technology both in a contributing and a damaging position. The neoclassical view lays stress on the role of the production center and the externality of technology (Kliman 1997). The Schumpeterian view centers on the business mindset that develops technology, and in the new form, the technology as one of the greatest intrinsic variables of growth. The Marxist view concentrates on the projection of the technology movement on its social transformation and Keynes defends the technology by pointing out that the labor would not be sufficient for industrial growth and the technical productivity was more prominent (Gera and Singh 2019).

The ways to address the concept within the political economy and economic sociology makes this complexity more inextricable. Meanwhile, despite being a social context-focused by different schools of economics, the effects of technical progress create a diversity of views (Campa 2017). Within this scope as an example, the Orthodox theory rejects permanent technological unemployment as possible (Neisser 1942). On the other hand, socialist theory promotes the idea that machine production had led to technological unemployment in Germany in the time before the world war (Kähler 1935). The technological unemployment within the economic system is addressed by designing it within individual actors, companies, profitable industries, countries or the global economy (Campa 2017). Furthermore, new technologies are being used with the thought of economizing the use of labor. However, there is no significant technological unemployment since the very beginning of the Industrial Revolution but rather the views on technological unemployment are important discussion topics (Vivarelli 2014). Although there was no response for Keynes' statement on common technological unemployment as "... *due to our discovery of means of economizing the use of labor outrunning the pace at which we can find new uses for labor.*" in 1931 under the conditions of that period, when it is seen that computers substituted for the jobs of bookkeepers, cashiers and telephone operators over the past few years, this debate has been reignited (Schwab 2016).

The place and importance of technology in human life are more centralized than ever before compared to the previous century. This central role makes the functionality of the technology in different structures visible and exists in every phase of the working life, especially in daily life. This central role brings the different structures of technology's functionality into view and exists in every stage of working life, especially in daily life. The use of automation, which is described as the product of the previous century in the development of humanity, creates micro-negative effects (Ansal and Cetindamar Karaomerlioglu 1999). At the macro level, it generates new employment fields and ensures significant prosperity (Van Roy et al. 2018). As an example, the Ford Motor Company increased the number of employees, which had been sharply reduced before the 1929 crisis, with approximately 100,000 labor force for newly opened areas after the crisis. On the other hand, the fact that the economical understanding, envisaged by the automation thread would not produce enough jobs in terms of prosperity increase, some of the existing jobs would be invalid, and to what extent the assumption of basic income guarantee would provide prosperity under the new economic management, calls up an important discussion topic (Walker 2014). In this manner, it is argued that a universal basic income or envisaged prosperity aids would be limited in terms of leveraging society, social and ethical problems based on the fact that the businesses mostly relinquish their workplaces to automation would even lead this situation into a dead-end (Kim and Scheller-Wolf 2019). Against the background, the assumption that high-income people would increase and accordingly would offer more donations to eliminate unemployment related to automation and there would be a large donation economy continues to be relevant (Chomanski 2019).

Meanwhile, the automation technology located in the middle of the multi-dimensional discussions expects a radical axis change; the machines are now conceived not as an extension of man as before, but as vehicles that are substituted for people themselves (Wajcman 2017). In the past two centuries, technological unemployment has revealed fear for an artificial future in terms of adapting to new developments and economizing the use of labor. Technological unemployment in the industrialization period is perceived as a serious problem (Mokyr et al. 2015). For example, the depression burst up by technological progress at the beginning of industrialization had triggered the machine destroying actions, known as Luddite Uprising in England (Postel-Vinay 2002). However, the translocation effect of machine use is dominant in the short term, while productivity is seen as a long-term effect (Krousie 2018).

On the other hand, there are two different views over against technological change and progress. The automation, according to the optimistic view, is placed in terms of life-facilitating arguments such as information technology and micro-chips; and of contribution to social life as leisure time, early retirement and return to "domestic values". Whereas the pessimistic view draws attention to possible consequences such as skill loss of new machines and organizations, reducing job creativity, creating mass unemployment and standardizing the consumption (Gajewska 2014; Standing 1984). In traditional literature, the view that supports the optimistic view of automation fear prevails (Acemoglu and Autor 2011). In other words, it is argued that the technological change would make a complementary contribution to any employee and no employee would be unemployed against this change and his condition would get worse (Susskind 2017). However, the reasons for being an optimistic change in the new work-based literature. Here, the technology is not complementary to all kinds of workers, but plays a complementary role only in jobs of a certain type and requiring some skills (Autor 2015).

The unprecedented progress of automation and digitalization in recent years revives this fear again (Arntz et al. 2016). In this manner, the fact that the machine gradually replacing the workforce triggers greater capital accumulation and significantly determines the winners of the development process (Brynjolfsson et al. 2014). The empirical scenarios regarding the losses of people who put their efforts against the innovation achievements of the capital owner attract more attention. Against the background, the automation technology highly, moderately and slightly threatens some professions within the next 10 or 20 years. In a study conducted in the USA, 47% of total employment is estimated to be in the high-risk category (Frey and Osborne 2017). This rate is predicted to be 35% in Finland and 33% in Norway (Pajarinen et al. 2015). In a more recent study, IPSOS Research Company has measured with a survey of people aged 18–74, conducted in 28 countries, primarily USA, Canada, Malaysia, mainly South Africa and Turkey whether the current job would be substituted for automation. Accordingly, 35% of the participants declare that their existing jobs would be substituted for automation technology in the next 10 years (IPSOS 2020).

On the other hand, the risk factor envisaged in the workforce is evaluated as an extension of the demographic transformation. According to this, the decrease in death rates and significant improvements in public health increase the life expectancy of the population and the population is getting old (Taşçı 2010). Meanwhile, the emerging perception of old age creates a dilemma in terms of the labor market and comes to the forefront with consumption patterns rather than producing (Taşçı 2013). With this regard, those, who are fully employed, are expected to be significantly reduced. Concordantly, it is estimated that losing ground to support the unemployed within the population structure by the working people would create a mass migration effect for young people (Peters 2019). The decrease in production load comes up with a decrease in workforce participation and productivity (Acemoglu and Restrepo 2017a, b). In this manner, rapidly aging countries' tendency to adopt automation technology is more powerful. Also, the possibility of spreading automation technology to countries with a young workforce is far ahead when compared with the potential of these countries to minimize labor inputs and increase total output (Acemoglu 2010; Acemoğlu and Restrepo 2016).

In other respects, The Fourth Industrial Revolution represents production and economic system in which the use of technology reaches the highest level. The developments in digital, physical and biological technologies have three basic technological dynamics of the Fourth Industrial Revolution (Li et al. 2017, p. 627). Therefore, it holds some opportunities and threats as a structure however, it is unable to go beyond the estimate for now (Hirschi 2018). Opportunities are as the elimination or reduction of barriers between inventors and markets, the active role of artificial intelligence, integration of different technical areas, improving the quality of life with robotic use, strengthening the internet connection (Marchant et al. 2014; Naastepad and Mulder 2018). Whereas the threads refer to as gradual growth of inequality, shrinking of potential workforce markets, substantial reduction especially in industry jobs, increasing the gap between labor and capital by the substitution of machine, training and time requirement to gain new skills (Peters 2017; Xu et al. 2018; Sanchez 2019; Kapeliushnikov 2019).

On the other hand, technological unemployment is associated with the Fourth Industrial Revolution. It is proposed in many studies done with this regard that the advantages, brought out by the overuse of innovation, should be limited. Therefore, training in technological unemployment without establishing new employment areas creates new winning classes in a labor market where the number of employees would gradually decrease (Peters and Jandrić 2019). Additionally, it is asserted that the utilization of the latest technology was used to create a disposable, precarious and always exploited workforce; long-term use would force more workers to work in poor working conditions over the long run (Spencer 2018). It is stressed that the work of low qualified workers in sectors that require low skill would increase physical addiction (Manning 2004). More importantly, it is stated that the lack of multiple skills required by new technologies would increase unemployment. Against the background, in a study conducted in Slovenia, 50% of more than 100 employers state that they had difficulties in finding the right person to work with new technologies (Novak and Dizdarevic 2018). According to the possible scenario for employment, workplaces and skills by 2020, directed to human resources managers of the largest companies from 10 sectors and 15 countries in the Future of Jobs report of World Economic Forum, while a slight improvement in wages and work-life balance is expected for many professions, occupational safety is expected to go worse in half of such sectors (Schwab 2016). Beyond all, the financial source is deemed to be a means for people to reach material means only. It is assumed that this situation would create technological unemployment and require more human capital in terms of capacity increase and creativity for future generations (Naastepad and Houghton Budd 2019). With this regard, it is pointed out that technology and innovation would lead to a dichotomy between highly and low-qualified people; the managers would like to work with groups that develop product innovation and thereby an exclusion would appear (Cirillo 2017).

The artificial intelligence, which is seen as one of the opportunities of the Fourth Industrial Revolution and expected to take on a more active role, when viewed from the point of mechanization, is considered as the substitution of mental tasks rather than physical tasks of human (Ernst et al. 2019). This functionality potentially transforms the nature of work and affects workforce types at different levels, from fields such as finance, information technologies, journalism to medical applications (Brynjolfsson and Mitchell 2017; Barlow 2016; Darcy et al. 2016; Scheinkman 2019; Barnhizer 2016). It is argued that such change, as opposed to popular belief, would not always create unemployment, on the contrary, the use of artificial intelligence would trigger the skill requirement of professions positively, encourage new investments, bear an additional employment potential, and reduce production costs and thereby would increase productivity (Bessen 2016; Autor et al. 2003; Acemoglu and Restrepo 2018a, b). However, the negative effects of such change are taken into consideration at all aspects like economic stability, especially at the macro level, negative effect on national budget revenues and accordingly disruption in outreach programs. Thereby it is thought that the current economic stakeholder relations in society would evolve into an unsustainable dead end and the common automation effect of artificial intelligence would require significant changes (Bruun and Duka 2018). Nonetheless, it is supposed that artificial intelligence would contribute to the enrichment of humanity and increase inequality on the other hand. Meanwhile, it is envisaged that the increased use of artificial intelligence tools would affect the future demand regarding factor labor in terms of survival and reproduction of Malthus's theory that *"Scarce consumer goods limit the survival and reproduction of people."* (Korinek and Stiglitz 2017). On the other hand, local economies in the USA were significantly affected in the post-1990 period with the robot technology and it currently exposes the reduction effects on workers' wages and employment (Acemoglu and Restrepo 2017a, b). On the other hand, possible contributions of artificial intelligence to economic growth are measured by the gross domestic product figures of countries with an increase in productivity (Pwc 2017). With this regard, it is discussed that the significant losses in the workforce might directly affect growth. Many future scenarios are put forward especially in this regard. Against the background, the possible skill failure/loss of the employee profiles in 9 of 21 countries are at risk and it is expected that 21% of Japan, 30% of the United Kingdom and 38% of the USA would be at risk of change (Lloyd and Payne 2019).

3 The Theoretical Information About Research and Development

Research and development (R&D) include the innovative studies carried out systematically to increase knowledge and thereby the human capital (including human, cultural and social information) and the use of this knowledge to design new applications. R&D activities are addressed as basic research, applied research and experimental development. In many studies, it is construed that R&D expenditures had a positive effect on economic growth and social prosperity, the public intervention has led to additional growth in R&D investments and such growth would have an additional contribution to social prosperity (Heijs 2003; Akcali and Sismanoglu 2015).

However, while R&D expenditures are compared in the international arena, they are considered as the national product expenditures and these consist of the expenditures for the studies carried out by the companies, research institutes, universities and government laboratories (OECD 2012). Expenditures that are spent generally by the companies are for measuring productivity, evaluating the quality and quantity and increasing profitability opportunities by properly building the technology strategies (Clausen 2009). Also, there is a positive relationship between total patent applications and innovation patent applications and R&D expenditures in the companies (Li and Tan 2019). There might be an R&D-based collaboration between companies operating in different sectors, for example; a company in the manufacturing sector may cooperate with companies providing information-intensive services to overcome customer uncertainty and eliminate its competitors (Bustinza et al. 2019; Dinçer et al. 2020). Besides, the subsidy policy of the government may channel the R&D activities of the companies. The technological policy initiatives adopted by the government are mostly in favor of growing companies by accelerating their dynamic, expanding and innovative activities, corporate differences between countries may affect additional R&D expenditures of subsidized companies, there may also be a strong relationship between the indebtedness of the companies and R&D investments (David et al. 2000; Hall 1992). The necessity of a policy, which is focused not only on the winners but also for those who fulfill the R&D criteria regardless of the size of the companies with this aspect, is elaborated (Heijs and Herrera Danny 2004).

On the other hand, the universities are described as organizations, which influence the growth of gross national product and increase in employment with their inventions and patents, with a dynamic process approach, having the power to fundamentally influence economic development, and also with entrepreneurial activities (Martin 1998; Guerrero et al. 2015). R&D perception and approach are mostly degraded only to studies in major science fields nevertheless, university-based R&D studies are not limited to technological infrastructure investments rather they are at the center of a broader knowledge generation process and in a position that contributes to the socio-economic development of its location (Link 2000; Pastor et al. 2013). Besides, the universities are likely to conduct joint research projects with companies and collaborations to invest in human capital by producing new know-how is usually encountered (Roessner et al. 2013). On the other hand, macro and local dynamics and corporate differences can bring the output of these investments into view either positively or negatively (Medda et al. 2004). In this manner, when it is viewed at the macro level, the public sector may tend to fund in times of economic crisis and the university can directly contribute to scientific production to increase industry interaction (Azagra-Caro et al. 2019; Kalkavan and Ersin 2019). Additionally, the R&D studies of the university may also affect the profit maximization decisions of an organization for location selection (Woodward et al. 2006).

4 Literature Review

When the literature is viewed, there are many studies that examine the effects of investments, such as R&D and innovation covering various periods on unemployment. The main theme of this study, focuses on examining the effects of R&D expenditures on unemployment, however, since indirect results are also possible, they are likely included in the literature. The effects of the expenditures, which are incurred by companies, government and universities, are usually discussed in the literature. In this respect, Aguilera and Ramos Barrera (2016) address the technological unemployment in the South American examples and examine the science and technology expenditures within the scope of the study, gross domestic product per capita, minimum nominal wage and domestic expenditures on education for the period of 1996–2011 by using panel data. According to the result obtained, it is mentioned that the science and technology investments were not at a level to significantly reduce employment however, innovations are the achievement for labor productivity.

Crespi and Tacsir (2011) examined the effects of innovation on employment in Latin America that the product innovation was important for employment in four Latin American countries, however, they draw attention to the necessity of this skilled workforce; and they come out with the solution that it was complementary to the skilled workforce in the sectors using high technology. Vivarelli (2012) focused on the relationship between innovation, employment, and skills in developing countries and stated that he remained incapable to explain the effects of innovation of economic theories on labor and draws attention to the necessity of total, sectoral and microeconomic, empirical analysis considering this relationship. Piva and

Vivarelli (2005) evaluated the correlation between innovation and employment with microdata in the Italian example and it is determined from the data of 575 Italian manufacturing companies by using panel data that there was a meaningful relationship to some extent. In another study examined at the micro-level, Ciriaci et al. (2016) made an analysis through the 2002–2009 data sets of 3304 Spanish companies whether the relationship between innovation and job creation is sustainable or not. Accordingly, it is concluded that innovative, small and more relative companies create higher employment growth rather than non-innovative companies. Bogliacino et al. (2014) evaluated the importance of R&D expenditures in job creation in terms of technology and employment and examines 677 European companies using panel data from 1990 through 2008. Accordingly, the positive effect of R&D on employment exists only in the tertiary sector and high technology production.

Feldmann (2013) analyzed the annual data of 21 countries for the period between 1985 and 2009 and states that according to the regression results, the increase in technological change revealed the unemployment effect for the last 3 years within the period studied, and stresses on that there was no long-term effect after all. Krousie (2018) examined technological unemployment in the US at the state level and analyzes workforce statistics and R&D expenditure data of each state from 2002 through 2013. According to the result obtained, it is stressed that the technological change altered the structure of labor in the USA; however, its effect was not strong. Matuzeviciute et al. (2017) focused on the effects of technological innovations in 25 European country examples by taking panel data from 2000 through 2012. Findings reveal that technological innovations had no effect on unemployment. Kwon et al. (2015) tried to analyze where the effects of innovation on creating new jobs in the examples of the manufacturing industry of South Korea were examined, reveals that the product innovation strategies of the companies had significant positive effects on creating new employment. Haile et al. (2017) examines the effect of imported technology on production employment in Ethiopia, by taking panel data from 1996 through 2004 and conclude that technology had a labor-increasing effect.

Lachenmaier and Rottmann (2011) analyzed the companies that have been in Germany for more than 20 years by dynamic panel data analysis concludes that there was a positive effect between innovation and employment. Stiglitz (2014) paid attention in his study, where the causality between technology and unemployment were addressed, that innovation might not be sufficient to increase the prosperity of all segments in the society, and would not bear conclusive results in even in obtaining maximum output. Kirchhoff et al. (2007) comes across a positive relationship in the study where the possible effects of universities' R&D expenditures on new company regulations and economic growth were examined and states that the universities made important contributions to the establishment of new companies, especially to local economic growth. Agovino et al. (2018) examined the role of patents in company's R&D expenditures and employment relations and for this purpose they analyzed 879 production companies from all over the world by using panel data for the busy period of 2002–2010 and reveals that the expansion of R&D had a significant effect on company employment.

5 Data Set

Depending on their desire to gain a competitive advantage in science and technology, the government and private sector attach importance to R&D activities and lay out money for R&D. According to a piece of information in the OECD database, a country's R&D expenditures consist of the total amount spent for R&D by all resident companies, research institutes, universities, government laboratories, and so on in that country.[1]

In academic studies that examine R&D activities from an economic perspective, R&D spending as a share of GDP is frequently used as an important parameter. Based on this general use, the ratio of R&D expenditures to GDP was considered as an independent variable within the scope of the study. However, to examine the effect of R&D expenditures on unemployment, the unemployment rate was included in the study as a dependent variable for the study.

Whereas the ratio of R&D expenditures to GDP was collected from UNESCO's database, the unemployment rate was obtained from the World Bank's database. Totally 15 countries are included in the study. The primary selection criterion of these countries is that they have the highest share of R&D expenditure in GDP. Another criterion is that the ratio of R&D expenditures to GDP is completed. Therefore, although 21 countries were planned to be included in the study, 15 countries with full data could be analyzed. The annual data set covering the period from 1996 to 2017 was tested in the study. Since the variables will be divided into positive and negative shocks or components in the econometric method to be used in the analysis, the variables have been used in the form of raw data and no transformation has been carried out for them. Also, both the ratio of R&D expenditure to GDP and unemployment rate are the same level variables expressed as a percentage.

6 Methods

In the study, the unemployment hypothesis based on R&D expenditures was investigated by using the panel hidden co-integration approach and panel asymmetric causality test. An introductory brief explanation of these methods is given.

6.1 Panel Hidden Co-Integration Test

Granger and Yoon (2002) introduced the concept of hidden co-integration. The feature of hidden co-integration is that it allows for potential asymmetry in a steady-state relationship between time series variables (Hatemi-J 2011). According to Panel

[1]https://data.oecd.org/rd/gross-domestic-spending-on-r-d.htm

Hidden Co-Integration Test, first, positive cumulative shocks and negative cumulative shocks are determined for each variable. And then Potential panel co-integration is tested. The variables for the co-integration relationship should be stationary at the first difference (I(1)). Then, the co-integration relationship between non-stationary variables at the level is examined. In addition to examining the co-integration relationship between only negative or positive shocks of variables, the relationship between positive component and negative component might also be tested.

6.2 Panel Asymmetric Causality Test

In the Granger Causality Test, there is the thought of investigating whether the historical data of one variable is predicted with another variable (Hatemi-J 2011). There is a similar logic under the asymmetric causality analysis. The difference here is that the causal effect of positive shocks may differ from the causal effect of negative shocks (vice versa). Here, first of all, the variables are divided into positive and negative components or shocks. Then their stationarity should be checked and they should be stationary at the level (I(0)). After completing all these processes, the causality relationship between positive and negative shocks is examined.

7 Pre-testing Results

The first process that should be checked at the beginning of the analysis phase is to test whether the variables are integrated at the same order. There are some panel unit root tests developed to check this process. As Asongu (2013) stated, the mechanics of the unit root test is usually not elaborated in detail because it is widely applied and only creates an exploratory analysis of the research. When viewed from this aspect, Table 1 presents the results of the panel unit root tests. No variable has a panel unit root at levels rejected by both tests. In other words, the results in Table 1 show that the zero hypotheses of a unit root cannot be rejected at a 5% significance level for all series. Thus, the series is not stationary at the level.

Moreover, in this study cross-sectional dependence and homogeneity test results were also examined. As stated by Hatemi-J et al. (2014), if the null hypothesis of cross-sectional dependence is rejected, a shock in a particular country is transmitted to other countries because of globalization, market integration and close economic connections among countries. In addition to this, rejection of homogeneity means that assuming homogeneity in panel causality analysis will lead to misleading inference and results. According to the results of the cross-sectional dependence and homogeneity tests, the null hypotheses of both tests were rejected.

When the original versions of variables were examined with standard co-integration tests, it was understood that there was no panel co-integration between the variables. In this case, it can be tested whether there is a hidden co-integration

Table 1 Panel unit root tests

H_0: Unit root	Levels				First differences			
	ADF-Fisher		Im, Pesaran & Shin		ADF-Fisher		Im, Pesaran & Shin	
Components of variables	Statistic	Prob.	Statistic	Prob.	Statistic	Prob.	Statistic	Prob.
R&D-GDP rate$^-$	3.6922	0.999	3.5124	0.999	−5.5792	0.000**	−5.5346	0.000**
R&D-GDP rate$^+$	3.2215	0.999	3.0952	0.999	−5.8184	0.000**	−5.7253	0.000**
Unemp. rate$^-$	3.7002	0.999	3.7141	0.999	−5.2834	0.000**	−5.0947	0.000**
Unemp. rate$^+$	0.4082	0.658	−0.3633	0.358	−9.9994	0.000**	−11.287	0.000**

Notes: ** denotes significance at 5%. To select the lag lengths, the Schwarz information criterion was used. Stationary test results in which trend and intercept are included in the model are reported

+ and − indicate positive and negative shocks respectively

Table 2 Hidden panel co-integration test results

H_0: No Co-integration	Kao Panel Co-integration Test	
Variables in the models	Statistic	Prob.
(Unemp. rate$^-$, R&D-GDP rate$^-$)	−1.82738	0.033**
(Unemp. rate$^-$, R&D-GDP rate$^+$)	−0.90109	0.183
(Unemp. rate$^+$, R&D-GDP rate$^-$)	−1.84709	0.032**
(Unemp. rate$^+$, R&D-GDP rate$^+$)	−1.48485	0.068*

Notes: *, ** denote significance at 10% and 5% respectively
+ and − indicate positive and negative shocks respectively

Table 3 Asymmetric panel causality test results

	First lag		Second lag		Third lag	
Null hypotheses	Statistic	Prob.	Statistic	Prob.	Statistic	Prob.
D(R&D-GDP rate$^-$) ≠ > D (Unemp. Rate$^-$)	3.9368	0.048**	3.4124	0.034**	2.5566	0.055*
D(Unemp. Rate$^-$) ≠ > D (R&D-GDP rate$^-$)	0.0451	0.831	2.7909	0.063*	2.6472	0.049**
D(R&D-GDP rate$^+$) ≠ > D (Unemp. Rate$^-$)	1.0531	0.861	2.1017	0.745	2.9358	0.470
D(unemp.t rate$^-$) ≠ > D (R&D-GDP rate$^+$)	1.8491	0.119	2.8271	0.488	5.2188	0.125
D(R&D-GDP rate$^-$) ≠ > D (Unemp. Rate$^+$)	2.1926	0.139	0.5815	0.559	0.3475	0.791
D(Unemp. Rate$^+$) ≠ > D (R&D-GDP rate$^-$)	5.2719	0.022**	4.2346	0.015**	2.8871	0.036**
D(R&D-GDP rate$^+$) ≠ > D (Unemp. Rate$^+$)	3.0608	3. E−05**	5.9727	3. E−07**	5.9194	0.026**
D(Unemp. Rate$^+$) ≠ > D (R&D-GDP rate$^+$)	2.0831	0.038**	2.6352	0.671	3.5603	0.916

Notes: *, ** denote significance at 10% and 5% respectively
+ and − indicate positive and negative shocks respectively

relationship between the positive or negative components of the variables. According to the results reported in Table 2, test statistics for all zero hypotheses of co-integration are rejected, except for one hypothesis. However, when the tests suggested by Hatemi-J (2018) were applied, a long-term co-integrated relationship was found between the negative and positive components of the panel data variables.

8 Estimation Results

In general, the existence of a co-integration relationship between the variables means that there is at least one-way causality relationship between these variables. In Table 3, asymmetric causality relationships between the shocks of the variables resulted in overlapping results of the co-integration analysis.

It has been determined by considering three different lags that there is a one-way causality in co-integrated components. In this case, it has been determined that there is causality from the ratio of R&D expenditures to GDP to the unemployment rate. There is only one exception. There is no causality from the negative shock of the ratio of R&D expenditures to GDP to the positive shock of the unemployment rate.

9 Discussion and Conclusion

R&D spending has an important place in the new economy concept, which is called the information society. Accordingly, one of the most fundamental dynamics measuring the economic competition between countries is the shares allocated to R&D expenditures. R&D expenditures are seen as a force both in different factions of the public sector and in the competitive strategies of the private sector among companies. It is considered an important factor especially in determining the market positions of the companies. Also, university-sector collaborations have been gained importance all over the world. The general idea on this subject is that the knowledge produced at the university has a very important function to increase the supply-demand compatibility and efficiency of the labor force in the market and to develop a need-oriented approach with an innovative approach.

Considering the results of studies conducted on a firm basis, Kirchhoff et al. (2007) found that universities' R&D spending positively influenced employment. Tamayo and Huergo (2016) also found a positive relationship between R&D spending and qualified employment. Similarly, Piva and Vivarelli (2017) found that R&D spending positively affects employment in companies, not producing low technology. In sector-based research, Brouwer et al. (1993) found a negative relationship between R&D spending and employment in the manufacturing industry. Conversely, Bogliacino and Vivarelli (2010) have discovered that R&D spending positively affects employment in the manufacturing and service sectors. Coad and Rao (2010) identified a significant relationship between R&D spending and employment for the manufacturing industry. Both firm and industry-based studies confirm that there is a relationship between R&D expenditure and employment.

When macro-scale studies are examined, Matuzeviciute et al. (2017) concluded that innovation investments do not affect unemployment in 25 selected European countries. On the other hand, Gerçeker et al. (2019) found that there is mutual causality between R&D expenditures and unemployment in some G-7 countries, while others have one-way causality. The empirical findings of this study also support the literature in general. However, there are also some original contributions. These contributions arise from the analysis used in the study. Co-integration findings prove the existence of a hidden co-integration between R&D spending and unemployment for the 15 countries with the highest R&D spending in GDP. When causality findings are analyzed, it shows that R&D spending is the Granger cause of unemployment in general. Accordingly, the negative shock of the ratio of R&D expenditures to GDP is the Granger cause of the negative shock of the unemployment rate. The positive shock of the ratio of R&D expenditures to GDP is the Granger cause of the positive shock of the unemployment rate. Apart from these, a causality finding from unemployment to R&D expenditures has also been identified in these developed countries. Accordingly, the positive shock of the unemployment rate is the Granger cause of the negative shock of the ratio of R&D spending to GDP.

The findings of this study are considered valuable. The reason for this is that if there is no relationship between variables in future macro-scale researches using classical co-integration methods, it is recommended to look for hidden co-integration. Besides, although it seems more logical to investigate the R&D-unemployment relationship in countries with high R&D expenditures, research might be conducted in developing countries.

References

Acemoglu, D. (2010). When does labor scarcity encourage innovation? *Journal of Political Economy, 118*(6), 1037–1078.

Acemoglu, D., & Autor, D. (2011). Skills, tasks and technologies: Implications for employment and earnings. In *Handbook of labor economics* (Vol. 4, pp. 1043–1171). New York: Elsevier.

Acemoğlu, D., & Restrepo, P. (2016). The race between machines and humans: Implications for growth, factor shares and jobs. Retrieved 6, 2019.

Acemoglu, D., & Restrepo, P. (2017a). *Robots and jobs: Evidence from US labor markets.*

Acemoglu, D., & Restrepo, P. (2017b). Secular stagnation? The effect of aging on economic growth in the age of automation. *American Economic Review, 107*(5), 174–179.

Acemoglu, D., & Restrepo, P. (2018a). The race between man and machine: Implications of technology for growth, factor shares, and employment. *American Economic Review, 108*(6), 1488–1542.

Acemoglu, D., & Restrepo, P. (2018b). *Artificial intelligence, automation and work (No. w24196).* National Bureau of Economic Research.

Agovino, M., Aldieri, L., Garofalo, A., & Vinci, C. P. (2018). R&D spillovers and employment: Evidence from European patent data. *Empirica, 45*(2), 247–260.

Aguilera, A., & Ramos Barrera, M. G. (2016). Technological unemployment: An approximation to the Latin American case. *AD-minister, 29*, 58–78.

Akcali, B. Y., & Sismanoglu, E. (2015). Innovation and the effect of research and development (R&D) expenditure on growth in some developing and developed countries. *Procedia-Social and Behavioral Sciences, 195*, 768–775.

Ansal, H. K., & Cetindamar Karaomerlioglu, D. (1999). New technologies and employment: Industry and firm level evidence from Turkey. *New Technology, Work and Employment, 14* (2), 82–99.

Arntz, M., Gregory, T., & Zierahn, U. (2016). *The risk of automation for jobs in OECD countries: A comparative analysis.*

Asongu, S. A. (2013). How would population growth affect investment in the future? Asymmetric panel causality evidence for Africa. *African Development Review, 25*(1), 14–29.

Autor, D. H. (2015). Why are there still so many jobs? The history and future of workplace automation. *Journal of Economic Perspectives, 29*(3), 3–30.

Autor, D. H., Levy, F., & Murnane, R. J. (2003). The skill content of recent technological change: An empirical exploration. *The Quarterly Journal of Economics, 118*(4), 1279–1333.

Azagra-Caro, J. M., Tijssen, R. J., Tur, E. M., & Yegros-Yegros, A. (2019). University-industry scientific production and the great recession. *Technological Forecasting and Social Change, 139*, 210–220.

Barlow, M. (2016). *AI and medicine: Data-driven strategies for improving healthcare and saving lives*.

Barnhizer, D. (2016, January 15). The future of work: Apps, artificial intelligence, automation and androids. *Artificial Intelligence, Automation and Androids. Cleveland-Marshall Legal Studies Paper, 289*.

Bessen, J. E. (2016). How computer automation affects occupations: Technology, jobs, and skills. *Boston University School of Law, Law and Economics Research Paper*, 15–49.

Bogliacino, F., & Vivarelli, M. (2010). The job creation effect of R&D expenditures. *IEB Working Paper 2010/55*.

Bogliacino, F., Piva, M., & Vivarelli, M. (2014). Technology and employment: The job creation effect of business R&D. *Rivista Internazionale di Scienze Sociali, 126*, 239–264.

Brouwer, E., Kleinknecht, A., & Reijnen, J. O. (1993). Employment growth and innovation at the firm level. *Journal of Evolutionary Economics, 3*(2), 153–159.

Bruun, E. P., & Duka, A. (2018). Artificial intelligence, jobs and the future of work: Racing with the machines. *Basic Income Studies, 13*(2), 1–15.

Brynjolfsson, E., & Mitchell, T. (2017). What can machine learning do? Workforce implications. *Science, 358*(6370), 1530–1534.

Brynjolfsson, E., McAfee, A., & Spence, M. (2014). New world order: Labor, capital, and ideas in the power law economy. *Foreign Affairs, 93*(4), 44–53.

Bustinza, O. F., Gomes, E., Vendrell-Herrero, F., & Baines, T. (2019). Product–service innovation and performance: The role of collaborative partnerships and R&D intensity. *R&D Management, 49*(1), 33–45.

Calvino, F., & Virgillito, M. E. (2018). The innovation-employment nexus: A critical survey of theory and empirics. *Journal of Economic Surveys, 32*(1), 83–117.

Campa, R. (2017). Technological unemployment: A brief history of an idea. *ISA eSymposium for Sociology, 7*(1), 57.

Chomanski, B. (2019). Massive technological unemployment without redistribution: A case for cautious optimism. *Science and Engineering Ethics, 25*(5), 1389–1407.

Ciriaci, D., Moncada-Paternò-Castello, P., & Voigt, P. (2016). Innovation and job creation: A sustainable relation? *Eurasian Business Review, 6*(2), 189–213.

Cirillo, V. (2017). Technology, employment and skills. *Economics of Innovation and New Technology, 26*(8), 734–754.

Clausen, T. H. (2009). Do subsidies have positive impacts on R&D and innovation activities at the firm level? *Structural Change and Economic Dynamics, 20*(4), 239–253.

Coad, A., & Rao, R. (2010). Firm growth and R&D expenditure. *Economics of Innovation and New Technology, 19*(2), 127–145.

Crespi, G., & Tacsir, E. (2011, September). Effects of innovation on employment in Latin America. In *2011 Atlanta Conference on Science and Innovation Policy* (pp. 1–11). IEEE.

Dankert, C. E. (1959). Technological change and unemployment. *Lab. LJ, 10*, 393.

Darcy, A. M., Louie, A. K., & Roberts, L. W. (2016). Machine learning and the profession of medicine. *JAMA, 315*(6), 551–552.

David, P. A., Hall, B. H., & Toole, A. A. (2000). Is public R&D a complement or substitute for private R&D? A review of the econometric evidence. *Research Policy, 29*(4–5), 497–529.

Dinçer, H., Yüksel, S., & Pınarbaşı, F. (2020). Kano-based measurement of customer expectations in retail service industry using IT2 DEMATEL-QUALIFLEX. In *Handbook of research on positive organizational behavior for improved workplace performance* (pp. 349–370). Hershey, PA: IGI Global.

Ernst, E., Merola, R., & Samaan, D. (2019). Economics of artificial intelligence: Implications for the future of work. *IZA Journal of Labor Policy, 9*(1), 7.

Ersin, İ., & Ergeç, E. H. (2018). Harcama Bileşenleri ve Sektörel İstihdam Arasındaki Nedensellik İlişkisi. *Yönetim ve Ekonomi Araştırmaları Dergisi, 16*(1), 161–180.

Eti, S., Kalkavan, H., Dinçer, H., & Yüksel, S. (2020). Predicting the role of Islamic banking on sustainable economic development: An analysis for Turkey with ARIMA model. In *Handbook of research on creating sustainable value in the global economy* (pp. 146–164). Hershey, PA: IGI Global.

Feldmann, H. (2013). Technological unemployment in industrial countries. *Journal of Evolutionary Economics, 23*(5), 1099–1126.

Frey, C. B., & Osborne, M. A. (2017). The future of employment: How susceptible are jobs to computerisation? *Technological Forecasting and Social Change, 114*, 254–280.

Gajewska, K. (2014). Technological unemployment but still a lot of work: Towards prosumerist services of general interest. *Journal of Evolution and Technology, 24*(1), 104–112.

Gera, I., & Singh, S. (2019). A critique of economic literature on technology and fourth industrial revolution: Employment and the nature of jobs. *The Indian Journal of Labour Economics, 62* (4), 715–729.

Gerçeker, M., Özmen, İ., & Mucuk, M. (2019). AR-GE harcamalari ve işsizlik arasindaki nedenselliğin ampirik analizi: G7 ülkeleri örneği. *Marmara Üniversitesi İktisadi ve İdari Bilimler Dergisi, 41*(2), 413–431.

Granger, C. W., & Yoon, G. (2002). Hidden cointegration. *University of California, Economics Working Paper, 2002-02.*

Gregory, T. E. (1930). Rationalisation and technological unemployment. *The Economic Journal, 40* (160), 551–567.

Guerrero, M., Cunningham, J. A., & Urbano, D. (2015). Economic impact of entrepreneurial universities' activities: An exploratory study of the United Kingdom. *Research Policy, 44*(3), 748–764.

Haile, G., Srour, I., & Vivarelli, M. (2017). Imported technology and manufacturing employment in Ethiopia. *Eurasian Business Review, 7*(1), 1–23.

Hall, B. H. (1992). *Investment and research and development at the firm level: Does the source of financing matter?* (No. w4096). National Bureau of Economic Research.

Hatemi-J, A. (2011). *Asymmetric panel causality tests with an application to the impact of fiscal policy on economic performance in Scandinavia.* Munich, Germany: University Library of Munich.

Hatemi-J, A. (2018). Hidden panel cointegration. *Journal of King Saud University-Science, 32*, 507–510.

Hatemi-J, A., Gupta, R., Ksango, A., Mboweni, T., & Netshitenzhe, N. (2014). *Are there asymmetric causal relationships between tourism and economic growth in a panel of G-7 countries.* University of Pretoria, Department of Economics Working Paper, 76, p. 18.

Heijs, J. (2003). Freerider behaviour and the public finance of R&D activities in enterprises: The case of the Spanish low interest credits for R&D. *Research Policy, 32*(3), 445–461.

Heijs, J., & Herrera Danny, L. (2004). *The distribution of R&D subsidies and its effect on the final outcome of innovation policy.*

Hirschi, A. (2018). The fourth industrial revolution: Issues and implications for career research and practice. *The Career Development Quarterly, 66*(3), 192–204.

Ipsos. (2020). *Global views on jobs and automation.* Retrieved January 28, 2020, from https://www.ipsos.com/sites/default/files/ct/news/documents/2020-01/report-jobs-and-automation-global-advisor.pdf

Kähler, A. (1935). The problem of verifying the theory of technological unemployment. *Social Research, 2*, 439–460.

Kalkavan, H., & Ersin, I. (2019). Determination of factors affecting the south east Asian crisis of 1997 probit-logit panel regression: The south east Asian crisis. In *Handbook of research on global issues in financial communication and investment decision making* (pp. 148–167). Hershey, PA: IGI Global.

Kapeliushnikov, R. (2019). The phantom of technological unemployment. *Russian Journal of Economics, 5*(1), 88–116.

Kim, T. W., & Scheller-Wolf, A. (2019). Technological unemployment, meaning in life, purpose of business, and the future of stakeholders. *Journal of Business Ethics, 160*(2), 319–337.

Kirchhoff, B. A., Newbert, S. L., Hasan, I., & Armington, C. (2007). The influence of University R&D Expenditures on new business formations and employment growth. *Entrepreneurship Theory and Practice, 31*(4), 543–559.

Kliman, A. J. (1997). Technological disemployment in the neoclassical model. *Review of Political Economy, 9*(1), 37–49.

Korinek, A., & Stiglitz, J. E. (2017). *Artificial intelligence and its implications for income distribution and unemployment (No. w24174)*. National Bureau of Economic Research.

Krousie, C. (2018). Technological unemployment in the United States: A state-level analysis. *Major Themes in Economics, 20*(1), 87–101.

Kwon, S. J., Park, E., Ohm, J. Y., & Yoo, K. (2015). Innovation activities and the creation of new employment: An empirical assessment of South Korea's manufacturing industry. *Social Science Information, 54*(3), 354–368.

Lachenmaier, S., & Rottmann, H. (2011). Effects of innovation on employment: A dynamic panel analysis. *International Journal of Industrial Organization, 29*(2), 210–220.

Li, X., & Tan, Y. (2019). University R&D activities and firm innovations. *Finance Research Letters, 28*, 328–336.

Li, G., Hou, Y., & Wu, A. (2017). Fourth industrial revolution: Technological drivers, impacts and coping methods. *Chinese Geographical Science, 27*(4), 626–637.

Link, A. N. (2000). Assessing the economic impacts of university R&D and identifying roles for technology transfer officers. *Industry and Higher Education, 14*(1), 24–32.

Lloyd, C., & Payne, J. (2019). Rethinking country effects: Robotics, AI and work futures in Norway and the UK. *New Technology, Work and Employment, 34*(3), 208–225.

Manning, A. (2004). We can work it out: The impact of technological change on the demand for low-skill workers. *Scottish Journal of Political Economy, 51*(5), 581–608.

Marchant, G. E., Stevens, Y. A., & Hennessy, J. M. (2014). Technology, unemployment & policy options: Navigating the transition to a better world. *Journal of Evolution and Technology, 24*(1), 26–44.

Martin, F. (1998). The economic impact of Canadian university R&D. *Research Policy, 27*(7), 677–687.

Matuzeviciute, K., Butkus, M., & Karaliute, A. (2017). Do technological innovations affect unemployment? Some empirical evidence from European countries. *Economies, 5*(4), 48.

Medda, G., Piga, C., & Siegel, D. S. (2004). University R&D and firm productivity: Evidence from Italy. *The Journal of Technology Transfer, 30*(1–2), 199–205.

Mokyr, J., Vickers, C., & Ziebarth, N. L. (2015). The history of technological anxiety and the future of economic growth: Is this time different? *Journal of Economic Perspectives, 29*(3), 31–50.

Naastepad, C. W. M., & Houghton Budd, C. (2019). Preventing technological unemployment by widening our understanding of capital and Progress: Making robots work for us. *Ethics and Social Welfare, 13*(2), 115–132.

Naastepad, C. W. M., & Mulder, J. M. (2018). Robots and us: Towards an economics of the 'good life'. *Review of Social Economy, 76*(3), 302–334.

Neisser, H. P. (1942). Permanent "technological unemployment:" demand for commodities is not demand for labor. *The American Economic Review*, 50–71.

Novak, V., & Dizdarevic, D. (2018). The future of work in the light of technological change. *International Journal of Economics and Law, 8*(23), 127–136.

Oberdabernig, D.A. (2016). Employment effects of innovation in developing countries: A summary, Swiss Programme for research on global issues for development, *Swiss Programme for Research on Global Issues for Development R4D Working Paper, 2016/2*.

OECD. (2012). *Main science and technology indicators*. OECD Publishing.

Pajarinen, M., Rouvinen, P., & Ekeland, A. (2015). Computerization threatens one-third of Finnish and Norwegian employment. *Etla Brief, 34*, 1–8.

Pastor, J. M., Pérez, F., & De Guevara, J. F. (2013). Measuring the local economic impact of universities: An approach that considers uncertainty. *Higher Education, 65*(5), 539–564.
Peters, M. A. (2017). Technological unemployment: Educating for the fourth industrial revolution. *Journal of Self-Governance and Management Economics, 5*(1), 25–33.
Peters, M. A. (2019). Beyond technological unemployment: The future of work. *Educational Philosophy and Theory.* https://doi.org/10.1080/00131857.2019.1608625.
Peters, M. A., & Jandrić, P. (2019). Posthumanism, open ontologies and bio-digital becoming: Response to Luciano Floridi's Onlife Manifesto.
Piva, M., & Vivarelli, M. (2005). Innovation and employment: Evidence from Italian microdata. *Journal of Economics, 86*(1), 65–83.
Piva, M., & Vivarelli, M. (2017). *Is R&D Good for Employment? Microeconometric Evidence from the* EU (No. 10581). IZA Discussion Papers.
Postel-Vinay, F. (2002). The dynamics of technological unemployment. *International Economic Review, 43*(3), 737–760.
Pwc. (2017). *The economic impact of artificial intelligence on the UK economy.* Retrieved January 28, 2020, from https://www.pwc.co.uk/economic-services/assets/ai-uk-report-v2.pdf
Roessner, D., Bond, J., Okubo, S., & Planting, M. (2013). The economic impact of licensed commercialized inventions originating in university research. *Research Policy, 42*(1), 23–34.
Sanchez, D. (2019, June). Sustainable development challenges and risks of industry 4.0: A literature review. In *2019 Global IoT Summit (GIoTS)* (pp. 1–6). IEEE.
Scheinkman, M. (2019). Intimacies: An integrative multicultural framework for couple therapy. *Family Process, 58*(3), 550–568.
Schwab, K. (2016). *Dördüncü sanayi devrimi.* Istanbul: Optimist Yayın Grubu.
Spencer, D. A. (2018). Fear and hope in an age of mass automation: Debating the future of work. *New Technology, Work and Employment, 33*(1), 1–12.
Standing, G. (1984). The notion of technological unemployment. *International Labour Review, 123*, 127.
Stiglitz, J. E. (2014). *Unemployment and innovation (No. w20670).* National Bureau of Economic Research.
Susskind, D. (2017). A model of technological unemployment. *Economics Series Working Papers, 819.*
Tamayo, M. P., & Huergo, E. (2016). The effect of R&D services offshoring on skilled employment: Firm evidence. *The World Economy, 39*(9), 1414–1433.
Taşçı, F. (2010). Yaşlılara yönelik sosyal politikalar: İsveç, Almanya, İngiltere ve İtalya örnekleri. *Çalışma ve Toplum, 1*, 175–202.
Taşçı, F. (2013). Refah devleti modelleri içinde Türkiye'nin pozisyonu:"yaşlı algısı" üzerinden değerlendirmeler. *İnsan & Toplum Dergisi, 3*(5), 5–35.
Van Roy, V., Vértesy, D., & Vivarelli, M. (2018). Technology and employment: Mass unemployment or job creation? Empirical evidence from European patenting firms. *Research Policy, 47* (9), 1762–1776.
Vivarelli, M. (2012). Entrepreneurship in advanced and developing countries: A microeconomic perspective. ISO 690. IZA discussion paper no. 6513.
Vivarelli, M. (2014). Innovation, employment and skills in advanced and developing countries: A survey of economic literature. *Journal of Economic Issues, 48*(1), 123–154.
Wajcman, J. (2017). Automation: Is it really different this time? *The British Journal of Sociology, 68*(1), 119–127.
Walker, M. (2014). BIG and technological unemployment: Chicken little versus the economists. *Journal of Evolution and Technology, 24*(1), 5–25.
Woodward, D., Figueiredo, O., & Guimaraes, P. (2006). Beyond the Silicon Valley: University R&D and high-technology location. *Journal of Urban Economics, 60*(1), 15–32.
Xu, M., David, J. M., & Kim, S. H. (2018). The fourth industrial revolution: Opportunities and challenges. *International Journal of Financial Research, 9*(2), 90–95.
Zhang, G., Zhou, S., Xia, X., Yüksel, S., Baş, H., & Dincer, H. (2020). Strategic mapping of youth unemployment with interval-valued intuitionistic hesitant fuzzy DEMATEL based on 2-tuple linguistic values. *IEEE Access, 8*, 25706–25721.

A CAMELS Analysis of Selected Banks in Turkey After the Crisis in 2008

Mustafa Eser Kurum and Eray Öztürk

Abstract Banking industry can be appeared as one of the most functional and dynamic engines of the economy; especially of the developing economies, by providing funds for growth. Hence, problems stemming from this industry tend to be more contagious. Therefore, monitoring banking system has become more vital in the light of fact that the world speed of experiencing crisis had increased. In that context one of the most popular supervision system, CAMELS analyses, provide researchers a comprehensive, standardized and effective way to monitor, and detect problems in banks. By this study four biggest bank in Turkey, in terms of their asset size and profitability, were analyzed for the period between 2011 and 2018, when the effect of the crisis in 2008 had started to diminish in Turkish Economy. A CAMELS analysis was employed with 30 ratios in order to evaluate banks performances. Results demonstrated that two out of four banks (Akbank and Ziraat Bank) seemed to improved and reached a satisfactory performance after the crisis in terms of all components of CAMELS, while Garanti Bank' performance fluctuated over the period and İşbank has not managed to increase its scores and forestall deteriorating.

1 Introduction

The financial institutions are vital for developed countries in order to maintain and enhance their economic activities and to fund their economic growth. It is an obvious fact that especially banking sector directly participates in a nation's gross domestic income as an industry in service production (Dash and Das 2009). Besides, its more important contribution is that it stimulates al other industries by providing money that they need for new investments or their other economic activities, and by financing new companies who enter into a new sector. Thus, banks are seemed as

M. E. Kurum (✉) · E. Öztürk
İstanbul Yeni Yüzyıl University, İstanbul, Turkey
e-mail: mustafaeser.kurum@yeniyuzyil.edu.tr; eray.ozturk@yeniyuzyil.edu.tr

H. Dincer, S. Yüksel (eds.), *Strategic Priorities in Competitive Environments*,
Contributions to Management Science, https://doi.org/10.1007/978-3-030-45023-6_15

the backbone of an economy that enables a country to use its monetary surplus efficiently and hence to fund its growth in a quality way (Dang 2011).

Since banks play increasing critical role in an economy their performance and its objective measurement have become a crucial debase in literature (Kalkavan and Ersin 2019). Actually, functions of banks exceeded their national limit which urges us to monitor and evaluate them in a global scale. Also, because they fund almost whole sectors in an economy a successful banking performance will encourage entire economic activity in a national scale (Nimalathasan 2008). Furthermore, due to costumers' changing and becoming more complex needs banks risks reached an intricate level that is to be evaluate properly, responsibly, beneficially and sustainably (Dang 2011; Eti et al. 2020; Dinçer et al. 2020).

In general bank performance measurements focus on objective financial organization such as earning reasonable return and minimizing risks (Hempel et al. 1986). Accordingly, methods like financial ratio analysis, benchmarking and evaluating budget risks are commonly used for that consideration (Avkiran 1994). Although methods are various it is clear that a strong, well-functioning and steady banking sector need to be promoted by a measurement system which should be successful in detecting and correcting errors smoothly and deal with vulnerabilities easily (Roman and Şargu 2013).

According to meet these criteria one of the most preferred method is CAMELS rating system that is developed by federal regulators in USA in 1970s. It measures the bank's creditworthiness via six fundamental factors: Capital adequacy, Asset quality, Management, Earnings, Liquidity, and market Sensitivity which constitute the acronym called CAMELS. By this system the bank performance can be analyzed with its interactions with country's economic, political and regulatory environment. Thanks to this it becomes possible to evaluate the county's noneconomic situations that strongly effect economy together with the bank's unique conditions. For instance, if a country does not have a free functioning financial market then banks in it cannot be estimated as having an acceptable credit risk even if its own conditions were sufficient (Grier 2007).

So, for a successful CAMELS analysis the bank is to be studied with the country's legal regulations and political climate. Then bank's relative performance needs to be compared over time and with other banks performance in the market. While explaining changes by time the analyst is to use qualitative and quantitative parameters and is to be careful about ratios which can change with market conditions. For last the analyst needs to be aware of that the final determination is to be based on common sense (Grier 2007).

However, an incisive common sense can obviously arise from proper and delicate parameters. In CAMELS analysis each factor scored from one to five where the point 1 represents the strongest conditions while the score 5 represents the poorest ones. The whole CAMELS score also derives from the components and shares the same logic. The analyst can determine the scores after both an on-site or off-site examination by evaluating the bank's general health, financial circumstance, and management quality (Wirnkar and Tanko 2008).

Here are the five composite rating levels defined by Board of Governors of the Federal Reserve System in USA.

Score 1: an institution that is basically sound in every respect.
Score 2: an institution that is fundamentally sound but has modest weaknesses.
Score 3: an institution with financial, operational, or compliance weaknesses that give cause for supervisory concern.
Score 4: an institution with serious financial weaknesses that could impair future viability.
Score 5: an institution with critical financial weaknesses that render the probability of failure extremely high in the near term (Siems and Barr 1998).

Or as Grier's (2007) defined: (1) is strong, (2) is satisfactory, (3) is fair, (4) is marginal and (5) is unsatisfactory.

The first component for the CAMELS analysis is the Capital adequacy. Actually, capital is seemed as the main guarantee for the depositors. A bank that has a strong capital sources is to be able to compensate large amount of losses and minimize depositors' risk (Grier 2007). This parameter represents the success of maintaining balance despite risks like credit risk, market risk, and operational risk against any potential losses in order to protect the depositors (Dang 2011). Therefore, the capital adequacy is generally calculated from the capital-deposit ratio (Mitchell 1984). As Uniform Financial Institutions Rating System reported in 1997 "Meeting statutory minimum capital requirement is the key factor in deciding the capital adequacy and maintaining an adequate level of capital is a critical element" (Uniform Financial Institutions Rating System 1997).

Secondly the asset quality needs to be scored. One of the major risks to which banks can exposure is the poor asset quality. And one of the main asset components is the loan portfolio. The delinquent loans therefore increase the bank's risk as well as decrease its asset quality. So, the asset quality measurement should include the score of credit risk management and the quality of loans. Especially loans that appeared to be doubtful and bank's provision against these loans are to be calculated by the asset quality score (Dang 2011).

The third category for the CAMELS rating system is the Management. Apart from other components an extensive set of ratios cannot be used while measuring the score for management because of the subjectivity about its mensuration. Managements are to be evaluated by their policies, systems, and controls. Lending, foreign exchange, and liquidity can be some of policies that the manager should be scored and bank's adherence to laws and regulations also can be approached as the systems and controls that the managers need to be responsible for. On the other hand it is a common approach that the category of management needs to be scored at last because the "well-managed banks should have adequate capital, good asset quality, adequate profits, sufficient liquidity, and a sustainable system to measure sensitivity to market risk" (Grier 2007).

The Earning abilities, or in other words profits, are the fourth components of the CAMELS analysis. New capitals can derive from new investors or earnings where both of these new entries are strongly related with how the bank profitable is. So, banks are expected to make profit and this profit constitutes public confidence and conduces to absorb loan losses. Also, the sustainability of profitability plays a significant role in computing the Earning score. Therefore, not only profits but also factors that generate profit together determine whether or not the bank's earnings will be sustainable and hence they should together take account while measuring the Earnings score (Grier 2007).

The fifth component of CAMELS is the risk of Liquidity which is represented by the bank's capacity of meet unexpected credit demands (Rostami 2015). Thereby a bank is required to meet its obligations without any loss in order to have high liquidity score. So, banks need to have liquid assets that can rapidly be change into cash (Grier 2007). Also, while evaluating liquidity the supervisor must be aware of the hazard of mismatching which derives from the differences of timing between short-term deposits and long-term credits. As a result, a successful fund management is expected to conduct the fund at a secure level that assure to meet its monetary obligations in a timely manner, and to rapidly unload troubled assets with minimum loss (Dang 2011).

The last component of CAMELS analysis is the sensitivity ratio, added into the analysis in 1997 by US regulators, which measures the sensitivity to market risk. It is an economic fact that "the changes in interest rates, foreign exchange rates, commodity prices or equity prices can adversely affect a financial institution's earnings or economic capital." Hence while evaluating this last category of CAMELS the analyst is to be focus on "management's ability to identify, measure, monitor and control market risk; the institution's size; the nature and complexity of its activities; and the adequacy of its capital and earnings in relation to its level of market risk exposure". Actually, the banks need to be careful about issues that create market risks like the bank's sensitivity to change in interest rates, foreign operations or trading activities (Grier 2007).

After the six of the components scored then the overall rating score, which is known as the composite rating, can be calculated. This overall rating that will provide the analyst an express indication is reached by dividing the sum of these six components is by six. This composite rating can provide a comparable and standardized parameter, but its efficiency is limited with the ability of supervisor to judgment, examining, and measuring (Grier 2007).

2 Literature Review

2.1 CAMELS Analysis in the World

The CAMELS system has been using all around the world as a comprehensive and functional tool which managed to detect and monitor deteriorating in banking sectors successfully. Thanks to this method bankruptcies could be realized and prevented, and stress in financial markets could be evaluated in such a sufficient way. Hence, in the USA. and in other advanced economies using the CAMELS analysis this information about banks contributed to stability of the economy (Yuksel et al. 2015). It can be approached as a common opinion that CAMELS system is one of the most popular and useful method, and it is employed not only by the USA. but also by countries such as Hong Kong, South Korea, Chili, and Argentina (Kaya 2001). Here are some studies using this analysis around the world.

In a study Ahsan (2016) conducted three Islamic Banks in Bangladesh for the years 2007 and 2014 using the system of CAMELS and determined that all banks performance's measured satisfactory. Another study was conducted by Roman and Şargu (2013) for 15 banks in Romania employing CAMELS analysis. They found that the banks were seemed satisfactory at Management and Earnings categories while not adequate in Liquidity.

The biggest investment bank in the USA, Lehman Brothers Investing Bank was studied by Christopoulos et al. (2011) for the years 2003 and 2007 via CAMELS method and its credits were reported as poor and doubtful just before the crisis in 2008. Also, the bank reported to be at risk of numerous of negative conditions while Managements were observed to be reluctant.

Nimalathasan (2008) conduct CAMELS analysis in order to evaluate 48 banks performance in Bangladesh for the years 1999 and 2006. With the study three banks performance were classified as strong, 31 banks as were satisfactory, seven banks as normal, five banks as marginal, and two banks as unsatisfactory.

Dang (2011) used CAMEL analysis (without the letter S –sensitivity-) in order to measure a bank oriented in Vietnam, whose majority shares are holed by the government. American International Assurance's CAMEL framework was employed for the data between 2007 and 2010. The analyst reached the conclusion that the CAMEL analysis is useful and popular for banking supervision because it is standardized internationally which enables compare bank from all over the world and also because it can be applied to both off-site and on-site examinations.

A CAMELS analysis was used by Dash and Das (2009) for 29 public and 29 private/foreign, total 54 banks operating in India between years 2003–2008. They concluded that private/foreign banks performed better in most categories of CAMELS, especially categories of management and earnings. They reported that there are significant differences between public and private banks especially in credit policy, costumer services, attaining and adopting of IT services.

Five strongest banks operating in North Cyprus Turkish Republic was investigated through CAMELS method for the period after 2001 by Atikogullari (2009). According to findings foreign capitalized banks were observed to be more Sensitive than others.

Another CAMELS analysis from India was studied by Raiyani (2010) for six merged banks. The researcher reported an increase was observed in profitability, liquidity, solvency, quality of assets and efficiency of the management after the merger. He also detected that private merged banks performed better than public ones.

Kumar et al. (2012) employed CAMELS analysis in order to evaluate 12 state and private banks in India for the period 2000 and 2011. According to the findings private banks which experienced a bigger growth during the period, appeared to have stronger structures than state banks.

CAMELS analysis was used in order to measure 19 conventional and 16 participation banks in Malaysia by Rozzani and Rahman (2013) for the years 2008 and 2009. According to the study banks' profitability due to ineffective loan conditions, and Liquidity managements due to unbalanced ratio of liquid and illiquid assets, emerged to be inadequate.

Çağıl and Mukhtarov (2014) compared domestic and foreign banks performance in Azerbaijan between years 2007 and 2010 employing CAMELS system and reached the conclusion that foreign owned banks performed better than domestic ones.

Hyz and Gikas (2015) studied four biggest Greek Banks for the period 2008 and 2013 by employing the CAMELS analysis. They reached the result that all of the four banks' performance deteriorated during the period. Although the decreasing trend of the Greek banks' performance could mostly be related with the diminishing GDP of the country, assets quality was detected as the major problem for the banks apart from the general conditions of Greece.

Six domestic and private banks operating in Georgia were studied by Helhel and Varshalomidze (2014) for the years between 2007 and 2013 with CAMELS analysis. Banks did not perform well in any components of CAMELS due to the global crisis in 2008 and war with Russia.

Ahmedov and Memmedov (2017) studied foreign owned ten banks in Azerbaijan for the years 2010 and 2014 and found that banks were operated with a high performance except for the component Capital and Earnings. Also, CAMELS analysis was reported as a healthy and fruitful system while evaluating banking performance by this study.

2.2 CAMELS Analysis in Turkey

Banks operations with other banks and financial institutions are shaped and limited by their creditworthiness which is measured via two methods in Turkey; the rating scores given by International Rating Bureaus and CAMELS analysis. The institution called BRSA, which is responsible for supervision of banks in Turkey, supervises banks though both on-site and off-site examinations. CAMELS system is employed by BRSA in order to do the off-site supervision twice a year (Kılıç and Fettahoğlu 2005). Here are some examples of CAMELS analysis conducted for Turkish banks.

A BRSA working report by Kaya (2001) studied CAMELS analysis in order to demonstrate 45 Turkish banks performance for the year between 1997 and 2000. Twenty two banks performances were determined as inadequate which 14 out of them were seized by Turkish State in 2000. So, the report highlighted that the CAMELS system detected the poor performance with a success of 60%.

Forty four private owned banks in Turkey were evaluated by Çinko and Avcı (2008) using 22 ratios of CAMELS analysis between 1996 and 2000. They tried to measure the success of CAMELS method though monitoring whether or not banks would be seized by government. However, they reported that the CAMELS system did not worked properly about providing accurate information before the banks seized by government.

In another study Sakarya (2010) aimed to investigate banks performance via CAMELS analysis in Turkey especially after financial liberation and foreign owned capital entrance into Turkish banking markets. The study was conducted for the period 2005 and 2007 in order to compare domestic owned and foreign owned banks performance. As a result, the superiority of domestic banks in Capital, Earnings and Liquidity categories and the superiority of foreign owned banks in Assets and Sensitivity categories were observed.

State owned and private banks were evaluated for between the years 2003 and 2007 by Tükenmez et al. (2010) with the help of analysis CAMELS. An increase in five out of eight banks performance parameters was observed. State banks emerged to be strong at the components of Capital and Liquidity, while private banks were strong at components Asset quality, Managements, and Earnings. In terms of Sensitivity to market risks all banks performed at nearly same level.

Dincer et al. (2011) applied a CAMELS analysis for Turkish banks for the years 2001 to 2009. Banks were categorized into three groups; state, private and foreign, in order to investigate the effect of crises in 2001 and 2008. As a result, all groups experienced an improvement in capital sufficiency, and efficient internal control, thanks to changing rules and regulations after crisis in 2001.

Another CAMELS analysis was applied by Şen and Solak (2011) for the period 1995–2008 in order to evaluate private, state and foreign owned banks performance. They demonstrated effects of crisis in 2001 with their CAMELS analysis and found that all banks, but particularly state-owned banks, improved their performance after the crisis. On the other hand, deterioration in profitability (Earnings), Capital adequacy, and Liquidity components were observed. According to their result CAMELS analysis recorded as successful about measuring bank risks, but incapable of forecasting the time of crisis.

Kandemir and Arıcı (2013) conducted CAMELS method between 2001 and 2010 for state, private, and foreign owned banks by using 19 ratios. Foreign owned banks in components Asset and Management, and state-owned banks in component Earnings appeared to have a better performance. Also, it was observed that banks in Turkey were not affected a lot from the crisis in 2008 thanks to the regulation in banking legislation.

CAMELS analysis was used by Abdullayev (2013) in order to detect the effects of disinflation on banking sector in Turkey for the period 2005 and 2008. With this study the CAMELS analysis was reported as working successfully especially about detecting problems before they emerge, just like an early warning system.

Yuksel et al. (2015) studied relationship between CAMLES ratios and credit ratings (given by credit agencies) of 20 deposit banks in Turkey for the period 2004 and 2014. They demonstrated that CAMELS system was not able to explain changes in credit ratings for the banks completely. However, three factors of CAMLES were detected as have a significant effect on credit ratings: Asset quality, Management, and Sensitivity.

Another CAMELS analysis of 29 Turkish banks was conducted by Gümüş and Nalbantoğlu (2015) for the years between 2002 and 2013. Banks were separated into four groups: public, private/domestic, foreign and participation banks. They reached the conclusion that domestic banks gained the highest score especially thanks to their strong Capital structure, quality Management, and profitability (Earnings). Public banks came in second thanks to their solid Capital structure and improvement in their Assets especially after the crisis in 2001. On the other hand, foreign banks performances were poor due to deterioration in their profits (Earnings) and quality of Managements derived from increase in the amount of non-performing credits. Likewise, participation banks' capital became inadequate compare to other groups of bank.

Ege et al. (2015) studied the period between 2002 and 2010 employing CAMELS method with 25 ratios. Components Capital, Earnings, and Sensitivity were measured better for state owned banks, while Asset quality and Liquidity were measured better for foreign owned banks than others. By contrast with others this study scored Management performance of state banks higher than other group of banks.

Güney and Ilgın (2015) evaluated banks operating in Turkey for the period 2002 and 2012. They detected that foreign owned banks have strong and private owned banks have inadequate performance. State owned banks performed powerful in component of Earnings, while private owned banks in Management quality and Sensitivity, and foreign banks in Capital, Assets and Liquidity.

Şimşek et al. (2017) compared private, state, foreign and participation banks in Turkey for the period 2001 and 2015 employing the method CAMELS. The study demonstrated that state banks were efficient in the category of Sensitivity but placed at the end of the list in terms of Assets quality. Foreign banks performed better at the Liquidity and Asset quality components, private banks were better at the component Earnings, while participation banks left behind their peers at the component Capital.

Bayramoglu and Gürsoy (2017) evaluated 25 banks performance via studying group values; state, private and foreign bank groups, by using 22 ratios. According to their results state banks appeared to be strongest group while foreign ones the weakest.

Gündoğdu (2017) studied the biggest ten banks of Turkey in terms of Asset amount for the period 2005 and 2015 employing CAMELS system with 29 ratios in order to illustrate the effect of the crisis in 2008. Results observed that Akbank, Garanti Bank, Ziraat Bank, Halkbank, İş Bank and Vakıf Bank reached high scores while Finansbank, Denizbank, TEB and Yapı Kredi Bank reached relatively insufficient scores. Garanti Bank and Halkbank seemed to improve their performances after the crisis in 2008 and Ziraat Bank performed best when all years took account.

3 Data and Model

3.1 *The Scope and Constraints of the Study*

Like any empirical study, this study also has some limitations. The banks included in the study are the first four banks with the largest asset size and profitability in the Turkish banking system. One of these banks is a state-owned bank and the other three are private banks. The findings obtained as a result of the analysis studied between the years 2011 and 2018. Therefore, the results of the analysis should be interpreted within the framework of the post-global crisis period. However, because the data was obtained from the period between 2011 and 2018, it is not possible to comment on the financial performance of the analyzed banks in the future periods.

3.2 *CAMELS Analysis*

CAMELS analysis of the four banks that we studied is conducted in eight steps. The data set consisting of 30 financial ratios for each six components of CAMELS was generated for each year at first step. Thirty ratios of each bank were analyzed separately for each year as second step. In order to do this arithmetic mean of 120 (30 ratio $\times$ 4 banks) ratios were calculated for each year, and hence the *reference value* for each ratio were determined.

The index value is computed at the third step. The index value is found separately for each year, by division of reference value by banks value of related year. At the fourth step the *deviation value* is calculated. The deviation value is determined as "index value − 100" if the financial ratio found positive (+), and as "100 − index value" if the ratio found negative (−).

At the fifth step deviation value is weighted: each deviation value is divided by financial ratio's weight into its group. Thereby *weighted deviation value* is reached. Then each component's sum of weighted deviation value is calculated as *the group's weighted deviation value* at step six. At seventh step, this group's weighted deviation value is multiplied by the percentage of each group' weight.

Finally, at the last step the sum of the six weighted deviation value is calculated and hence reached CAMELS value.

3.3 *Variables*

With this study, 30 financial ratios under the CAMELS system were calculated for Akbank, Ziraat Bank, Garanti Bank, and İş Bank which are deposit banks operating in Turkey, for the period between 2011 and 2018. The data used in the analysis was obtained from the Banks Association of Turkey's (TBB) annual report. While calculating ratios and weights used in our analysis other CAMELS studies ratios and weights were taken account. As a result, categories of capital adequacy's, and asset quality's weights were decided to be (20%), while all others were decided to be 15%.

Table 1 shows the proportions chosen for the analysis, the weights given to these rates, and the direction of the relationship between the financial rate and the component to which it belongs. The direction of the relationship was interpreted according to whether or not it increases the component. If it increases the value of the component, it is determined as "+" and if it decreases, it is determined as "−".

3.4 Results of the Model

The second step of CAMELS analysis, namely calculation of the reference values is shown in Table 2 below.

In this study four banks performance were measured for the period 2011 and 2018. As an example, for reference value 2011s calculated data was illustrated with Table 2. Here at Table 2, arithmetic mean of financial values found for each bank, was calculated. So, this arithmetic mean shows reference value for each financial ratio. On the other hand, reference value computed for each year is demonstrated by Table 3.

All steps regarding CAMELS analysis of Akbank is given as an example in Table 4. Bank value in column four in the table shows the financial ratios of the bank for the calculated year.

Regarding Table 4, proportion of each reference value to bank value was multiplied by 100. And the result gives us the index value. The calculation of (index value − 100) is used if the relationship's direction is (+), and (100 − index value) is used if the direction is (−). Hence the deviation value is calculated. Each ratio is given equal weight into the groups which can be monitored from the column 'subgroup impact'. This means each calculated deviation value's 20% is found. The results give weighted value for each ratio. And then group weighted value is calculated by finding sum of ratios into a group (for instance weighted value of group c/ namely Capital). At the last stage each group's weighted value are calculated; 20% of group C's weighted value and A, and 15% of other groups' weighted value. At the end sum of these group's weighted values gives us related bank's CAMELS score for related year.

When we examine Table 5, we can say that Akbank has shown a strong performance since 2013 after the Global Crisis. The most important reason for this is the improvement of the bank's ratios regarding capital adequacy and sensitivity to market risk. Akbank is the only bank who has a steady rise among the analyzed banks.

In Ziraat Bank, which is the only state-owned bank in our example, stable trend was experienced until 2018. However, in 2018, a sharp decline in the liquidity and market risk sensitivity of the bank turned the CAMELS score into a negative

Table 1 Ratios

CAMELS ratios	Abbreviations	The direction of the relationship	Impact (%)
C-Capital adequacy			**20**
Capital adequacy ratio	CAR	+	20
Shareholders equity/total assets	SETA	+	20
Shareholders equity – tangible assets/ total assets	SETT	+	20
Net profit/total assets	NPTA	+	20
FX position/shareholders equity	FXSE	–	20
A-Asset quality			**20**
Financial assets (net)/total assets	FAT	+	20
Total loans/total assets	TLTA	+	20
Total loans/total deposits	TLTD	+	20
Tangible assets/total assets	TATA	–	20
Consumer loans/total loans	CLTL	–	20
M-Management capability			**15**
Net profit per branch	NPPB	+	20
Personnel expenses/other operating expenses	PEOOE	–	20
Non-performing loans/total loans	NLTL	–	20
Non interest income/other operating expenses	NIIOOE	+	20
Other operating expenses/total assets	OOETA	–	20
E-Earnings			**15**
Average return on assets	ARA	+	20
Average return on equity	ARE	+	20
Pretax profit/total assets	PPTA	+	20
Net profit/paid-in capital	NPPC	+	20
Total income/total expenses	TITE	+	20
L-Liquidity			**15**
Liquid assets/total assets	LATA	+	20
Liquid assets/short-term liabilities	LASL	+	20
TL liquid assets/total assets	TLATA	+	20
Liquid assets/(deposits + non-deposit sources)	LADNDS	+	20
FX liquid assets/FX liabilities	FXLAFXL	+	20
S-Sensitivity			**15**
Interest income/total assets	IITA	+	20
FX assets/FX liabilities	FXAFXL	+	20
Non-interest income/total assets	NIITA	+	20
Net balance position/shareholders equity	NBPSE	–	20
FX position/shareholders equity	FXPSE	–	20

Table 2 The calculation of the reference value for the year 2011

Ratios	AKBNK	TCZB	GARAN	ISBNK	Ref.
C-Capital adequacy					
Capital adequacy ratio	17.0	15.6	16.9	14.1	15.9
Shareholders equity/total assets	13.1	8.2	12.0	11.1	11.1
Shareholders equity – tangible assets/total assets	11.6	6.9	9.3	6.0	8.46
Net profit/total assets	1.9	1.3	2.3	1.8	1.84
FX position/shareholders equity	73.5	9.0	4.3	14.2	25.2
A-Assets					
Financial assets (net)/total assets	32.7	44.0	24.1	27.0	32
Total loans/total assets	52.6	44.5	57.2	56.7	52.7
Total loans/total deposits	91.5	63.2	99.1	93.2	86.8
Tangible assets/total assets	2.4	1.7	3.5	6.3	3.48
Consumer loans/total loans	35.8	42.5	33.1	27.5	34.7
M-Management capability					
Net profit per branch	3	1	3	2	2.4
Personnel expenses/other operating expenses	39.5	50.1	38.9	52.3	45.2
Non-performing loans/total loans	1.8	1.2	1.8	2.2	1.75
Non-interest income/other operating expenses	85.9	36.9	101.3	103.5	81.9
Other operating expenses/total assets	1.8	1.6	2.2	2.2	1.95
E-Earnings					
Average return on assets	1.9	1.9	2.3	1.8	1.99
Average return on equity	13.6	13.6	18.0	15.3	15.1
Pretax profit/total assets	2.2	2.2	2.7	2.0	2.3
Net profit/paid-in capital	59.9	59.9	73.1	59.3	63
Total income/total expenses	148.4	148.4	152.6	147.7	149
L-Liquidity					
Liquid assets/total assets	41.6	33.5	36.2	28.6	35
Liquid assets/short-term liabilities	73.3	44.6	63.5	47.3	57.2
TL liquid assets/total assets	28.5	25.1	21.4	15.1	22.5
Liquid assets/(deposits + non-deposit sources)	50.1	37.6	44.3	34.9	41.7
FX liquid assets/FX liabilities	28.8	49.4	36.0	37.7	38
S-Sensitivity					
Interest income/total assets	6.8	8.5	7.1	6.7	7.31
FX assets/FX liabilities	78.7	95.7	98.7	95.6	92.2
Non interest income/total assets	1.6	0.6	2.2	2.2	1.65
Net balance position/shareholders equity	−64.1	−8.8	13.2	3.9	−14
FX position/shareholders equity	73.5	9.0	4.3	14.2	25.2

Table 3 Reference values calculated for 2011–2018

Years	2011	2012	2013	2014	2015	2016	2017	2018
C-Capital adequacy								
Capital adequacy ratio	15.9	18.0	14.2	16.2	15.1	16.1	15.9	15.4
Shareholders equity/ total assets	11.1	12.7	10.8	12.0	11.4	11.6	11.7	11.5
Shareholders equity – tangible assets/ total assets	8.5	9.9	8.2	9.0	8.1	8.89	8.81	8.56
Net profit/total assets	1.8	1.9	1.7	1.6	1.5	1.77	1.68	1.64
FX position/share-holders equity	25.2	19.9	40.8	44.6	40.6	32.6	36.4	39.6
A-Assets								
Financial assets (net)/ total assets	32.0	29.0	23.3	22.0	19.8	26.5	23.5	22.9
Total loans/total assets	52.7	54.6	59.6	61.4	62.3	57.1	59.5	60.1
Total loans/total deposits	86.8	92.1	101.7	108.0	107.7	97.1	102	104
Tangible assets/total assets	3.5	3.7	3.5	3.9	4.4	3.64	3.86	3.85
Consumer loans/total loans	34.7	35.8	33.9	31.4	28.5	33.9	32.4	31.9
M-Management capability								
Net profit per branch	2	3	3	3	3	2.63	2.77	2.75
Personnel expenses/ other operating expenses	45.2	42.8	43.4	41.8	39.0	43.3	41.8	41.9
Non-performing loans/ total loans	1.7	2.1	1.9	1.9	2.2	1.91	2.03	1.99
Non-interest income/ other operating expenses	81.9	75.7	75.2	66.1	55.2	74.7	68	67.8
Other operating expenses/total assets	1.9	2.1	2.0	2.0	2.0	2.02	2.04	2.02
E-Earnings								
Average return on assets	2.0	2.0	1.7	1.6	1.3	1.82	1.66	1.61
Average return on equity	15.1	15.5	13.6	13.3	11.3	14.4	13.4	13.2
Pretax profit/Total assets	2.3	2.4	2.0	1.9	1.6	2.16	1.98	1.91
Net profit/paid-in capital	63.0	73.5	72.2	77.3	74.8	71.5	74.5	74
Total income/total expenses	149.3	150.6	157.6	149.7	145.1	152	151	151
L-Liquidity								
Liquid assets/total assets	35.0	35.2	30.6	30.1	28.9	32.7	31.2	30.6
Liquid assets/short-term liabilities	57.2	59.7	56.5	56.6	52.9	57.5	56.4	55.9
TL liquid assets/total assets	22.5	21.0	15.4	14.8	11.9	18.4	15.8	15.2

(continued)

Table 3 (continued)

Years	2011	2012	2013	2014	2015	2016	2017	2018
Liquid assets/ (deposits + non-deposit sources)	41.7	43.3	36.7	36.5	34.9	39.6	37.8	36.9
FX liquid assets/FX liabilities	38.0	43.2	38.5	36.4	37.8	39	39	37.9
S-Sensitivity								
Interest income/total assets	7.3	8.0	6.5	7.0	6.9	7.19	7.08	6.89
FX assets/FX liabilities	92.2	92.8	89.7	88.0	90.1	90.7	90.1	89.6
Non-interest income/ total assets	1.7	1.6	1.5	1.3	1.1	1.53	1.4	1.38
Net balance position/ shareholders equity	−14.0	−8.0	−26.9	−28.3	−28.0	−19.3	−22.8	−25.6
FX position/share-holders equity	25.2	19.9	40.8	44.6	40.6	32.6	36.4	39.6

outlook. In addition, it can be recommended that the bank needs to improve the quality of management that dropped in 2018.

Although Garanti Bank appears to be the bank that recovered most quickly after the Global Crisis, the bank's decline in CAMELS score since 2014 is standing out. The most important reason for this is that the sensitivity of the bank against market risk diminished sharply. Although there has been a decrease in the liquidity ratios of the bank in recent years, it is observed that it recovered in 2018. Thus, Garanti Bank managed to enhance its CAMELS score in 2018. In addition, Garanti Bank was observed as the most successful one in terms of profitability.

It is detected that İşbank exhibited the worst performance in terms of composite score of CAMELS analysis among the banks examined. After the global crisis, İşbank's capital adequacy and sensitivity to market risk fell dramatically. Besides, a steady decline in İşbank's management quality observed to be a striking feature of it.

4 Conclusion

By this study Turkey's four biggest banks performances in terms of size of asset and profitability were evaluated for the period after the crisis. Thirty ratios were calculated for each six groups of components in order to conduct CAMELS analysis.

According to these ratios of CAMELS, İşbank was determined as the worst performed one for the period of 8 years. It emerged as a fact that İşbank needs to make provision for all components of CAMLES. The management quality which was already scored low and has been continuing to decrease, can be a proper study case to recover, particularly if it takes account that the interaction between the management and all other categories of CAMELS.

Table 4 Calculation of Akbank's CAMELS score for 2018

	Group impact (%)	The direction of the relationship	Subgroup impact (%)	Ref.	Bank value	Index value	Deviation value	Weighted value	CAMELS score
C-Capital adequacy	**20**							5.14	7.07
CAR		+	20	16.95	18.20	107.36	7.36	1.47	
SETA		+	20	12.25	13.37	109.18	9.18	1.84	
SETT		+	20	8.48	10.28	121.24	21.24	4.25	
NPTA		+	20	1.77	1.77	99.82	−0.18	−0.04	
FXSE		−	20	53.58	59.95	111.88	−11.88	−2.38	
								0.00	
A-Asset quality	**20**							6.82	
FAT		+	20	31.67	38.48	121.49	21.49	4.30	
TLTA		+	20	62.54	56.50	90.34	−9.66	−1.93	
TLTD		+	20	104.70	98.27	93.86	−6.14	−1.23	
TATA		−	20	3.77	3.09	82.03	17.97	3.59	
CLTL		−	20	24.86	22.26	89.54	10.46	2.09	
								0.00	
M-Management capability	**15**							15.28	
NPPB		+	20	5.97	7.29	122.04	22.04	4.41	
PEOOE		−	20	40.35	38.40	95.17	4.83	0.97	
NLTL		−	20	3.91	4.23	108.19	−8.19	−1.64	
NIIOOE		+	20	79.06	120.51	152.42	52.42	10.48	
OOETA		−	20	1.78	1.69	94.68	5.32	1.06	
								0.00	
E-Earnings	**15**							−2.21	
ARA		+	20	1.80	1.77	98.04	−1.96	−0.39	

(continued)

Table 4 (continued)

	Group impact (%)	The direction of the relationship	Subgroup impact (%)	Ref.	Bank value	Index value	Deviation value	Weighted value	CAMELS score
ARE		+	20	14.17	13.51	95.32	−4.68	−0.94	
PPTA		+	20	2.12	2.13	100.62	0.62	0.12	
NPPC		+	20	148.24	142.24	95.95	−4.05	−0.81	
TITE		+	20	169.71	168.06	99.03	−0.97	−0.19	
								0.00	
L-Liquidity	**15**							14.72	
LATA		+	20	13.15	14.85	112.97	12.97	2.59	
LASL		+	20	24.79	29.69	119.74	19.74	3.95	
TLATA		+	20	1.29	1.58	122.44	22.44	4.49	
LADNDS		+	20	16.85	19.21	114.00	14.00	2.80	
FXLAFXL		+	20	23.88	24.95	104.45	4.45	0.89	
								0.00	
S-Sensitivity	**15**							3.40	
IITA		+	20	10.06	10.25	101.94	1.94	0.39	
FXAFXL		+	20	86.77	84.93	97.88	−2.12	−0.42	
NIITA		+	20	0.89	1.25	141.37	41.37	8.27	
NBPSE		–	20	−45.74	−51.38	112.32	−12.32	−2.46	
FXPSE		–	20	53.58	59.95	111.88	−11.88	−2.38	

Table 5 CAMELS scores of Turkey's four big banks after the global crisis

CAMELS ratios	2011	2012	2013	2014	2015	2016	2017	2018
AKBANK	**−18.44**	**−4.89**	**−8.57**	**0.92**	**5.35**	**8.85**	**8.08**	**7.07**
C-capital adequacy	−24.61	−8.16	−16.58	−3.66	1.61	4.61	4.78	5.14
A-asset quality	7.26	12.44	9.56	10.34	11.08	10.87	8.27	6.82
M-management capability	5.79	17.86	13.23	10.57	9.80	14.46	18.04	15.28
E-earnings	−4.09	0.33	2.71	3.02	2.20	1.81	4.92	−2.21
L-liquidity	13.94	9.45	−0.23	2.95	9.21	13.49	14.10	14.72
S-sensitivity	−115.42	−65.97	−63.49	−19.32	−2.48	8.60	−0.60	3.40
ZIRAAT BANK	**0.12**	**−0.95**	**6.81**	**9.98**	**12.61**	**21.23**	**7.27**	**−5.12**
C-capital adequacy	−1.81	1.25	5.98	16.81	18.33	32.91	7.76	0.89
A-asset quality	4.75	0.43	5.59	1.37	4.38	2.20	3.43	6.36
M-management capability	−11.71	−22.21	−11.93	−5.02	5.41	2.16	3.51	−6.85
E-earnings	−4.09	0.33	2.71	3.02	2.20	1.81	4.92	−2.21
L-liquidity	1.08	11.28	21.63	19.37	13.12	11.35	2.98	−31.59
S-sensitivity	11.61	2.03	17.58	24.90	33.07	79.41	22.16	−3.18
GARANTI	**18.95**	**6.12**	**6.21**	**−5.66**	**−4.14**	**−15.15**	**−3.59**	**9.85**
C-capital adequacy	26.12	7.03	12.51	−6.63	0.95	−14.99	3.30	7.27
A-asset quality	0.40	−0.34	−4.38	−2.99	−6.78	−6.45	−6.53	−3.89
M-management capability	12.15	3.29	2.67	−2.90	−6.64	−5.15	−6.66	8.08
E-earnings	13.42	0.15	−0.92	−1.12	5.56	4.49	6.02	8.19
L-liquidity	2.11	4.65	−6.62	−16.09	−18.86	−22.32	−12.94	22.40
S-sensitivity	63.30	23.82	35.41	−4.79	0.15	−49.46	−6.07	22.48
İş BANK	**−0.63**	**−0.28**	**−4.45**	**−5.24**	**−13.82**	**−14.92**	**−11.76**	**−11.80**
C-capital adequacy	0.30	−0.12	−1.91	−6.52	−20.88	−22.53	−15.84	−13.30
A-asset quality	−12.40	−12.53	−10.78	−8.72	−8.68	−6.63	−5.16	−9.30
M-management capability	−6.23	1.07	−3.97	−2.66	−8.57	−11.47	−14.89	−16.51

(continued)

Table 5 (continued)

CAMELS ratios	2011	2012	2013	2014	2015	2016	2017	2018
E-earnings	−5.24	−0.81	−4.50	−4.91	−9.96	−8.10	−15.87	−3.78
L-liquidity	−17.14	−25.38	−14.78	−6.23	−3.47	−2.52	−4.14	−5.53
S-sensitivity	40.52	40.12	10.51	−0.80	−30.74	−38.55	−15.49	−22.70

On the other hand, even though Ziraat Bank's scores are satisfactory for all components of CAMELS except for the year 2018, it needs to improve its liquid quality that has fallen, rapidly. Also, Akbank seems to reach the best scores for all years in all components, but nevertheless it needs to improve its profitability. On the other hand, although Garanti Bank's performance is not inadequate for recently, it fluctuated when all years take account.

Consequently, CAMELS analysis approached as one of the powerful and most explanatory methods in order to evaluate and compare banks situation. Although a brief but clear investigation about four biggest banks in Turkey was presented with this study, another aim of it should be lighten other studies. So, it can be expected from it to encourage future CAMELS studies which can include a more comprehensive data containing all other banks' value in Turkish banking sector by using ratios more than 30.

References

Abdullayev, M. (2013). Türk bankacılık sektöründe dezenflasyon sürecinde camels analizi. *Dumlupınar Üniversitesi Sosyal Bilimler Dergisi, 37*, 97–112.

Ahmedov, T., & Memmedov, E. (2017). Azerbaycan Bankacılık Sektörünün CAMELS Analizi: Yabancı Sermayeli 10 Banka. *İktisadi İdari ve Siyasal Araştırmalar Dergisi, 2*(4), 97–109.

Ahsan, M. K. (2016). Measuring financial performance based on CAMEL: A study on selected Islamic banks in Bangladesh. *Asian Business Review, 6*(1), 7–56.

Atikogullari, M. (2009). An analysis of the northern Cyprus banking sector in the post-2001 period through the CAMELS approach. *International Research Journal of Finance and Economics, 32* (10), 212–229.

Avkiran, N. K. (1994). Developing an instrument to measure customer service quality in branch banking. *The International Journal of Bank Marketing, 12*(6), 10–18.

Bayramoglu, M. F., & Gürsoy, İ. (2017). Türkiye'de Faaliyet Gösteren Mevduat Bankalarinin Bireysel ve Sektörel Risk Derecelendirmesi: Bir Camels Analizi Uygulaması. *Yönetim ve Ekonomi Araştırmaları Dergisi, 15*(1), 1–19.

Çağıl, G., & Mukhtarov, S. (2014). Azerbaycan Ticari Bankacılık Sektörünün CAMELS Yöntemi ile Performans Analizi. *Öneri Dergisi, 11*(41), 77–94.

Caton, W. F. (1997). Uniform financial institutions rating system. *Federal Register, 62*(3), 752–757.

Christopoulos, A. G., Mylonakis, J., & Diktapanidis, P. (2011). Could Lehman Brothers' collapse be anticipated? An examination using CAMELS rating system. *International Business Research, 4*(2), 11.

Çinko, M., & Avcı, E. (2008). CAMELS Derecelendirme Sistemi ve Türk Ticari Bankacılık Sektöründe Başarısızlık Tahmini. *BDDK Bankacılık ve Finansal Piyasalar Dergisi, 2*(2), 25–48.

Dang, U. (2011). The CAMEL rating system in banking supervision: A case study of Arcada University of applied sciences. *International Business, 5*(3), 82–103.

Dash, M., & Das, A. (2009). *A CAMELS analysis of the Indian banking industry*. Available at SSRN 1666900.

Dincer, H., Gencer, G., Orhan, N., & Sahinbas, K. (2011). A performance evaluation of the Turkish banking sector after the global crisis via CAMELS ratios. *Procedia-Social and Behavioral Sciences, 24*, 1530–1545.

Dinçer, H., Yüksel, S., & Pınarbaşı, F. (2020). Kano-based measurement of customer expectations in retail service industry using IT2 DEMATEL-QUALIFLEX. In E. Baykal (Ed.), *Handbook of research on positive organizational behavior for improved workplace performance* (pp. 349–370). Hershey, PA: IGI Global.

Ege, İ., Topaloğlu, E., & Karakozak, Ö. (2015). CAMELS performans değerleme modeli: Türkiye'deki mevduat bankalari üzerine ampirik bir uygulama. *Niğde Üniversitesi İktisadi ve İdari Bilimler Fakültesi Dergisi, 8*(4), 109–126.

Eti, S., Kalkavan, H., Dinçer, H., & Yüksel, S. (2020). Predicting the role of Islamic banking on sustainable economic development: An analysis for Turkey with ARIMA model. In U. Akkucuk (Ed.), *Handbook of research on creating sustainable value in the global economy* (pp. 146–164). Hershey, PA: IGI Global.

Grier, W. A. (2007). *Credit analysis of financial institutions*. London: Euromoney Books.

Gümüş, F. B., & Nalbantoğlu, Ö. (2015). Türk Bankacılık Sektörünün CAMELS Analizi Yöntemiyle 2002–2013 Yılları Arasında Performans Analizi. *Journal of Economics & Administrative Sciences/Afyon Kocatepe Üniversitesi Iktisadi ve Idari Bilimler Fakültesi Dergisi, 17* (2).

Gündoğdu, A. (2017). Türkiye'de Mevduat Bankalarının CAMELS Analizi. *Bankacılık ve Finansal Araştırmalar Dergisi (BAFAD), 4*(2), 26–43.

Güney, S., & Ilgın, K. S. (2015). Finansal Krizlerin Bankalarin Performanslarina Etkisi: Türk Mevduat Bankalarinda Camels Modelinin İncelenmesi Ve Örnek Bir Uygulama. *Dokuz Eylül Üniversitesi Sosyal Bilimler Enstitüsü Dergisi, 17*(3), 303–331.

Helhel, Y., & Varshalomidze, M. (2014). Gürcistan'da faaliyet gösteren yerli sermayeli özel ticari bankaların CAMELS derecelendirme sistemi ile değerlendirilmesi. *Finans Sempozyumu Denizli/15–18 Ekim* (pp. 413–424).

Hempel, G., Coleman, A., & Smon, D. (1986). *Bank management text and cases*. New York: Wiley.

Hyz, A., & Gikas, G. (2015). CAMELS and Greek banking sector performance during the crisis an analysis and review of the evidence. *Acta Universitatis Lodziensis. Folia Oeconomica, 5*(316), 27–39.

Kalkavan, H., & Ersin, I. (2019). Determination of factors affecting the South East Asian crisis of 1997 probit-logit panel regression: The South East Asian crisis. In H. Dinçer & S. Yuksel (Eds.), *Handbook of research on global issues in financial communication and investment decision making* (pp. 148–167). Hershey, PA: IGI Global.

Kandemir, T., & Arıcı, A. G. N. D. (2013). Mevduat Bankalarında Camels Performans Değerleme Modeli Üzerine Karşılaştırmalı Bir Çalışma (2001–2010). *Suleyman Demirel University Journal of Faculty of Economics & Administrative Sciences, 18*(1), 61–87.

Kaya, Y. T. (2001). Türk Bankacılık Sektöründe CAMELS Analizi. *Bankacılık Düzenleme ve Denetleme Kurumu, MSPD Çalışma Raporları, 6*, 1–20.

Kılıç, Ç., & Fettahoğlu, A. (2005). Türk Bankacılık Sektörünün CAMELS Analizi İle Değerlendirilmesi. *Ulusal Finans Sempozyumu*, 89–128.

Kumar, M. A., Harsha, G. S., Anand, S., & Dhruva, N. R. (2012). Analyzing soundness in Indian banking: A CAMEL approach. *Research Journal of Management Sciences ISSN, 2319*, 1171.

Mitchell, K. (1984). Capital adequacy at commercial banks. *Economic Review, Sep*, 17–30.

Nimalathasan, B. (2008). A comparative study of financial performance of banking sector in Bangladesh. An application of CAMELS rating system. *Universitatii Bucuresti. Analele. Seria Stiinte Economice si Administrative, 2*, 133.

Raiyani, J. R. (2010). Effect of mergers on efficiency and productivity of Indian banks: A CAMELS analysis. *Asian Journal of Management Research, 1*(2), 772–794.

Roman, A., & Şargu, A. C. (2013). Analysing the financial soundness of the commercial banks in Romania: An approach based on the camels framework. *Procedia Economics and Finance, 6*, 703–712.

Rostami, M. (2015). Determination of Camels model on bank's performance. *International Journal of Multidisciplinary Research and Development, 2*(10), 652–664.

Rozzani, N., & Rahman, R. A. (2013). Camels and performance evaluation of banks in Malaysia: Conventional versus Islamic. *Journal of Islamic Finance and Business Research, 2*(1), 36–45.

Sakarya, Ş. (2010). Camels Derecelendirme Sistemine Göre İMKB'deki Yerli ve Yabancı Sermayeli Bankaların Karşılaştırmalı Analizi. *Akademik Araştırmalar ve Çalışmalar Dergisi (AKAD)*, 7–21.

Şen, A., & Solak, S. (2011). Ticari bankacılık sektörünün CAMELS analizi: Türkiye örneği. *Finans Politik & Ekonomik Yorumla, 2011*, 554.

Siems, T. F., & Barr, R. S. (1998). Benchmarking the productive efficiency of US banks. *Financial Industry Studies, 4*, 11–24.

Şimşek, T., Aslan, E., & Şahin, A. (2017). Türk Bankacılık Sektörünün 2001–2015 Dönemi İçin CAMELS Yöntemiyle Performans Analizi. *Bilgi Ekonomisi ve Yönetimi Dergisi, 12*(2), 155–167.

Tükenmez, N. M., Kutay, N., & Akkaya, G. C. (2010). Kamu ve özel sermayeli ticari bankalarda CAMELS Performans Değerleme Modeli üzerine bir inceleme. *Iktisat Isletme ve Finans, 25* (293), 95–112.

Wirnkar, D., & Tanko, M. (2008). *CAMELs and banks performance evaluation: The way forward.* Viewed August 5, 2014.

Yuksel, S., Dincer, H., & Hacioglu, U. (2015). CAMELS-based determinants for the credit rating of Turkish deposit banks. *International Journal of Finance & Banking Studies (2147–4486), 4*(4), 1–17.

The Effects of Trade Wars Between US and China on the Financial Performances of the Companies

Selman Duran and İrfan Ersin

Abstract Tariffs that the USA has implemented in some products toward China have recently caused trade wars. Trump, who was elected US president in 2016, triggered trade wars due to his protectionist attitude towards China. That's why trade wars officially started in 2018. This attitude of Trump influenced also the stock exchanges of the two countries as well as the trade relations of the two major economies. While our study provides information about the US-China trade wars, it empirically tested the relationship of this war with the stock markets of both countries. The relationship between exports made mutually by the USA and China and the stock exchange is analyzed using the Engle-Granger cointegration method. In this study, which was used monthly data for the period 2016–2019, a long-term relationship between exports and stock market is detected for both countries. Considering the global economy within the framework of this relationship, it is seen important that the two countries withdraw commercial wars and go for an agreement.

1 Introduction

At the beginning of March 2018, the trade war came to light when President Trump announced that additional tariffs will be applied on aluminum and steel imported from China. In fact, it is known that there was a serious struggle felt by all parties before this announcement. However, mutual high-level commercial relations were suppressing both China and the United States in order not to declare war. The declaration of such a struggle undoubtedly posed serious risks for both sides and even the global economy. It is inevitable that such a trade war will affect other

S. Duran (✉)
The School of Business, İstanbul Medipol University, İstanbul, Turkey
e-mail: sduran@medipol.edu.tr

İ. Ersin
Vocational School of Social Sciences, İstanbul Medipol University, İstanbul, Turkey
e-mail: iersin@medipol.edu.tr

H. Dincer, S. Yüksel (eds.), *Strategic Priorities in Competitive Environments*,
Contributions to Management Science, https://doi.org/10.1007/978-3-030-45023-6_16

regions and countries of the world. In fact, one of these countries has the highest foreign trade deficit, and the other is the country with the largest foreign trade surplus.

The competition between the USA and China, which have the two largest economies in the world, is getting worse day by day. Therefore, the problems experienced in the economies of these two countries might affect other countries with commercial or financial ties. In this section, the effects of the US-China trade wars on their own stock market is analyzed. In the first part of the study, the conceptual framework and background are explained. In the second part, concepts related to trade wars are mentioned. In the third and fourth sections, while giving information about the US-Chinese economies, the economic relationship between them is discussed. In the fifth chapter, empirical application is carried out, which analyzes the effect of US-China trade wars on the stock market. In the last section, evaluation and conclusion are mentioned.

2 Conceptual Framework and Historical Background

2.1 Trade Wars and Related Concepts

It can be said that the first systematic economic thought and doctrine in which protectionist foreign trade policies were applied can be seen in the Mercantilist period. The economic thought /doctrine called Mercantilism has marked a long period that started in 1500 years and lasted until 1776, when Adam Smith's The Wealth of Nations was published. Mercantilism is a concept that enables the spread of capitalism, which experienced the crawling period in the second half of the sixteenth century, to all of Western Europe, but includes the policies that were intensely implemented by gaining its real content in the seventeenth century. The interaction of economic events with each other and their handling in cause and effect relation started with the current of Mercantilism. In the historical process, it can be seen that the mercantilist movement generally took place between the fifteenth and eighteenth centuries and the period of strict protectionist policies was applied (Chong and Li 2019).

Another important point is that neo mercantilism is the embodiment of mercantilist thought in the context of recent history and trade wars. It is thought that neo-mercantilism is based on win-lose economic nationalism with old and new protectionism tools in order to become or maintain power of Hegenomic power. The dominant view in international economic theory is that free trade will maximize the welfare of nations. Both the Theory of Absolute Advantages, and the Comparative Advantages Theory, which were later proposed by David Ricardo, forms the basis of the free trade view. These theories have intrinsically criticized the previous Mercantilist view, contrary to what is believed, argue that protectionism does not provide efficiency. In general, the strong advocates of this view were England until World War II, and then the USA took over this banner. In this process, although preventative measures such as quota applications for imports and the increase of customs duties were expressed to encourage the use of domestic goods in both countries, the dominant view in these countries was free trade (Rassekh 2015).

The trade war means that a country's restriction on its imports for various reasons, and its partner, who trades with it, retaliates by following a similar path and applies for customs duties, quotas and other similar imports from that country. With this practice, the trade volume between countries is getting narrower. However, the examples experienced in the past show that even if protectionism can benefit countries in the short term, it causes a narrowing of the country's economies and crises in the long term (Yılmaz et al. 2019). It can be seen that the general reason for trade wars in the history was the economic policies of the states by considering their own interests. Even though these wars generally occur among developed countries throughout the history of humanity, it is seen that the destruction caused by the results of wars affects poorly developed and poor societies as in actual wars.

In today's world, while the party that started the trade war was a strong and developed country, it is not possible to make such a distinction for the countries that have faced the war. The main reason is that the US protectionist policies, while applying a developing country like Turkey, may also include developed countries such as the EU. Although economic reasons are mentioned in the background of the trade war initiated by the USA, it is thought that there is a rush to restore the hegemonic power that the USA thinks is losing in the political context. As stated earlier, the main tools used in Trade wars are protectionism policies. How, during which periods did protectionism policies have been used in the historical process and have survived to the present day? The answer to the question is of special importance in order to understand the phenomenon of trade war today. It can be said that the first systematic protection trend (in thought/doctrine) started in the Mercantilist period. Therefore, it is not wrong to say that the "zero sum" mercantilist thought is the first period of the trade wars (Yılmaz and Divani 2018).

2.2 *Historical Background of the Struggle*[1]

There are some strategies in order to overcome the negative effects of the financial crisis. The most popular strategies are monetary and fiscal policy tools. Moreover, some new strategies, such as guaranteeing the deposit of the customers by government and liquidity injection were also used especially in last financial crisis (Dinçer et al. 2020; Kalkavan and Ersin 2019). This war started in March 2018 with the announcement of 25% and 10% additional customs duties on imported steel and aluminum, respectively, to all trading partners (Öztürk and Altınöz 2019a, b). The measures announced covered about $48 billion in imports beyond the measures

[1]The chronological information in this section has been compiled by using databases of reputable news agencies that are internationally accepted.

suggested in the investigation report, and, unlike what is believed, mostly included products from allies such as Canada, the EU, Mexico, and South Korea. Only 6% of imports were from China (Mallick 2018).

If the protection measures to be taken are implemented, the EU applied to the WTO and stated that it will immediately apply a 25% additional customs tax on products worth $3.4 billion, including whiskey, jeans, peanut butter and motorcycles imported from the USA. Trump announced that protection measures will come into force on 23 March, by exempting Canada and Mexico from the decision, until the conclusion of the ongoing NAFTA renewal negotiations. Trump expanded the list of exemptions, noting that until May 1, 2018, the EU, South Korea, Brazil, Argentina and Australia will also be exempted from protection measures. Outside the determined exemption list, measures have entered into force for countries exporting $ 10.2 billion of steel and $ 7.7 billion of aluminum products to the US. No explanation was given as to when or under what conditions the measures would be lifted.

South Korea agreed with the United States on the permanent exemption from the measures, adopting a quota of 2.68 million tons, which means a 21.2% cut from its exports last year. China responded to the imports of US $ 2.8 billion worth of Chinese aluminum and steel products by imposing taxes on imports of aluminum scrap, fruit, etc., which was $ 2.4 billion in 2017. The exemption granted to the EU, Canada and Mexico was extended until June 1, 2018. South Korea and Argentina were saved from enforcement with a quota they agreed to restrict exports. While Brazil exempted these products with quotas on steel products, aluminum was subjected to a 10% tax application. Australia remained the only trading partner whose precautions were lifted without any restrictions.

After the EU, Canada also applied to the WTO to resolve the dispute. Canada has previously announced that the United States will respond by applying customs to the step it has taken. The application, which will come into force on July 1, is reported to include products imported from the US and amount to $ 16 billion 600 million. Customs measures to be implemented by Mexico against the USA include steel and aluminum, as well as agricultural products such as lamps, cheese and apples. The EU enacted the measures it threatened to implement on March 7 to import US products worth $3.2 billion. While only 1/3 of the products are steel and aluminum products, the rest of the products were targeted at traditional US products such as whiskey, jeans, yacht, motorcycle, corn, peanut oil. Trump added $60 billion in additional taxes to Chinese products, litigation and investments in WTO, based on the report of the investigation commission established by the Minister of Commerce on his own initiative on August 18, 2017, accusing China of unfair practices in the areas of technology transfer, intellectual property rights and innovation. He announced that he would introduce measures in the form of new rules. China responded to this move of the United States by bringing 25% tax to 106 US products worth $ 49.8 billion, mostly land, air and sea transportation vehicles and soy products.

Starting on July 6, the U.S. Department of Commerce released a revised product list that brought 25% additional tax to various products with a total value of $46.3 billion in two stages. The revised list contained more intermediate products than the list announced on April 3. Interestingly, 95% of the products were intermediate products, with companies based in the US dependent on China for production. China, like the US, has renewed about $45 billion—659 countermeasures to implement two stages. While the list of products planned to come into effect on July 6, mostly containing means of transportation and soy, was worth $29.6 billion, oil, chemicals, plastics and liquid propane weighed approximately $15.3 billion, later depending on Trump's practices announced that it will come into force. Unlike the first list envisaged by China on April 4, petroleum products, some consumer goods and medical equipment were added to the list, while aviation products that were $16.3 billion in 2017 were removed from the list.

The U.S. government has officially started applying 25% additional customs duty to more than 800 products worth $ 34 billion, which is the first phase of measures to be applied on $50 billion products imported from China. Upon Trump's request dated June 18, the Ministry announced an additional list of 5000 products, consisting of nearly 47% of the products, such as IT products and auto spare parts, to be discussed by the relevant parties in August. Consumer products such as telephones ($45 billion), computers ($37 billion), furniture, garments ($27 billion), lighting products and suitcases were heavily targeted. Thus, the list of measures that reached a total of $250 billion, along with a $50 billion worth of list determined on June 15, covered nearly half of the $504 billion imports from China in 2017.

In the direction of Trump, USTR is considering a 25% tariff instead of 10% in List 3, first announced on July 10, 2018. The list targets about $200 billion worth of goods and includes categories such as consumer products, chemical and construction materials, textiles, tools, food and agriculture products, commercial electronic equipment and vehicle/automotive parts. The U.S. Department of Commerce adds 44 Chinese units to the export checklist, which pose a "significant risk" for US national security. In response to potential US tariffs for products worth $200 billion announced on August 1, 2018 (List 3), the China Department of Commerce offers a number of additional tariffs for 5207 products of US origin (worth $ 60 billion):

- 25% of 2493 products (agriculture, products, foods, textiles and products, chemicals, metal products, machinery);
- 20% on 1078 products (foods, cardboard, chemical artworks);
- 10% on 974 products (agricultural products, chemicals, glassware); and
- 5% on 662 products (chemicals, machines, medical devices).

The United States and China agreed to a temporary ceasefire to increase trade tensions after a working dinner at the G20 Summit in Buenos Aires on December 1, 2018. According to the agreement, both the US and China are new tariffs for 90 days (until March 1, 2019), as the two parties working on a larger trade agreement will avoid increasing or imposing tariffs. More specifically, the US will avoid increasing the tariffs announced in Listing 3, which is scheduled to increase from 10% to 25% on January 2019 and will not be able to withstand previously threatened tariffs on an additional $ 267 billion of Chinese goods. China will purchase more US products—especially agricultural and energy products—and will break down the production and distribution of Fentanyl, a synthetic opioid produced primarily in China.

On Thursday, February 21, the US and Chinese negotiators resumed their trade talks in Washington. The next day, Friday, February 22, Trump met Liu He and expressed optimism about a trade deal. On Sunday, February 24, Trump announced the progress in trade negotiations and announced that the March 1 trade agreement would extend the cease-fire date. Trump does not give a concrete date for a new deadline, but says he hopes that Xi will visit the town of Mar-a-Lago in Florida in March to conclude a trade deal. The US and China are unable to reach an agreement after the end of the eleventh round of the top trade talks, so the US raises tariffs on $200 billion of Chinese goods (List 3) from 10% to 25%. The tariff increase will be effective from May 10, 2019, before China's goods are dropped from the previous 10% before midnight. In response, the China Ministry of Commerce issued a statement stating that it "deeply regrets" the tariffs and that "necessary measures" will be taken. China announced that it will increase tariffs on US goods as of June 1, 2019 in response to the tariff increases applied by the USA on May 10. The tariffs were announced last September. Affected products include beef, lamb, pork, vegetables, juice, cooking oil, tea, coffee, refrigerators and furniture.

"The USA will start by placing a small additional 10% Tariff on the remaining $ 300 billion goods and products from China on September 1," Trump said. The surprise tariff announcement comes after the US and China have finished their trade talks in Shanghai the day before. After the meeting, the White House described the debates as "constructive", adding that China has confirmed its commitments to increase US agricultural export purchases. When these round tariffs are applied, it will affect China's imports to almost the entire US, including electronics and apparel consumer goods. Trump also threatened to raise tariffs by up to 25% in goods worth $250 billion, if China could not move faster to reach a trade agreement.

3 Economic Structure of China

The Chinese economy, which is the beginning of the historical silk road, has a considerable background. The country has competitive power in silk, porcelain and tea production between the sixteenth and eighteenth centuries and sells these products to the whole world. Until the end of the twentieth century, it maintained its agricultural structure and failed to achieve industrialization. Before the introduction of economic reforms and trade liberalization nearly 40 years ago, China pursued policies that were too weak, stagnant, centrally controlled, largely inefficient, and relatively isolated from the global economy. Since opening to foreign trade and investment and implementing free market reforms in 1979, China has been among the fastest growing economies in the world, and the average annual gross domestic product (GDP) growth by 2018 is 9.5% on average it was. This growth has helped China to double its GDP on average every 8 years on average, and about 800 million people from poverty. China has become the world's largest economy (on the basis of purchasing power parity), producer, commercial trader and foreign exchange reserves. This made China an important trading partner of the USA. China is the

USA's largest trading partner, the largest import source, and the third largest US export market. China is also the largest foreign owner of U.S. Treasury securities, which helps finance federal debt and keeps U.S. interest rates low (CRS 2019).

Deng Shiaoping, who passed to the government in the last quarter of the twentieth century, initiated radical economic reforms. In this period, the Chinese market has entered a transition period from a controlled economy to a structure that is gradually opening up (Deniz 2014). The commercial and economic development of the country is generally based on these reforms and the strategy of opening up abroad. In China, while the central planning and control of the state prevailed until that period, collective companies and foreign capital institutions, which were under the control of local governments, draw attention as the main dynamics in the economy. The success of the reforms in these years are the effective taxation system, gradual price reforms, the introduction of new firms in the private sector and the increase in the efficiency of public firms (Kızıltan 2004). With the transition to the market system, the foundations of a state-controlled banking system in China have been laid and its economy has become even stronger.

During this period, China succeeded in attracting more foreign investments to its country, acquiring technology through imitation, reducing the burden on the public and providing support to large and efficient ones, especially by privatizing public economic enterprises that do not operate efficiently in imports. In 2001, China became a member of the World Trade Organization (WTO) and achieved faster integration into the global economy. Thus, the country has entered certain obligations on issues such as making its market more liberal and open to foreign capital (TOBB 2019). With this membership, a new period has started in China, serious increases have been seen in private sector investments, and the country's exports and economic growth have increased. With China's WTO membership, export figures have increased by $500 billion from 2001 to 2005. In the period of 2005–2011, Table 1 has doubled compared to the previous period and approached 1.9 trillion dollars.

Looking at the general economic indicators of China, it has been in an important economic development in the last 20 years. It is in steady development in almost all areas of the economy. In the process in question, it is one of the leading countries in the rare countries with such a picture worldwide. The gross domestic growth rate is above 9% on average in this 20-year period. It has reached incredible levels, especially in the process until 2007. Although it declined towards 7%, it achieved a certain stability. In fact, the density of its population keeps the country under pressure in this sense. It has also proved to be a very enviable success in per capita income. In the period from 2000 to 2018, per capita income increased by ten times and approached the level of developed countries. The income distribution problem is seen as a critical issue that needs more attention in the coming years.

Except for 3 years, it is not seen that China's exports decreased compared to the previous year, and it is constantly increasing. One of these years is the 2009 crisis year, the others are 2015 and 2016. Accordingly, it should be stated that its imports have increased in a similar way. Therefore, it can be said that its export is partly based on imports. The good thing is that it always gives foreign trade surplus. One of

Table 1 Economic indicators of China

Years	GDP growth (%)	GNI per cap. ($)	Export ($ billions)	Import ($ billions)	Trade balance ($ billions)	Global merchandise export (%)	Unemployment (%)
2000	8.4	940	249.2	225.1	24.1	4	3.1
2001	8.3	1010	266.2	243.6	22.6	4.4	3.6
2002	9.1	1110	325.6	295.2	30.4	5.2	4
2003	10	1280	438.4	412.8	25.6	6	4.3
2004	10.1	1510	593.4	561.4	32	6.7	4.2
2005	11.3	1760	762	660.1	101.9	7.5	4.2
2006	12.7	2060	969.1	791.5	177.6	8.2	4.1
2007	14.2	2510	1218.0	955.8	262.2	8.9	4
2008	9.6	3100	1428.9	1131.5	297.4	9.1	4.2
2009	9.2	3690	1202.0	1003.9	198.1	9.8	4.3
2010	10.6	4340	1578.4	1393.9	184.5	10.7	4.1
2011	9.5	5060	1899.3	1741.4	157.9	10.7	4.1
2012	7.9	5940	2050.1	1817.3	232.8	11.4	4.1
2013	7.8	6800	2210.7	1949.3	261.4	12	4.05
2014	7.3	7520	2343.2	1963.1	380.1	12.6	4.1
2015	6.9	7950	2280.5	1601.8	678.7	14.1	N/A
2016	6.7	8250	2135.3	1524.7	610.6	13.4	N/A
2017	6.8	8690	2279.2	1790	489.2	13.2	3.9
2018	6.6	9771	2491.4	2109	382.4	12.8	3.8

Source: GDP growth data from IMF (2019), Gross national income per capita and unemployment data from Worldbank (2020), Exports, imports and trade balance data from Global Trade Atlas and China's Customs Administration (GACC 2020), Global merchandise exports data from Economist Intelligence Unit

the most important indicators that make China stand out in the world economy is its share in global exports. Since 2000, it has become one of the leading countries by increasing its share in 4% levels by three times to 13%. Unemployment, which is one of the most important problems of developing countries, continues to be an important issue for China (Zhang et al. 2020). Despite the increase in the skilled workforce, the fact that there are still serious unemployment points to social problems in this field. Unemployment, which is one of the most important problems of developing countries, continues to be an important issue for China. Despite the increase in the skilled workforce, the fact that there are still serious unemployment points to social problems in this field.

According to Table 2, China's biggest three foreign trade markets were the United States, the European Union, ASEAN, 42 while its top sources for imports were the EU28, ASEAN, and South Korea. According to data, it maintained large trade surpluses with the United States ($323 billion), Hong Kong ($294 billion) and the European Union 28 ($135 billion) and reported large trade imbalances with Taiwan ($129 billion) and South Korea ($95 billion). China's trade data differs

Table 2 China's main merchandise trade partners in 2018 ($ billions)

Country	Total trade amount	Exports	Imports	Trade balance
EU (28)	681	408	273	135
USA	631	477	154	323
ASEAN	575	318	257	61
Japan	327	147	180	−33
South Korea	313	109	204	−95
Hong Kong	310	302	8	294
Taiwan	225	48	177	−129

Source: China's Customs Administration (GACC 2020)

significantly from those of many of its trading partners. These differences appear to be largely caused by how China's trade via Hong Kong is counted in official Chinese trade data. China treats a large share of its exports through Hong Kong as Chinese exports to Hong Kong for statistical purposes, while many countries that import Chinese products through Hong Kong generally attribute their origin to China for statistical purposes, including the United States.

4 Economic Relations Between China and USA

Since the last quarter of the twentieth century, China's growth rates are generally above the US and world growth rates. On the other hand, this country has only encountered almost no negative growth. Although the USA and the world displayed negative growth rates in the 2008–2009 Global Financial Crisis years, the Chinese economy continued to grow steadily. 1970s are accepted as the beginning of China and USA trade relations. In this process, China started to get closer with the USA and steered its foreign policy by recognizing the sovereignty of the USA in the international arena. While providing security against the Soviet Union, it used various privileges that its alliance gave to it to stabilize its economy. With the collapse of the Soviet Union, the interest of the USA in the central Asian region has increased. The reason for this is that China and Russia are trying to fill the power gap in this region. The USA started to fight with these countries by seeing the possibility of being a competitor in the future. This situation pushed China and Russia into an effort to balance the struggle. Geographically distant from this region has created a disadvantage for the USA until the September 11 attacks, but with the September 11 attacks, the USA has found the opportunity to besiege China and Russia by settling both in Afghanistan and Central Asia within the scope of the fight against terrorism (Aydın 2015).

The Beijing administration plays an active role in organizations especially in the East Asia Summit, the Shanghai Cooperation Organization, the China-Africa Cooperation Form. With this policy, China can reach its regional and global goals more easily, especially in foreign policy, it is in tighter relations with countries where the

Table 3 Foreign trade of China to USA (billions of US $)

Year	Total rrade	Exports	Imports	Trade balance
2012	536.1	425.6	110.5	315.1
2013	562.1	440.4	121.7	318.7
2014	592.1	468.4	123.7	344.7
2015	599	483.2	115.8	367.4
2016	578	462.5	115.5	347
2017	635.5	505.6	129.9	375.7
2018	659.8	539.5	120.3	419.2

Source: United States Census Bureau

USA does not develop good relations (IBP 2011). Another problem between the USA and China is that China entered into currency manipulation from 2003 to 2014. This manipulation is shown as the reason for most of the trade surplus, which constitutes 10% of China's GDP. During this period, the Obama administration took a tough attitude towards China. Obama Administration, which wants China to increase the value of its money, has passed laws calling on the US President to enforce tariffs on imports from China until the Yuan is adequately valued. Desiring to consolidate their presence in the global economy during this period, policy makers in China encouraged their companies to increase their strength in this economy. Within the framework of the globalization strategy, foreign investments, which are mainly under the control of the state, increased during the global crisis period and made China the capital exporter of the world.

From an economic perspective, trade relations with China benefit the US economy from the following aspects (Economics 2017). First, China is one of the main export markets to support the US market, and its importance as a commercial partner will continue to grow. Chinese investment in the United States supports the US market and overall economic growth. Second, Chinese investments keep the interest rates of the USA low, which provides more incentives for businesses and consumers in the USA. Third, China's role in the global supply chain increases US competitiveness and lowers inflation in the USA. Economic cooperation of these two countries can be defined as a relationship that includes hegemonic competition in the Pacific and includes suspicious approaches to each other. While one country sees its partner as a strong economic partner in this relationship, it also thinks as a potential competitor and develops policy accordingly.

As it can be understood from Table 3, China constantly has foreign trade surplus against the USA. This surplus is stable at around 350 billion dollars on average. Since it is not possible for the United States to eliminate such a deficit in the long term, it has become imperative that at some point it should stop. Therefore, trade wars emerged from here.

5 Literature Review

There are studies examining the effects of the US-China trade wars on the stock market. One of these works belongs to Öztürk and Altınöz (2019a, b). They examined the effects of the US-China trade war on the Shanghai Stock Exchange. In this study using ARDL bounds test, the period of 1991–2016 was taken into consideration. According to the results of the study, it was determined that the US-China trade war damaged the Chinese stock market. In addition, according to this study, it was emphasized that China was the loser in the trade war. Additionally, no comments were made for the USA on this issue such as the winner or the loser.

Moreover, Özer (2020) examined the effect of the US-China trade war on global trade. In this study, US export data to China and global export data were used as variables. In addition, the linear regression model was taken into account. The results of the analysis show that if the value of US exports to China increases by one unit, the value of global goods exports increased to 58 units. Furthermore, while trade wars reduce the export of goods from the USA to China, they have also declining effect on the export of global goods. Robinson and Thierfelder (2019) stated that the US-China trade war negatively affected both countries. According to the authors, the high tariffs of the USA and China increase the prices and this situation affects the demand negatively.

Mao and Görg (2019) examined the countries most affected by the US-China trade war. In the study, how the other countries are affected by this tariff was analyzed due to the import tariff applied by the USA to China. In the study where input-output tables were used, data analysis was also performed. As a result of the study, it was determined that the third most affected countries are Canada and Mexico which are the USA's trade partners. It is estimated that the tariffs bring about 500 to 600 million dollars overhead to these two countries (Mao and Görg 2019). Similarly, Pangestu (2019) examined the impact of the US-China trade war on the Indonesian economy. In the study, in which data analysis and literature review were conducted, it was revealed that the effect of the Chinese economy in the trade war of the USA had a negative effect on the Indonesian economy. Bolt et al. (2019) analyzed the impact of the US-China trade war on other regional and country economies. It was determined that the war in question created an opportunity for the European regional economy. As a result of this war, countries in the European region were able to import cheaper than China.

On the other side, Huang et al. (2018) tried to understand the market reactions of firms in the trade war. They reached the conclusion that the US firms that trade with China tend to perform lower on stock and bond returns in the financial market with the start of the trade war. For example, it is predicted that a 10% increase in the sales of companies in America to China reduces the average cumulative revenues in the stock market by 0.8%. Guo and Liu (2019) investigated the impact of the US-China trade war on domestic brands of consumers in China. In the analysis process, the survey method was taken into consideration. It is determined that the demand of Chinese consumers for domestic brands in the trade war increased and national consciousness was created in this issue. Similarly, Waugh (2019) analyzed the impact of the US-China trade war on automobile consumption by mathematical calculation. Consequently, it is identified that China's import policy against the import tariff of the USA caused a 3.8% decrease in automobile consumption imported from the USA.

Satoru et al. (2019) analyzed the impact of the US-China trade war on both countries using the IDE-GSM simulation model. According to the calculations made as a result of the study, the effect was found to be −0.4% for America and −0.6% for China. In addition, the US-China trade wars were found to have a 1.7% negative impact on the global economy. Moosa (2020) has criticized the assumption that import tariffs reduce the current account deficit and increase growth. In other words, the author has stated that the tariffs put on foreign trade affect the economic growth of the countries negatively. Ibrahim and Benjamin (2019) also examined the effect of US-China trade wars on the economies of the two countries using the literature review method. According to the results of the study, the import tariffs of the USA will affect the US economy negatively, but it will affect China positively. Therefore, it was emphasized that the trade war would be a policy in favor of China.

He et al. (2019) examined the US-China trade wars over agricultural trade. In this study, it is determined that soybean production in China is at a level that can respond to the trade war of the USA. However, it is seen as an important problem that soybean production also increases China's environmental costs. In this study, scenario and data analysis were used as a methodology. It was revealed that economic war damaged the sustainability of global agricultural production. Besides, it was stated that the trade barrier increased global environmental costs due to soybeans. The study recommends that China produce corn instead of soybeans in agriculture against the trade war of the USA.

Yu (2019) examined the effects that caused the US-China trade war. According to the study in question, the most important reason for this war is the increase of China's effectiveness in global markets. In the study using the literature review, it was suggested that China should increase its effectiveness in the markets with structural reforms. In the study using the literature review, it was suggested that China should require to increase its effectiveness in the markets with structural reforms. When the studies in the literature are evaluated, it is seen that there are very few studies examining the effect of the US-China trade war on the stock market. In this part of the book where the US-China trade war is described, testing the stock market effect with an empirical application will make also an important contribution to the literature.

6 Empirical Application

6.1 Data Set and Method

For the empirical application within the framework of the US and Chinese trade wars, the export data of the USA to China and the S&P 500 index, which is seen as the important stock exchange of the USA, is taken into consideration. Furthermore, China's export to the US and Shanghai stock market index, which is seen as the important stock exchange of China, is also used in the empirical application. In addition, four variables are taken into account. The first variable has called "cinex" that represents China's exports to the US in dollars. The second variable, "abdex" which is considered for the export of the USA to China. The variable "sp500" has represented the stock market index of the USA and the variable "shanghai" has represented the stock market index of China. US exports to China and Shangai Stock Exchange index data is used in the study. The data cover the period from November 2016 to June 2019. In the empirical application, the data is taken into account monthly. The reason why the beginning of the semester is preferred as 2016 in the study can be shown as the start of the US-China trade wars as of this year (Gün 2019; Ertürk 2017; Aran 2018; Kaya 2019; Gün 2018).

Engle-Granger cointegration test is used as a method in the study. The Engle-Granger cointegration test is a method that measures the presence of a long-term relationship between two variables which was brought to stability for the same level. In this regard, this method is taken into consideration in this study (Engle and Granger 1987). In the first stage of cointegration analysis, a regression is established between the two variables that are the first-order stationary.

In the second stage, the error terms are obtained from this analysis. If the residues contain a unit root, therefore there is no cointegration relationship between the two variables (Alhan and Yüksel 2018; Külünk 2018; Yıldırım 2016). In this study, unit root and cointegration tests were done on Eviews 9 program. Using the mentioned models, the hypotheses below have been tested:

H_0: There is no long-term relationship between China's export to the US and the Chinese stock market.

H_0: There is no long-term relationship between US exports to China and the US stock exchange.

6.2 Findings

In this section, which examines the effect of the US-China trade wars on the stock exchanges, unit root tests of the variables were made. The prerequisite for performing the Engle-Granger cointegration test is that the variables subject to the analysis are the first-degree stationary. The unit root test shows whether the series are stationary. If there is no stationarity in a time series, the difference of that series is

Table 4 ADF unit root test

	İntercept and trend		İntercept	
Variable	*t*-statistic I(0)	Prob. I(0)	*t*-statistic I(1)	Prob. I(1)
Cinex	−2.222725	0.4607	−4.778145	0.0006*
Abdex	−3.320089	0.0817***	−6.248741	0.0000*
Shanghai	−2.000949	0.5780	−5.440026	0.0001*
sp500	−2.940793	0.1643	−6.787324	0.0000*

Note: *, *** symbols represent 1% and 10% significance levels, respectively

Table 5 Engle-Granger cointegration results

	Level	
	Residuals series	Prob.
Cinhata	−4.679860 (7)	0.0008*
Abdhata	−5.913681(7)	0.0000*

Note: * symbol represents 1% significance levels

taken until it is stationary. Different tests can be used for stationary research. The most basic of these are Dickey and Fuller (1979) and Augmented Dickey–Fuller Test (1981). In our study, the Augmented Dickey-Fuller (ADF) Test, which is one of the unit root test applications and used widely in the literature, is taken into consideration (Ersin 2018; Kurum and Oktar 2019; Canöz 2018; Baş and Kocakaya 2020; Ersin and Karakeçe 2020).

When the unit root test results given in Table 4 are analyzed, it is seen that other variables other than "abdex" are not stationary at the level. Moreover, the "abdex" variable seems to be also stationary at a level of 10% significance. But, in accordance with the Engle-Granger cointegration prerequisite, the first-degree difference of the "abdex" variable was taken. Thus, all the variables to be analyzed are brought stationary from the first degree.

After the unit root tests of the variables are taken, the regression model is established for the Engle-Granger test as we mentioned earlier. After the regression model is also established, the residual series is created, and the stationarity of the residual series is checked. Engle-Granger cointegration test results are given in Table 5. The variable "cinhata" in Table 5 constitutes the residual series of the regression model based on the variables "cinex" and "shanghai". The variable "abdhata" in Table 5 represents the residual series of the regression model based on the variables "abdex" and "sp500".

In other words, a long-term relationship has been detected between China's exports to the USA and the Chinese stock market. Similarly, a long-term relationship has been detected also between the export of the USA to China and the US stock exchange. These results show that trade wars affect both countries mutually. It is seen important that is considered the USA and China economy, which have a significant impact on the world economy, take this relationship into consideration. Because the damage of the two major economies of the world due to this war can affect the economies of interrelated other countries.

7 Conclusion

China is one of the fastest rising economies in the world economy that has not shrunk in terms of economic performance for a long time. In addition, the fact that the USA, which is the strongest economy in the world, had serious problems in the economy with the 2007 global crisis, weakened the USA's effectiveness in the market. Using this gap, China has made a rapid rise in the economy. With the introduction of the Trump administration, economic relations between China and the US have experienced problematic processes since 2016. The trade war officially started with the import tariffs applied by Trump to China. The impact of the trade war on the economies of the two countries is discussed in point of can affect other countries as well.

The important economic institutions that the US-China trade war will affect are undoubtedly the stock exchanges. In this section, the relationship of the export of the USA to China with the S&P 500 stock exchange and the relationship of the export of China to the US with the Shanghai stock exchange has been examined empirically. Analysis results show that there is a long-term relationship between exports and stock markets. According to these results, the stock markets of the USA and China are affected by trade wars. Therefore, both countries need a mutual agreement on this issue. This agreement is necessary with the idea that the economies of other countries may also be affected.

References

Alhan, O., & Yüksel, S. (2018). Kadın Çalışanların Banka Büyüklüğü ve Karlılığına Etkisi: Engle-Granger Eş Bütünleşme Analizi İle Türkiye Üzerine Bir Uygulama. *İş'te Davranış Dergisi, 3*(2), 140–147.

Aran, B. (2018). ABD Çin Ticaret Savaşları ve Türkiye. Türkiye Ekonomi Politikaları Araştırma Vakfı Değerlendirme Notu, https://www.tepav.org.tr/tr/haberler/s/4331. *Erişim tarihi, 12*(07), 2019.

Aydın, A. (2015). Küresel Mücadele Politikaları: Orta Asya'da Rusya, ABD ve Çin. Suleyman Demirel University. *The Journal of Visionary, 6*(13), 1–11.

Baş, H., & Kocakaya, M. E. (2020). Identifying the relationship between health expenditures and life expectancy at birth: A Cointegration analysis for MENA countries. In Y. D. Uslu, H. Dinçer, & S. Yüksel (Eds.), *Multidimensional perspectives and global analysis of universal health coverage* (pp. 285–308). Hershey, PA: IGI Global.

Bolt, W., Mavromatis, K., & van Wijnbergen, S. (2019). *The global macroeconomics of a trade war: The EAGLE model on the US-China trade conflict* (DNB Working Papers 623). Netherlands Central Bank, Research Department.

Canöz, İ. (2018). Borsa İstanbul 100 Endeksi ile Tüketici Güven Endeksleri Arasındaki Nedensellik İlişkisi: Türkiye Örneği. *Fiscaoeconomia, 2*(1), 136–153.

Chong, T. T.-L., & Li, X. (2019, February). Understanding China-US trade war: Causes, economic impact, and the worst-case scenario. *Economic and Political Studies, 7*(2), 1–21.

CRS. (2019). *China's economic rise: History, trends, challenges, and implications for the United States*. Washington, DC: Congressional Research Service.

Deniz, T. (2014). Yükselen Güç Çin Halk Cumhuriyeti'nin Stratejik Hamleleri. *Electronic Journal of Social Sciences, 13*(50), 188–212.

Dickey, D. A., & Fuller, W. A. (1979). Distribution of the estimators for autoregressive time series with a unit root. *Journal of the American Statistical Association, 74*(366a), 427–431.

Dıckey, D., & Fuller, W. (1981). Likelihood ratio statistics for autogressive time series with a unit root. *Econometrica, 49*, 1052–1072.

Dinçer, H., Yüksel, S., & Pınarbaşı, F. (2020). Kano-based measurement of customer expectations in retail service industry using IT2 DEMATEL-QUALIFLEX. In E. Baykal (Ed.), *Handbook of research on positive organizational behavior for improved workplace performance* (pp. 349–370). Hershey, PA: IGI Global.

Engle, R. F., & Granger, C. W. (1987). Co-integration and error correction: Representation, estimation, and testing. *Econometrica: Journal of the Econometric Society, 55*, 251–276.

Ersin, İ. (2018). İhracata Dayalı Büyüme Hipotezinin Test Edilmesi: MINT Ülkeleri Örneği. *Ekonomi İşletme ve Maliye Araştırmaları Dergisi, 1*(1), 26–38.

Ersin, İ., & Karakeçe, E. (2020). Analysis of the effects of macroeconomic factors on entrepreneurship: An application on E7 countries. In H. Dinçer & S. Yüksel (Eds.), *Handbook of research on decision-making techniques in financial marketing* (pp. 412–428). Hershey, PA: IGI Global.

Ertürk, N. (2017). Ticaret Savaşları ve Dünya Ekonomisine Etkileri. *Fiscaoeconomia, 1*(2), 88–112.

GACC. (2020, January 25). *The General Administration of Customs of the People's Republic of China (GACC)*. Tarihinde the general Administration of Customs of the People's Republic of China website: http://english.customs.gov.cn/about/annualReports/adresinden alındı

Gün, M. (2018). The co-movement of credit default swaps and stock markets in emerging economies. *Fınance & Econometrıcs, 55*. https://doi.org/10.2139/ssrn.2000057.

Gün, M. (2019). Cointegration between carbon emission, economic growth, and energy consumption: A comparative study on Georgia and Turkey. *International Journal of Economic & Administrative Studies, 22*. https://doi.org/10.18092/ulikidince.397486.

Guo, H., & Liu, Z. Y. (2019). A study of consumers' purchasing intention for national brands in the context of Sino-US trade war-take China Huawei Company as an exle. *Journal of the Korea Society of Computer and Information, 24*(9), 127–134.

He, R., Zhu, D., Chen, X., Cao, Y., Chen, Y., & Wang, X. (2019). How the trade barrier changes environmental costs of agricultural production: An implication derived from China's demand for soybean caused by the US-China trade war. *Journal of Cleaner Production, 227*, 578–588.

Huang, Y., Lin, C., Liu, S., & Tang, H. (2018). *Trade linkages and firm value: Evidence from the 2018 US–China trade war*. Available at SSRN 3227972.

IBP. (2011). *China foreign policy and government guide* (Vol. 1). Washington, DC: International Business.

Ibrahim, S. G., & Benjamin, M. U. (2019). Us-Chına trade war: Makıng Amerıca great again or a symbolic decline of an Empıre? *African Journal of Economics and Sustainable Development, 2* (2), 39–55.

IMF. (2019). *World economic outlook database*. Washington, DC: International Monetary Fund.

Kalkavan, H., & Ersin, I. (2019). Determination of factors affecting the South East Asian crisis of 1997 probit-logit panel regression: The South East Asian crisis. In H. Dinçer & S. Yuksel (Eds.), *Handbook of research on global issues in financial communication and investment decision making* (pp. 148–167). Hershey, PA: IGI Global.

Kaya, M. (2019). ABD-Çin Ticaret Savaşları ve Türkiye. *Türkiye Mesleki ve Sosyal Bilimler Dergisi, 2*, 18–30.

Kızıltan, A. (2004). Tek Kutuplu Bir Dünyada Çin Halk Cumhuriyeti'nin "Süpergüç" Olabilirliği. *C.Ü. İktisadi ve İdari Bilimler Dergisi, 5*(1), 45–66.

Külünk, İ. (2018). Türkiye'de Ekonomik Büyüme ve Karbon Salınımı İlişkisi: Engle-Granger Eşbütünleşme Analizi (1960–2013). *Yönetim ve Ekonomi Araştırmaları Dergisi, 16*(1), 193–205.

Kurum, M. E., & Oktar, S. (2019). Zorunlu Karşılık Politikasının Enflasyon Üzerindeki Etkisi: Türkiye Örneği. *Ekonomi İşletme ve Maliye Araştırmaları Dergisi, 1*(3), 186–204.

Mallick, M. G. (2018). *US-China trade war: Analyses of deeper nuances and wider implications*. New Delhi: Vivekananda International Foundation.

Mao, H., & Görg, H. (2019). *Friends like this: The impact of the US-China trade war on global value chains* (KCG Working Papers No. 17). Kiel Centre for Globalization (KCG).

Moosa, I. A. (2020). The Thucydides trap as an alternative explanation for the US–China trade war. *Global Journal of Emerging Market Economies, 12*(1), 42–55. https://doi.org/10.1177/0974910119896644.

Özer, A. C. (2020). The effect of the US-China trade war on global trade. In A. Coskun Özer (Ed.), *International trade policies in the era of globalization* (pp. 56–70). Hershey, PA: IGI Global.

Öztürk, S., & Altınöz, B. (2019a). The effect of US-Chına trade wars on Shanghaı stock exchange Composıte index. *Afyon Kocatepe Üniversitesi İktisadi ve İdari Bilimler Fakültesi Dergisi, 21* (1), 59–69.

Öztürk, S., & Altınöz, B. (2019b). The effect of US-China trade wars on Shanghai stock exchange composite index. *KOCATEPEİİBF Dergisi, 21*(1), 59–69.

Pangestu, M. (2019). China–US trade war: An Indonesian perspective. *China Economic Journal, 12*(2), 208–230.

Rassekh, F. (2015). Comparative advantage in Smith's wealth of nations and Ricardo's principles: A brief history of its early development. *History of Economic Ideas, 23*(1), 59–75.

Robinson, S., & Thierfelder, K. (2019). *US-China trade war: Both countries lose, world markets adjust, others gain* (No. PB19-17).

Satoru, K., Toshitaka, G., Kenmei, T., Ikumo, I., & Kazunobu, H. (2019). *Economic impacts of the US-China trade war on the Asian economy: An applied analysis of IDE-GSM* (No. 760). IDE Discussion Paper.

TOBB. (2019). *2018 Ekonomik Raporu*. Ankara: TOBB Yayınları.

Waugh, M. E. (2019). *The consumption response to trade shocks: Evidence from the US-China trade war* (No. w26353). National Bureau of Economic Research.

Worldbank. (2020). *World development report 2020: Trading for development in the age of global value chains*. Washington, DC: World Bank Group.

Yıldırım, C. (2016). Tüketici Fiyat Endeksi ile Faiz Orani İlişkisinin Ekonometrik Bir İncelemesi. *Kastamonu Üniversitesi İktisadi ve İdari Bilimler Fakültesi Dergisi, 12*(2), 431–445.

Yılmaz, M., & Divani, E. (2018). Trade wars, economic nationalism, neo mercantilism and Disfunctionality of the World Trade Organization. *İzmir Katip Çelebi Üniversitesi İktisadi ve İdari Bilimler Fakültesi Dergisi, 1*(1), 10–24.

Yılmaz, S. S., Özdemir, M. G., & Gencer, Ü. (2019). *USA-China Trade Wars. UBAK Uluslararası Bilimler Akademisi- Munzur 1. Uluslararası Sosyal Bilimler Kongresi* (pp. 296–316). Tunceli: UBAK Uluslararası Bilimler Akademisi.

Yu, M. (2019). The status of China's market economy and structural reforms: The issues behind the US–China trade war. *Asian Economic Papers, 18*(3), 34–51.

Zhang, G., Zhou, S., Xia, X., Yüksel, S., Baş, H., & Dincer, H. (2020). Strategic mapping of youth unemployment with interval-valued intuitionistic hesitant fuzzy DEMATEL based on 2-tuple linguistic values. *IEEE Access, 8*, 25706–25721.

Brand Coolness in a Competitive Environment: An Empirical Study on Starbucks Turkey

Ayşen Akyüz and Fatih Pınarbaşı

Abstract Brand-consumer relationship is a major area of research for many years and many aspects of brand related concepts have been studied in different contexts. As being one of the fundamental brand phenomenons, brand personality has long been a question of interest among researchers. Brand coolness is a new topic in brand literature and a few studies have explored this concept empirically. In this exploratory study, the brand coolness of Starbucks, the significance levels related to frequency of coffee consumption and brand coolness' characteristics and the relationship of brand coolness and attitude towards Starbucks Turkey are being explored. Three hundred and seven surveys, collected from university students between the dates of 17th and 20th of November, 2019, were taken into analysis. *t*-test and correlation analysis were conducted and findings have been indicated in the study.

1 Introduction

Managing brand-consumer relationships in a competitive market environment with increasing technology and volatile economic conditions is a main task and a real challenge for marketing decision-makers in recent years. As the environmental conditions are instable, the changing needs of consumers and actions of competitors are becoming compelling for marketers. According to Nielsen (2019), 42% of global consumers love trying new things, search actively for new products or brands, while 49% of them are more conventional and they prefer "known". Brand-consumer relationships are more evident and mandatory for today's marketing, and it is

A. Akyüz (✉)
School of Communication, Istanbul Medipol University, İstanbul, Turkey
e-mail: aakyuz@medipol.edu.tr

F. Pınarbaşı
School of Business, Istanbul Medipol University, İstanbul, Turkey
e-mail: fpinarbasi@medipol.edu.tr

H. Dincer, S. Yüksel (eds.), *Strategic Priorities in Competitive Environments*, Contributions to Management Science, https://doi.org/10.1007/978-3-030-45023-6_17

essential to evaluate consumers in various modes both positive (Batra et al. 2012) and negative (Pinarbasi and Enginkaya 2019) side and for several situations like crisis communication (Akyüz 2019).

Brand-consumer relationship includes a variety of demands and conditions. Understanding the customer insight, solve the buyer's black box riddle, discerning their needs, wants and demands are the focal point for marketing and branding efforts today.

In brand-consumer relationship, brand personality always have had a prominent role with regards to its unique contributions to brand equity development for brand management. Brand personality concept includes characteristics associated with brand (Aaker 1997), and it reflects the attributes of brands from consumers' perceptions. Understanding how consumers perceive brands, how they link images/identities with brand associations are important topics for marketing decision making. On the other hand, brand coolness -a relatively new concept- refers to positive and distinctive attributes for brands. Coolness is a social construction. It is an attribution bestowed by the consumers to the brand. As consumers value brand coolness for decision making, it is essential to understand how coolness is constructed and how brands can differentiate in terms of coolness. Brand coolness has important contributions to marketing research related to consumer decision making and buying process, furthermore managerial implications can also be derived.

This study examines brand coolness from the consumer perspective and aims to understand the perceived brand coolness towards Starbucks Turkey. It starts with literature review, which includes brand identity, personality and brand coolness concepts. Brand personality reflects the traits for brands in general, while brand coolness concept is related to the positive side of brand traits perceived by consumers. Following the theoretical section, an empirical research section with findings is included to present results for Starbuck Turkey's brand coolness.

2 Literature Review

Brand identity is a broader term than brand personality. Brand identity covers personality; so the authors find relevant to start with brand identity before elaborating personality.

Aaker (1996, p. 68), defines brand identity as "*a unique set of brand associations that the brand strategist aspires to create or maintain. These associations represent what the brand stands for and imply a promise to customers from organization members*". Kapferer (2012), indicates that brand identity is a key concept of brand management and it is on the sender's side. The goal is to determine the brand's meaning, aim and self-image.

Roll (2015), states that internally, the identity guides all strategic branding decisions, such as communication and brand/line extension and externally, it provides customers with what the brand stands for, its essence, promises, and personality. Corporate management should always consider six facets while developing brand identity: (1). Brand vision: an internal document that shows the future direction for the brand, its desired role and status that the brand hopes to achieve. It describes the brand's objectives relates to strategy and finance. (2). Brand scope: a detailed subset of brand vision and describes growth opportunities for the brand. (3). Brand positioning: the place a brand endeavors to occupy in the minds of the customers. (4). Brand personality: the set of human characteristics associated with a brand. (5). Brand essence: covers what the brand is all about, what makes it unique and what it stands for; illustrating the core of the brand. (6). Brand guardrails: basic and clear articulation of what the brand "is" and what the brand "is not." (Roll 2015).

Kapferer (2012) as well mentions about six facets which define the identity of a brand. The brand identity prism demonstrates that the facets are all interrelated and form a highly organized entity. First of all, a brand, has physique. It has physical specificities and qualities. Physique is the brand's backbone and also its tangible added value. Second, a brand has a personality which can grow into a character. Third, a brand is a culture. A brand represents much more than personality or product benefits; it represents an ideology and major brands convey their cultures. Fourth, a brand is a relationship. Brands are often at the core of transactions and exchanges between people. Fifth, a brand is a customer reflection. It is the outward mirror of the customer. A brand will always tend to create an image of the buyer which it seems to be addressing. Finally, a brand addresses to an individual's self-image. Self-image is the target's own internal mirror. Through their attitudes towards certain brands, individuals develop a certain type of inner relationship with themselves.

According to Kapferer (2012), the product is the first source of brand identity. A brand displays its uniqueness through the products it chooses to endorse. It puts its values in the production and distribution process and its values must therefore be represented in the brand's highly symbolic products. Second source of brand identity is the name of the brand. Names can be selected with rational reasons (implying what the product does or the function of it) and with subjective reasons. Examining a brands name can lead individuals to learn its program and intentions. Brand characters serve as a source of identity as well. An emblem serves to symbolize brand identity through a visual figure and it has functions as helping to identify brand, guaranteeing the brand, differentiating the brand or giving the brand durability. An emblem transfers its personality to the brand and therefore enhances brand value. Some brands have chosen to be represented by a character. A character can be the brand's creator, a celebrity endorser or the direct symbol of the brand's qualities as the Michelin bibendum. Some characters serve to establish build an emotional link between the brand and its target market; on the other hand other characters might serve as brand ambassadors. Visual symbols and logos play an important role as being source of brand identity along with geographical and historical roots and the brand's creators (Kapferer 2012).

Akyüz and Akgün (2011) states that, there are many brands introduced to the market by small and large companies in present day and not all these brands can create the same effect on consumers. Brands that are able to develop successful brand personality would gain advantage in competitive environment, and loyal customer communities who match themselves with the personality of those brands would be formed (Dinçer et al. 2020). The concept of brand personality is based on the assumption that brands have personality traits and emotions like people. A brand can carry characteristics such as gender, age, and it can also be associated with personality traits such as cheerful or intelligent.

Brand personality is one of the main concepts in brand literature, and it is defined as "the set of human characteristics associated with a brand" (Aaker 1997). In another definition, brand personality refers to "the unique set of human personality traits both applicable and relevant to brands" (Azoulay and Kapferer 2003). Brand personality concept reflects the personal traits/characteristics for brands and consistent to the aim of the study; it is the starting point for understanding evaluation of brand coolness for consumers.

Beyond the definitions of brand personality, the exact position of brand personality for brand-consumer relationships is essential. Schmitt (2012) presents a model for consumers' psychology of brands and segments the consumers' psychology into five main parts; identifying, connecting, experiencing, signifying and integrating. Each part has three different engagement levels, and brand personality concept in the model refers to self-centered engagement level and integrating part of consumers' psychology. Self-centered engagement level implies the stage that brands are relevant to consumers and the integration part refers to combining process of brand information into overall brand concept, personality and relationship with the brand.

In historical perspective, Lara-Rodríguez et al. (2019) investigate brand personality concept in their bibliometric analysis and presented a timeline for the concept beginning from 1957. Wells et al. (1957)'s study which presents adjective check list for product personality is the starting point of the timeline. On the other side, Ekinci and Hosany (2006), points out that product/brand personality studies go back to the '60s with two main approaches; idiographic and nomothetic. They imply that the idiographic approach is related to capturing of uniqueness of each product, while the nomothetic approach refers to a collection of distinctive traits defining product personality with abstractions.

The theoretical framework proposed by Aaker (1997) includes five main dimensions for brand personality; sincerity, excitement, competence, sophistication and ruggedness as called The Big Five. Each of the five factors have been divided into facets as, Sincerity is related to down-to-earth, sincere, real and wholesome attributes, while excitement dimension refers to exciting, daring, imaginative and up-to-date traits. Competence dimension includes the facets as reliable, intelligent and successful traits, while sophistication refers to upper class, charming characteristics and ruggedness is related to outdoorsy and tough traits. According to (Aaker 1996), product related characteristics of a brand can be primary driver of personality. For ex, a bank company would tend to have a "banker" personality as serious, masculine, etc.; or Nike would tend to have personality traits such as ruggedness, young and lively. Non-product related characteristics such as CEO identification, country of origin or advertising strategies, sponsorship, etc. affect personality as well.

As Aaker (1997)'s framework is mostly used framework for measuring brand personality, there are some studies which re-evaluate or examine the topic with different contexts. For example, Grohmann (2009) evaluates gender dimensions of brand personality in terms of self congruity and consumers responses. In 2009, Geuens et al. (2009) re-examine brand personality measurement phenomenon and conclude five factors for brand personality; activity, responsibility, aggressiveness, simplicity and emotionality.

Relationship of brand personality with other brand constructs and consumer-related concepts has been interest of many studies as they employ several variables. For example, Sung and Kim (2010) study brand personality with brand trust and brand affect while they conclude sincerity and ruggedness are more likely to be related to brand trust level (than brand affect), excitement and sophistication are more likely to be related to brand affect (than brand trust). Other researchers evaluate different variables for brand personality-related studies, like brand loyalty (Lin 2010), attachment styles (Swaminathan et al. 2008) and perceived quality (Ramaseshan and Tsao 2007). The variety and scope of brand personality concepts indicate possible brand/consumer related outcomes or antecedents for future research. This study focuses on brand coolness concept in terms of brand-related dimension.

Apart from concepts/constructs side of brand personality, the concept has been subject of interest in several contexts including; tourism (Ekinci and Hosany 2006; Murphy et al. 2007), sport (Lee and Cho 2009; Carlson and Donavan 2013), restaurant (Murase and Bojanic 2004; Musante et al. 2008) and education (Watkins and Gonzenbach 2013; Rauschnabel et al. 2016).

Aaker (1996), proposed three models exhibiting brand personality's effect on consumer buying process. The first model is "Self Expression Model". Self-expression model remarks that a person can express himself over a brand; a brand can be a vehicle for articulating their self-identities and life styles. If a brand fits one's ideal self or own self, individuals experience satisfaction and feel comfortable. Substantial social impacts can come with badge brands. Consumers can evaluate each other's personal identities via the car driven or the bag worn. The second model is "Relationship Basis Model" which refers to the emotional bond established between the individual and brand. Aaker (1996) defines the brand as a friend of the consumer. In this relationship, both sides act as active partners. A brand has an identity and this identity helps creating its personality along with the strategies held by the company. So if a brand advertises widely, it can be perceived as outgoing or if it undertakes frequent discounts it can be thought to be a cheap brand. So not only an individual's actions influence other people's perception of his or her personality; but also a brand's behavior can influence the perceptions about its personality. The third model is "Functional Benefit Representational Model". It points out that a brand personality can act as a means of representing and suggesting brand attributes as well as functional benefits. The capability to strengthen brand attributes would be greater if there is a visual symbol or image exists which can cues or create personality like Michelin man's personality cueing a tire with energy and strength. In addition, country of origin can suggest attributions about quality and credibility about a brand and help brand differentiate itself among others (Aaker 1996).

It is paramount to define brand personality which can also be called as personification for companies in order to establish meaningful relations with its consumers.

Companies use brand personality to differentiate themselves from the competitors, to be recognized immediately, to establish emotional bond with consumer which can then create brand loyalty.

Understanding consumers' minds in a competitive marketplace is a significant process for today's marketing decision making. Coolness concept is one of the crucial elements in brand management practices as it is related to consumers' minds and perceptions. Today's marketing decision-makers must understand how consumers perceive brands as cool/uncool, authentic, likeable or not. For example, CoolBrands (2019) presents top coolest brands with a selection process including both experts and public votes.

Defining cool concept is a complicated process since it has been defined in various ways and expressions. Warren et al. (2019) include 70 different definitions for coolness concept in their study while they focus on one definition for their study developing a scale for brand coolness. The selected definition refers to; "a subjective and dynamic, socially constructed positive trait attributed to cultural objects inferred to be appropriately autonomous" (Warren and Campbell 2014). The main points indicated in definition; subjective, dynamic, positivity and autonomy can be studied in marketing and brand contexts.

The subjective side of coolness is consistent to the historical investigation of coolness concept in marketing and consumer contexts starts with individual perspective and "current"/"trend" perspective. For example, O'Donnell and Wardlow (2000) evaluate roots of coolness concept as they examine individuals' early adolescence and discrepancy between actual and ideal selves. Becoming cool in youth or a group environment is one of the starting points in coolness research. In addition to the individual perspective, brands as the entities which have "personalities" are the other side of coolness concept.

The positive side of coolness refers to positive traits/features of brands perceived by consumers. For instance; Rahman (2013) examines cool meaning for marketing while reviewing describing terms for the term cool and concludes them as; fashionable, amazing, sophisticated, unique, entertaining, eye-catching and composed. These findings emphasize the positive side of coolness.

Dynamic or time dimension is one of the essential elements for brand coolness concept, and it is consistent to the dynamic nature of coolness. Warren et al. (2019) indicate a lifecycle which brand coolness follow a path starting from niche cool to mass cool and finishes with losing coolness. Managing coolness for brand is difficult as Belk et al. (2010) states "...today's cool becomes tomorrow's uncool". This study focuses on the overall brand coolness of a brand rather than dynamic side of brand coolness.

Beyond the main elements of coolness, the construction of coolness by parties arises as an important issue. Constructing of coolness in brand context is examined in Gurrieri (2009)'s study with three different parties; marketers, cool hunters and consumers. Discourse analysis is employed in the study for evaluating the construction of coolness and discourses founds in the study refer to value, social networks, progressiveness and unconventionality. Marketers and cool hunters share common discourses, while the consumer party uses varying language and meanings for constructing a cool brand identity, in addition to having common discourses. Difference between the marketer side and consumer side needs to be researched as cool construct is subjective and socially constructed. On the other hand, Runyan et al. (2013) review coolness and classify as hedonic cool and utilitarian cool. In the study, five first-order factors are concluded; singular, personal, aesthetic, quality and functional cool.

Brand coolness concept has been evaluated with different sub-dimensions in marketing research. For example, Sriramachandramurthy and Hodis (2010) propose brand coolness with five dimensions; uniqueness, excitement, authenticity, innovation and self-image congruity. On the other hand, brand coolness is formed and examined with ten sub-dimensions in Warren et al. (2019)'s study. They conclude dimensions as extraordinary, energetic, aesthetically appealing, original, authentic, energetic, rebellious, high status, subcultural, iconic and popular.

Cultures are important factors affecting brand personality construct (Aaker et al. 2001; Sung and Tinkham 2005; Matzler et al. 2016). Warren et al. (2019) also conclude evaluating brand coolness in cross-cultural way would help to improve understanding of brand coolness construct. This study starts with the extending construct with different context idea and aims to evaluate brand coolness concept in Turkey context with Starbucks coffee brand.

3 Research Design and Methodology

The purpose of the study is to measure brand coolness perception of Turkish university students towards Starbucks; determining which brand coolness characteristics are prominent and explore the relationship of coolness characters with attitude.

In this study, questionnaire which was prepared in a single form was used in order to collect data. During the preparation of the survey questions, care was taken to ensure that the respondents easily understand the statements. Twenty-seven questions were prepared as in the form of dual-choice, closed-ended, and 5-point Likert scale. Respondents rate the degree to which they agree or disagree with each statement on a 5-point Likert scale going from "strongly agree" to "strongly disagree". The data collection phase of the study was performed between the dates, 17–20 of November, 2019. The selection of respondents was made by simple sampling method and sampling group was selected among university students. Within the above-mentioned period, the respondents were reached via Instagram, and they were requested to answer the questionnaire by giving link to Webanketa site where the questionnaire was hosted. In order to enable the completion of the questionnaire for only one time by each user, IP protected limitation was arranged. A total of 307 questionnaires were filled and later on, the statistical analyses were performed on these questionnaires. Survey covers both the coffee drinkers and non-coffee drinkers.

In the preparation stage of the survey questions, the scale developed by Warren et al. (2019) has been adapted for measuring coolness. The variables in the study "Brand Coolness" have been taken and a pre-test was applied on 60 students. According to the results of the pre-test, the questionnaire for our study has been developed by taking out some sub-themes tested in Warren et al.'s (2019) "Brand Coolness" study. The authors developed a model that includes ten brand coolness themes. In Warren et al.'s study "extraordinary" theme of brand coolness includes useful/exceptional, helps people/superb, valuable/fantastic, extraordinary characteristics; in our study we used valuable and extraordinary. "Energetic" theme includes energetic, outgoing, lively, vigorous; we included energetic and lively variables in our study depending on pre-test results. "Aesthetically Appealing" theme includes looks good, aesthetically appeling, attractive, has a really nice appearance; we took out aesthetically appealing and has a really nice appearance since they did not present a meaningful result in pre-test. "Original" theme includes innovative, original, does its own thing, we took original and innovative characteristics in our study. "Authentic" theme includes the titles, authentic, true to its roots, does not seem artificial, does not try to be something it's not in Warren et al.'s study. In our study we tested authentic and true to its roots under authentic theme. "Rebellious" includes rebellious, defiant, nonconformist and not afraid to break rules. We tested defiant and rebellious characteristics of brand coolness. "High status" component of brand coolness has chick, glamorous, ritzy, sophisticated and we took sophisticated and glamorous titles. "Popular" theme consists of liked by most people, in style, popular and widely accepted. While developing the final questionnaire, we took popular and liked by most people titles in to our research. "Subcultural" theme includes makes people who use it different from other people, if I were to use it, it would make me stand apart from others, helps people who use it stand apart from the crowd, people who use this brand are unique. Our study comprised, makes people who use it different from other people and helps people who use it stand apart from the crowd statements. "Iconic" theme included cultural and iconic characteristics and both were used in our research. Survey also includes questions regarding attitude towards Starbucks. Attitude questions have been adapted from Gwinner and Bennett (2008).

3.1 Statistical Analysis of the Data

For statistical analyses, SPSS 22.0 program is used. Descriptive statistical methods are used such as percentage, mean, standard deviation while assessing the data. The *t*-test was used to compare quantitative continuous data between two independent groups, and the One-way Anova test was used to compare quantitative continuous data between more than two independent groups. Scheffe test was used as a complementary post-hoc analysis to determine the differences after the Anova test. Pearson correlation analysis was applied among the continuous variables of the study. Reliability analysis of the scale regarding brand coolness and attitude are found to be high with a Cronbach's Alpha = 0.931 and 0.852 respectively.

3.2 Findings

This section includes the findings obtained as a result of the analysis of the data collected from the participants participating in the research. Explanations and comments were made based on the findings obtained (Tables 1, 2, 3, 4, and 5).

Table 1 Descriptive data

Group	Frequency (*n*)	Percentage (%)
Gender		
Women	213	69.4
Men	94	30.6
Coffee consumption		
Consuming	289	94.1
Not consuming	18	5.9
Routine of coffee consumption		
I do not drink coffee	18	5.9
I drink coffee every few months	5	1.6
I drink coffee once or more than once in a month	26	8.5
I drink coffee once or more than once in a week	98	31.9
I drink coffee everyday	160	52.1
Frequency of coffee consumption		
Not drinking coffee everyday	147	47.9
Drinking coffee everyday	160	52.1
Reasons for drinking coffee		
To stay awake	55	19.0
To get rid of drowsiness	81	28.0
For gaining energy	93	32.2
Liking its taste	203	70.2
Rewarding oneself	73	25.3
To have a break from daily rush	132	45.7
To focus better	68	23.5

Results as can be seen in Table 1, show that the 69.4% of the respondents are women and 30.6% of the respondents are consisting of men. 5.9% of the respondents stated that they do not consume coffee in contrast to 94.1% who consume coffee. According to frequency of coffee consumption variable, it is observed that 52.1% of the participants are every day coffee drinkers whereas 1.6% consume coffee every few months. Majority of the respondents (70.2%) drink coffee because they like its taste; nonetheless 45.7% drink coffee to have a break from daily rush and 32.2% of respondents for gaining energy

Table 2 Mean scores of brand coolness factors and attitude

	N	Mean	SD	Min.	Max.
Attitude	307	3.806	0.925	1.000	5.000
Extraordinary • Is valuable • Is extraordinary	307	3.393	0.935	1.000	5.000
Energetic • Is energetic • Is lively	307	3.467	0.938	1.000	5.000
Aesthetically appealing • Is attractive • Looks good	307	3.528	1.065	1.000	5.000
Original • Is original • Is innovative	307	3.603	0.990	1.000	5.000
Authentic • Is authentic • Is true to its roots	307	3.484	0.913	1.000	5.000
Rebellious • Is defiant • Is rebellious	307	3.098	0.893	1.000	5.000
High status • Is sophisticated • Is glamorous	307	3.098	1.001	1.000	5.000
Popular • Is popular • Liked by most people	307	4.295	0.801	1.000	5.000
Subcultural • Makes people who use it different from other people -helps people who use it stand apart from the crowd	307	2.562	1.208	1.000	5.000
Iconic • Is iconic • Is cultural	307	2.995	1.021	1.000	5.000

As shown in Table 2, Mean of the variable "popular" is found to be very high with 4.295 ± 0.801 (Min = 1; Max = 5), Mean of "attitude" (3.806 ± 0.925 (Min = 1; Max = 5), "extraordinary" 3.393 ± 0.935 (Min = 1; Max = 5), "energetic" 3.467 ± 0.938 (Min = 1; Max = 5), "aesthetically appealing" 3.528 ± 1.065 (Min = 1; Max = 5), "original" 3.603 ± 0.990 (Min = 1; Maks = 5), "authentic" 3.484 ± 0.913 (Min = 1; Max = 5) are found to be high. On the other hand, mean of "rebellious" 3.098 ± 0.893 (Min = 1; Max = 5), "high status" 3.098 ± 1.001 (Min = 1; Max = 5), "iconic" 2.995 ± 1.021 (Min = 1; Max = 5) are found to be moderate. Finally, "subcultural" is found to be weak 2.562 ± 1.208 (Min = 1; Max = 5)

4 Conclusion

Brand coolness concept in brand management practices includes various conditions because of competitiveness and dynamic market environment. Warren et al. (2018) review expression construct with coolness in their study while they find that being inexpressive is useful for competitive context as it makes parties seem dominant. But

Table 3 Correlation analysis

		Attitude
Extraordinary	R	0.696**
	P	0.000
Energetic	R	0.681**
	P	0.000
Aesthetically appealing	R	0.620**
	P	0.000
Original	R	0.627**
	P	0.000
Authentic	R	0.586**
	P	0.000
Rebellious	R	0.354**
	P	0.000
High status	R	0.564**
	P	0.000
Popular	R	0.510**
	P	0.000
Subcultural	R	0.365**
	P	0.000
Iconic	R	0.394**
	P	0.000

According to the findings displayed in Table 3, there is a positive correlation between "extraordinary" variable ($r = 0.696$; $p = 0.000 < 0.05$) "energetic" variable ($r = 0.681$; $p = 0.000 < 0.05$). "aesthetically appealing" variable ($r = 0.62$; $p = 0.000 < 0.05$) "original" variable ($r = 0.627$; $p = 0.000 < 0.05$) "authentic" variable ($r = 0.586$; $p = 0.000 < 0.05$) "rebellious" variable ($r = 0.354$; $p = 0.000 < 0.05$) "high status" variable ($r = 0.564$; $p = 0.000 < 0.05$) "Popular" variable ($r = 0.51$; $p = 0.000 < 0.05$) "Subcultural" variable ($r = 0.365$; $p = 0.000 < 0.05$). "iconic" ($r = 0.394$; $p = 0.000 < 0.05$) and attitude towards Starbucks

in noncompetitive contexts, being inexpressive is related to cold image. Thus, brand managers and marketing decision makers must use brand coolness concept in consistent to competitiveness and market environments.

In this study, authors use an empirical study to develop a better understanding about brand coolness concepts. Three hundred and seven surveys were taken into research to find out which characteristics of brand coolness are more effective in the formation of brand coolness. Research reveals that there is a positive correlation with all the characteristics of brand coolness such as "energetic" and "authentic" with attitude. Though all the themes' mean scores are high; subcultural theme's score found to have a weak score in contrast to "popular" theme having a very high score. Respondents' attitude, extraordinary, aesthetically appealing, original, authentic, high status, popular, subcultural and iconic scores do not exhibit significant

Table 4 Differentiation of brand coolness and attitude scores by gender

	Group	n	Mean	SD	T	df	p
Attitude	Women	213	3.819	0.927	0.372	305	0.710
	Men	94	3.777	0.923			
Extraordinary	Women	213	3.345	0.916	−1.340	305	0.181
	Men	94	3.500	0.973			
Energetic	Women	213	3.547	0.915	2.251	305	0.025
	Men	94	3.287	0.969			
Aesthetically appealing	Women	213	3.549	1.028	0.535	305	0.593
	Men	94	3.479	1.148			
Original	Women	213	3.608	0.989	0.143	305	0.886
	Men	94	3.590	0.997			
Authentic	Women	213	3.444	0.894	−1.158	305	0.248
	Men	94	3.575	0.953			
Rebellious	Women	213	3.092	0.882	−0.182	305	0.856
	Men	94	3.112	0.922			
High status	Women	213	3.096	0.998	−0.039	305	0.969
	Men	94	3.101	1.012			
Popular	Women	213	4.298	0.796	0.110	305	0.913
	Men	94	4.287	0.818			
Subcultural	Women	213	2.580	1.184	0.391	305	0.696
	Men	94	2.521	1.266			
Iconic	Women	213	2.986	0.978	−0.237	305	0.813
	Men	94	3.016	1.118			

Independent samples *t*-test

As Table 4 indicates, Respondents' energetic scores are significantly different in terms of gender energetic scores ($t_{(305)} = 2.251; p = 0.025 < 0.05$). Women's energetic score ($\bar{x} = 3.547$), is found higher than men's ($\bar{x} = 3.287$)

Respondents' attitude, extraordinary, aesthetically appealing, original, authentic, high status, popular, subcultural and iconic scores do not exhibit significant difference in terms of gender ($p > 0.05$)

difference in terms of gender. Finally, according to the findings, participants do not differ significantly on aesthetics, originality, rebelliousness, high status, popularity, and subcultural scores in terms of coffee consumption frequency.

Future research might include three main topics as extending brand coolness concept to other contexts, comparing brand coolness's of different brands and evaluating brand coolness concept with other brand/consumer related constructs. This study is thought to make significant contribution in terms of expanding and complementing the current brand coolness literature.

Table 5 Differentiation of brand coolness and attitude scores according to coffee consumption frequency

	Group	*n*	Mean	SD	*t*	df	*p*
Attitude	Not drinking coffee everyday	147	3.663	0.913	−2.620	305	0.009
	Drinking coffee everyday	160	3.938	0.919			
Extraordinary	Not drinking coffee everyday	147	3.279	0.937	−2.051	305	0.041
	Drinking coffee everyday	160	3.497	0.924			
Energetic	Not drinking coffee everyday	147	3.330	0.934	−2.483	305	0.014
	Drinking coffee everyday	160	3.594	0.927			
Aesthetically appealing	Not drinking coffee everyday	147	3.463	1.049	−1.027	305	0.305
	Drinking coffee everyday	160	3.588	1.079			
Original	Not drinking coffee everyday	147	3.483	0.985	−2.039	305	0.042
	Drinking coffee everyday	160	3.713	0.985			
Authentic	Not drinking coffee everyday	147	3.405	0.911	−1.455	305	0.147
	Drinking coffee everyday	160	3.556	0.911			
Rebellious	Not drinking coffee everyday	147	3.136	0.894	0.720	305	0.472
	Drinking coffee everyday	160	3.063	0.893			
High status	Not drinking coffee everyday	147	3.061	0.995	−0.612	305	0.541
	Drinking coffee everyday	160	3.131	1.009			
Popular	Not drinking coffee everyday	147	4.208	0.833	−1.836	305	0.067
	Drinking coffee everyday	160	4.375	0.765			
Subcultural	Not drinking coffee everyday	147	2.490	1.180	−1.003	305	0.317
	Drinking coffee everyday	160	2.628	1.233			

(continued)

Table 5 (continued)

	Group	n	Mean	SD	t	df	p
Iconic	Not drinking coffee everyday	147	2.867	0.978	−2.113	305	0.035
	Drinking coffee everyday	160	3.113	1.049			

Independent samples t-test
As shown in Table 5, following results are obtained: Respondents' attitude scores demonstrate significant difference in terms of coffee consumption frequency ($t_{(305)} = -2.620$; $p = 0.009 < 0.05$). Everyday coffee drinkers' attitude score ($\bar{x} = 3.938$), is found higher than the ones who do not drink coffee everyday ($\bar{x} = 3.663$). Extraordinary scores also show significant difference ($t_{(305)} = -2.051$; $p = 0.041 < 0.05$). Everyday coffee drinkers' score ($\bar{x} = 3.497$), is found to be higher than the respondents'' extraordinary theme scores who stated that they do not consume coffee everyday ($\bar{x} = 3.279$) Energetic scores of participants of the research exhibit significant difference in terms of consumption frequency as well ($t_{(305)} = -2.483$; $p = 0.014 < 0.05$). Everyday coffee drinkers' scores for energetic variable ($\bar{x} = 3.594$), found higher than the other group ($\bar{x} = 3.330$). Additionally original ($t_{(305)} = -2.039$; $p = 0.042 < 0.05$) and iconic ($t_{(305)} = -2.113$; $p = 0.035 < 0.05$) scores exhibit significant difference. Both themes are found to be having higher scores (original ($\bar{x} = 3.713$), iconic ($\bar{x} = 3.113$)) for everyday coffee drinkers
However, participants do not differ significantly on aesthetics, originality, rebelliousness, high status, popularity, and subcultural scores in terms of coffee consumption frequency ($p > 0.05$)

References

Aaker, D. A. (1996). *Building strong brands*. New York: The Free Press.

Aaker, J. L. (1997). Dimensions of brand personality. *Journal of Marketing Research, 34*(3), 347–356.

Aaker, J. L., Benet-Martinez, V., & Garolera, J. (2001). Consumption symbols as carriers of culture: A study of Japanese and Spanish brand personality constructs. *Journal of Personality and Social Psychology, 81*(3), 492–508.

Akyüz, A. (2019). Corporate scandals involving social media: Cases from Turkey. In H. Dinçer & S. Yuksel (Eds.), *Handbook of research on global issues in financial communication and investment decision making* (pp. 442–456). Hershey, PA: IGI Global.

Akyüz, A., & Akgün, S. (2011). Marka Kişiliği ve Tüketici Kişiliği Arasındaki İlişkinin Boyutlarını Belirlemeye Yönelik Bir Araştırma. In N. Uray, Ş. Burnaz, E. Karaosmanoğlu, B. E. Baş, G. Ulubaşoğlu, C. Aktan, & M. Demiray (Eds.), *Pazarlama İşletme Yönetimi ve Eğitiminde Seçilmiş Yazılar*. İstanbul: Beta Basım Yayın.

Azoulay, A., & Kapferer, J. N. (2003). Do brand personality scales really measure brand personality? *Journal of Brand Management, 11*(2), 143–155.

Batra, R., Ahuvia, A., & Bagozzi, R. P. (2012). Brand love. *Journal of Marketing, 76*(2), 1–16.

Belk, R. W., Tian, K., & Paavola, H. (2010). Consuming cool: Behind the unemotional mask. In R. W. Belk (Ed.), *Research in consumer behavior* (pp. 183–208). Bingley: Emerald Group Publishing.

Carlson, B. D., & Donavan, D. T. (2013). Human brands in sport: Athlete brand personality and identification. *Journal of Sport Management, 27*(3), 193–206.

CoolBrands. (2019). *An insight into some of Britain's coolest brands*. Retrieved from https://www.coolbrands.uk.com/

Dinçer, H., Yüksel, S., & Pınarbaşı, F. (2020). Kano-based measurement of customer expectations in retail service industry using IT2 DEMATEL-QUALIFLEX. In E. Baykal (Ed.), *Handbook of research on positive organizational behavior for improved workplace performance* (pp. 349–370). Hershey, PA: IGI Global.

Ekinci, Y., & Hosany, S. (2006). Destination personality: An application of brand personality to tourism destinations. *Journal of Travel Research, 45*(2), 127–139.

Geuens, M., Weijters, B., & De Wulf, K. (2009). A new measure of brand personality. *International Journal of Research in Marketing, 26*(2), 97–107.

Grohmann, B. (2009). Gender dimensions of brand personality. *Journal of Marketing Research, 46* (1), 105–119.

Gurrieri, L. (2009, November). Cool brands: A discursive identity approach. In *ANZMAC 2009: Sustainable management and marketing conference proceedings*.

Gwinner, K., & Bennett, G. (2008). The impact of brand cohesiveness and sport identification on brand fit in a sponsorship context. *Journal of Sport Management, 22*(p), 410–426.

Kapferer, J. N. (2012). *The new strategic brand management: Advanced insights and strategic thinking* (5th ed.). Kogan: Page.

Lara-Rodríguez, J. S., Rojas-Contreras, C., & Oliva, E. J. D. (2019). Discovering emerging research topics for brand personality: A bibliometric analysis. *Australasian Marketing Journal, 27*, 261–272.

Lee, H. S., & Cho, C. H. (2009). The matching effect of brand and sporting event personality: Sponsorship implications. *Journal of Sport Management, 23*(1), 41–64.

Lin, L. Y. (2010). The relationship of consumer personality trait, brand personality and brand loyalty: An empirical study of toys and video games buyers. *Journal of Product & Brand Management, 19*(1), 4–17.

Matzler, K., Strobl, A., Stokburger-Sauer, N., Bobovnicky, A., & Bauer, F. (2016). Brand personality and culture: The role of cultural differences on the impact of brand personality perceptions on tourists' visit intentions. *Tourism Management, 52*, 507–520.

Murase, H., & Bojanic, D. (2004). An examination of the differences in restaurant brand personality across cultures. *Journal of Hospitality & Leisure Marketing, 11*(2–3), 97–113.

Murphy, L., Moscardo, G., & Benckendorff, P. (2007). Using brand personality to differentiate regional tourism destinations. *Journal of Travel Research, 46*(1), 5–14.

Musante, M. D., Bojanic, D. C., & Zhang, J. (2008). A modified brand personality scale for the restaurant industry. *Journal of Hospitality & Leisure Marketing, 16*(4), 303–323.

Nielsen. (2019). *Battle of the brands: Consumer disloyalty is sweeping the globe*. Retrieved from https://www.nielsen.com/us/en/insights/article/2019/battle-of-the-brands-consumer-disloyalty-is-sweeping-the-globe/

O'Donnell, K. A., & Wardlow, D. L. (2000). A theory on the origins of coolness. In S. J. Hoch & R. J. Meyer (Eds.), *NA – Advances in Consumer Research*. Provo, UT: Association for Consumer Research.

Pinarbasi, F., & Enginkaya, E. (2019). Consumer negativity towards brands: Brand hate or brand switch? *Press Academia Procedia, 9*(1), 78–80.

Rahman, K. (2013). "Wow! It's cool": The meaning of coolness in marketing. *Marketing Intelligence & Planning, 31*(6), 620–638.

Ramaseshan, B., & Tsao, H. Y. (2007). Moderating effects of the brand concept on the relationship between brand personality and perceived quality. *Journal of Brand Management, 14*(6), 458–466.

Rauschnabel, P. A., Krey, N., Babin, B. J., & Ivens, B. S. (2016). Brand management in higher education: The University brand personality scale. *Journal of Business Research, 69*(8), 3077–3086.

Roll, M. (2015). *Asian brand strategy: Building and sustaining strong global brands in Asia*. New York: Palgrave Macmillan.

Runyan, R. C., Noh, M., & Mosier, J. (2013). What is cool? Operationalizing the construct in an apparel context. *Journal of Fashion Marketing and Management: An International Journal, 17* (3), 322–340.

Schmitt, B. (2012). The consumer psychology of brands. *Journal of Consumer Psychology, 22*(1), 7–17.

Sriramachandramurthy, R., & Hodis, M. (2010). Why is apple cool? An examination of brand coolness and its marketing consequences. In *Proceedings from the American Marketing Association summer academic conference*. Chicago, IL: American Marketing Association.

Sung, Y., & Kim, J. (2010). Effects of brand personality on brand trust and brand affect. *Psychology & Marketing, 27*(7), 639–661.

Sung, Y., & Tinkham, S. F. (2005). Brand personality structures in the United States and Korea: Common and culture-specific factors. *Journal of Consumer Psychology, 15*(4), 334–350.

Swaminathan, V., Stilley, K. M., & Ahluwalia, R. (2008). When brand personality matters: The moderating role of attachment styles. *Journal of Consumer Research, 35*(6), 985–1002.

Warren, C., Batra, R., Loureiro, S. M. C., & Bagozzi, R. P. (2019). Brand coolness. *Journal of Marketing, 4*(4), 409–421.

Warren, C., & Campbell, M. C. (2014). What makes things cool? How autonomy influences perceived coolness. *Journal of Consumer Research, 41*(2), 543–563.

Warren, C., Pezzuti, T., & Koley, S. (2018). Is being emotionally inexpressive cool? *Journal of Consumer Psychology, 28*(4), 560–577.

Watkins, B. A., & Gonzenbach, W. J. (2013). Assessing university brand personality through logos: An analysis of the use of academics and athletics in university branding. *Journal of Marketing for Higher Education, 23*(1), 15–33.

Wells, W. D., Andriuli, F. J., Goi, F. J., & Seader, S. (1957). An adjective check list for the study of product personality. *Journal of Applied Psychology, 41*(5), 317.

The manufacturer's authorised representative in the EU is Springer Nature Customer Service Centre GmbH, Europaplatz 3, 69115 Heidelberg, Germany. If you have any concerns regarding our products, please contact ProductSafety@springernature.com

Printed and bound by CPI Group (UK) Ltd, Croydon, CR0 4YY
30/09/2026
02225697-0012